I'LL BE REJECTING ANSWERS LIKE, "THE DANGER HAS PASSED DUE TO ALL OUR PRAYERS"!
YOU SEEM TO BE QUITE A TWISTED SOUL.
SMIRK

和月伸宏

NOBUHIRO WATSUKI

THE END OF THE CENTURY

THE FIRST JAPANESE EDITION OF THIS VOLUME WILL BE RELEASED IN JULY 1999. YES, IT IS THE TIME OF THE GREAT PROPHECY! NOW IS THE TIME!!

WATSUKI ABSOLUTELY DOES NOT BELIEVE IN IT, BUT IF IT HAPPENS, I WILL BE HAPPY TO BE THE LAST OF HUMANITY ALIVE. AND IF IT DOESN'T HAPPEN, I WILL BE LOOKING SO VERY FORWARD TO THE EXCUSES THE CHARLATANS AND EXPERTS MAKE UP TO COVER THEMSELVES.

ALTHOUGH IT IS THE END OF THE CENTURY, IT IS JUST ANOTHER DATE. RUN RIGHT THROUGH IT WITH VIGOR AND ELEGANCE!

Rurouni Kenshin, which has found fans not only in Japan but around the world, first made its appearance in 1992, as an original short story in ***Weekly Shonen Jump Special***. Later rewritten and published as a regular, continuing ***Jump*** series in 1994, ***Rurouni Kenshin*** ended serialization in 1999 but continued in popularity, as evidenced by the 2000 publication of ***Yahiko no Sakabatô*** ("Yahiko's Reversed-Edge Sword") in ***Weekly Shonen Jump***. His most current work, ***Buso Renkin*** ("Armored Alchemist"), began publication in June 2003, also in ***Jump***.

RUROUNI KENSHIN
VOL. 26: A MAN'S BACK
The SHONEN JUMP Manga Edition

STORY AND ART BY
NOBUHIRO WATSUKI

English Adaptation/Pancha Diaz
Translation/Kenichiro Yagi
Touch-Up Art & Lettering/Steve Dutro
Design/Matt Hinrichs
Editor/Kit Fox

Managing Editor/Elizabeth Kawasaki
Director of Production/Noboru Watanabe
Vice President of Publishing/Alvin Lu
Vice President & Editor in Chief/Yumi Hoashi
Sr. Director of Acquisitions/Rika Inouye
Vice President of Sales & Marketing/Liza Coppola
Publisher/Hyoe Narita

Printed in the U.S.A.

Published by VIZ Media, LLC
P.O. Box 77010
San Francisco, CA 94107

SHONEN JUMP Manga Edition
10 9 8 7 6 5 4 3 2 1
First printing, May 2006

www.viz.com

PARENTAL ADVISORY
RUROUNI KENSHIN is rated T+ for Older Teen and is recommended for ages 16 and up. This volume contains realistic violence and alcohol and tobacco use.

SHONEN JUMP MANGA

Rurouni Kenshin™

STORY & ART BY
NOBUHIRO WATSUKI

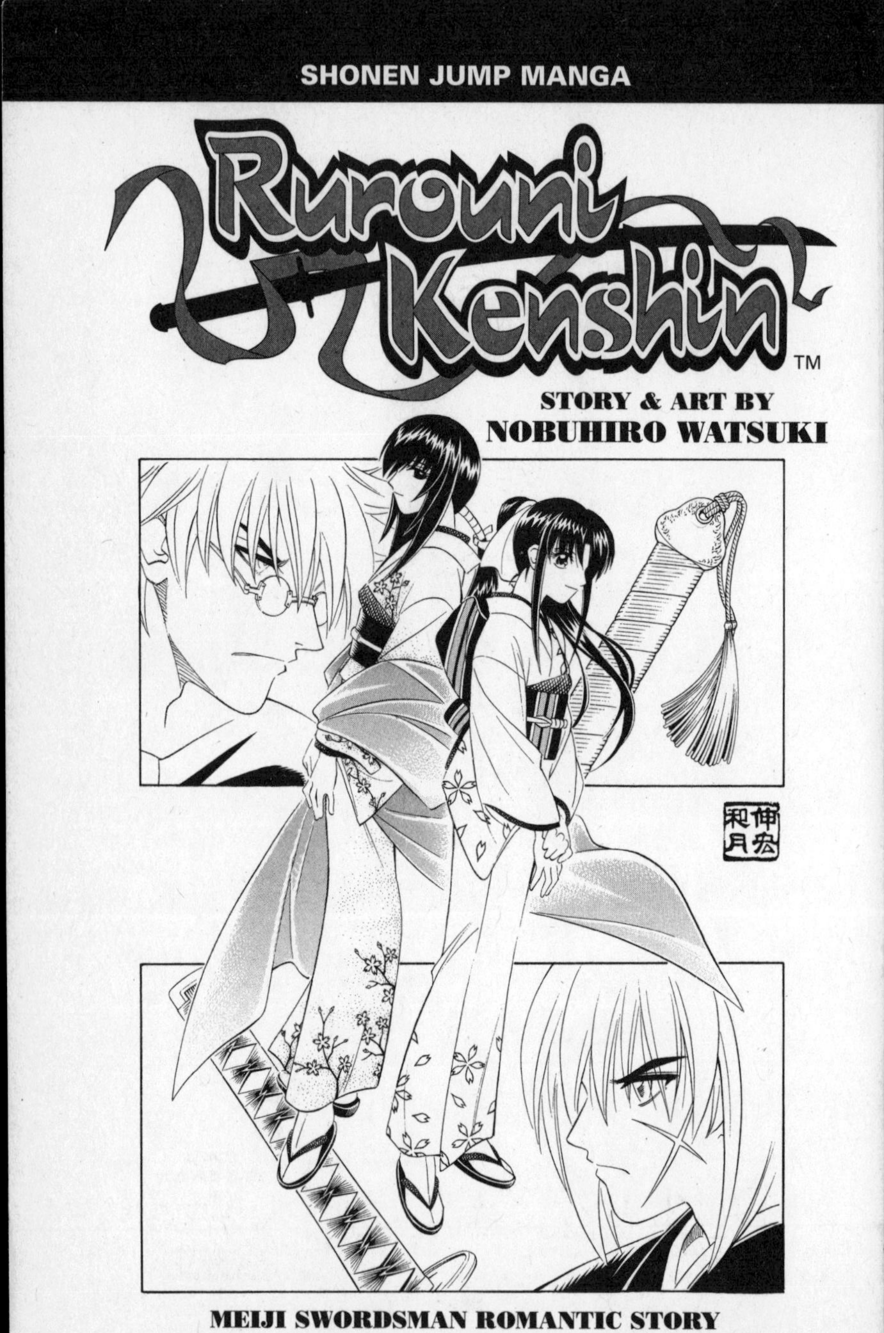

MEIJI SWORDSMAN ROMANTIC STORY

Vol. 26: A MAN'S BACK

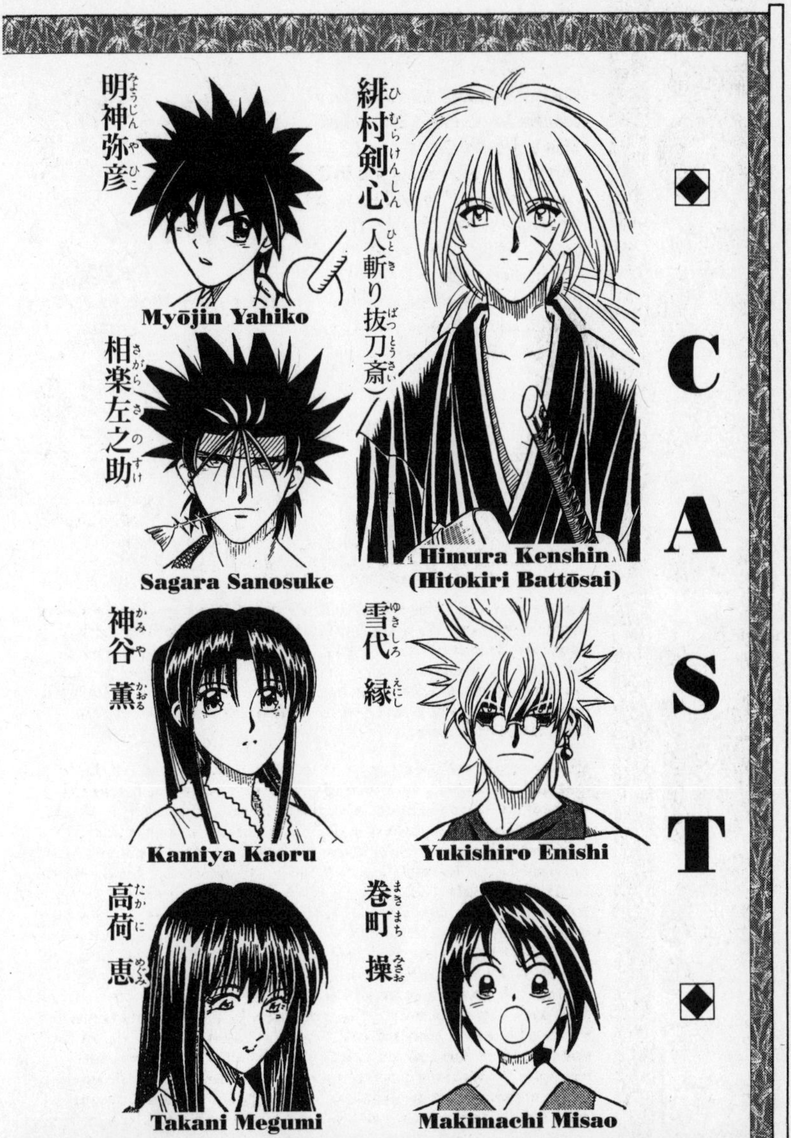
CAST
緋村剣心（人斬り抜刀斎）
Himura Kenshin
(Hitokiri Battōsai)
明神弥彦
Myōjin Yahiko
相楽左之助
Sagara Sanosuke
雪代縁
Yukishiro Enishi
神谷薫
Kamiya Kaoru
巻町操
Makimachi Misao
高荷恵
Takani Megumi

Once he was *hitokiri*, an assassin, called Battōsai. His name was legend among the pro-Imperialist or "patriot" warriors who launched the Meiji Era. Now, Himura Kenshin is *rurouni*, a wanderer, and carries a reversed-edge *sakabatō* blade, vowing to never kill another soul.

呉黒星（ウーヘイシン）

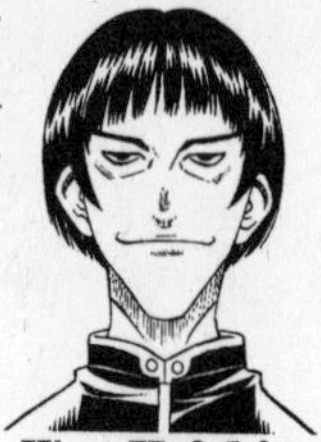

Woo Heishin

不動沢（ふどうさわ）

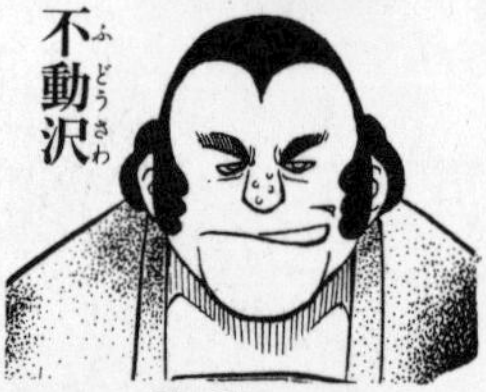

Fudōsawa

THUS FAR

Those with grudges against Battōsai have gathered to take their revenge. To make matters worse, Kenshin finds out that the mastermind of this new attack is Enishi, the brother of Kenshin's deceased wife Tomoe—who died at Kenshin's own hand. And yet Kenshin decides to fight in order to protect the present and begins by telling his friends of his past.

Enishi and his crew appear midair above Kamiya Dojo in hot air balloons. In the midst of the battle that follows, Enishi murders Kaoru. Overwhelmed by the guilt of not saving Kaoru, Kenshin exiles himself to the "Fallen Village." However, the others discover that Kaoru's body is actually one of the "corpse dolls" created by Gein. Aoshi, while searching for Kaoru's whereabouts, defeats Gein and joins Saitō on the way to Enishi's organization's new hide-out. In the meantime, the crazed Kujiranami escapes from jail. Tsubame, worried about Yahiko fighting Kujiranami along with the police, runs to Kenshin in the Fallen Village. Kenshin, who did not react to the call for revenge, finally responds when the girl pleads for help. Kenshin's revived sword saves Yahiko and returns Kujiranami to sanity. Kujiranami desires a warrior's death, but he accepts Kenshin's appeal to "live in the new era" and remands himself to justice. Meanwhile, Sanosuke is in a travelers' town in Shinshū, unaware of Kenshin's return.

CONTENTS

RUROUNI KENSHIN

Meiji Swordsman Romantic Story

BOOK TWENTY-SIX: A MAN'S BACK

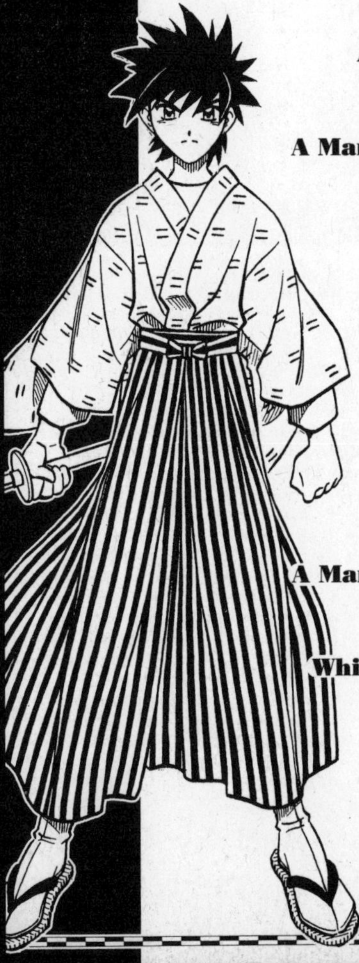

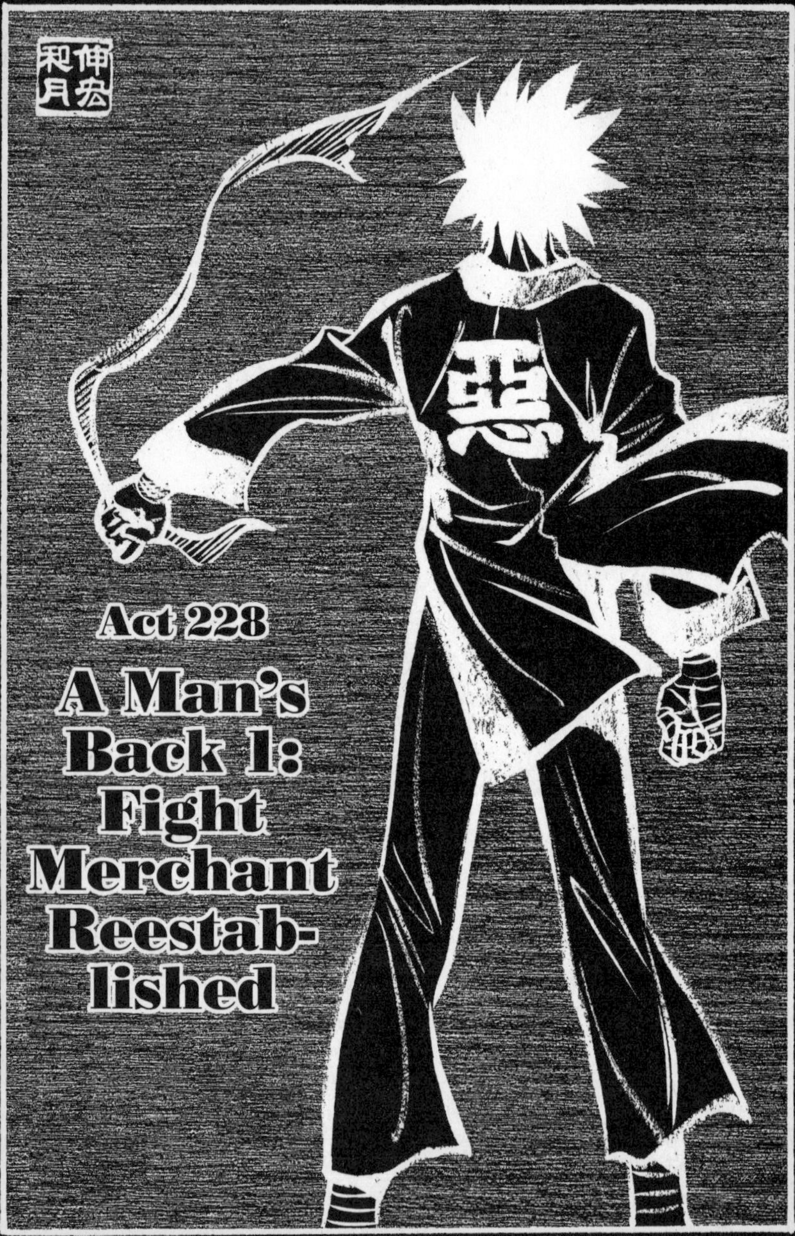
Act 228
A Man's Back 1: Fight Merchant Reestablished

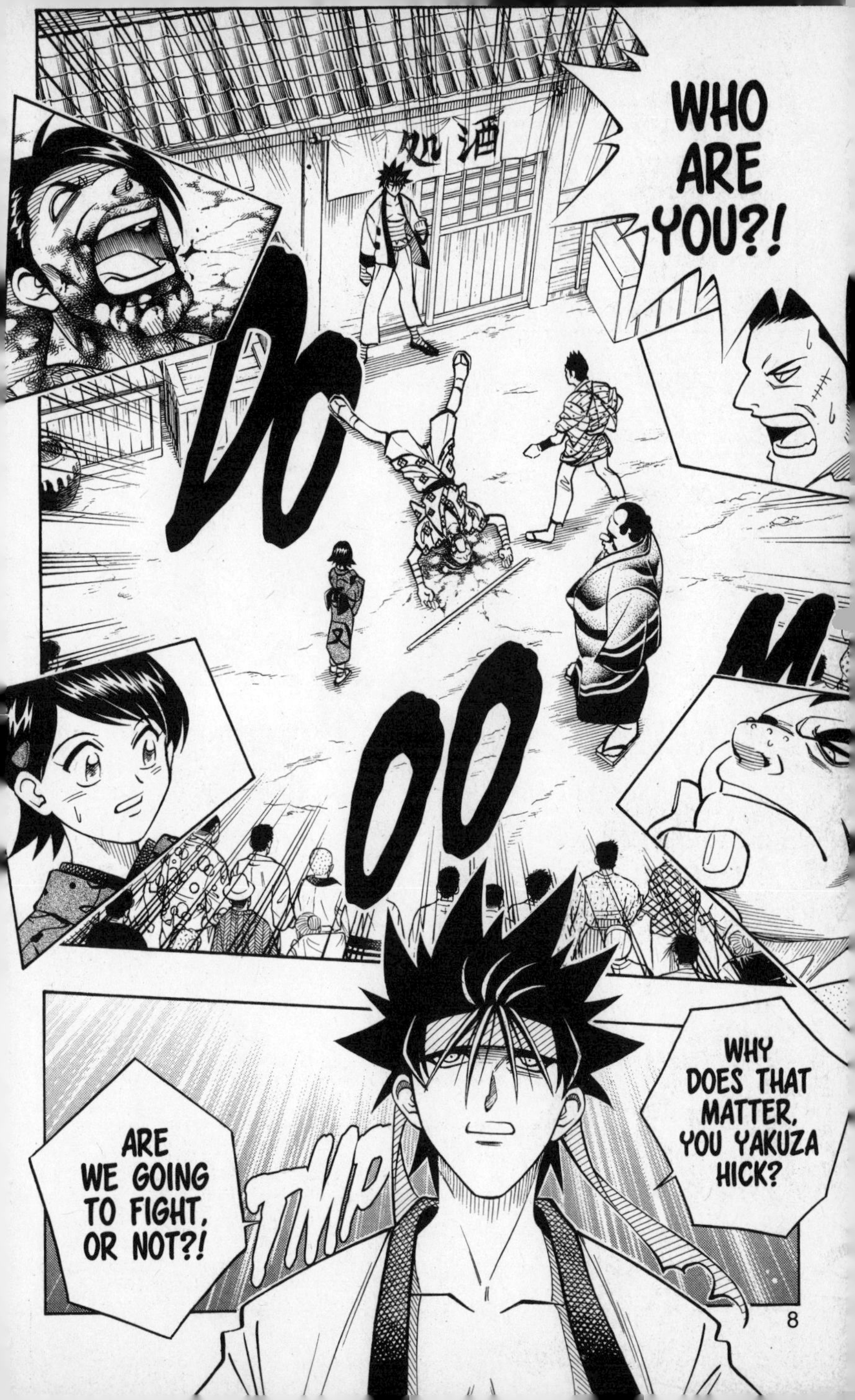
WHO ARE YOU?!
酒処
WHY DOES THAT MATTER, YOU YAKUZA HICK?
ARE WE GOING TO FIGHT, OR NOT?!

READ THIS WAY

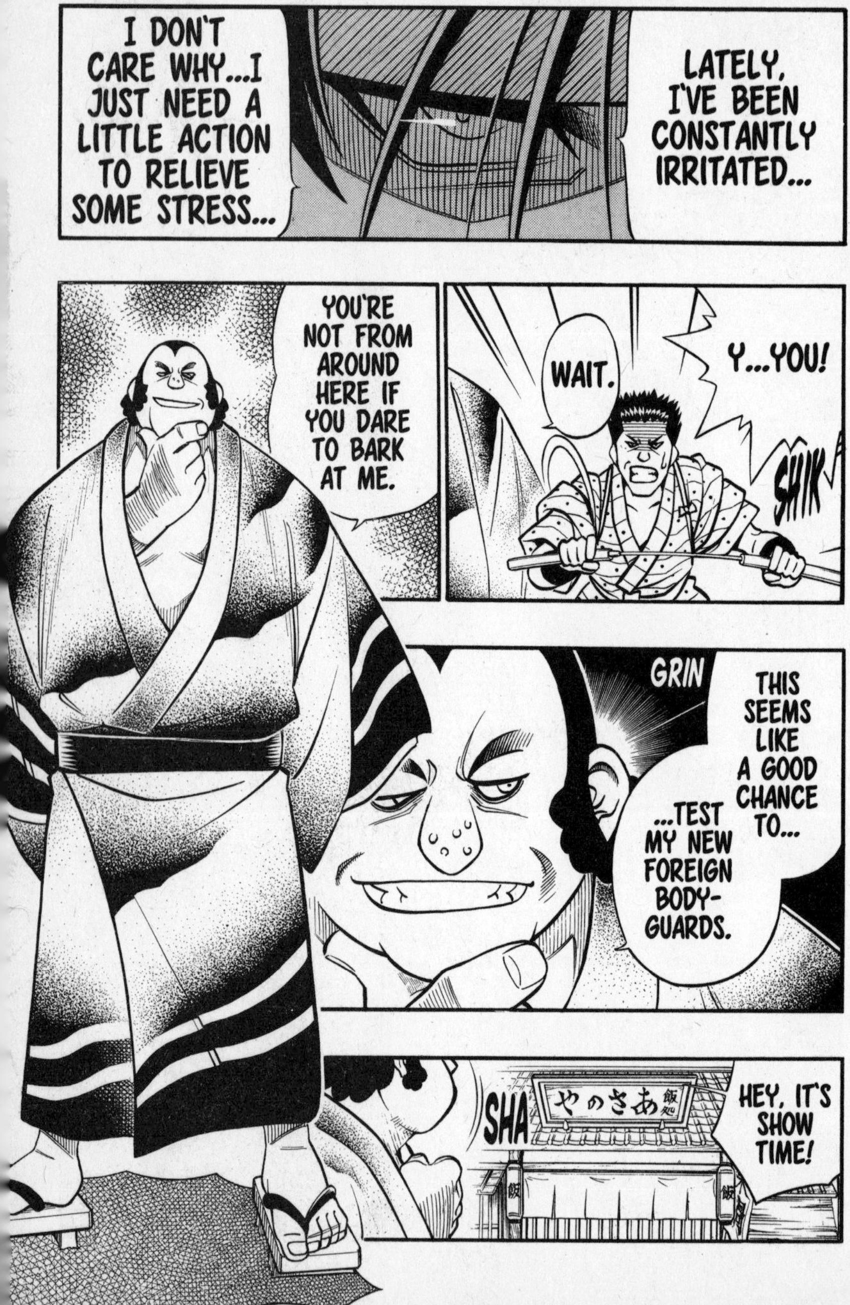
LATELY, I'VE BEEN CONSTANTLY IRRITATED...
I DON'T CARE WHY...I JUST NEED A LITTLE ACTION TO RELIEVE SOME STRESS...
Y...YOU!
SHIK
WAIT.
GRIN
THIS SEEMS LIKE A GOOD CHANCE TO...
...TEST MY NEW FOREIGN BODY-GUARDS.
HEY, IT'S SHOW TIME!
SHA
やのさあ 飯処
YOU'RE NOT FROM AROUND HERE IF YOU DARE TO BARK AT ME.

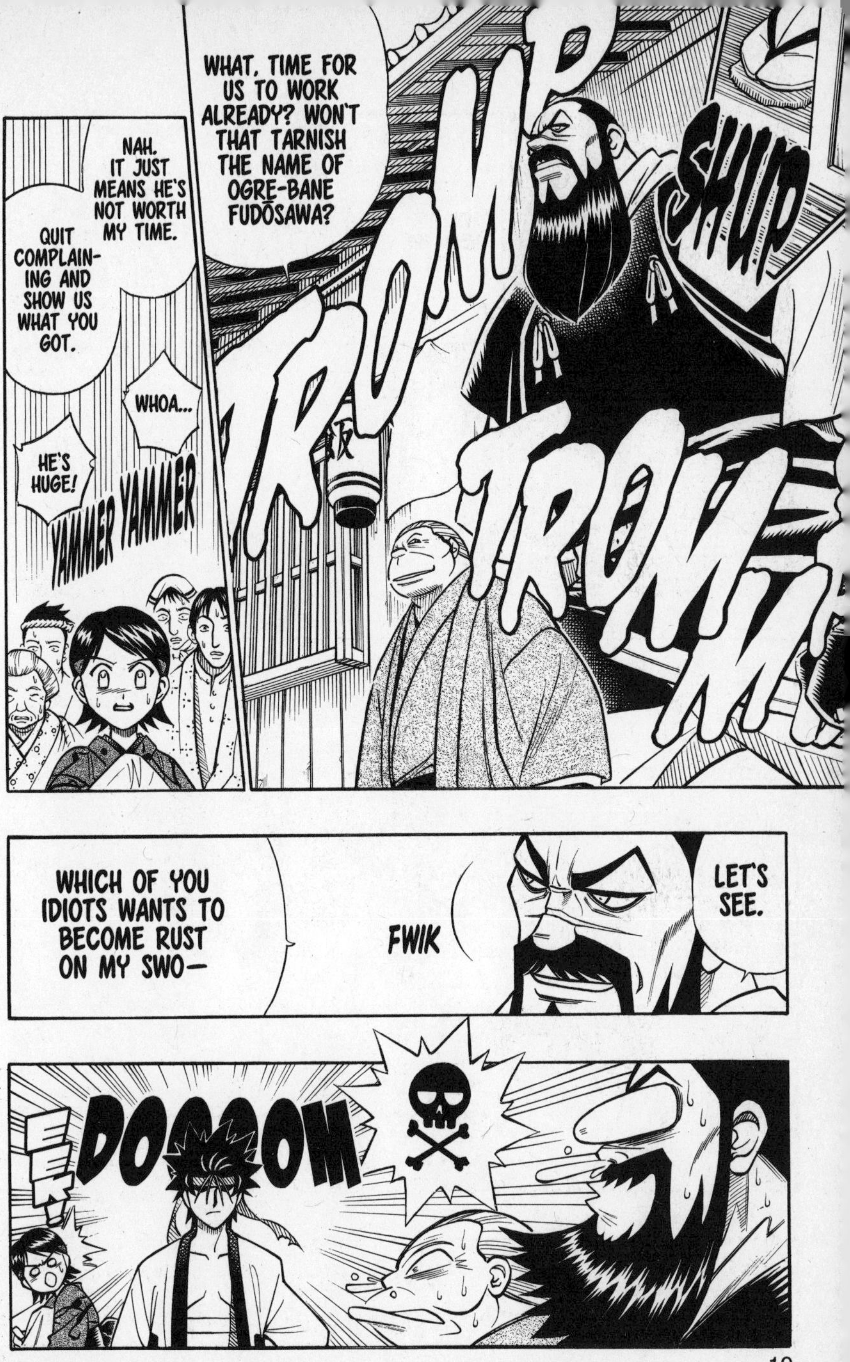
TROMP
SHUP
WHAT, TIME FOR US TO WORK ALREADY? WON'T THAT TARNISH THE NAME OF OGRE-BANE FUDŌSAWA?
TROMP
NAH. IT JUST MEANS HE'S NOT WORTH MY TIME.
QUIT COMPLAINING AND SHOW US WHAT YOU GOT.
WHOA...
HE'S HUGE!
YAMMER YAMMER
LET'S SEE.
FWIK
WHICH OF YOU IDIOTS WANTS TO BECOME RUST ON MY SWO—
DOOOOM
EEK!

READ THIS WAY

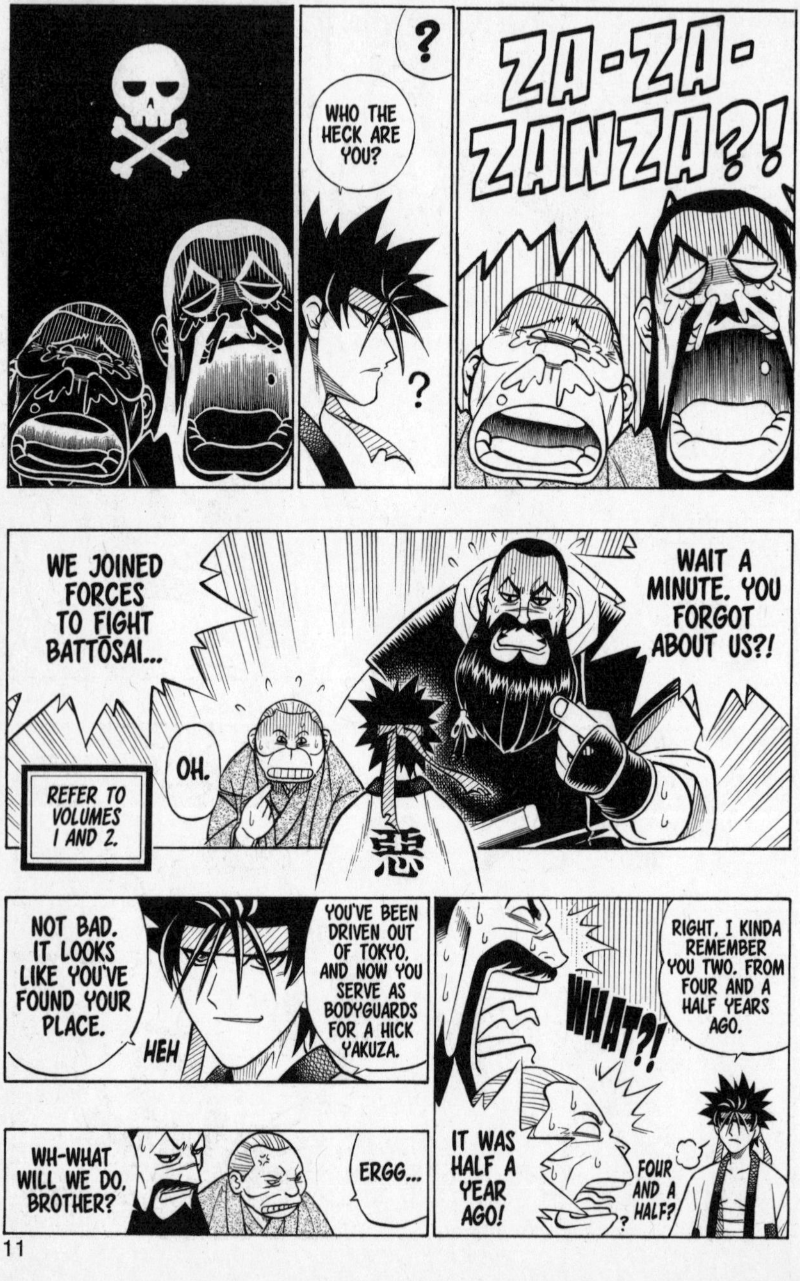
ZA-ZA-ZANZA?!
?
WHO THE HECK ARE YOU?
?
WAIT A MINUTE. YOU FORGOT ABOUT US?!
WE JOINED FORCES TO FIGHT BATTŌSAI...
OH.
REFER TO VOLUMES 1 AND 2.
悪
RIGHT, I KINDA REMEMBER YOU TWO. FROM FOUR AND A HALF YEARS AGO.
WHAT?!
IT WAS HALF A YEAR AGO!
FOUR AND A HALF?
?
YOU'VE BEEN DRIVEN OUT OF TOKYO, AND NOW YOU SERVE AS BODYGUARDS FOR A HICK YAKUZA.
NOT BAD. IT LOOKS LIKE YOU'VE FOUND YOUR PLACE.
HEH
ERGG...
WH-WHAT WILL WE DO, BROTHER?

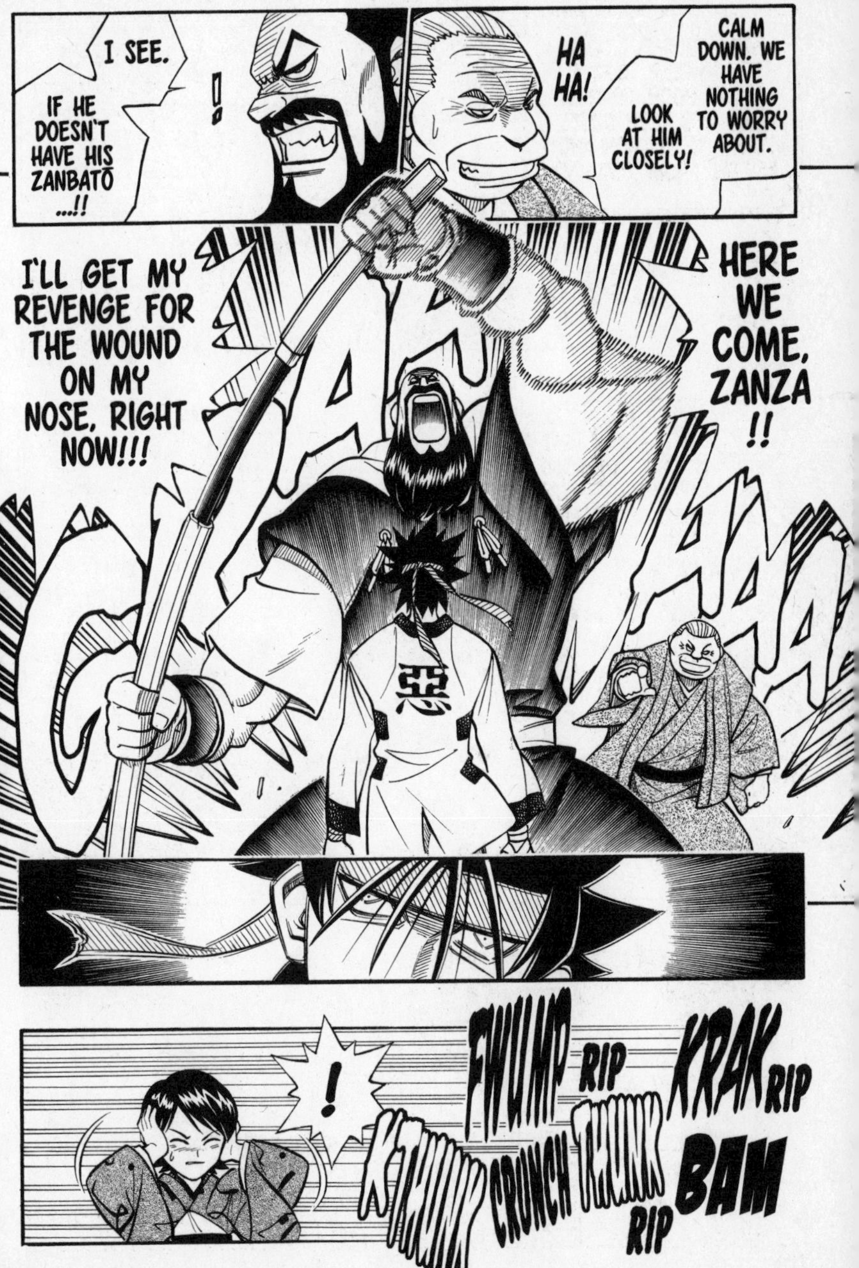
CALM DOWN. WE HAVE NOTHING TO WORRY ABOUT.
HA HA!
LOOK AT HIM CLOSELY!
I SEE.
!
IF HE DOESN'T HAVE HIS ZANBATŌ ...!!
HERE WE COME, ZANZA!!
I'LL GET MY REVENGE FOR THE WOUND ON MY NOSE, RIGHT NOW!!!
KRAK
RIP
BAM
RIP
THUNK
RIP
FWUMP
RIP
CRUNCH
!

READ THIS WAY

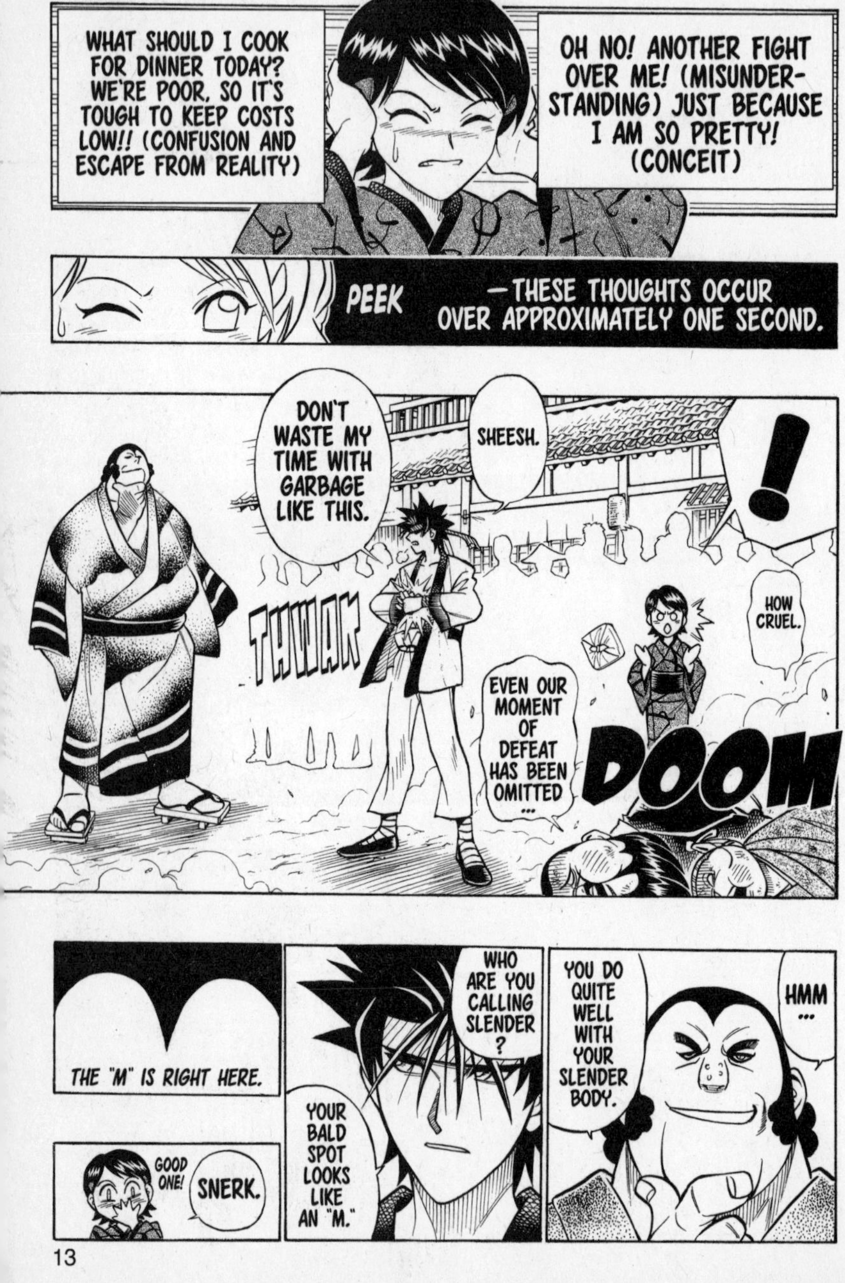

OH NO! ANOTHER FIGHT OVER ME! (MISUNDER-STANDING) JUST BECAUSE I AM SO PRETTY! (CONCEIT)
WHAT SHOULD I COOK FOR DINNER TODAY? WE'RE POOR, SO IT'S TOUGH TO KEEP COSTS LOW!! (CONFUSION AND ESCAPE FROM REALITY)
—THESE THOUGHTS OCCUR OVER APPROXIMATELY ONE SECOND.
PEEK
!
HOW CRUEL.
DOOM
EVEN OUR MOMENT OF DEFEAT HAS BEEN OMITTED...
SHEESH.
DON'T WASTE MY TIME WITH GARBAGE LIKE THIS.
THWAK
HMM...
YOU DO QUITE WELL WITH YOUR SLENDER BODY.
WHO ARE YOU CALLING SLENDER?
YOUR BALD SPOT LOOKS LIKE AN "M."
THE "M" IS RIGHT HERE.
SNERK.
GOOD ONE!

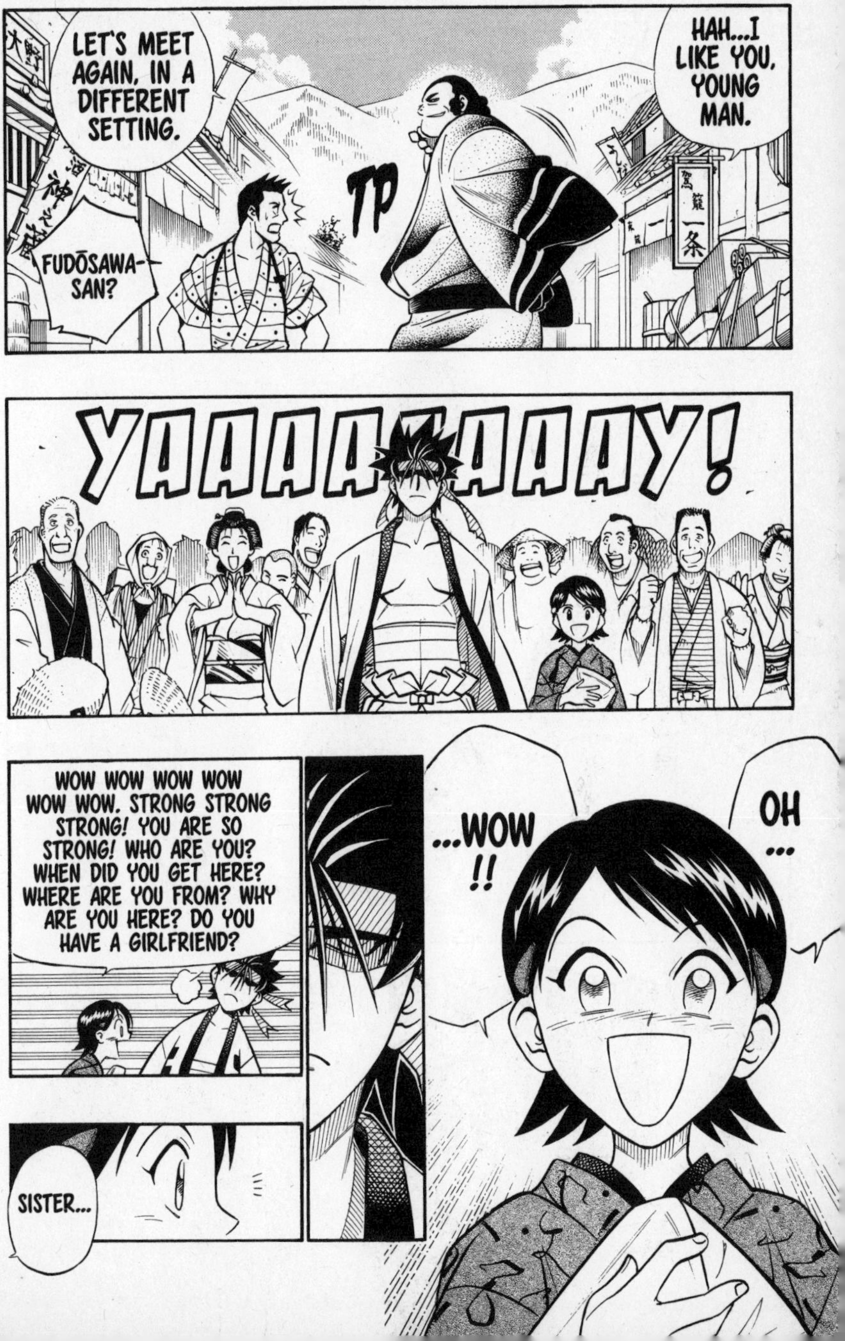
HAH...I LIKE YOU, YOUNG MAN.
LET'S MEET AGAIN, IN A DIFFERENT SETTING.
TP
FUDŌSAWA-SAN?
YAAAAAAAAY!
OH ...
...WOW !!
WOW WOW WOW WOW WOW WOW. STRONG STRONG STRONG! YOU ARE SO STRONG! WHO ARE YOU? WHEN DID YOU GET HERE? WHERE ARE YOU FROM? WHY ARE YOU HERE? DO YOU HAVE A GIRLFRIEND?
SISTER...

READ THIS WAY

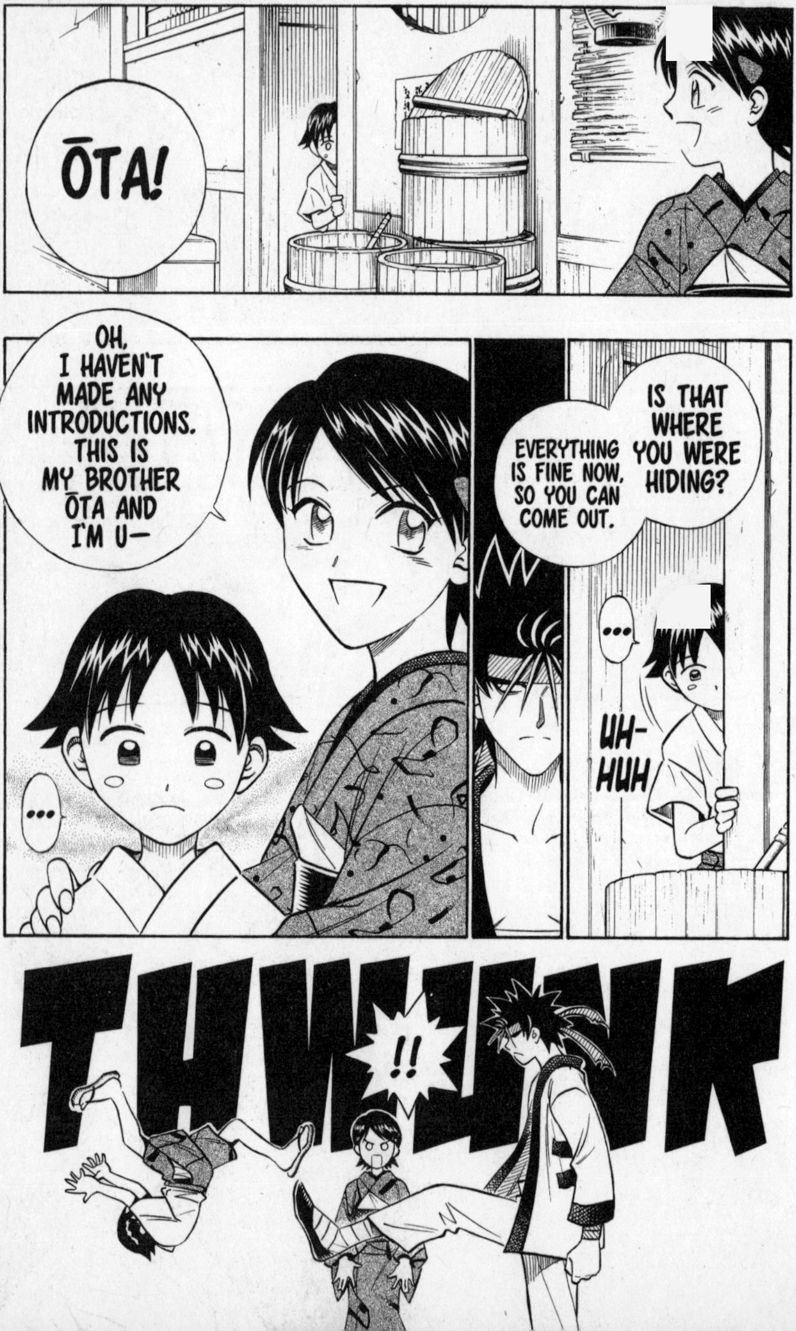
ŌTA!
IS THAT WHERE YOU WERE HIDING?
EVERYTHING IS FINE NOW, SO YOU CAN COME OUT.
...
UH-HUH
OH, I HAVEN'T MADE ANY INTRODUCTIONS. THIS IS MY BROTHER ŌTA AND I'M U—
...
THW NK
!!

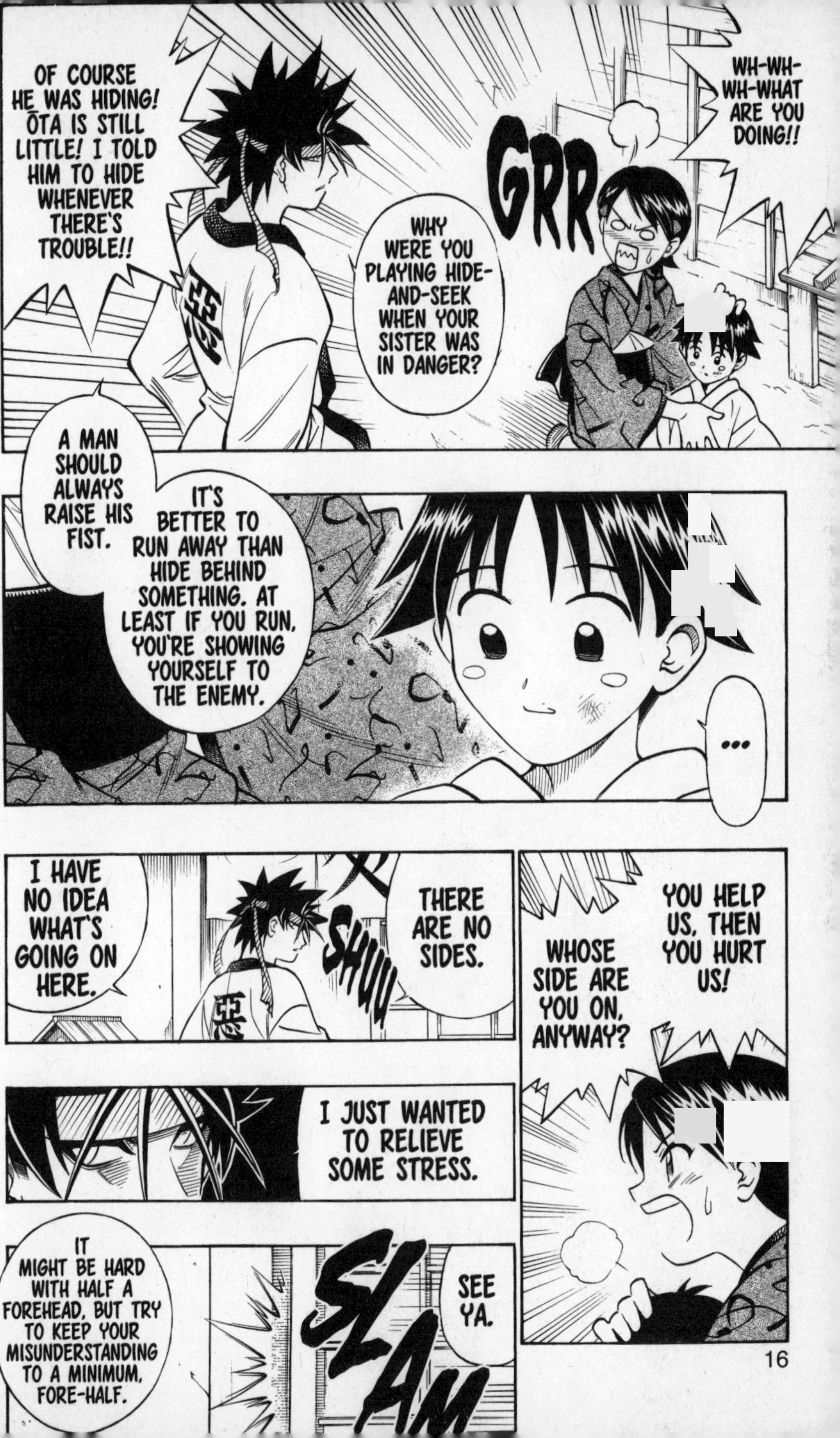
WH-WH-WH-WHAT ARE YOU DOING!!
GRR
WHY WERE YOU PLAYING HIDE-AND-SEEK WHEN YOUR SISTER WAS IN DANGER?
OF COURSE HE WAS HIDING! ŌTA IS STILL LITTLE! I TOLD HIM TO HIDE WHENEVER THERE'S TROUBLE!!
IT'S BETTER TO RUN AWAY THAN HIDE BEHIND SOMETHING. AT LEAST IF YOU RUN, YOU'RE SHOWING YOURSELF TO THE ENEMY.
A MAN SHOULD ALWAYS RAISE HIS FIST.
...
YOU HELP US, THEN YOU HURT US!
WHOSE SIDE ARE YOU ON, ANYWAY?
THERE ARE NO SIDES.
SHUU
I HAVE NO IDEA WHAT'S GOING ON HERE.
I JUST WANTED TO RELIEVE SOME STRESS.
SEE YA.
SLAM
IT MIGHT BE HARD WITH HALF A FOREHEAD, BUT TRY TO KEEP YOUR MISUNDERSTANDING TO A MINIMUM, FORE-HALF.

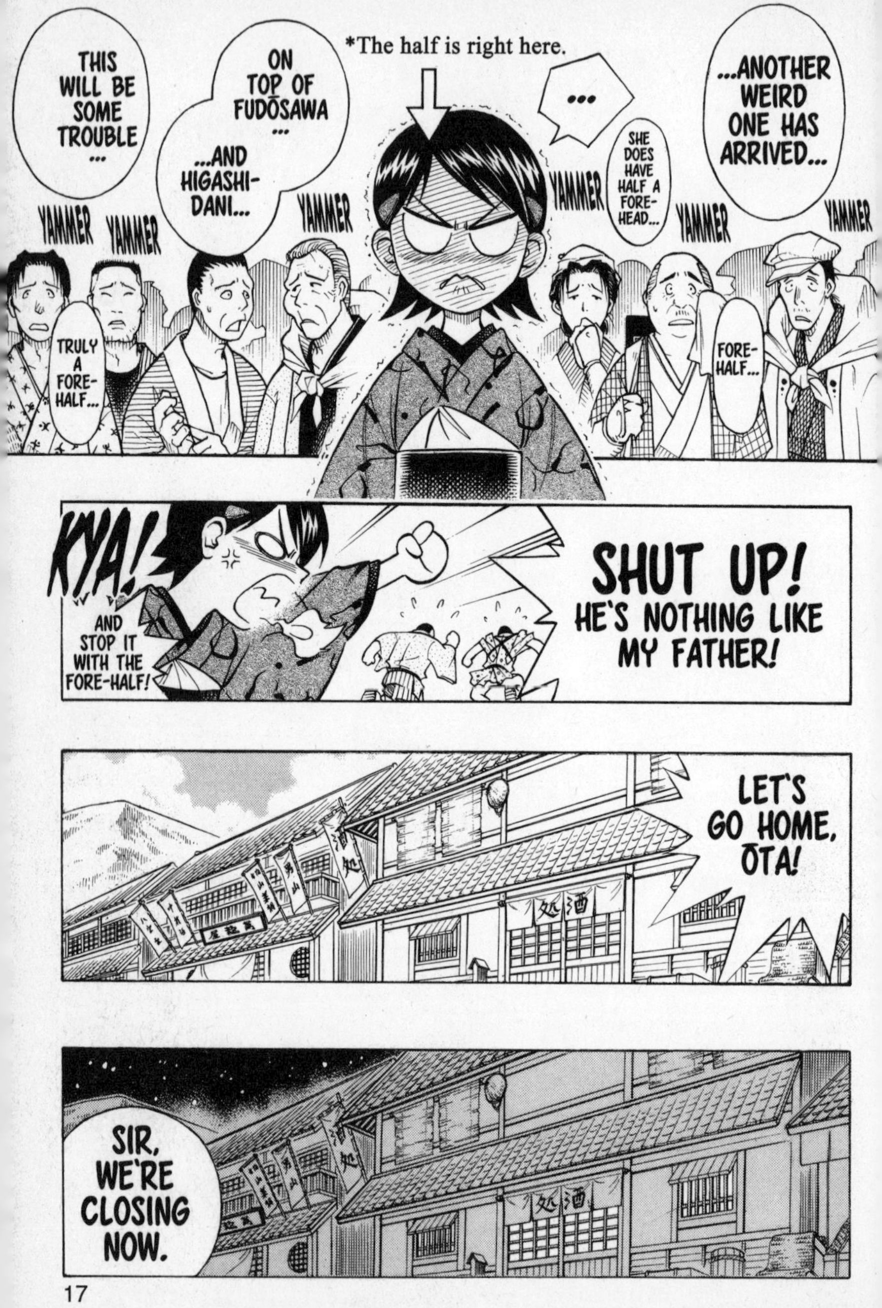
...ANOTHER WEIRD ONE HAS ARRIVED...
YAMMER
FORE-HALF...
YAMMER
SHE DOES HAVE HALF A FORE-HEAD...
YAMMER
...
*The half is right here.
YAMMER
ON TOP OF FUDŌSAWA...
...AND HIGASHI-DANI...
YAMMER
THIS WILL BE SOME TROUBLE...
YAMMER
TRULY A FORE-HALF...
SHUT UP! HE'S NOTHING LIKE MY FATHER!
AND STOP IT WITH THE FORE-HALF!
KYA!
LET'S GO HOME, ŌTA!
SIR, WE'RE CLOSING NOW.

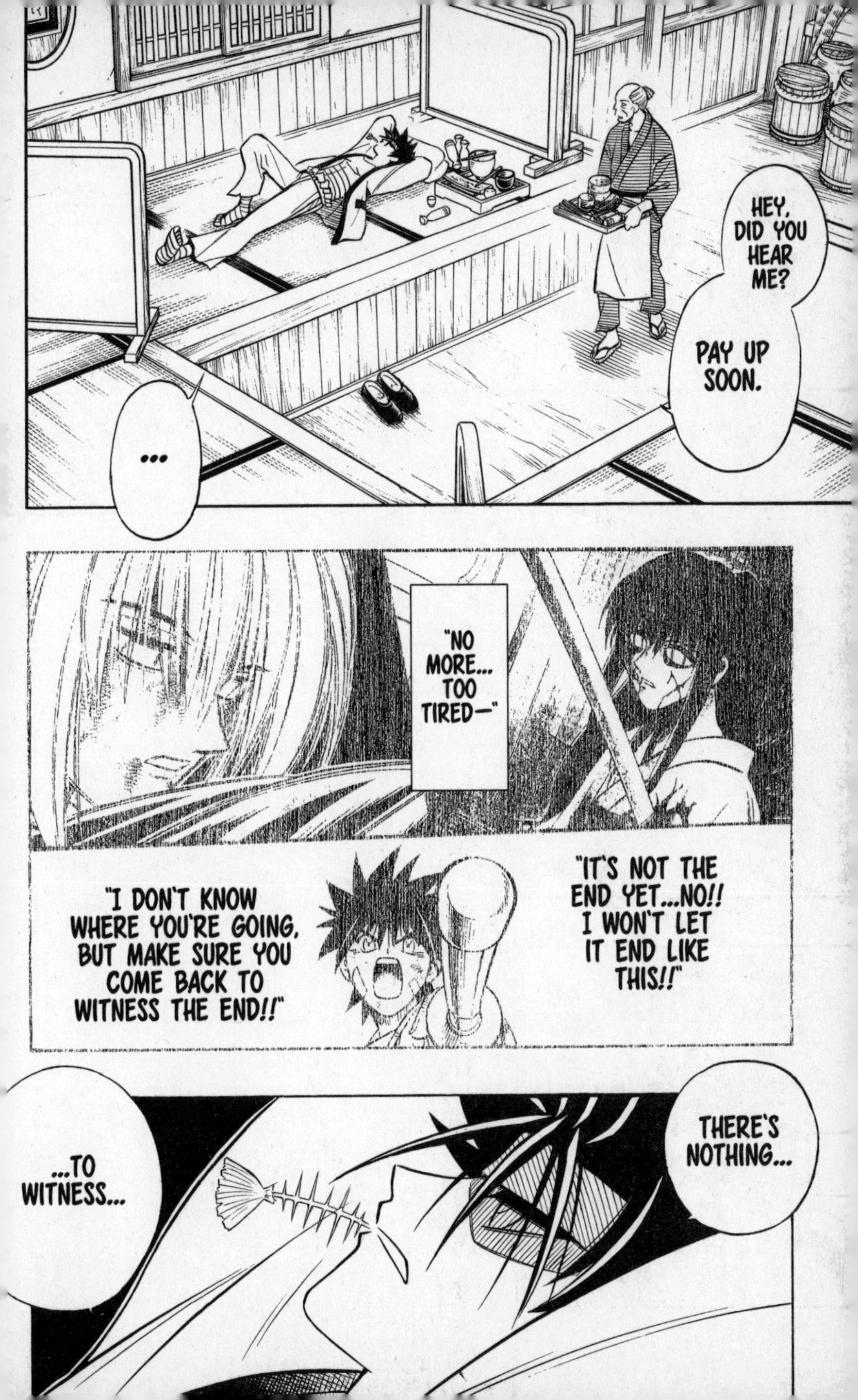
HEY, DID YOU HEAR ME?
PAY UP SOON.
...
"NO MORE... TOO TIRED—"
"IT'S NOT THE END YET...NO!! I WON'T LET IT END LIKE THIS!!"
"I DON'T KNOW WHERE YOU'RE GOING, BUT MAKE SURE YOU COME BACK TO WITNESS THE END!!"
THERE'S NOTHING...
...TO WITNESS...

READ THIS WAY

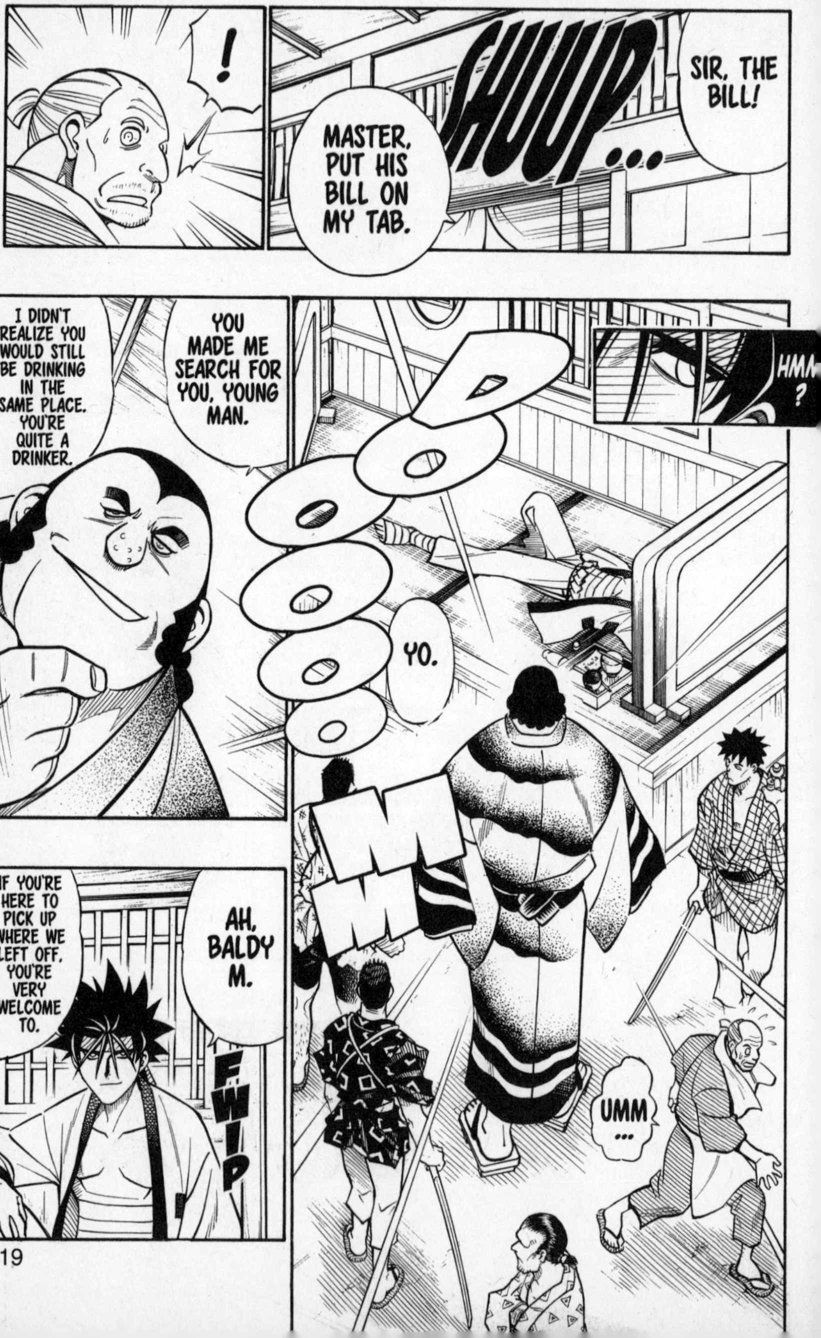
SIR, THE BILL!
SHUUP...
MASTER, PUT HIS BILL ON MY TAB.
!
HMM?
DOOOOOO
YO.
MMM
UMM...
YOU MADE ME SEARCH FOR YOU, YOUNG MAN.
I DIDN'T REALIZE YOU WOULD STILL BE DRINKING IN THE SAME PLACE. YOU'RE QUITE A DRINKER.
AH, BALDY M.
IF YOU'RE HERE TO PICK UP WHERE WE LEFT OFF, YOU'RE VERY WELCOME TO.
FWIP

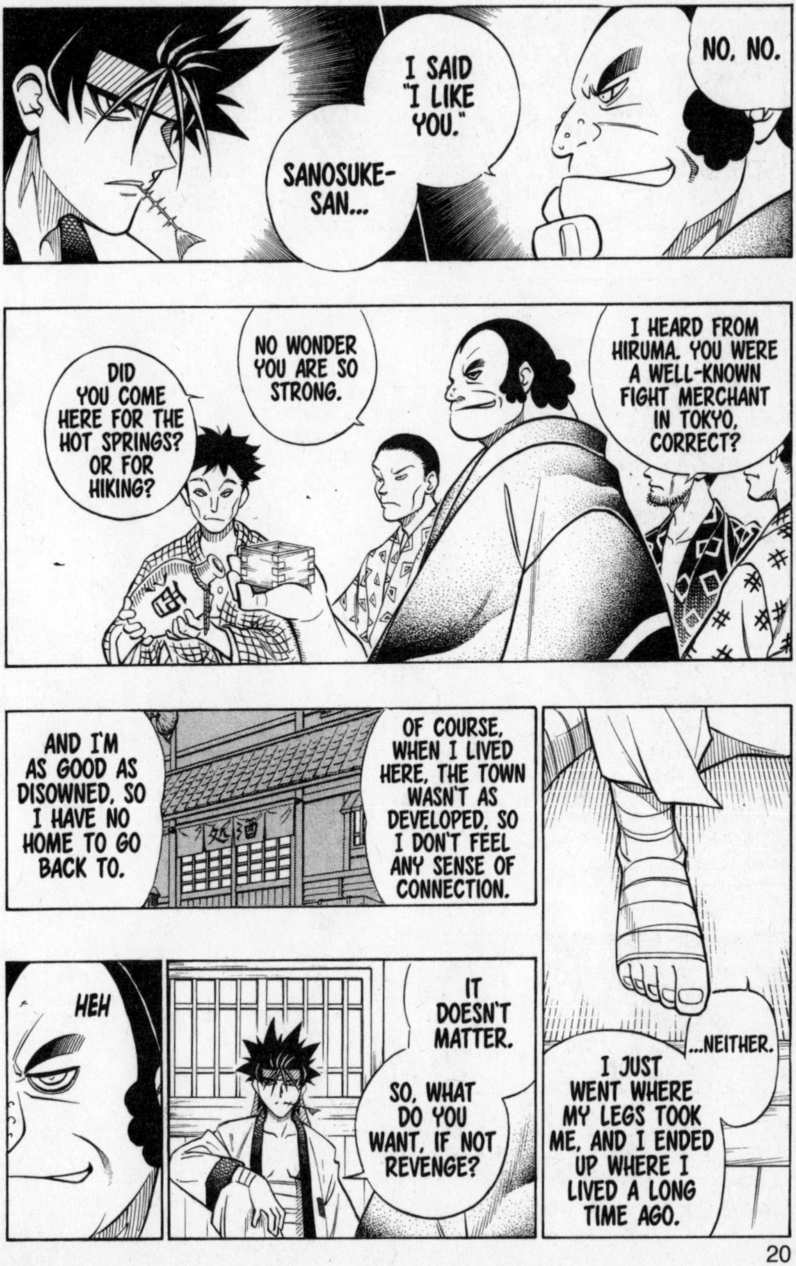
NO, NO.
I SAID "I LIKE YOU."
SANOSUKE-SAN...
I HEARD FROM HIRUMA. YOU WERE A WELL-KNOWN FIGHT MERCHANT IN TOKYO, CORRECT?
NO WONDER YOU ARE SO STRONG.
DID YOU COME HERE FOR THE HOT SPRINGS? OR FOR HIKING?
...NEITHER.
I JUST WENT WHERE MY LEGS TOOK ME, AND I ENDED UP WHERE I LIVED A LONG TIME AGO.
OF COURSE, WHEN I LIVED HERE, THE TOWN WASN'T AS DEVELOPED, SO I DON'T FEEL ANY SENSE OF CONNECTION.
AND I'M AS GOOD AS DISOWNED, SO I HAVE NO HOME TO GO BACK TO.
IT DOESN'T MATTER.
SO, WHAT DO YOU WANT, IF NOT REVENGE?
HEH

READ THIS WAY

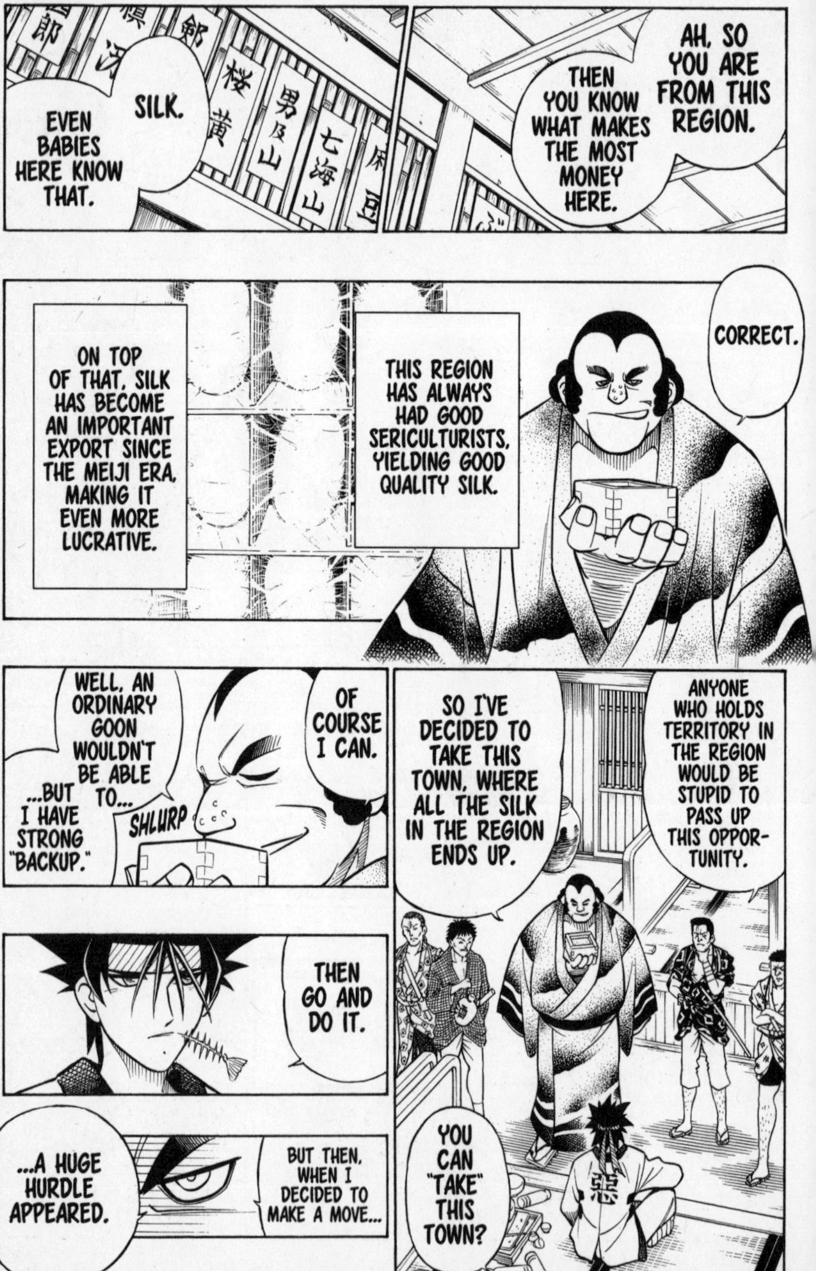
AH, SO YOU ARE FROM THIS REGION.
THEN YOU KNOW WHAT MAKES THE MOST MONEY HERE.
SILK.
EVEN BABIES HERE KNOW THAT.
CORRECT.
THIS REGION HAS ALWAYS HAD GOOD SERICULTURISTS, YIELDING GOOD QUALITY SILK.
ON TOP OF THAT, SILK HAS BECOME AN IMPORTANT EXPORT SINCE THE MEIJI ERA, MAKING IT EVEN MORE LUCRATIVE.
ANYONE WHO HOLDS TERRITORY IN THE REGION WOULD BE STUPID TO PASS UP THIS OPPOR-TUNITY.
SO I'VE DECIDED TO TAKE THIS TOWN, WHERE ALL THE SILK IN THE REGION ENDS UP.
YOU CAN "TAKE" THIS TOWN?
OF COURSE I CAN.
WELL, AN ORDINARY GOON WOULDN'T BE ABLE TO...
SHLURP
...BUT I HAVE STRONG "BACKUP."
THEN GO AND DO IT.
BUT THEN, WHEN I DECIDED TO MAKE A MOVE...
...A HUGE HURDLE APPEARED.

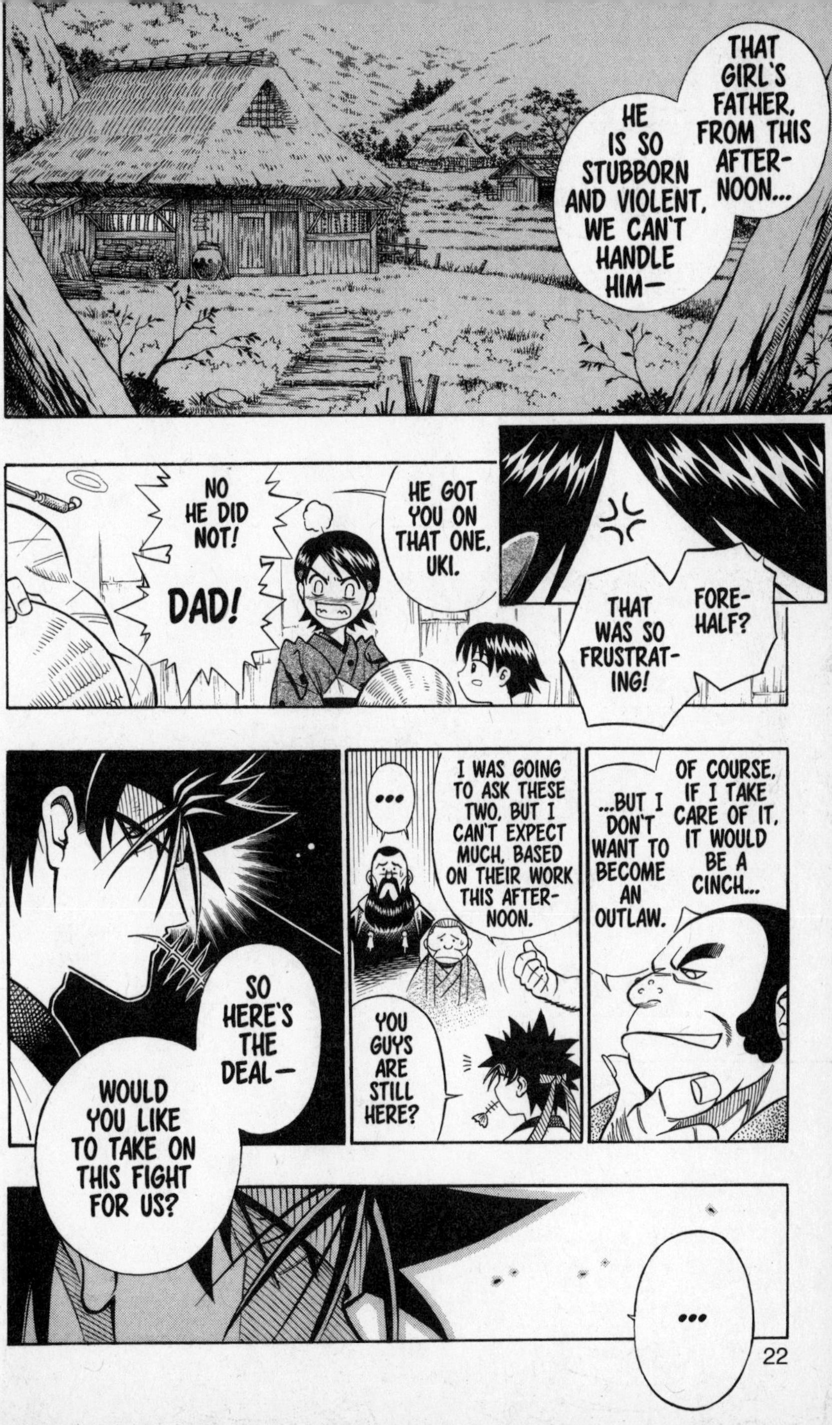
THAT GIRL'S FATHER, FROM THIS AFTERNOON...
HE IS SO STUBBORN AND VIOLENT, WE CAN'T HANDLE HIM—
FORE-HALF?
THAT WAS SO FRUSTRATING!
HE GOT YOU ON THAT ONE, UKI.
NO HE DID NOT!
DAD!
OF COURSE, IF I TAKE CARE OF IT, IT WOULD BE A CINCH...
...BUT I DON'T WANT TO BECOME AN OUTLAW.
I WAS GOING TO ASK THESE TWO, BUT I CAN'T EXPECT MUCH, BASED ON THEIR WORK THIS AFTERNOON.
...
YOU GUYS ARE STILL HERE?
SO HERE'S THE DEAL—
WOULD YOU LIKE TO TAKE ON THIS FIGHT FOR US?
...

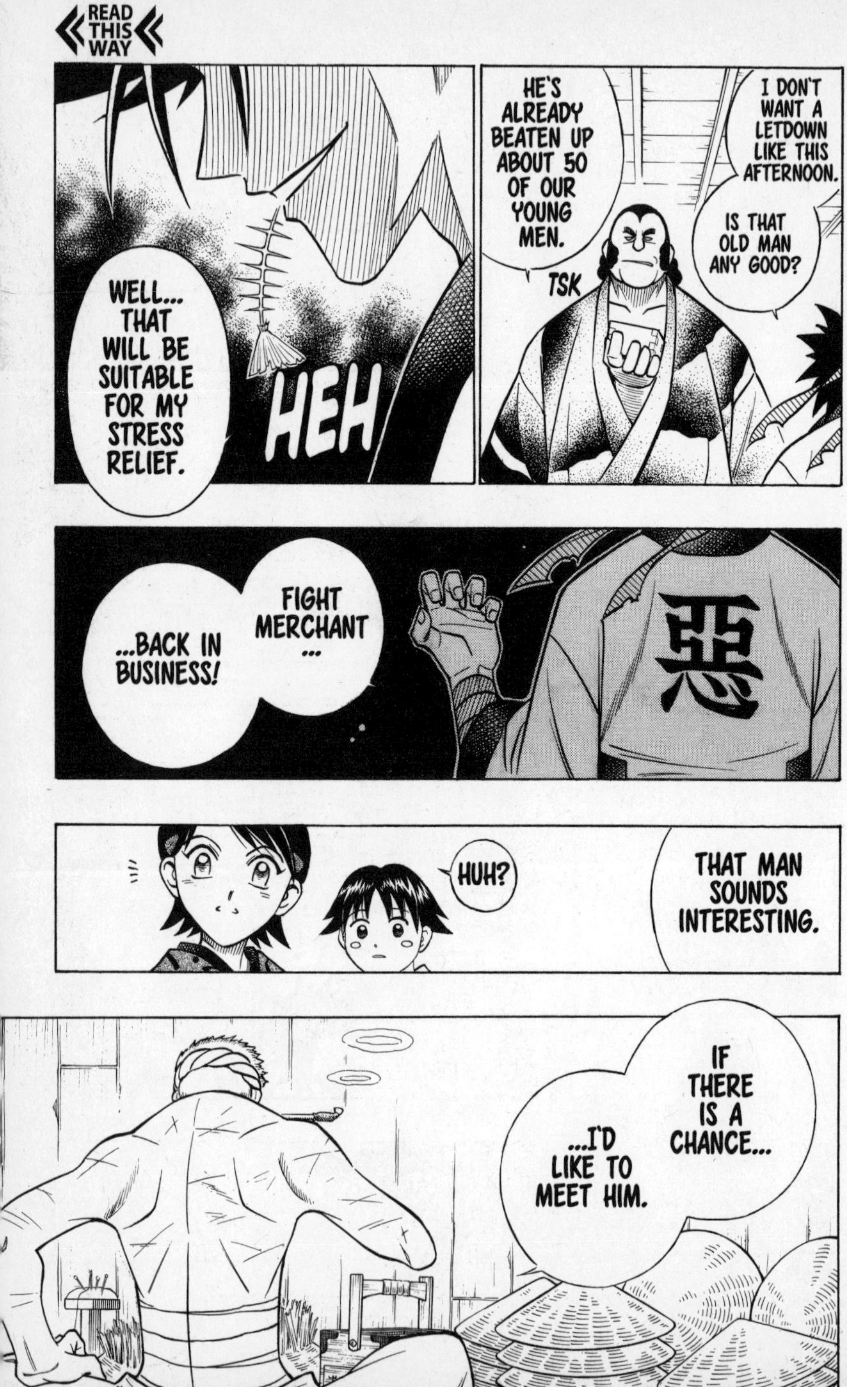
READ THIS WAY
I DON'T WANT A LETDOWN LIKE THIS AFTERNOON.
IS THAT OLD MAN ANY GOOD?
HE'S ALREADY BEATEN UP ABOUT 50 OF OUR YOUNG MEN.
TSK
WELL... THAT WILL BE SUITABLE FOR MY STRESS RELIEF.
HEH
悪
FIGHT MERCHANT ...
...BACK IN BUSINESS!
THAT MAN SOUNDS INTERESTING.
HUH?
IF THERE IS A CHANCE...
...I'D LIKE TO MEET HIM.

Rurouni Kenshin

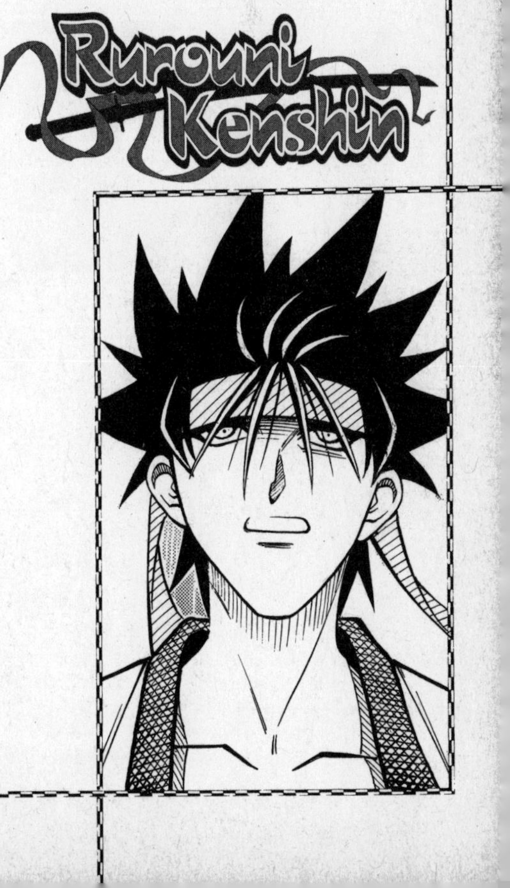

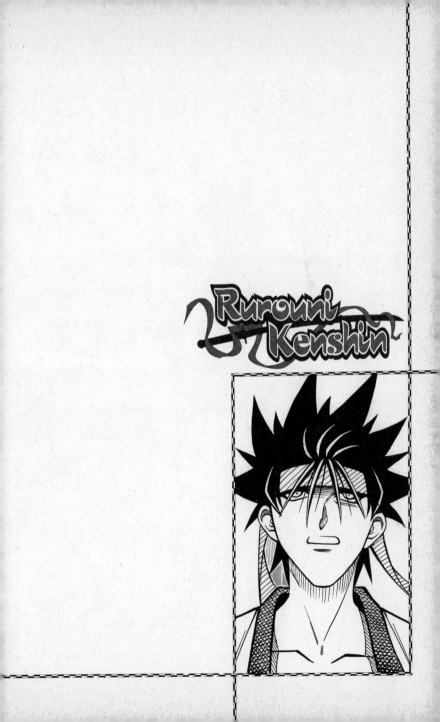

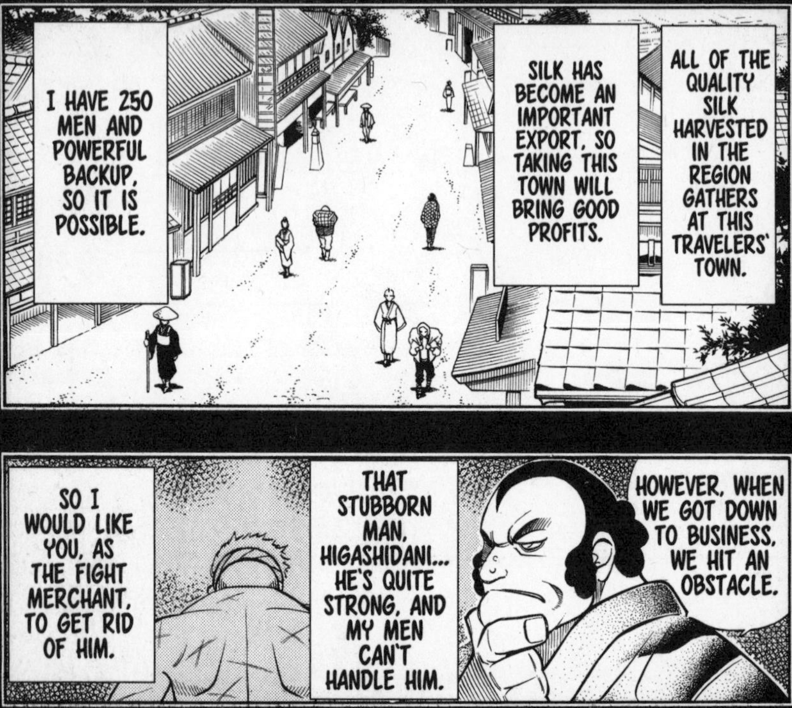
ALL OF THE QUALITY SILK HARVESTED IN THE REGION GATHERS AT THIS TRAVELERS' TOWN.
SILK HAS BECOME AN IMPORTANT EXPORT, SO TAKING THIS TOWN WILL BRING GOOD PROFITS.
I HAVE 250 MEN AND POWERFUL BACKUP, SO IT IS POSSIBLE.
HOWEVER, WHEN WE GOT DOWN TO BUSINESS, WE HIT AN OBSTACLE.
THAT STUBBORN MAN, HIGASHIDANI... HE'S QUITE STRONG, AND MY MEN CAN'T HANDLE HIM.
SO I WOULD LIKE YOU, AS THE FIGHT MERCHANT, TO GET RID OF HIM.

Act 229

A Man's Back 2: Two Alike

伸宏和月

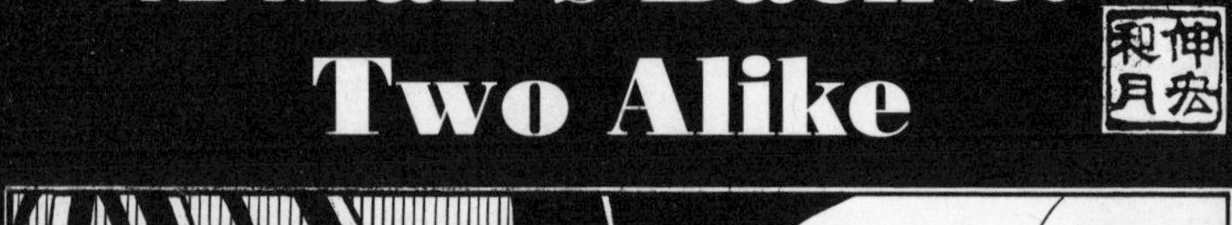
DON'T TALK TO ME LIKE A HIRED KILLER.
LIFE OR DEATH DEPENDS ON HIS LUCK, NOT ME.

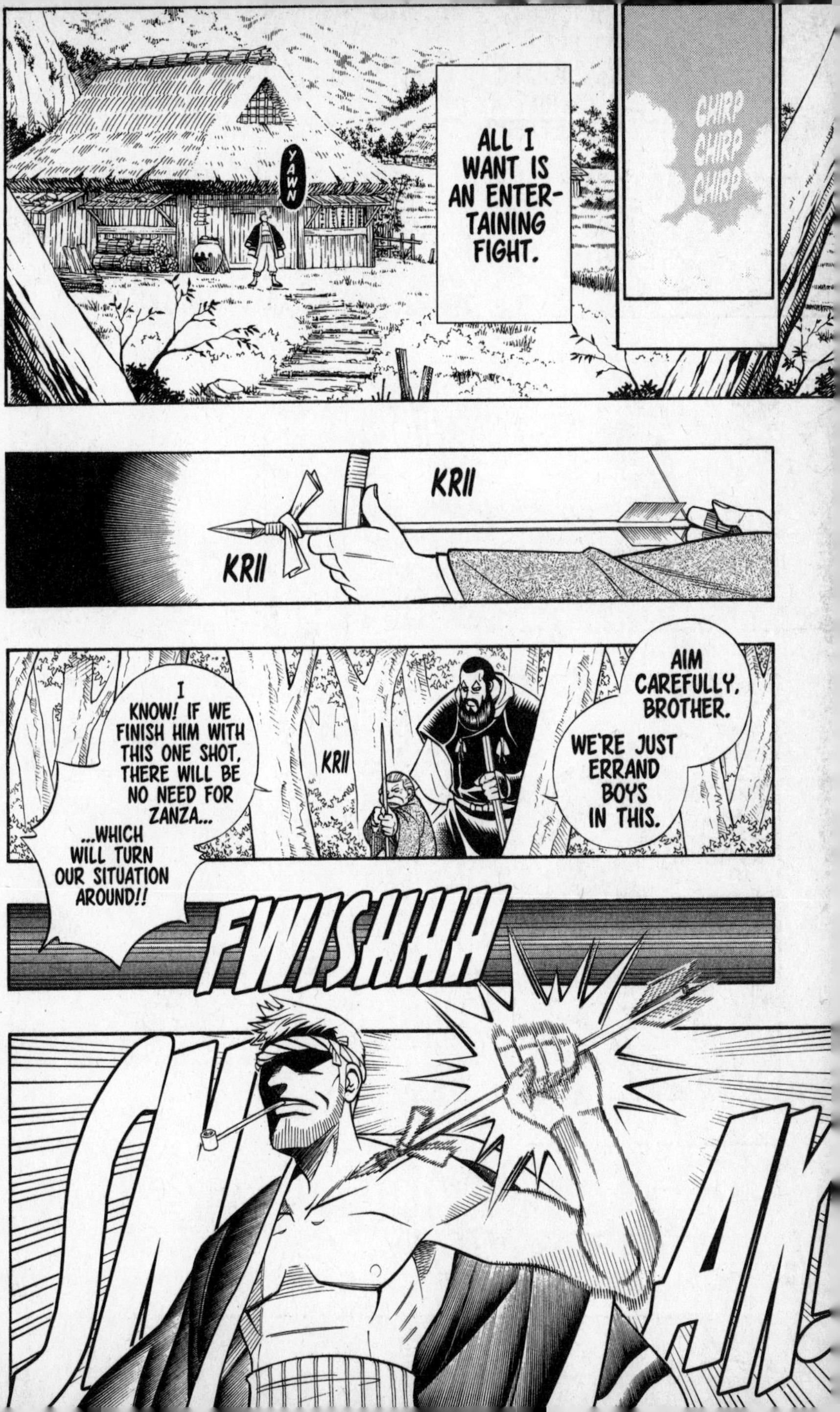
CHIRP CHIRP CHIRP
ALL I WANT IS AN ENTER-TAINING FIGHT.
YAWN
KRII
KRII
AIM CAREFULLY, BROTHER.
WE'RE JUST ERRAND BOYS IN THIS.
KRII
I KNOW! IF WE FINISH HIM WITH THIS ONE SHOT, THERE WILL BE NO NEED FOR ZANZA...
...WHICH WILL TURN OUR SITUATION AROUND!!
FWISHHH

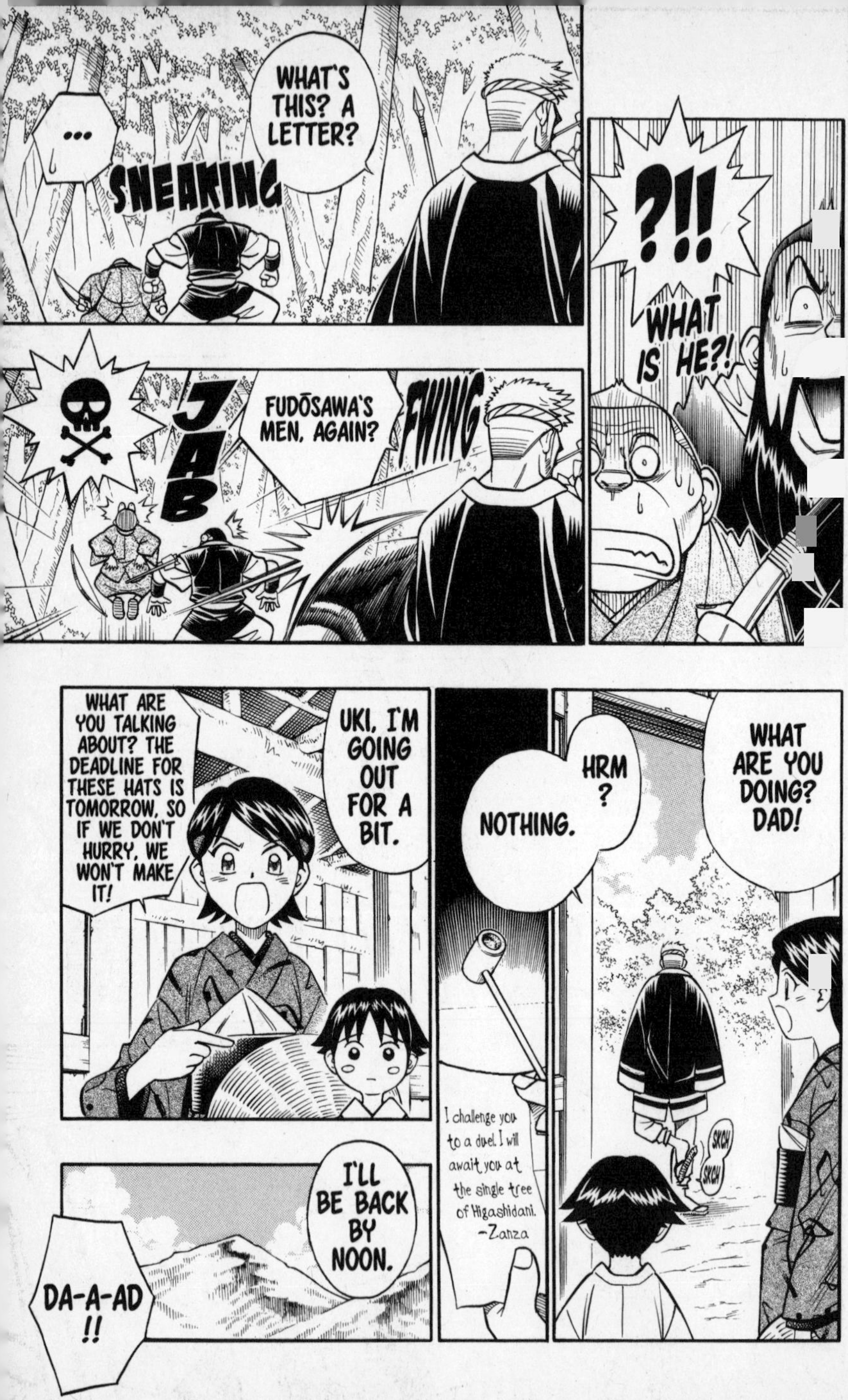
?!!
WHAT IS HE?!
WHAT'S THIS? A LETTER?
...
SNEAKING
FWING
FUDŌSAWA'S MEN, AGAIN?
JAB
WHAT ARE YOU DOING? DAD!
HRM?
SKCH
SKCH
NOTHING.
I challenge you to a duel. I will await you at the single tree of Higashidani. -Zanza
UKI, I'M GOING OUT FOR A BIT.
WHAT ARE YOU TALKING ABOUT? THE DEADLINE FOR THESE HATS IS TOMORROW, SO IF WE DON'T HURRY, WE WON'T MAKE IT!
I'LL BE BACK BY NOON.
DA-A-AD !!

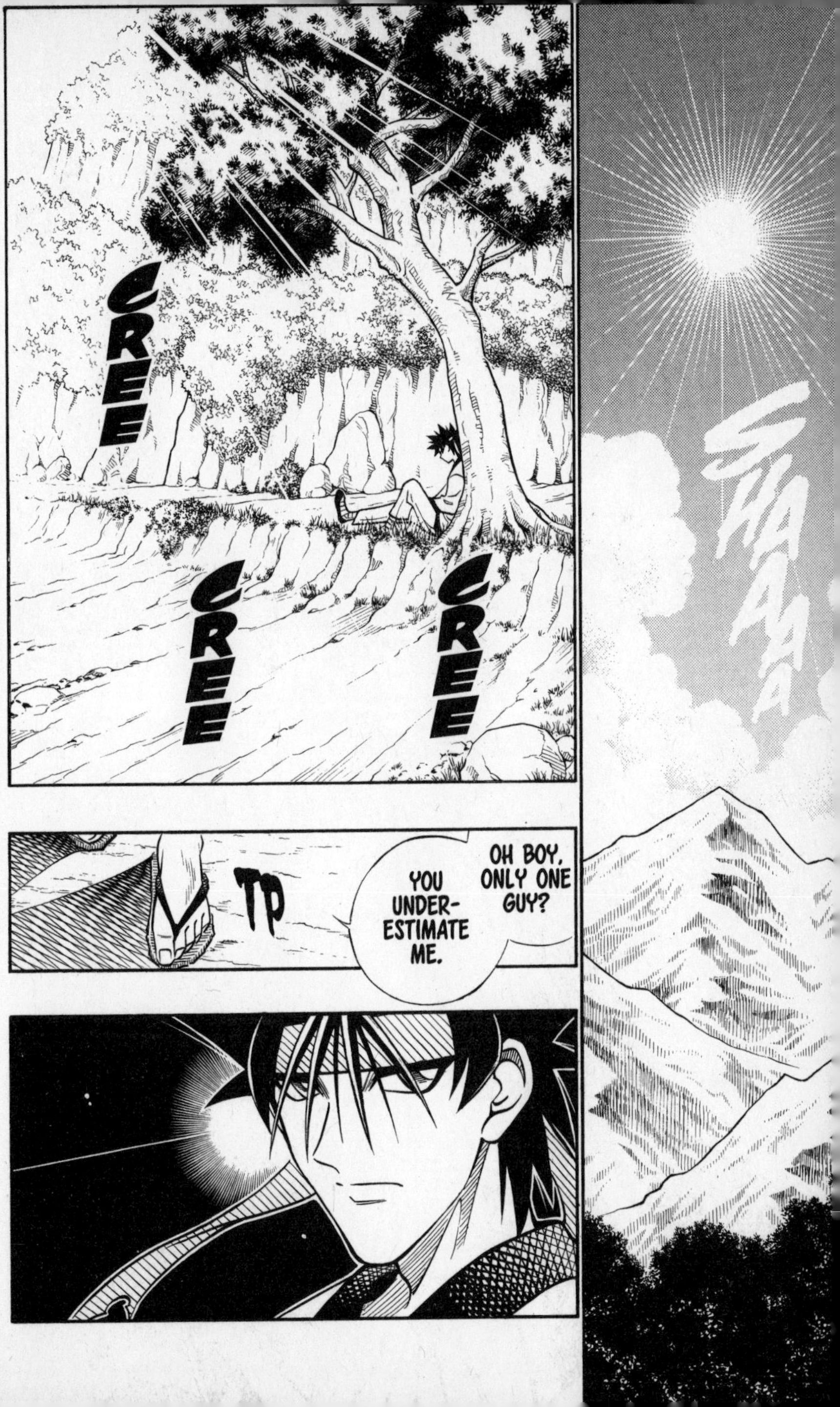
SHAAAA
CREE
CREE
CREE
TP
OH BOY, ONLY ONE GUY?
YOU UNDER-ESTIMATE ME.

READ THIS WAY

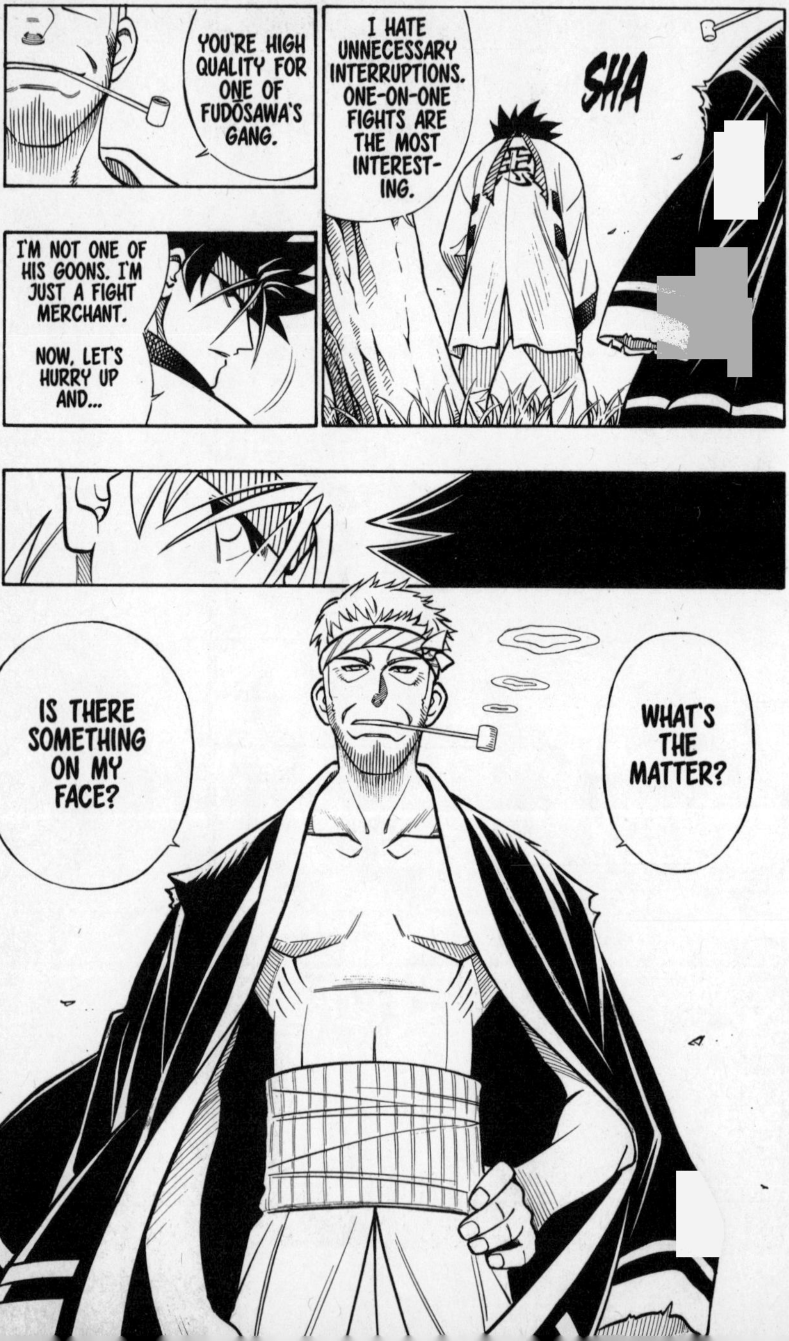
I HATE UNNECESSARY INTERRUPTIONS. ONE-ON-ONE FIGHTS ARE THE MOST INTEREST-ING.
SHA
YOU'RE HIGH QUALITY FOR ONE OF FUDŌSAWA'S GANG.
I'M NOT ONE OF HIS GOONS. I'M JUST A FIGHT MERCHANT.
NOW, LET'S HURRY UP AND...
WHAT'S THE MATTER?
IS THERE SOMETHING ON MY FACE?

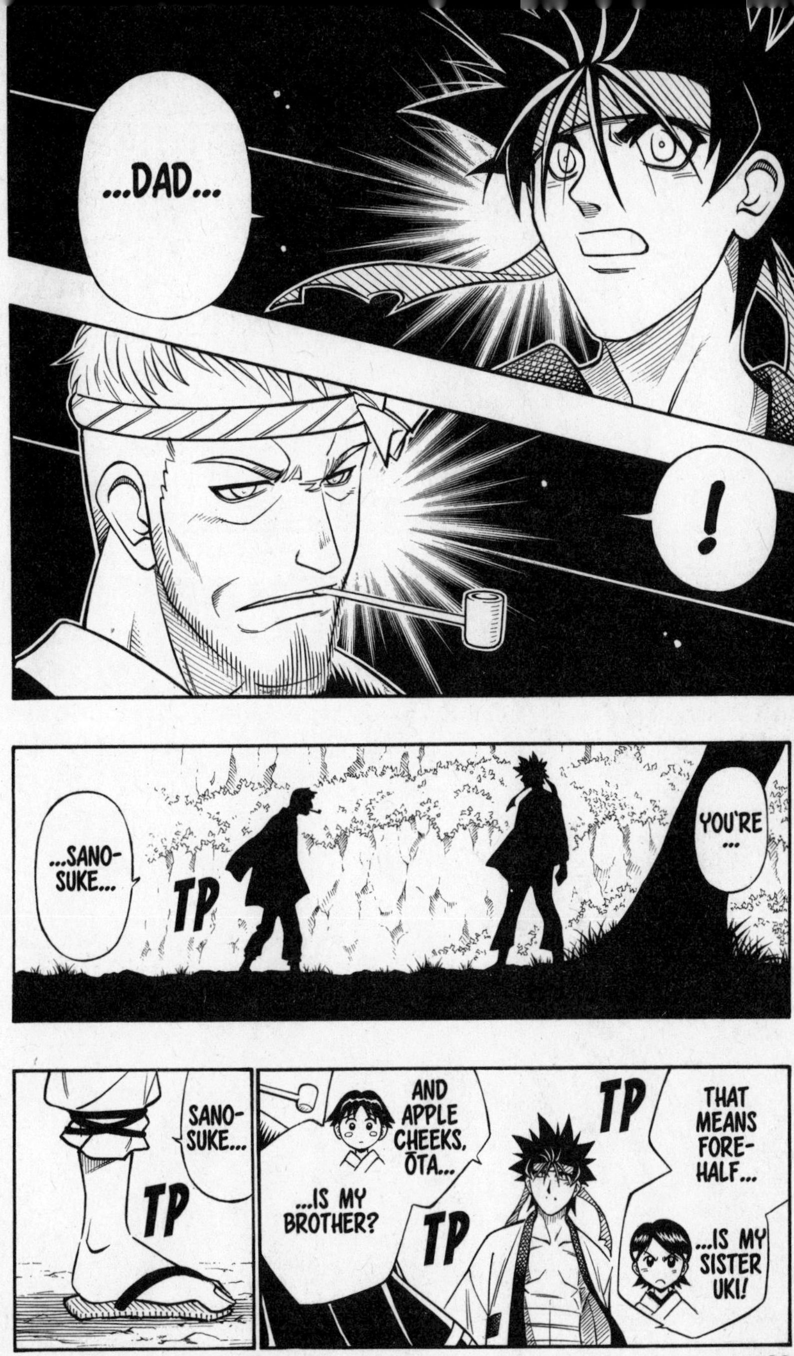
...DAD...
!
YOU'RE ...
TP
...SANO-SUKE...
THAT MEANS FORE-HALF...
...IS MY SISTER UKI!
TP
TP
AND APPLE CHEEKS, ŌTA...
...IS MY BROTHER?
SANO-SUKE...
TP

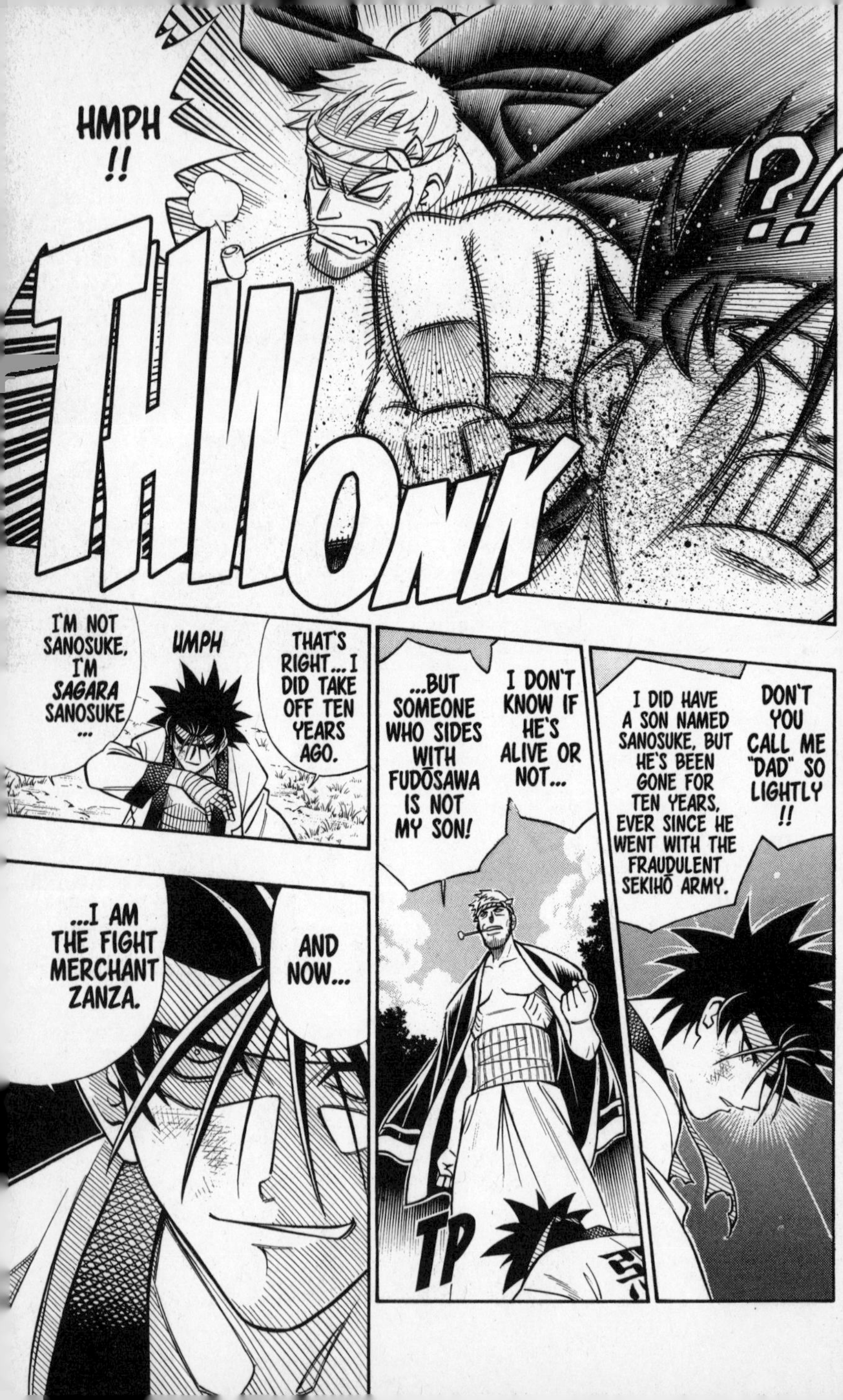
HMPH !!
?!
THWONK
DON'T YOU CALL ME "DAD" SO LIGHTLY !!
I DID HAVE A SON NAMED SANOSUKE, BUT HE'S BEEN GONE FOR TEN YEARS, EVER SINCE HE WENT WITH THE FRAUDULENT SEKIHŌ ARMY.
I DON'T KNOW IF HE'S ALIVE OR NOT...
...BUT SOMEONE WHO SIDES WITH FUDŌSAWA IS NOT MY SON!
TP
THAT'S RIGHT... I DID TAKE OFF TEN YEARS AGO.
UMPH
I'M NOT SANOSUKE, I'M SAGARA SANOSUKE ...
AND NOW...
...I AM THE FIGHT MERCHANT ZANZA.

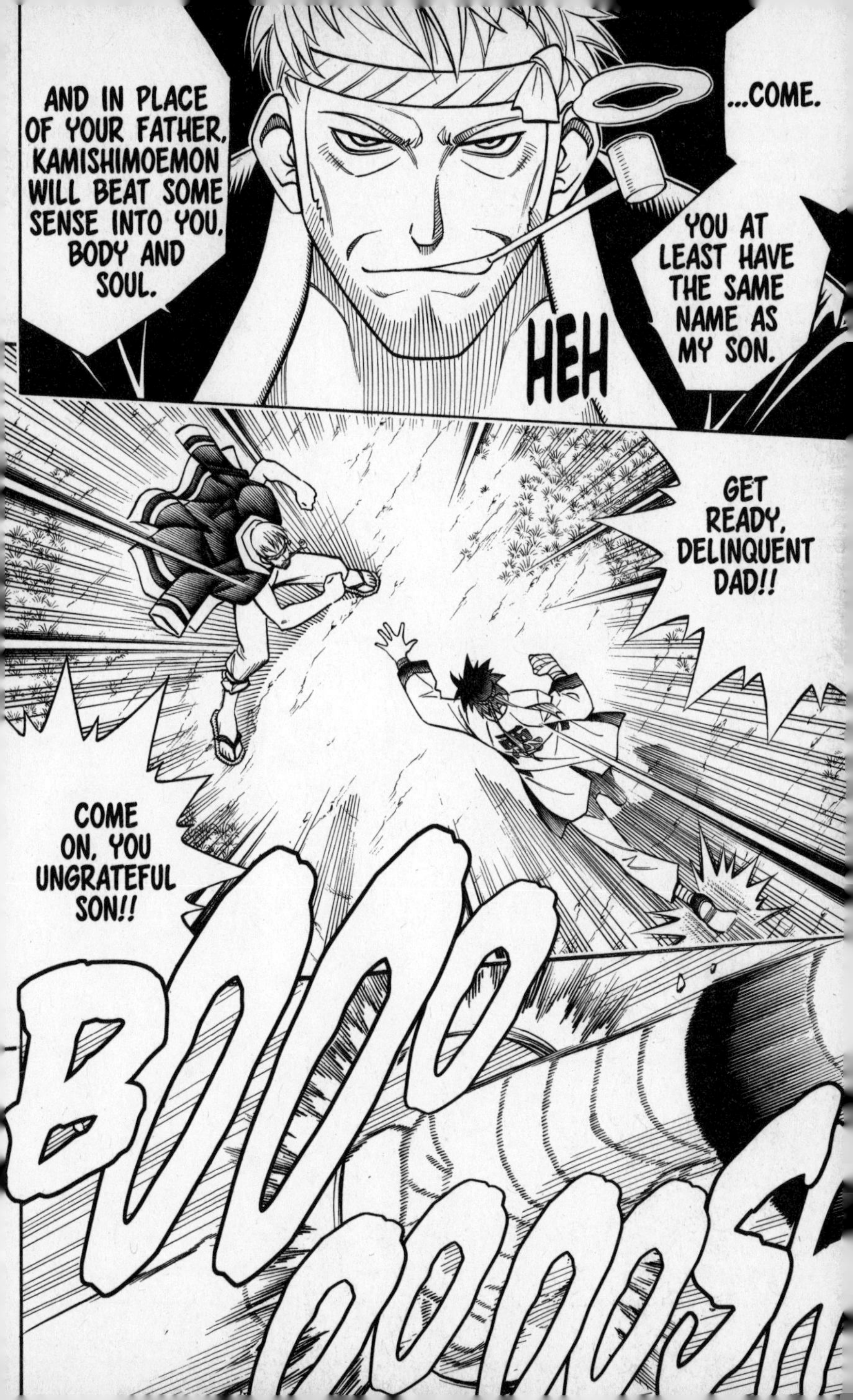
...COME.
YOU AT LEAST HAVE THE SAME NAME AS MY SON.
HEH
AND IN PLACE OF YOUR FATHER, KAMISHIMOEMON WILL BEAT SOME SENSE INTO YOU, BODY AND SOUL.
GET READY, DELINQUENT DAD!!
COME ON, YOU UNGRATEFUL SON!!
BOOOOOOOO

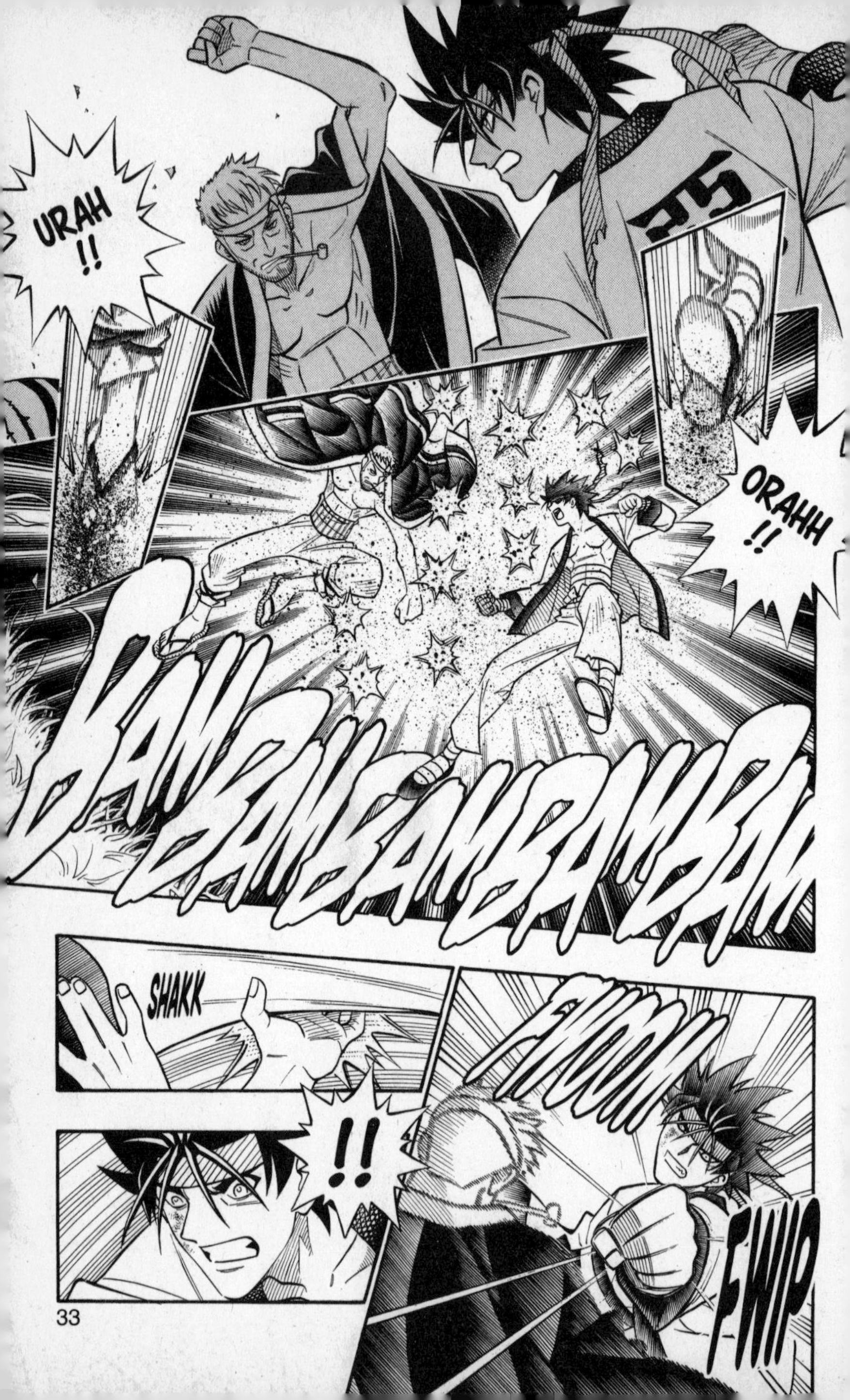
URAH !!
ORAHH !!
BAMBAMBAMBAMBAM
FWOOM
FWIP
SHAKK
!!

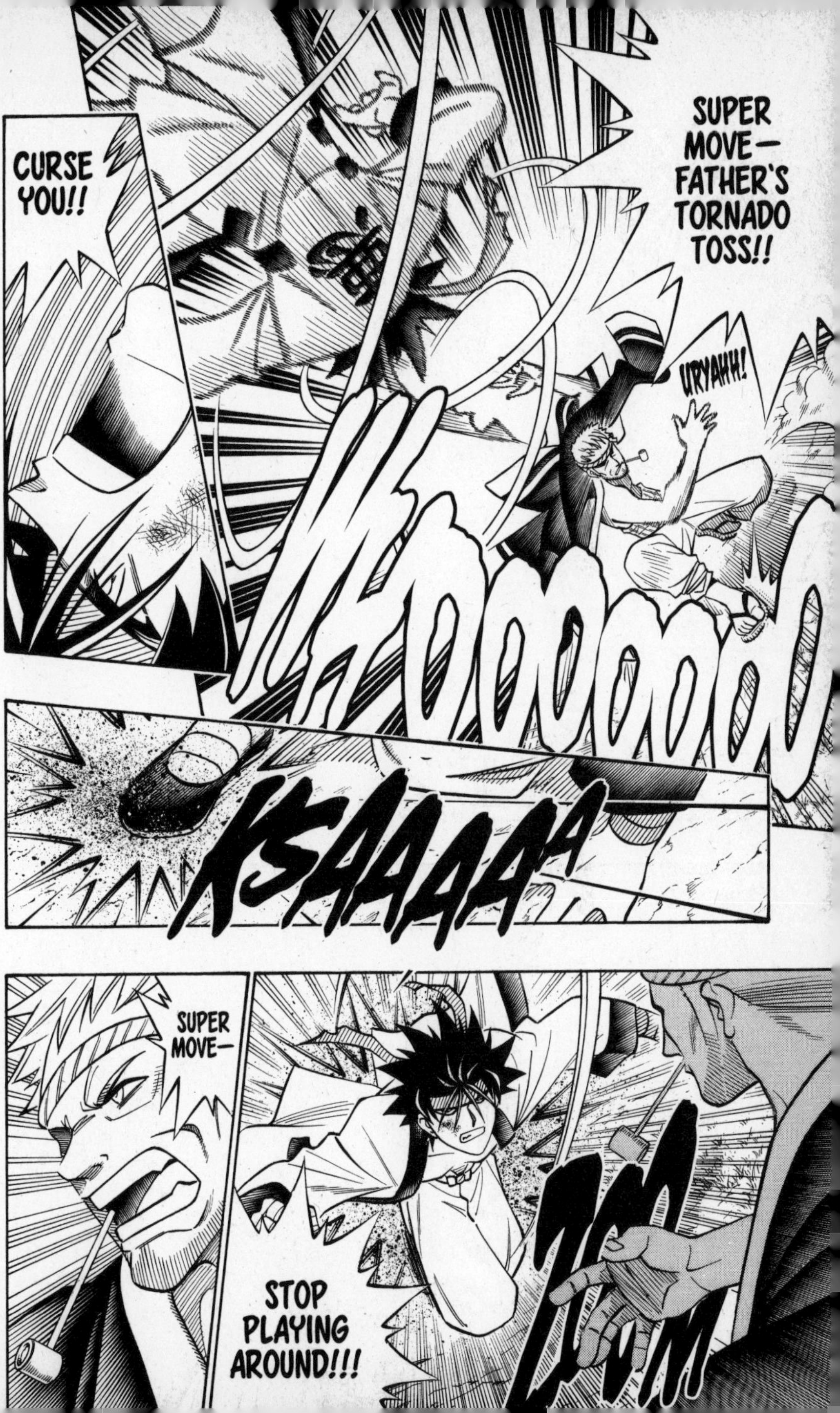
SUPER MOVE—FATHER'S TORNADO TOSS!!
URYAHH!
CURSE YOU!!
STOP PLAYING AROUND!!!
ZOOM
SUPER MOVE—

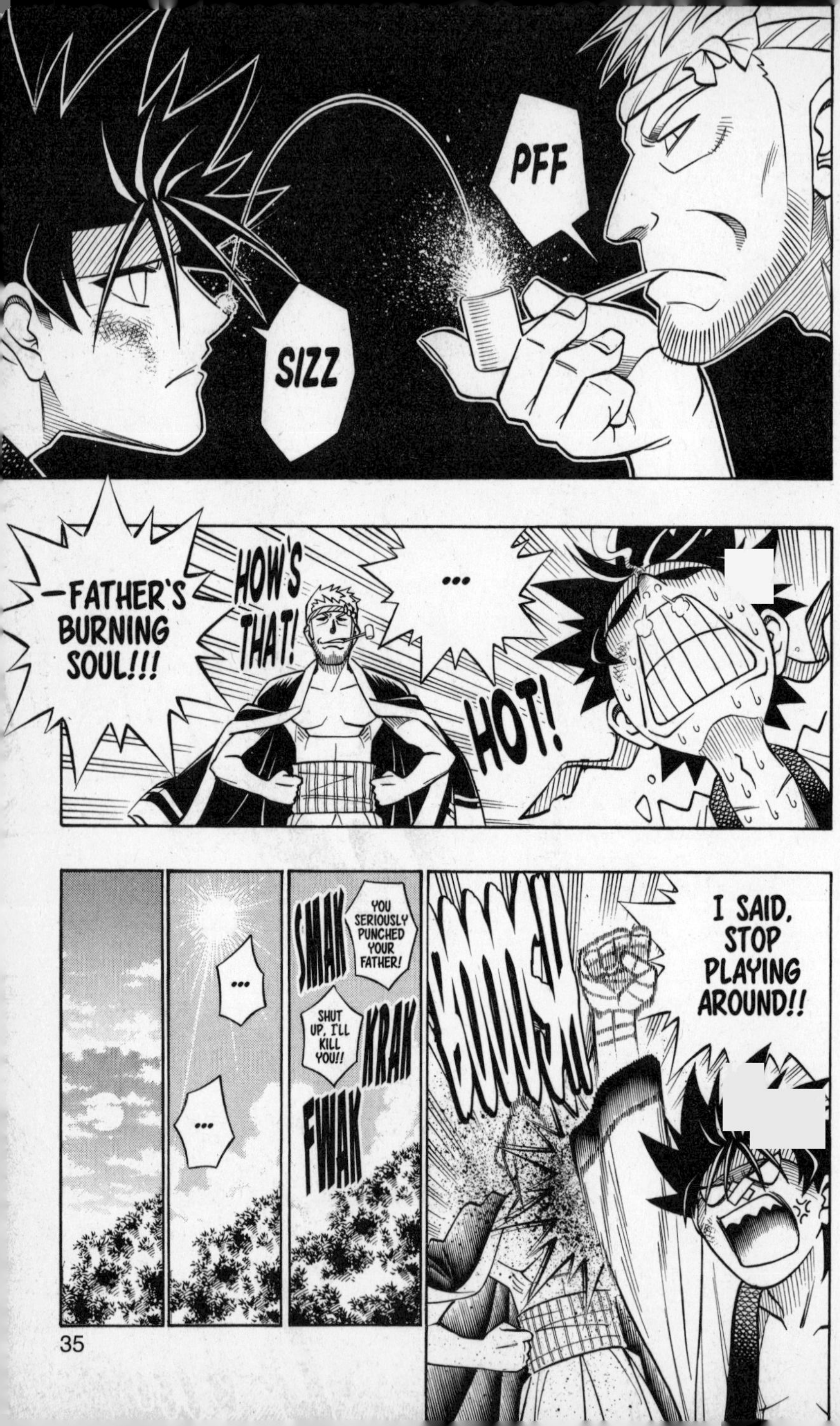
PFF
SIZZ
...
HOT!
HOW'S THAT!
—FATHER'S BURNING SOUL!!!
I SAID, STOP PLAYING AROUND!!
YOU SERIOUSLY PUNCHED YOUR FATHER!
SMAK
KRAK
SHUT UP, I'LL KILL YOU!!
FWAK
...
...

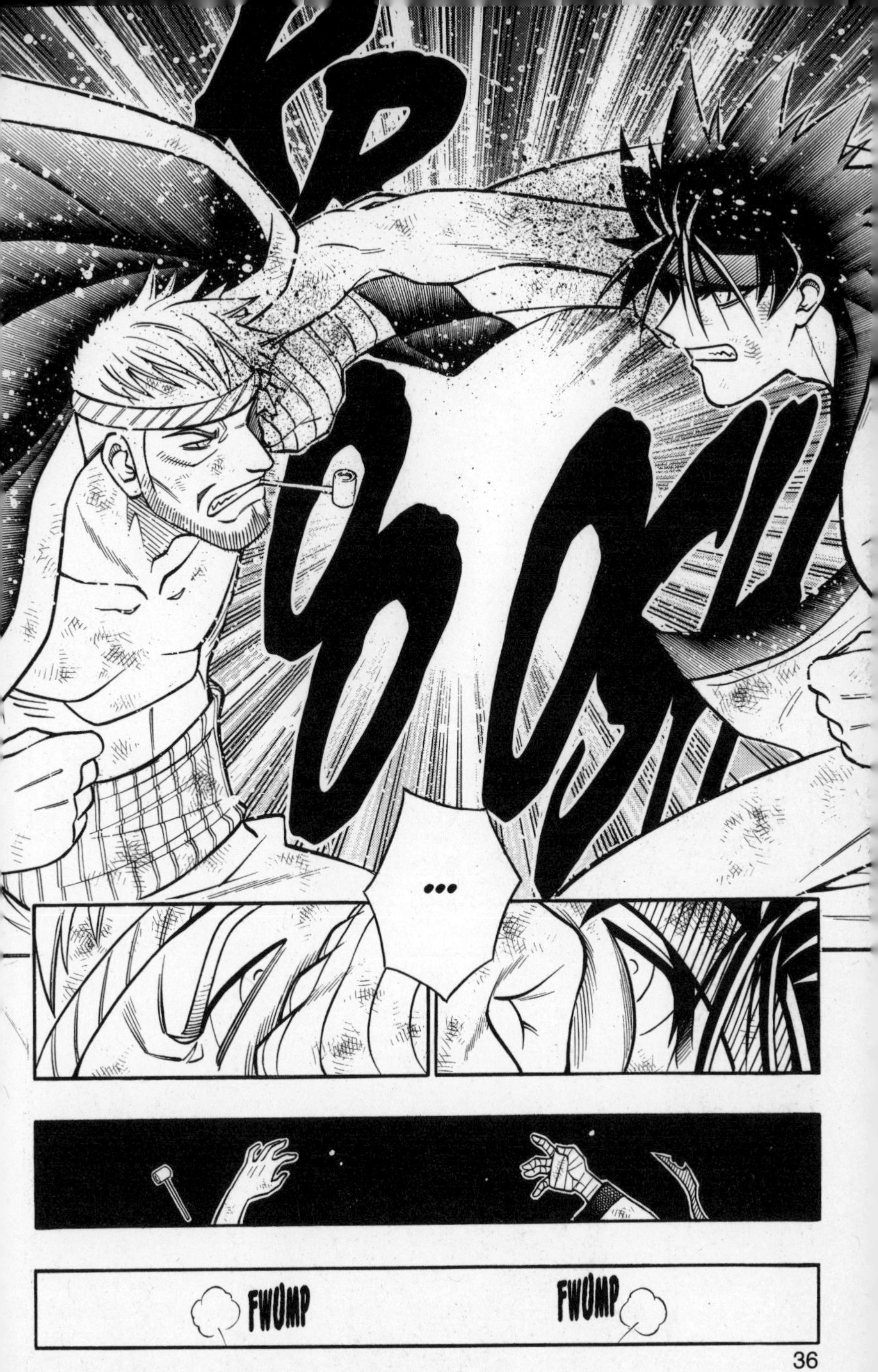
...
FWUMP
FWUMP

READ THIS WAY

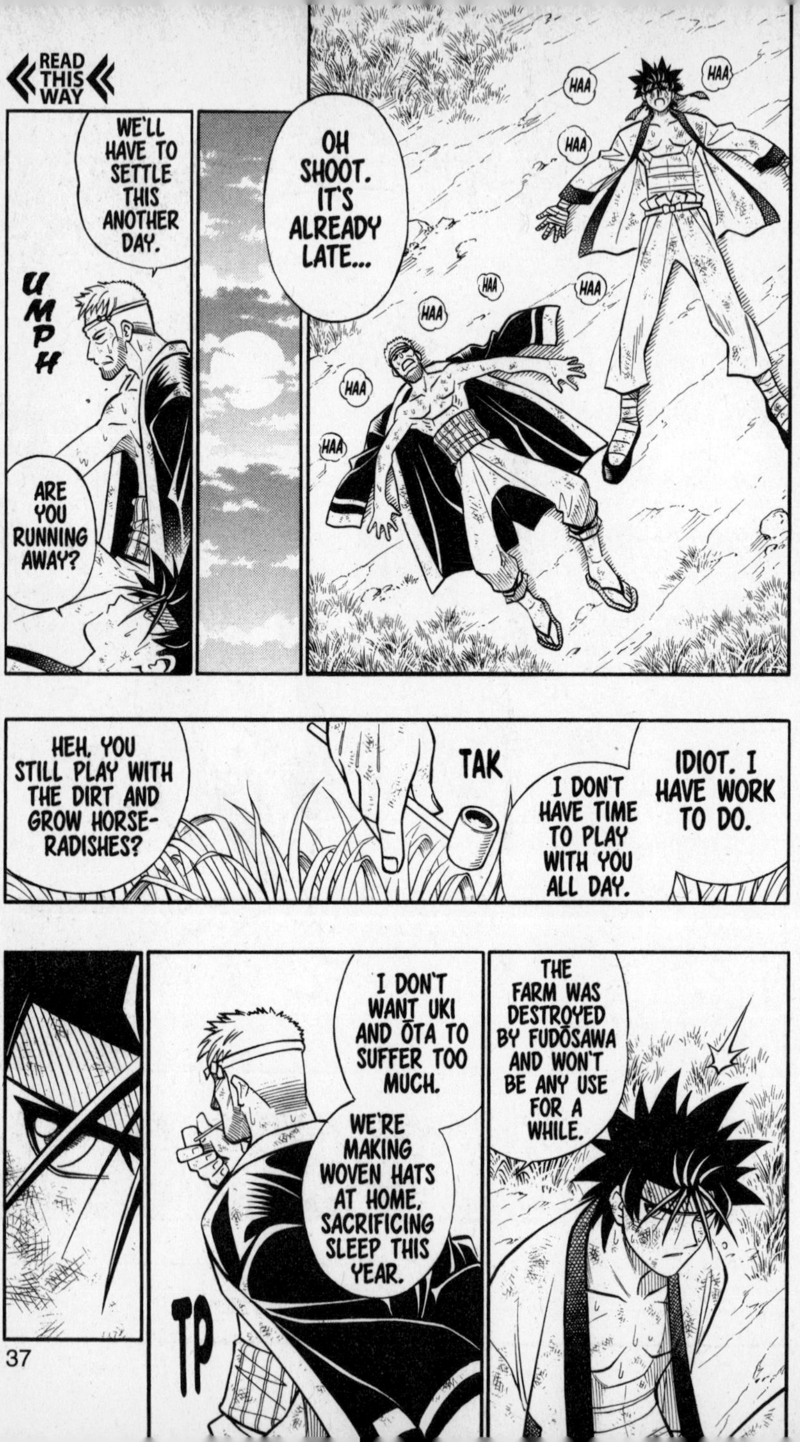
HAA
HAA
HAA
OH SHOOT. IT'S ALREADY LATE...
HAA
HAA
HAA
HAA
HAA
WE'LL HAVE TO SETTLE THIS ANOTHER DAY.
UMPH
ARE YOU RUNNING AWAY?
IDIOT. I HAVE WORK TO DO.
I DON'T HAVE TIME TO PLAY WITH YOU ALL DAY.
TAK
HEH, YOU STILL PLAY WITH THE DIRT AND GROW HORSE-RADISHES?
THE FARM WAS DESTROYED BY FUDŌSAWA AND WON'T BE ANY USE FOR A WHILE.
I DON'T WANT UKI AND ŌTA TO SUFFER TOO MUCH.
WE'RE MAKING WOVEN HATS AT HOME, SACRIFICING SLEEP THIS YEAR.
TP

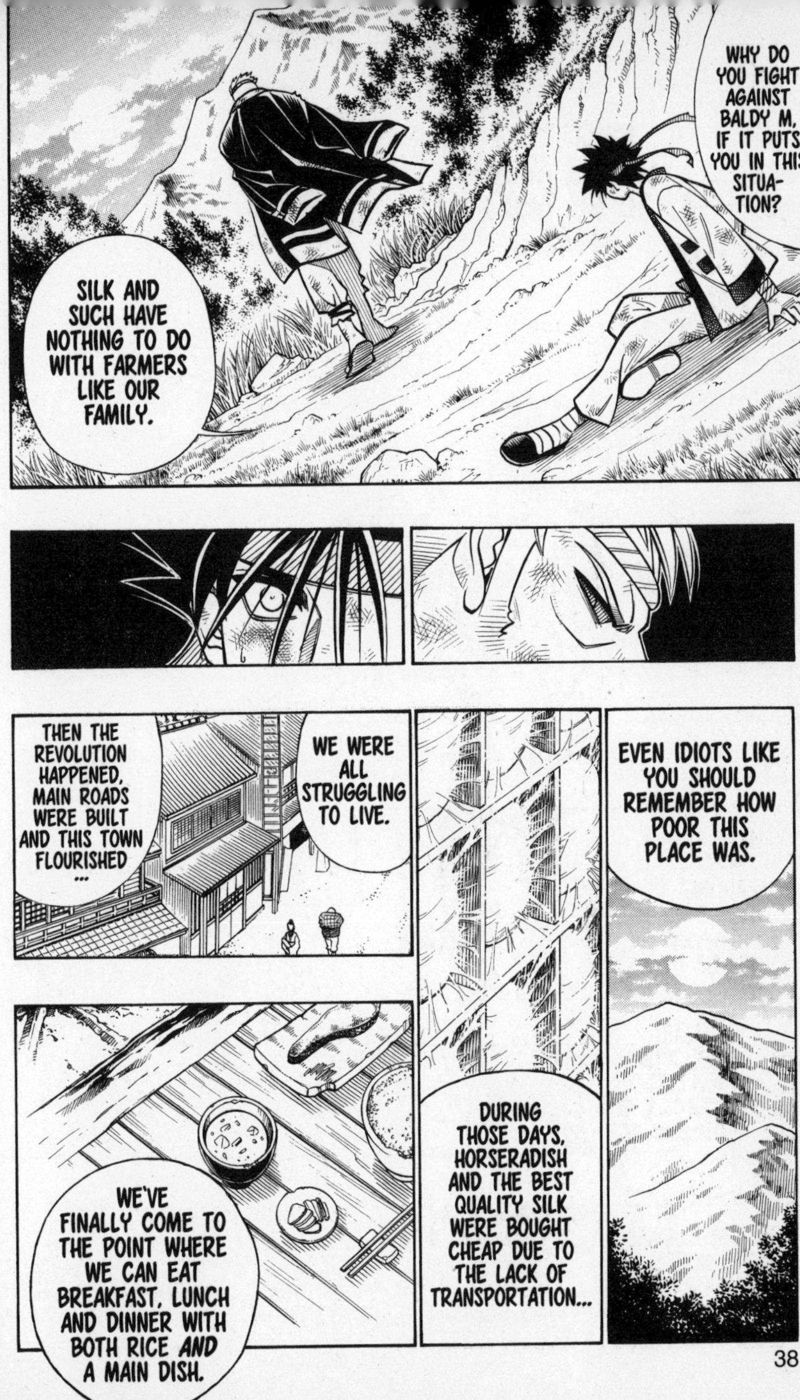
WHY DO YOU FIGHT AGAINST BALDY M, IF IT PUTS YOU IN THIS SITUATION?
SILK AND SUCH HAVE NOTHING TO DO WITH FARMERS LIKE OUR FAMILY.
EVEN IDIOTS LIKE YOU SHOULD REMEMBER HOW POOR THIS PLACE WAS.
DURING THOSE DAYS, HORSERADISH AND THE BEST QUALITY SILK WERE BOUGHT CHEAP DUE TO THE LACK OF TRANSPORTATION...
WE WERE ALL STRUGGLING TO LIVE.
THEN THE REVOLUTION HAPPENED, MAIN ROADS WERE BUILT AND THIS TOWN FLOURISHED...
WE'VE FINALLY COME TO THE POINT WHERE WE CAN EAT BREAKFAST, LUNCH AND DINNER WITH BOTH RICE *AND* A MAIN DISH.

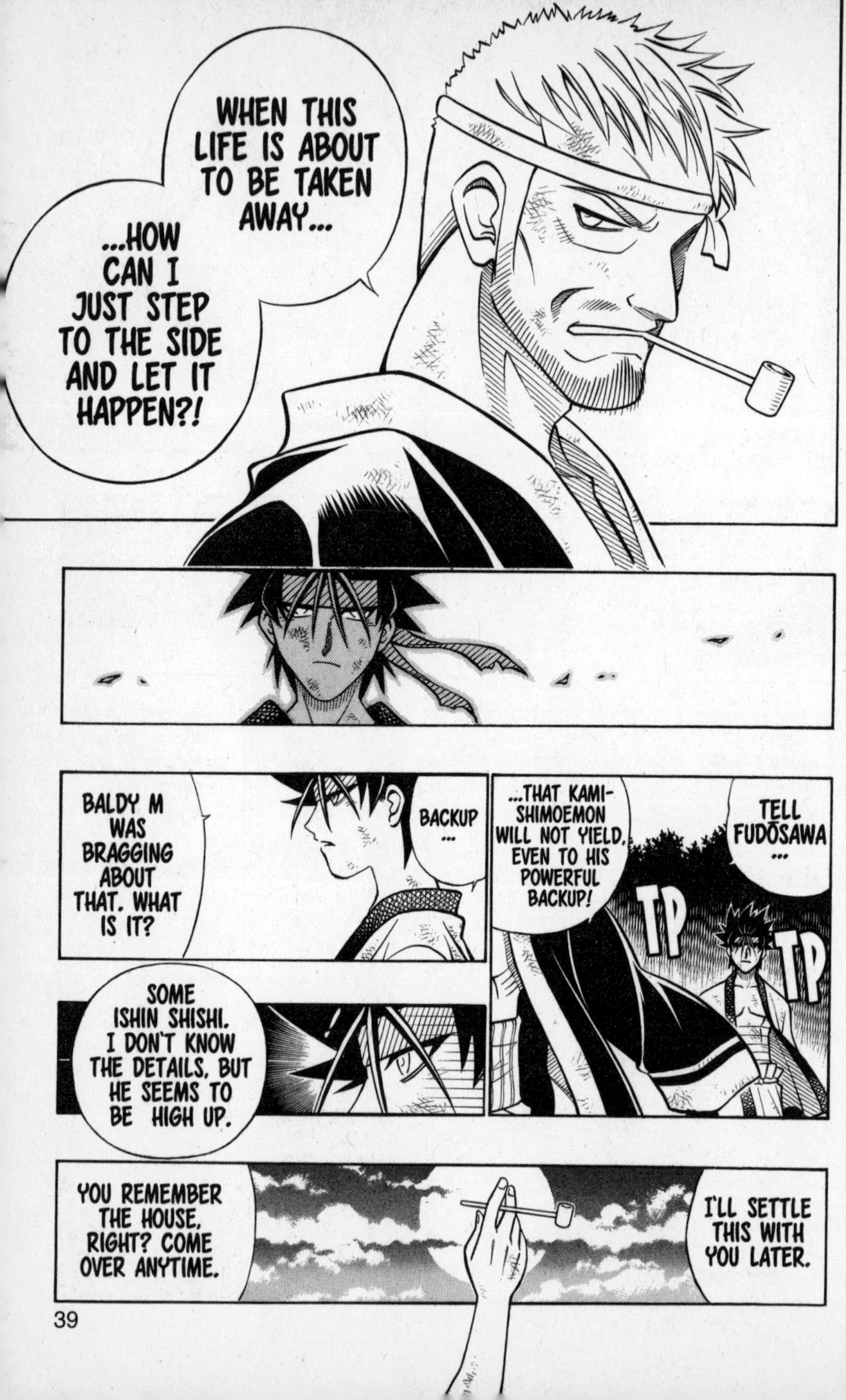
WHEN THIS LIFE IS ABOUT TO BE TAKEN AWAY...
...HOW CAN I JUST STEP TO THE SIDE AND LET IT HAPPEN?!
TELL FUDŌSAWA...
...THAT KAMI-SHIMOEMON WILL NOT YIELD, EVEN TO HIS POWERFUL BACKUP!
TP
TP
BACKUP...
BALDY M WAS BRAGGING ABOUT THAT. WHAT IS IT?
SOME ISHIN SHISHI. I DON'T KNOW THE DETAILS, BUT HE SEEMS TO BE HIGH UP.
I'LL SETTLE THIS WITH YOU LATER.
YOU REMEMBER THE HOUSE, RIGHT? COME OVER ANYTIME.

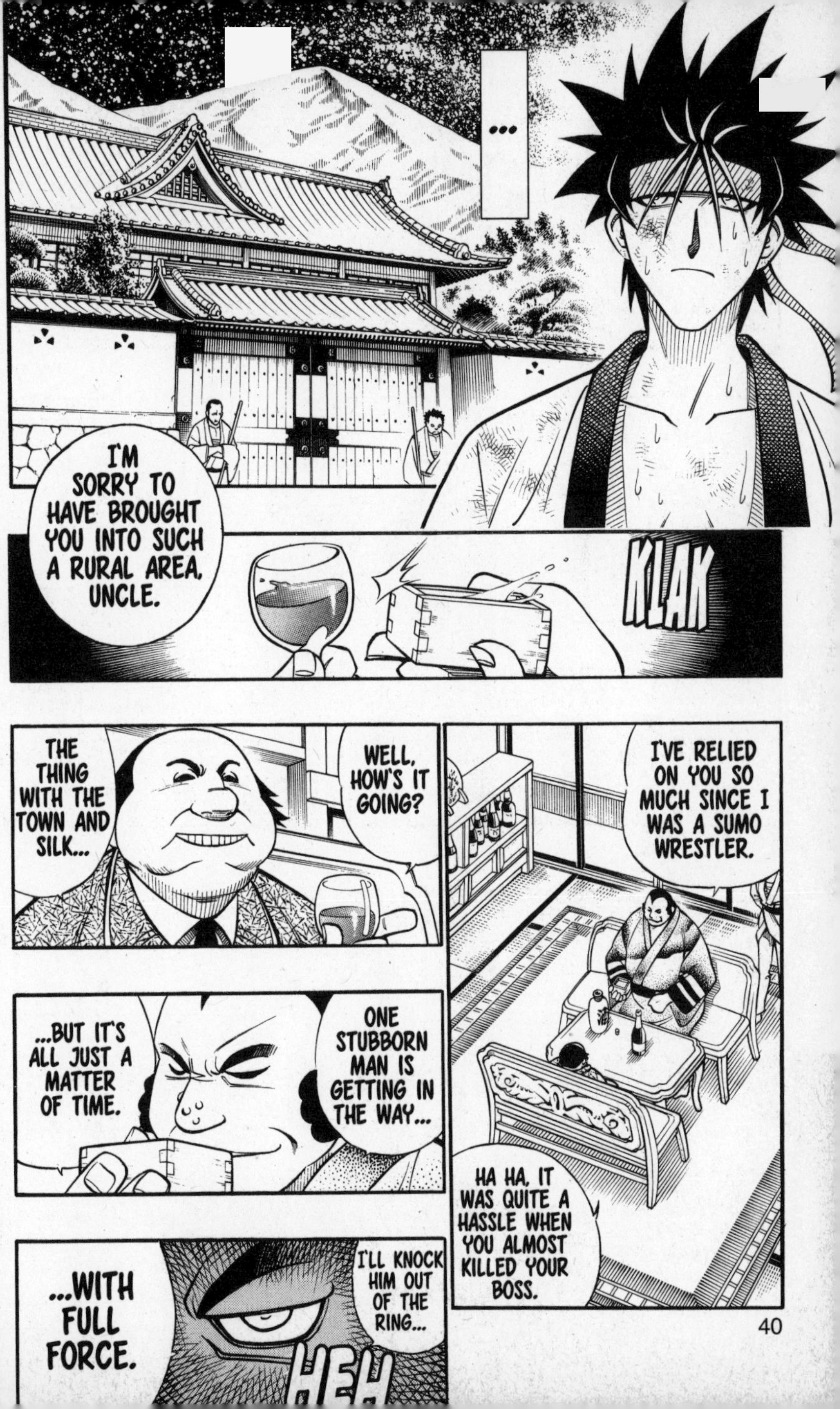
...
I'M SORRY TO HAVE BROUGHT YOU INTO SUCH A RURAL AREA, UNCLE.
KLAK
I'VE RELIED ON YOU SO MUCH SINCE I WAS A SUMO WRESTLER.
HA HA, IT WAS QUITE A HASSLE WHEN YOU ALMOST KILLED YOUR BOSS.
WELL, HOW'S IT GOING?
THE THING WITH THE TOWN AND SILK...
ONE STUBBORN MAN IS GETTING IN THE WAY...
...BUT IT'S ALL JUST A MATTER OF TIME.
I'LL KNOCK HIM OUT OF THE RING...
...WITH FULL FORCE.
HEH

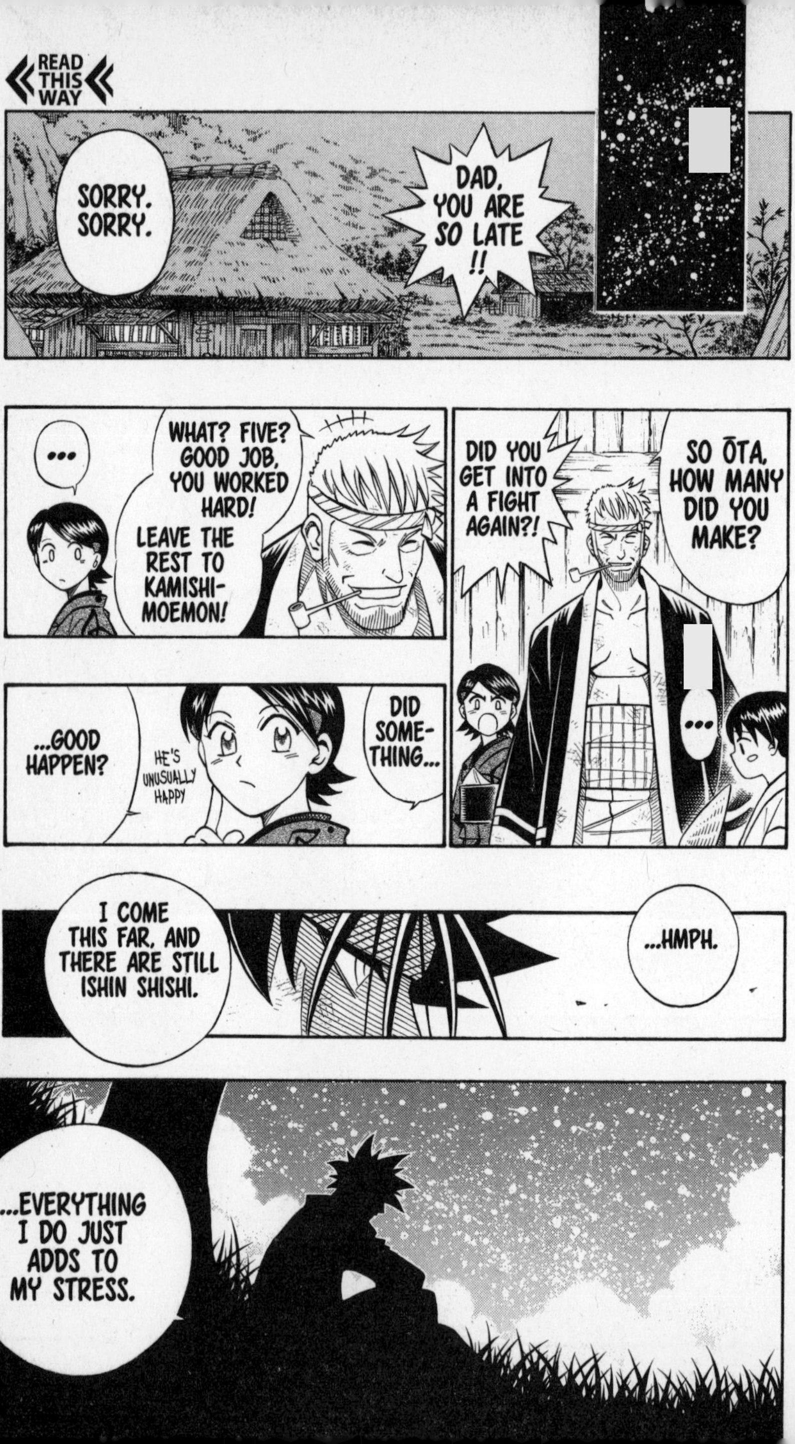
READ THIS WAY
DAD, YOU ARE SO LATE !!
SORRY. SORRY.
SO ŌTA, HOW MANY DID YOU MAKE?
DID YOU GET INTO A FIGHT AGAIN?!
...
WHAT? FIVE? GOOD JOB, YOU WORKED HARD!
LEAVE THE REST TO KAMISHI-MOEMON!
...
DID SOME-THING...
HE'S UNUSUALLY HAPPY
...GOOD HAPPEN?
...HMPH.
I COME THIS FAR, AND THERE ARE STILL ISHIN SHISHI.
...EVERYTHING I DO JUST ADDS TO MY STRESS.

Rurouni Kenshin

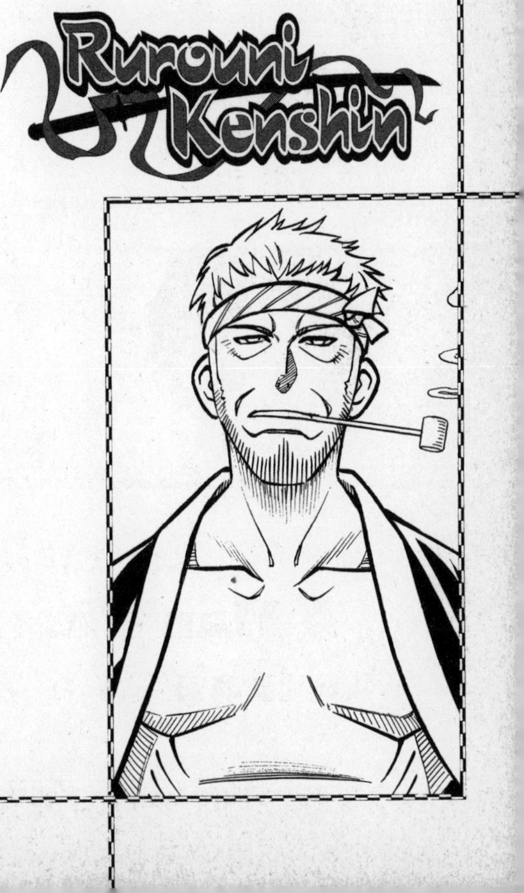

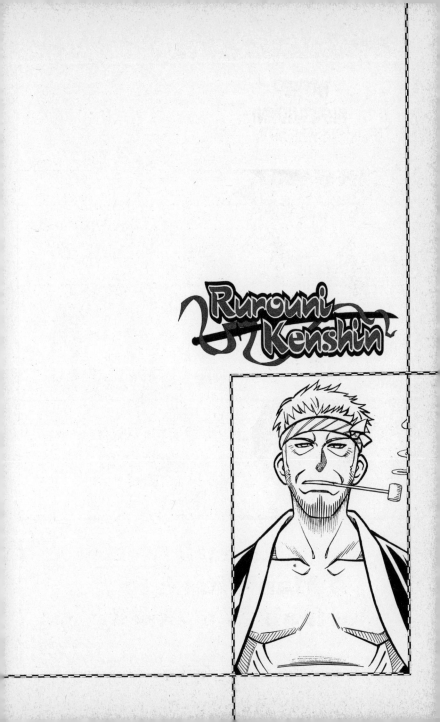

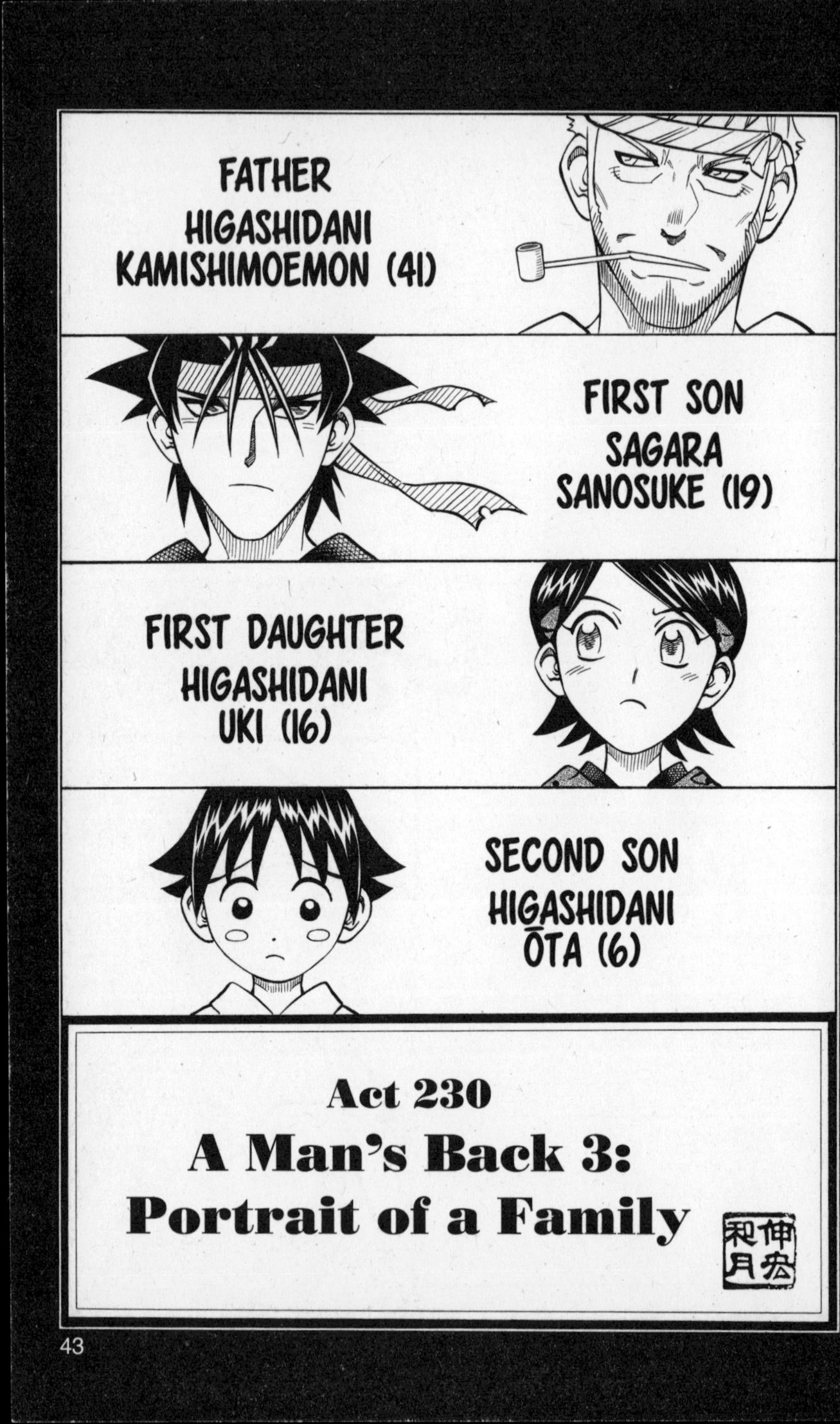
FATHER
HIGASHIDANI
KAMISHIMOEMON (41)
FIRST SON
SAGARA
SANOSUKE (19)
FIRST DAUGHTER
HIGASHIDANI
UKI (16)
SECOND SON
HIGASHIDANI
ŌTA (6)

Act 230

A Man's Back 3: Portrait of a Family

伸宏
和月

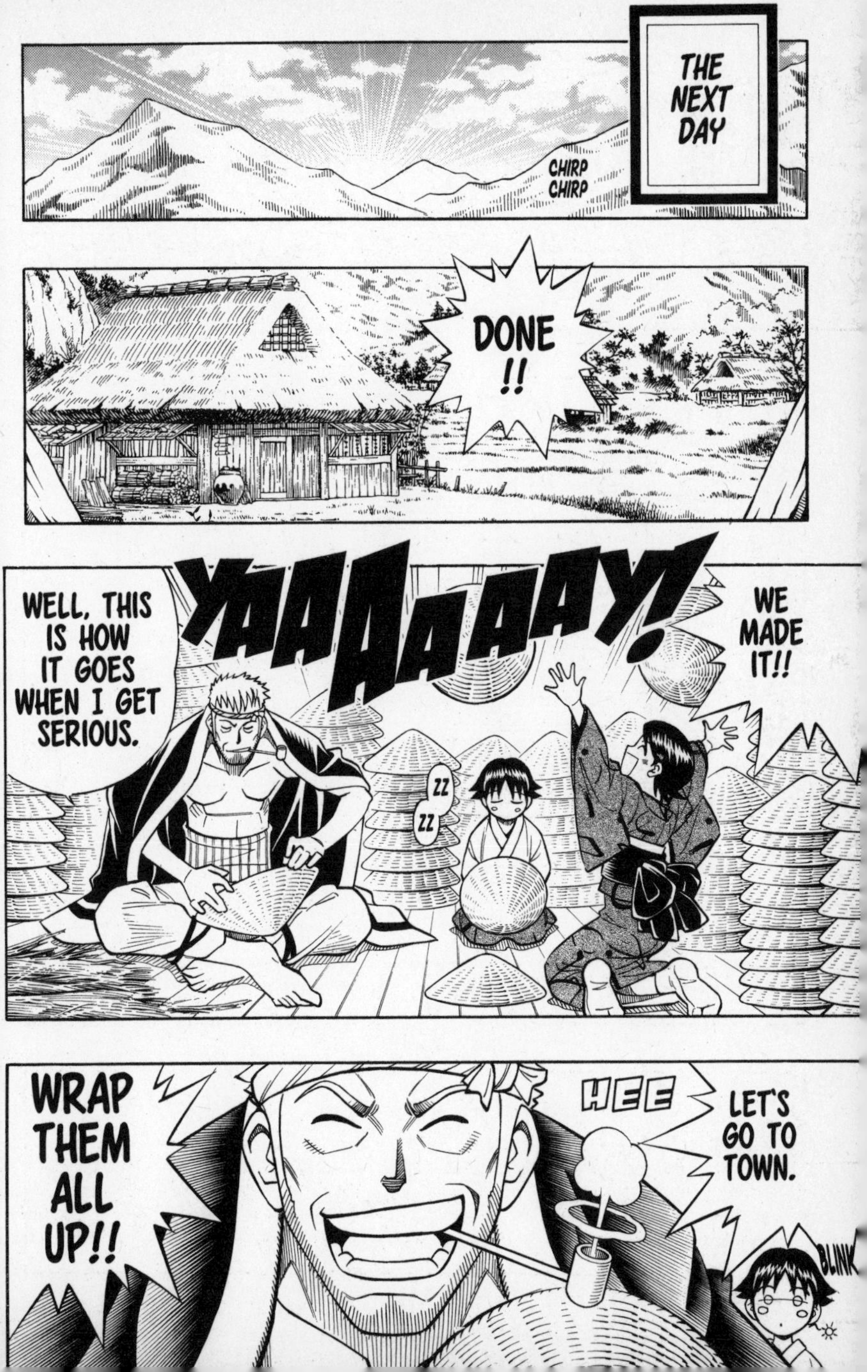

THE NEXT DAY
CHIRP CHIRP
DONE!!
WE MADE IT!!
YAAAAAAY!
WELL, THIS IS HOW IT GOES WHEN I GET SERIOUS.
ZZ ZZ
BLINK
LET'S GO TO TOWN.
HEE
WRAP THEM ALL UP!!

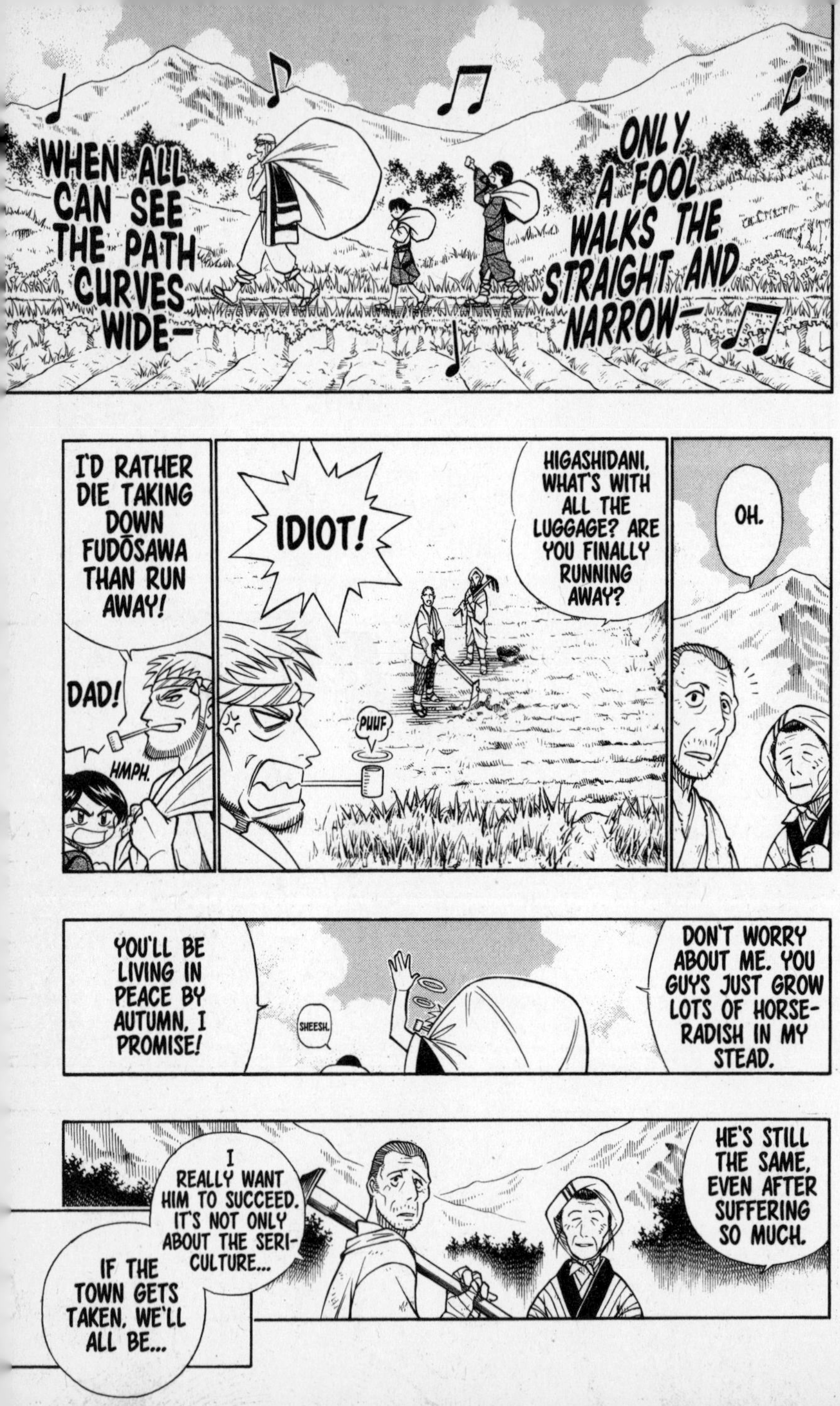
ONLY A FOOL WALKS THE STRAIGHT AND NARROW—
WHEN ALL CAN SEE THE PATH CURVES WIDE—
OH.
HIGASHIDANI, WHAT'S WITH ALL THE LUGGAGE? ARE YOU FINALLY RUNNING AWAY?
IDIOT!
PUUF
I'D RATHER DIE TAKING DOWN FUDŌSAWA THAN RUN AWAY!
DAD!
HMPH.
DON'T WORRY ABOUT ME. YOU GUYS JUST GROW LOTS OF HORSE-RADISH IN MY STEAD.
SHEESH.
YOU'LL BE LIVING IN PEACE BY AUTUMN, I PROMISE!
HE'S STILL THE SAME, EVEN AFTER SUFFERING SO MUCH.
I REALLY WANT HIM TO SUCCEED. IT'S NOT ONLY ABOUT THE SERI-CULTURE...
IF THE TOWN GETS TAKEN, WE'LL ALL BE...

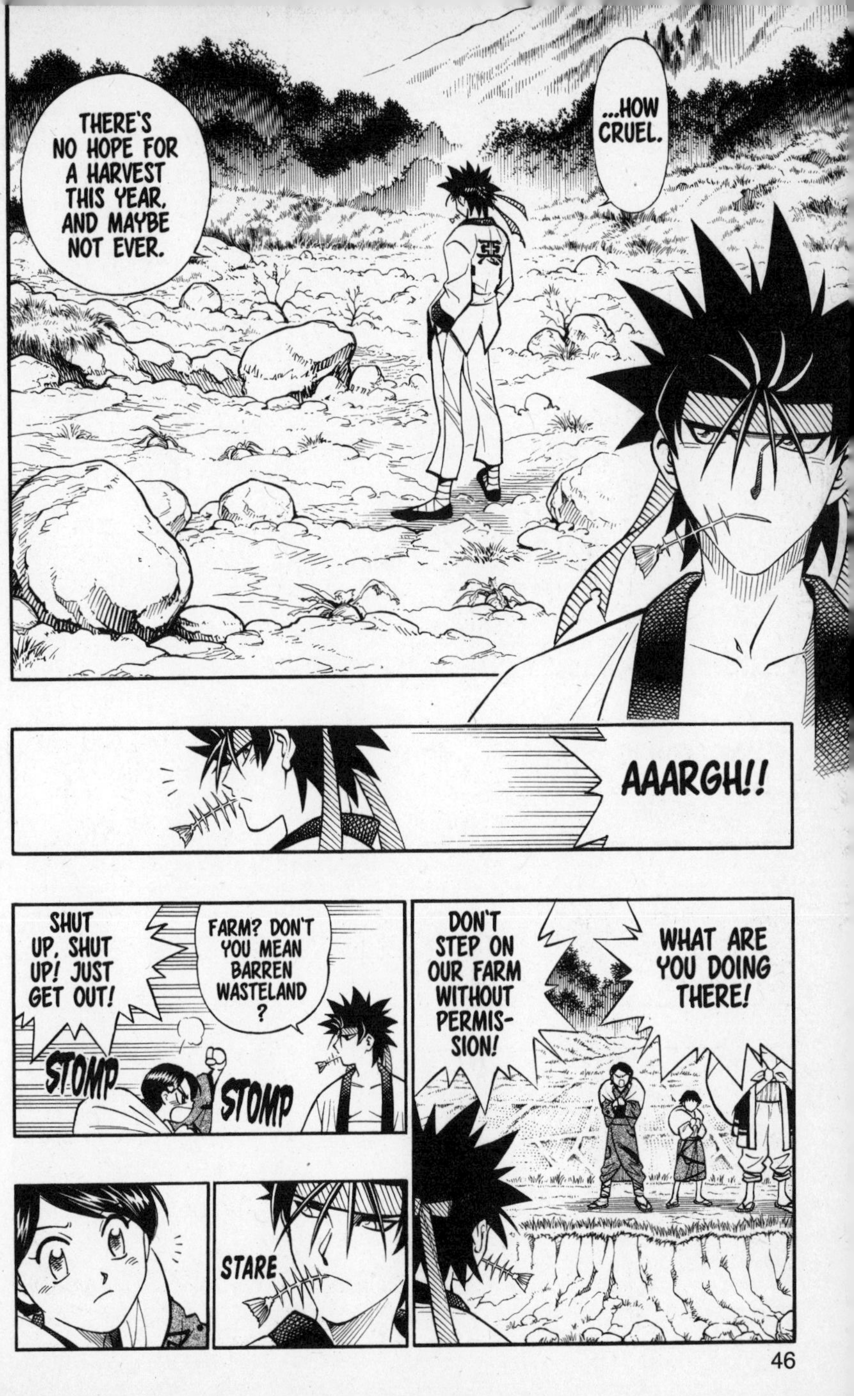
...HOW CRUEL.
THERE'S NO HOPE FOR A HARVEST THIS YEAR, AND MAYBE NOT EVER.
AAARGH!!
WHAT ARE YOU DOING THERE!
DON'T STEP ON OUR FARM WITHOUT PERMISSION!
FARM? DON'T YOU MEAN BARREN WASTELAND?
SHUT UP, SHUT UP! JUST GET OUT!
STOMP
STOMP
STARE

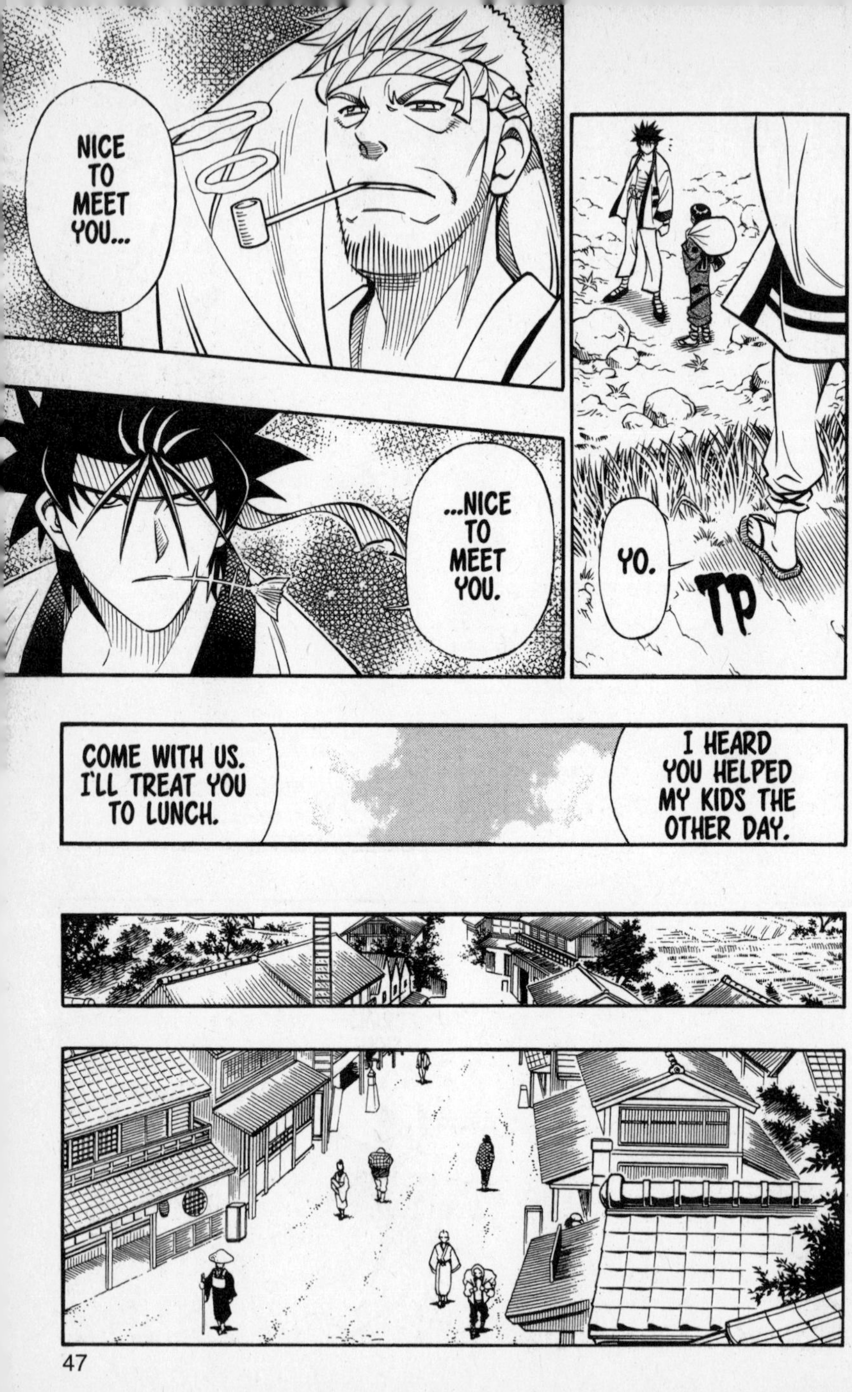
YO.
TP
NICE TO MEET YOU...
...NICE TO MEET YOU.
I HEARD YOU HELPED MY KIDS THE OTHER DAY.
COME WITH US. I'LL TREAT YOU TO LUNCH.

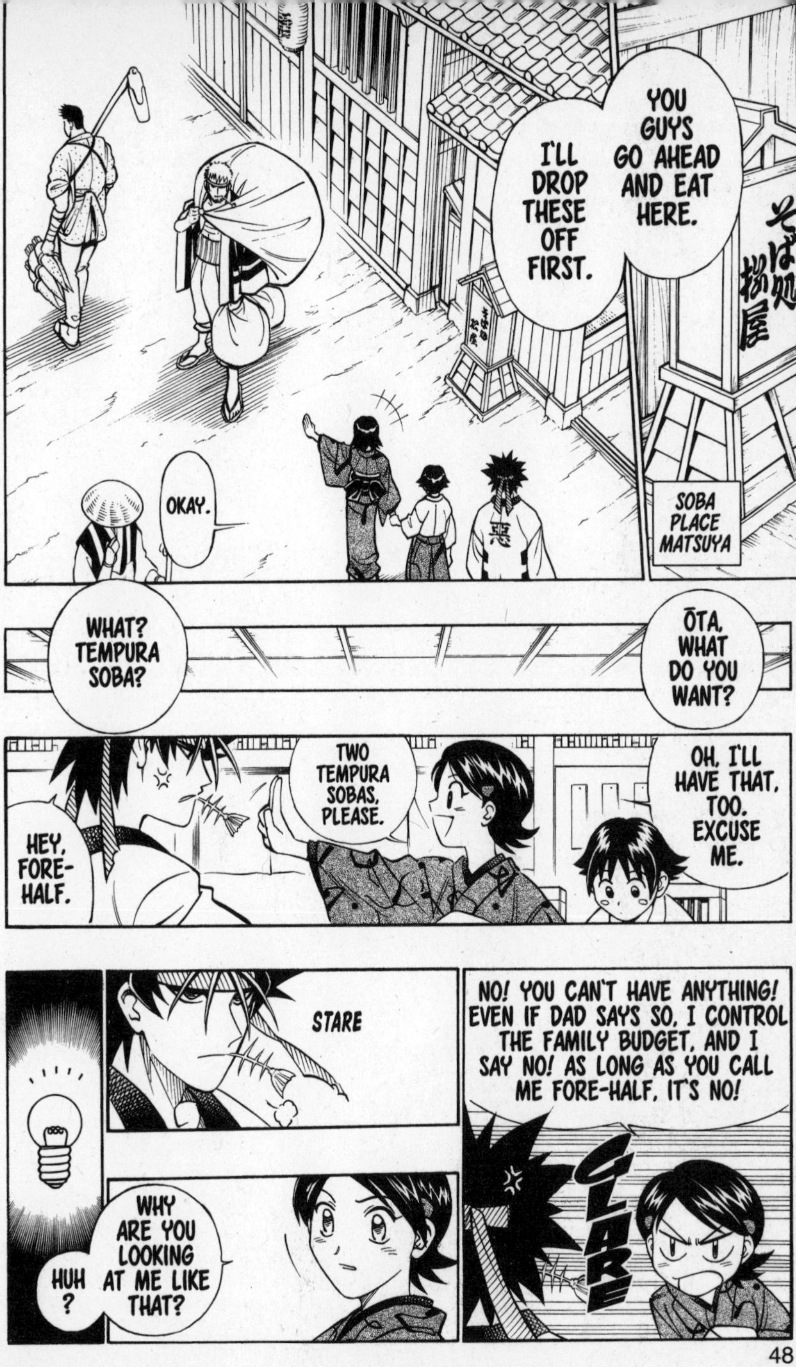
YOU GUYS GO AHEAD AND EAT HERE.
I'LL DROP THESE OFF FIRST.
そば処 松屋
SOBA PLACE MATSUYA
OKAY.
ŌTA, WHAT DO YOU WANT?
WHAT? TEMPURA SOBA?
OH, I'LL HAVE THAT, TOO. EXCUSE ME.
TWO TEMPURA SOBAS, PLEASE.
HEY, FORE-HALF.
NO! YOU CAN'T HAVE ANYTHING! EVEN IF DAD SAYS SO, I CONTROL THE FAMILY BUDGET, AND I SAY NO! AS LONG AS YOU CALL ME FORE-HALF, IT'S NO!
GLARE
STARE
WHY ARE YOU LOOKING AT ME LIKE THAT?
HUH?

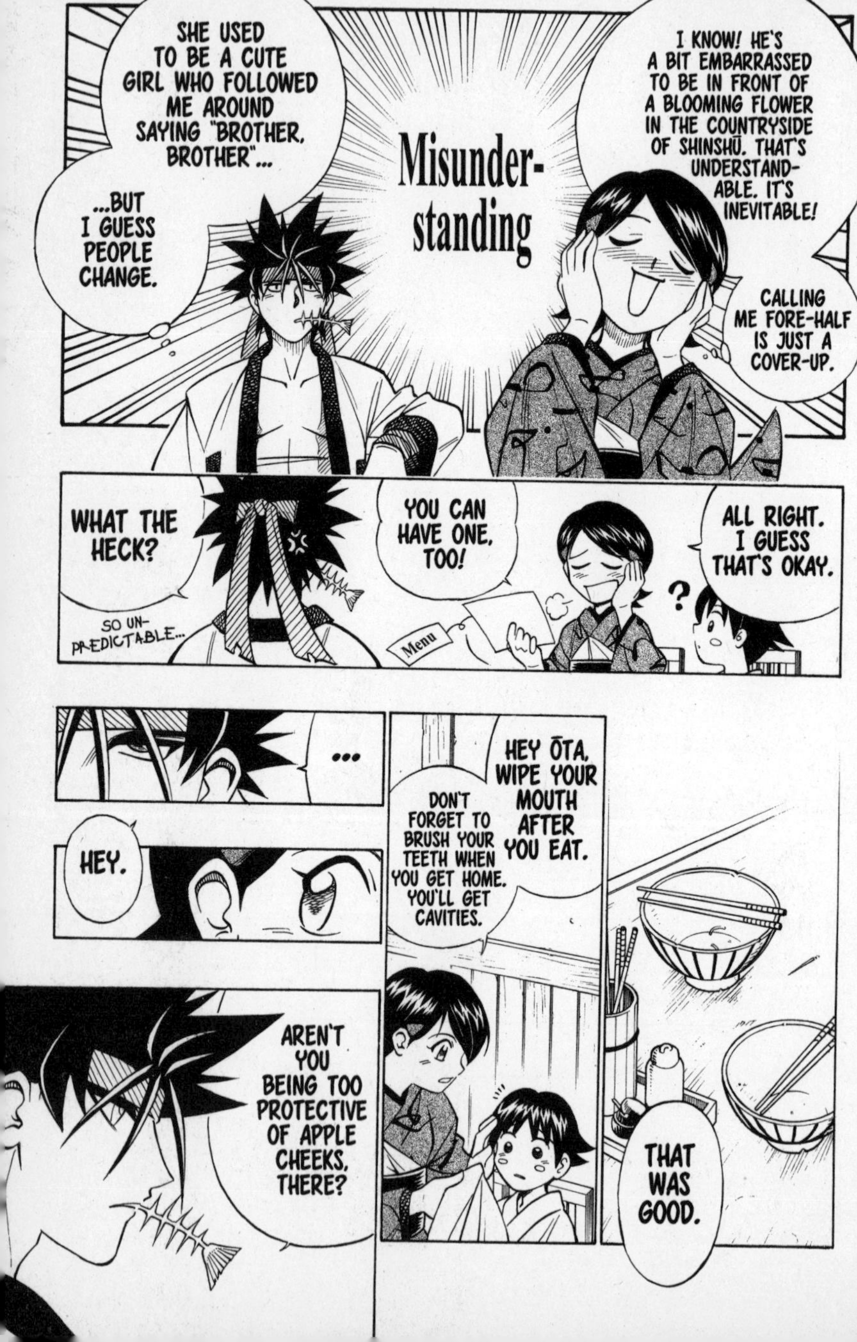
I KNOW! HE'S A BIT EMBARRASSED TO BE IN FRONT OF A BLOOMING FLOWER IN THE COUNTRYSIDE OF SHINSHŪ. THAT'S UNDERSTANDABLE. IT'S INEVITABLE!
CALLING ME FORE-HALF IS JUST A COVER-UP.
Misunder-standing
SHE USED TO BE A CUTE GIRL WHO FOLLOWED ME AROUND SAYING "BROTHER, BROTHER"...
...BUT I GUESS PEOPLE CHANGE.
ALL RIGHT. I GUESS THAT'S OKAY.
?
YOU CAN HAVE ONE, TOO!
Menu
WHAT THE HECK?
SO UN-PREDICTABLE...
HEY ŌTA, WIPE YOUR MOUTH AFTER YOU EAT.
DON'T FORGET TO BRUSH YOUR TEETH WHEN YOU GET HOME. YOU'LL GET CAVITIES.
THAT WAS GOOD.
...
HEY.
AREN'T YOU BEING TOO PROTECTIVE OF APPLE CHEEKS, THERE?

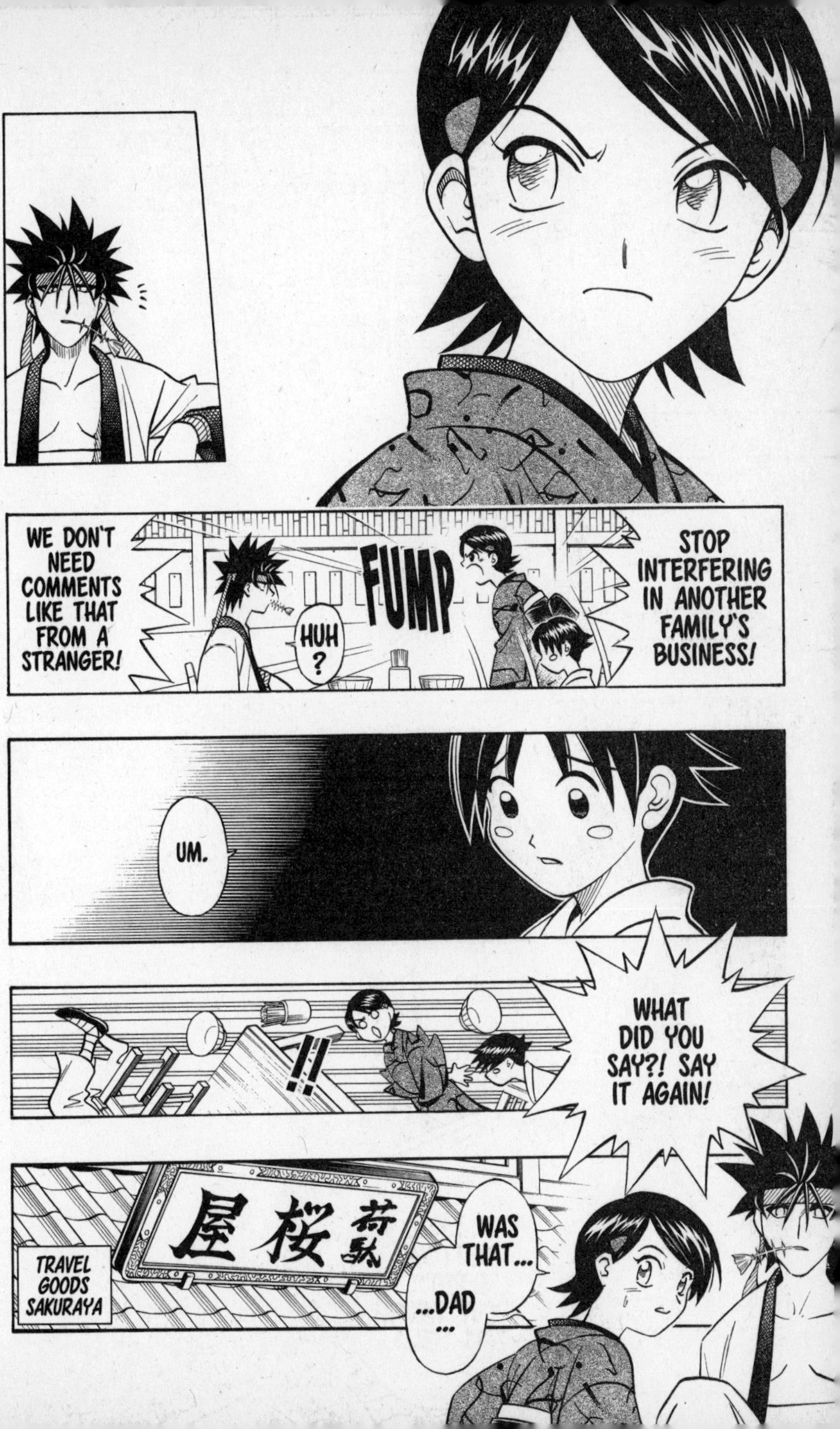
STOP INTERFERING IN ANOTHER FAMILY'S BUSINESS!
FUMP
WE DON'T NEED COMMENTS LIKE THAT FROM A STRANGER!
HUH?
UM.
WHAT DID YOU SAY?! SAY IT AGAIN!
!!
WAS THAT...
...DAD...
荷駄桜屋
TRAVEL GOODS SAKURAYA

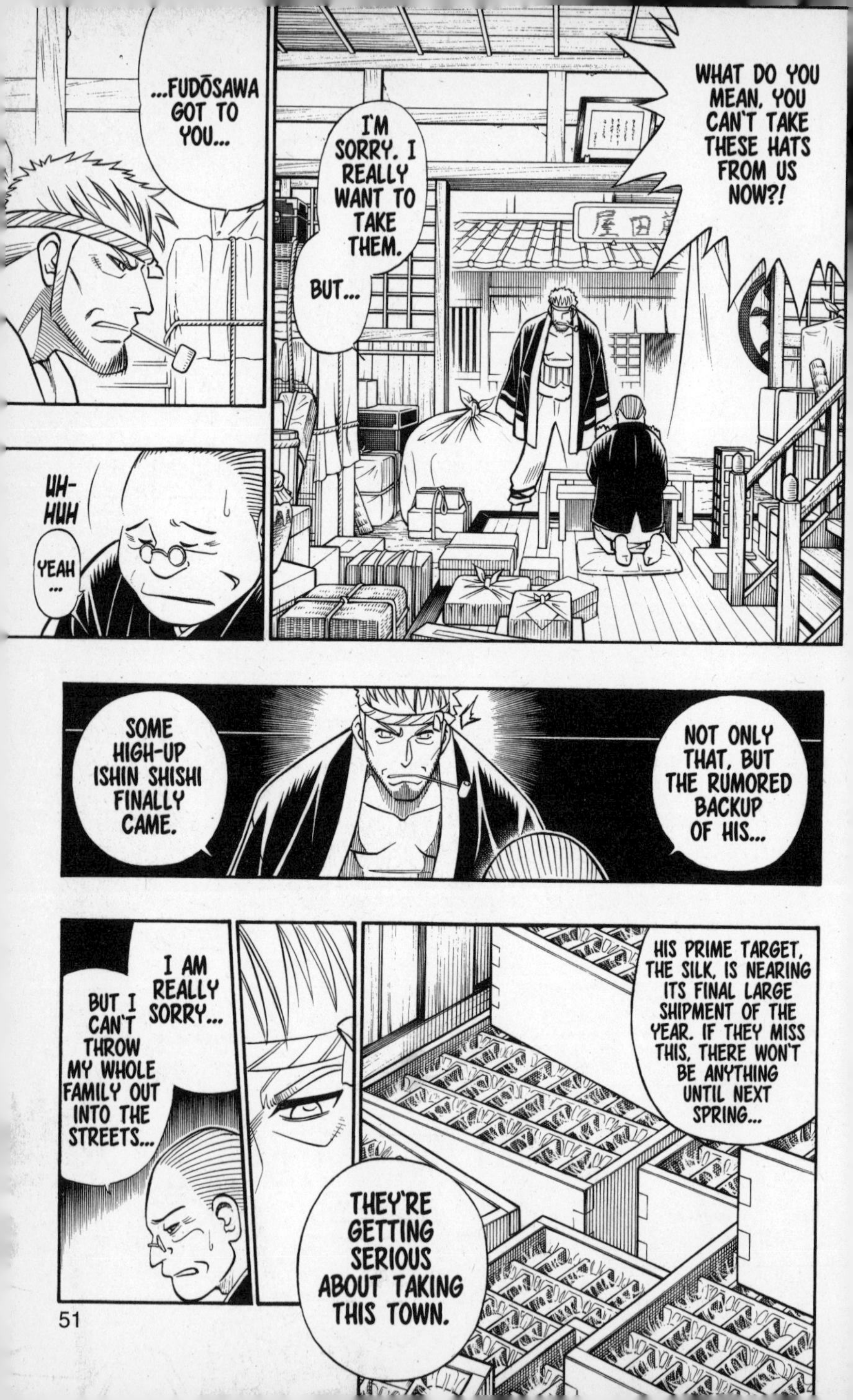
WHAT DO YOU MEAN, YOU CAN'T TAKE THESE HATS FROM US NOW?!
I'M SORRY. I REALLY WANT TO TAKE THEM.
BUT...
...FUDŌSAWA GOT TO YOU...
UH-HUH
YEAH...
SOME HIGH-UP ISHIN SHISHI FINALLY CAME.
NOT ONLY THAT, BUT THE RUMORED BACKUP OF HIS...
HIS PRIME TARGET, THE SILK, IS NEARING ITS FINAL LARGE SHIPMENT OF THE YEAR. IF THEY MISS THIS, THERE WON'T BE ANYTHING UNTIL NEXT SPRING...
THEY'RE GETTING SERIOUS ABOUT TAKING THIS TOWN.
I AM REALLY SORRY...
BUT I CAN'T THROW MY WHOLE FAMILY OUT INTO THE STREETS...

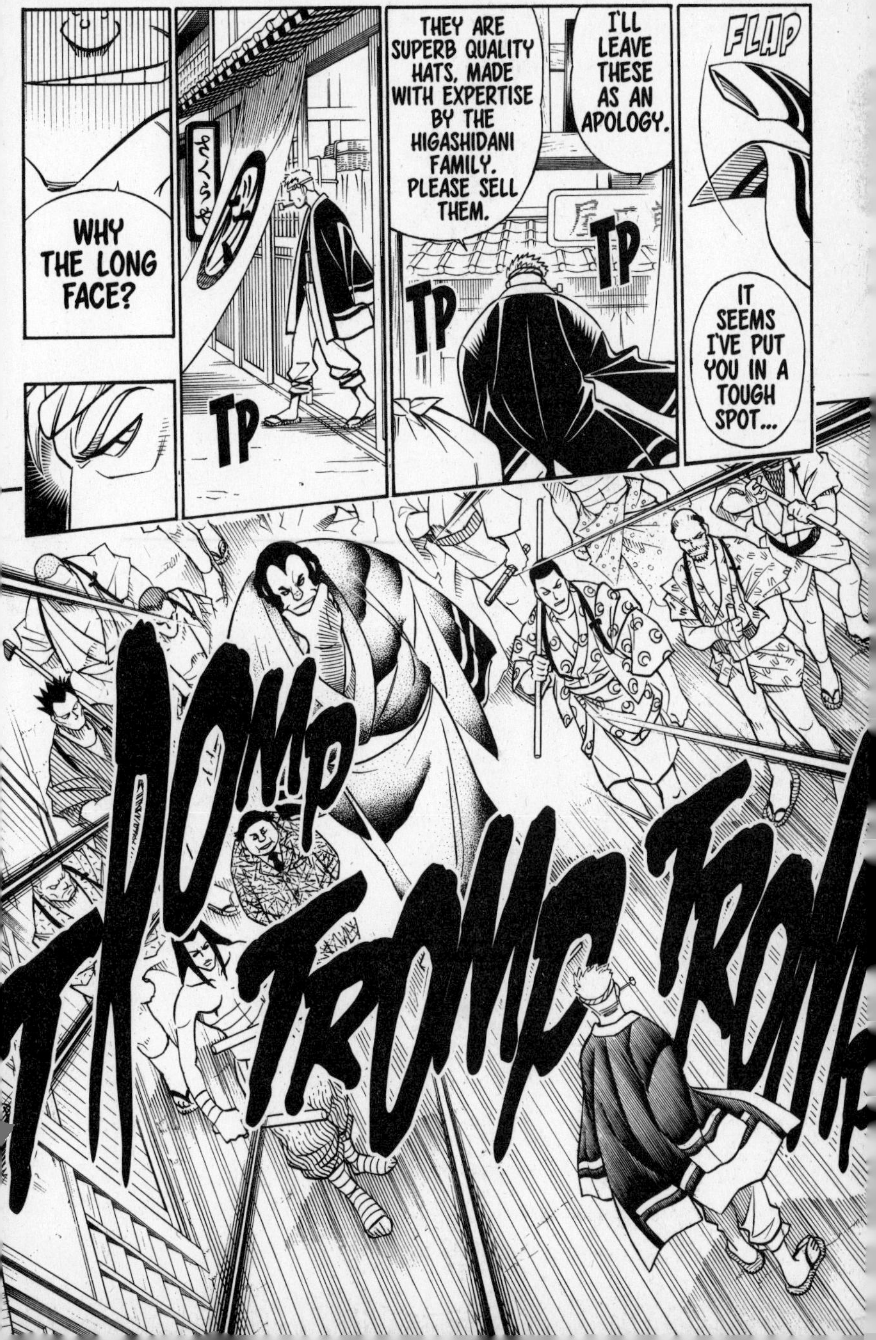
FLAP
IT SEEMS I'VE PUT YOU IN A TOUGH SPOT...
I'LL LEAVE THESE AS AN APOLOGY.
THEY ARE SUPERB QUALITY HATS, MADE WITH EXPERTISE BY THE HIGASHIDANI FAMILY. PLEASE SELL THEM.
TP
TP
TP
WHY THE LONG FACE?
THOMP
TROMP
TROMP

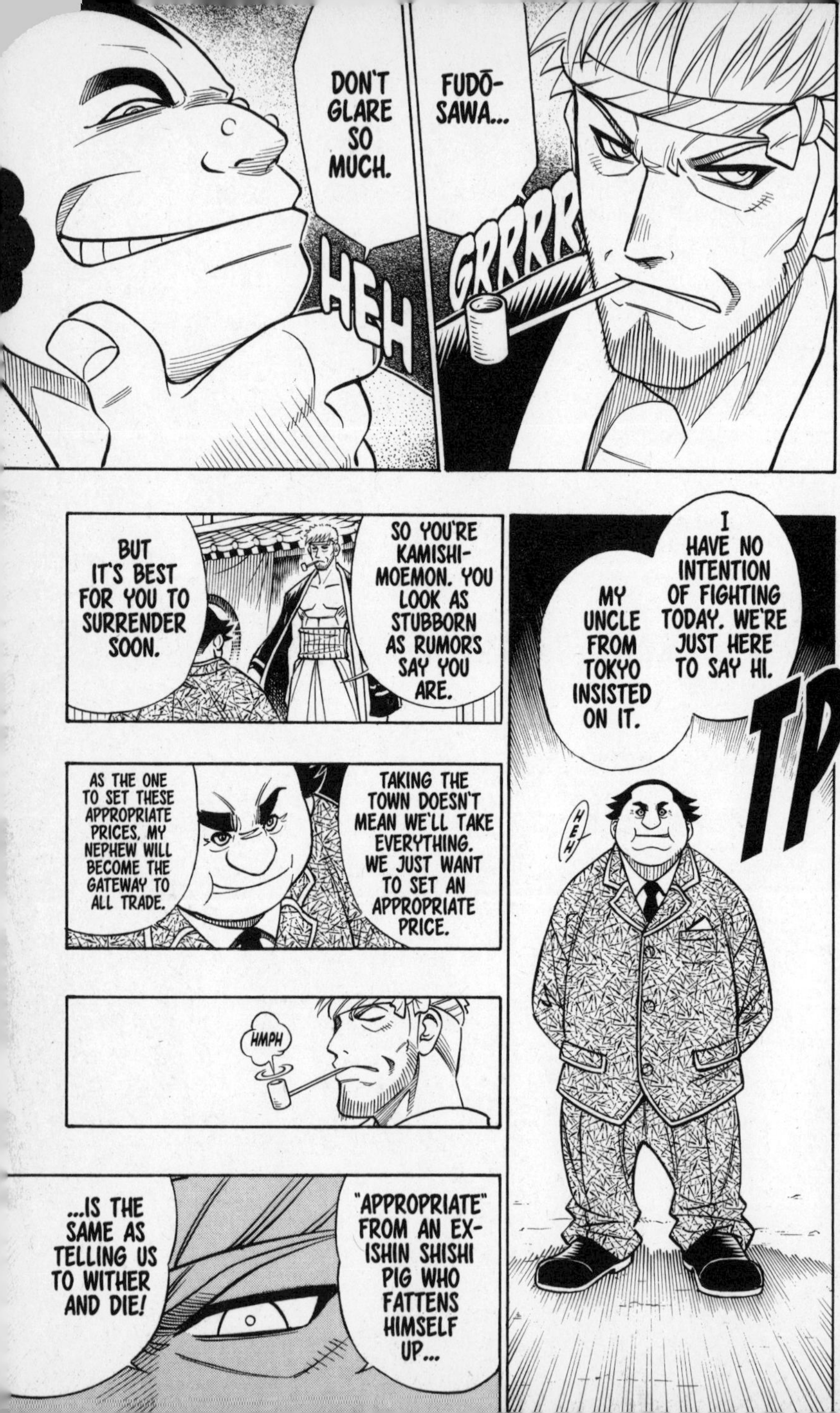
FUDŌ-SAWA...
GRRRR
DON'T GLARE SO MUCH.
HEH
I HAVE NO INTENTION OF FIGHTING TODAY. WE'RE JUST HERE TO SAY HI.
MY UNCLE FROM TOKYO INSISTED ON IT.
TP
HEH
SO YOU'RE KAMISHI-MOEMON. YOU LOOK AS STUBBORN AS RUMORS SAY YOU ARE.
BUT IT'S BEST FOR YOU TO SURRENDER SOON.
TAKING THE TOWN DOESN'T MEAN WE'LL TAKE EVERYTHING. WE JUST WANT TO SET AN APPROPRIATE PRICE.
AS THE ONE TO SET THESE APPROPRIATE PRICES, MY NEPHEW WILL BECOME THE GATEWAY TO ALL TRADE.
HMPH
"APPROPRIATE" FROM AN EX-ISHIN SHISHI PIG WHO FATTENS HIMSELF UP...
...IS THE SAME AS TELLING US TO WITHER AND DIE!

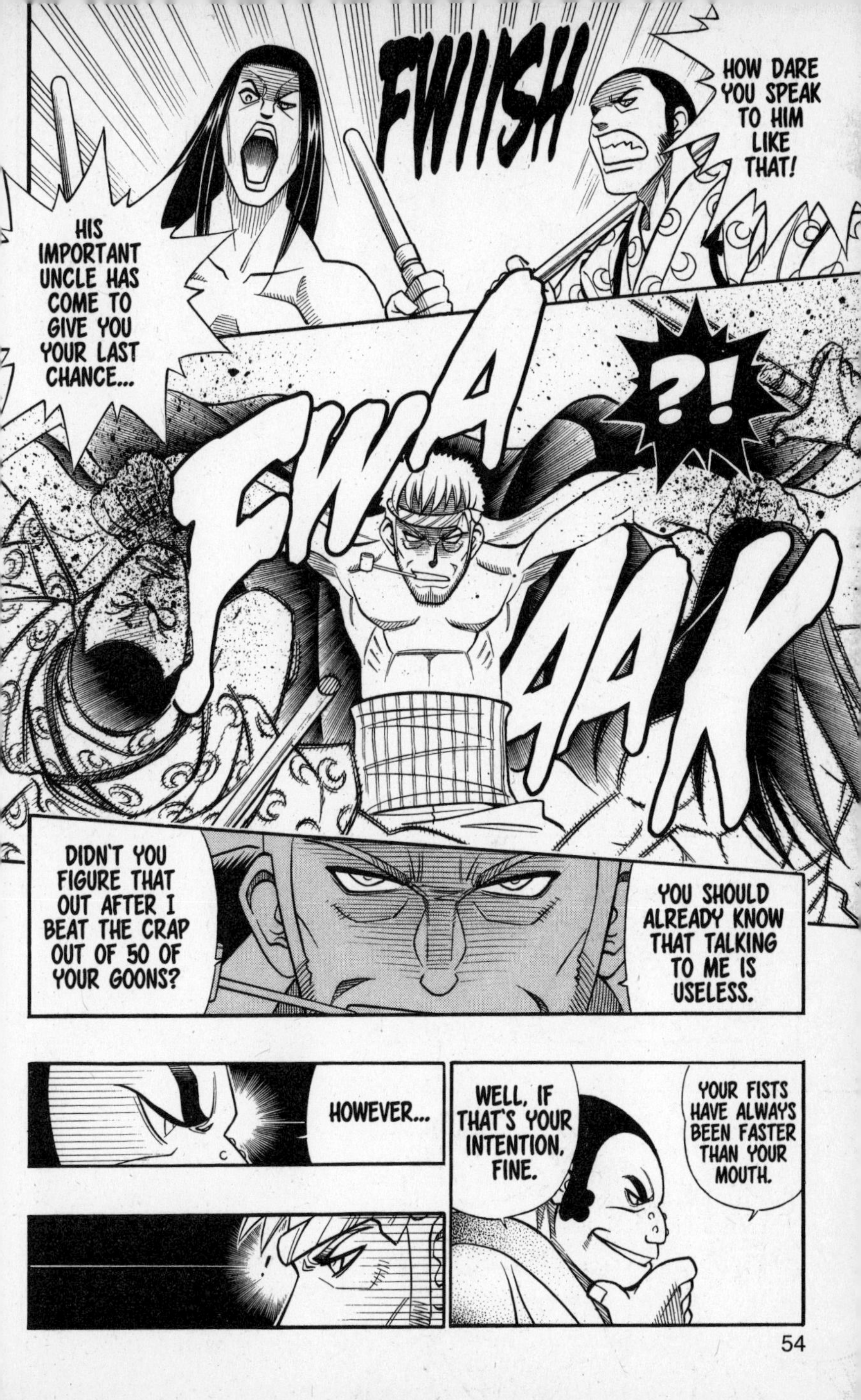
HOW DARE YOU SPEAK TO HIM LIKE THAT!
FWISH
HIS IMPORTANT UNCLE HAS COME TO GIVE YOU YOUR LAST CHANCE...
?!
FWAAAK
YOU SHOULD ALREADY KNOW THAT TALKING TO ME IS USELESS.
DIDN'T YOU FIGURE THAT OUT AFTER I BEAT THE CRAP OUT OF 50 OF YOUR GOONS?
YOUR FISTS HAVE ALWAYS BEEN FASTER THAN YOUR MOUTH.
WELL, IF THAT'S YOUR INTENTION, FINE.
HOWEVER...

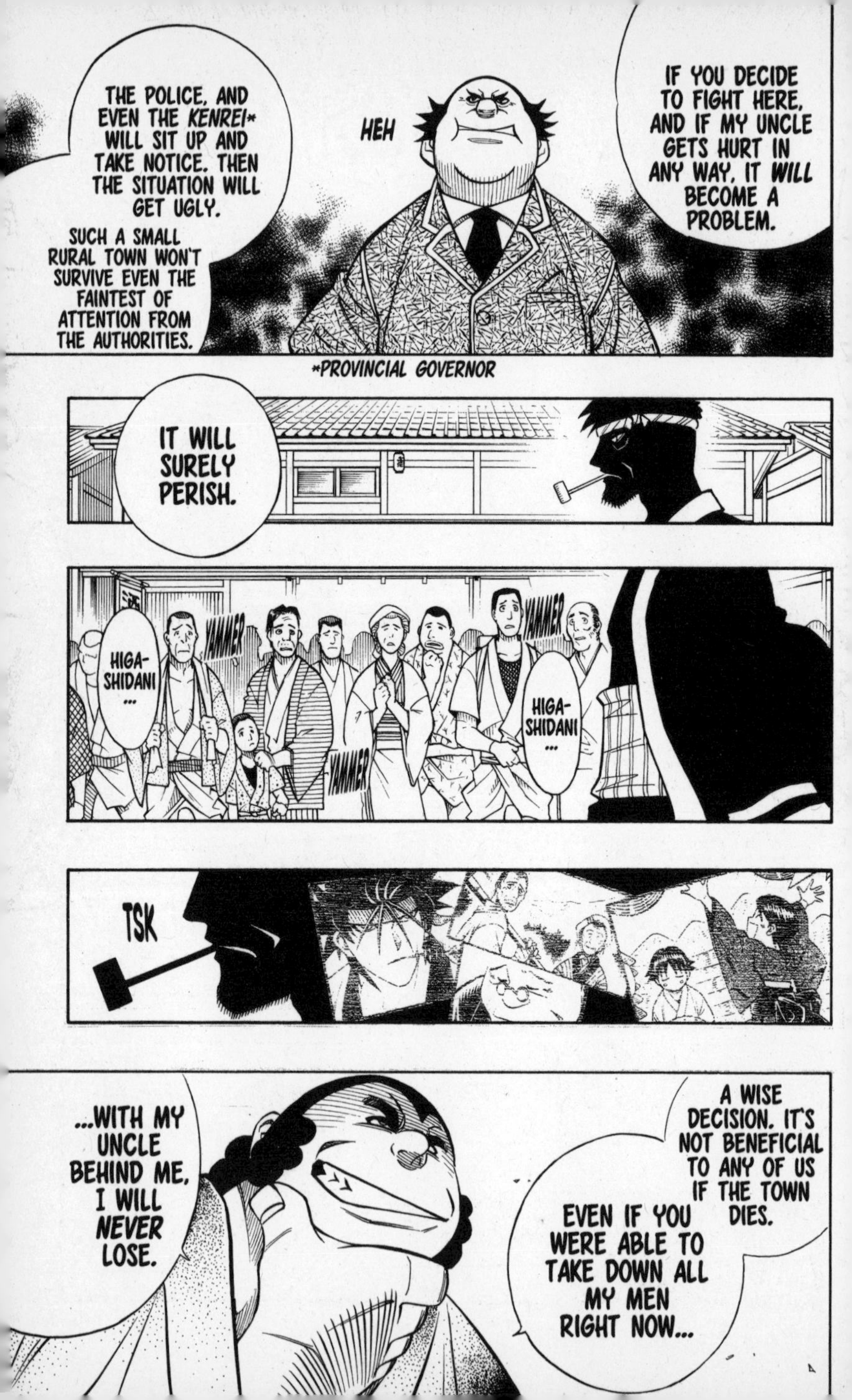
IF YOU DECIDE TO FIGHT HERE, AND IF MY UNCLE GETS HURT IN ANY WAY, IT *WILL* BECOME A PROBLEM.
HEH
THE POLICE, AND EVEN THE *KENREI** WILL SIT UP AND TAKE NOTICE. THEN THE SITUATION WILL GET UGLY.
SUCH A SMALL RURAL TOWN WON'T SURVIVE EVEN THE FAINTEST OF ATTENTION FROM THE AUTHORITIES.
*PROVINCIAL GOVERNOR
IT WILL SURELY PERISH.
YAMMER
HIGA-SHIDANI...
YAMMER
YAMMER
HIGA-SHIDANI...
TSK
A WISE DECISION. IT'S NOT BENEFICIAL TO ANY OF US IF THE TOWN DIES.
EVEN IF YOU WERE ABLE TO TAKE DOWN ALL MY MEN RIGHT NOW...
...WITH MY UNCLE BEHIND ME, I WILL *NEVER* LOSE.

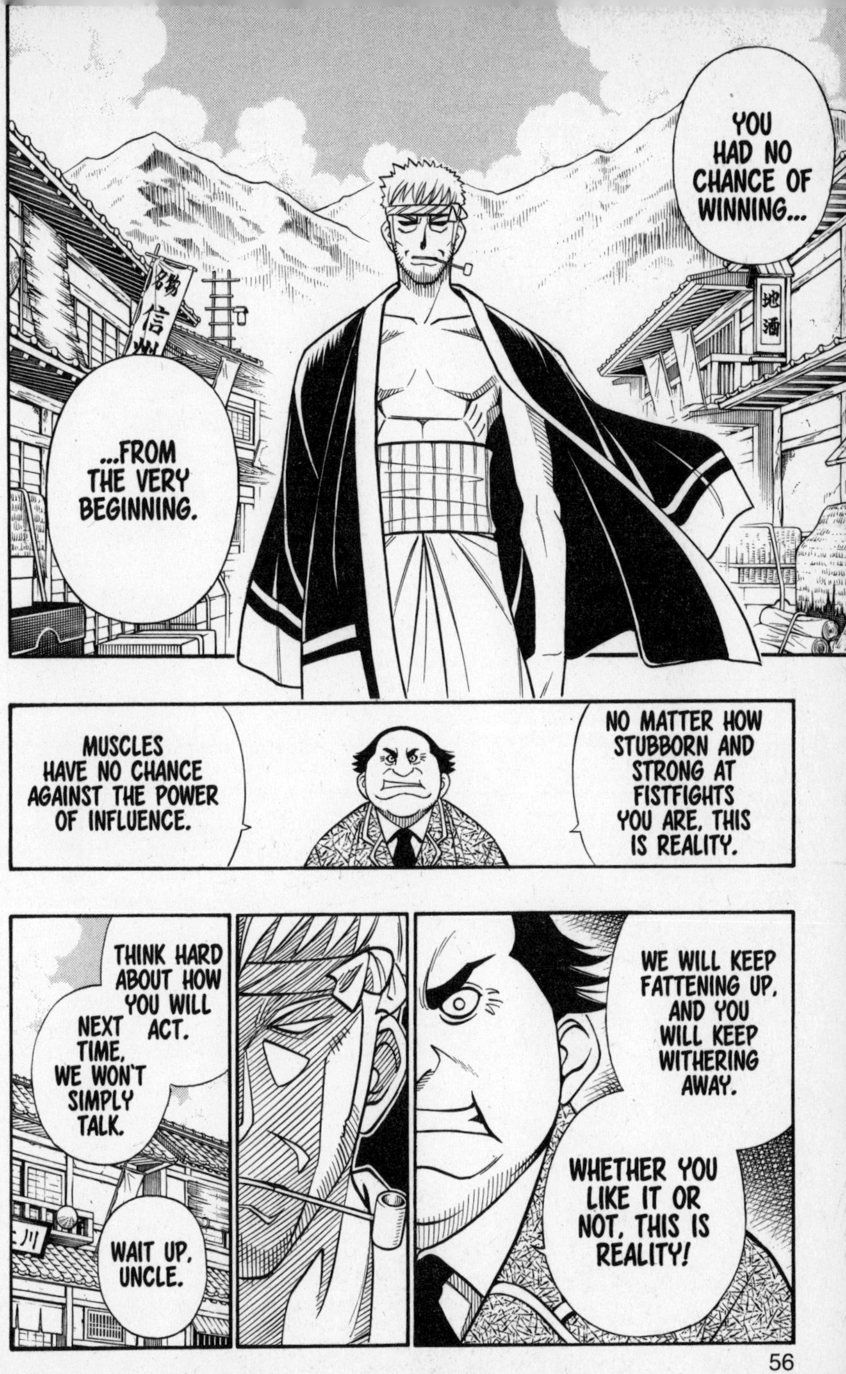
YOU HAD NO CHANCE OF WINNING...
...FROM THE VERY BEGINNING.
NO MATTER HOW STUBBORN AND STRONG AT FISTFIGHTS YOU ARE, THIS IS REALITY.
MUSCLES HAVE NO CHANCE AGAINST THE POWER OF INFLUENCE.
WE WILL KEEP FATTENING UP, AND YOU WILL KEEP WITHERING AWAY.
WHETHER YOU LIKE IT OR NOT, THIS IS REALITY!
THINK HARD ABOUT HOW YOU WILL ACT.
NEXT TIME, WE WON'T SIMPLY TALK.
WAIT UP, UNCLE.

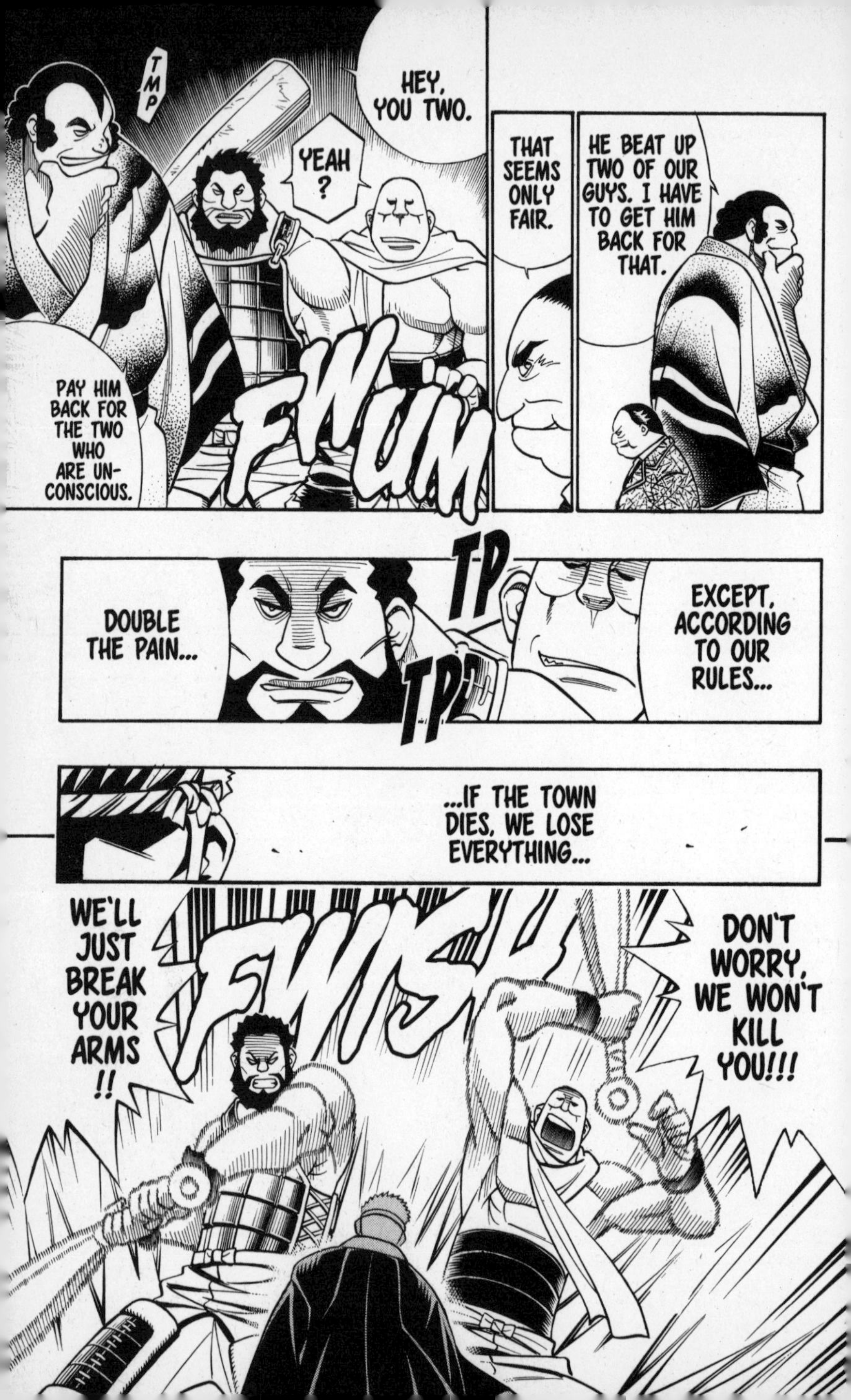
HE BEAT UP TWO OF OUR GUYS. I HAVE TO GET HIM BACK FOR THAT.
THAT SEEMS ONLY FAIR.
HEY, YOU TWO.
TMP
YEAH?
FWUM
PAY HIM BACK FOR THE TWO WHO ARE UN-CONSCIOUS.
EXCEPT, ACCORDING TO OUR RULES...
TP
TP
TP
DOUBLE THE PAIN...
...IF THE TOWN DIES, WE LOSE EVERYTHING...
DON'T WORRY, WE WON'T KILL YOU!!!
FWIS
WE'LL JUST BREAK YOUR ARMS!!

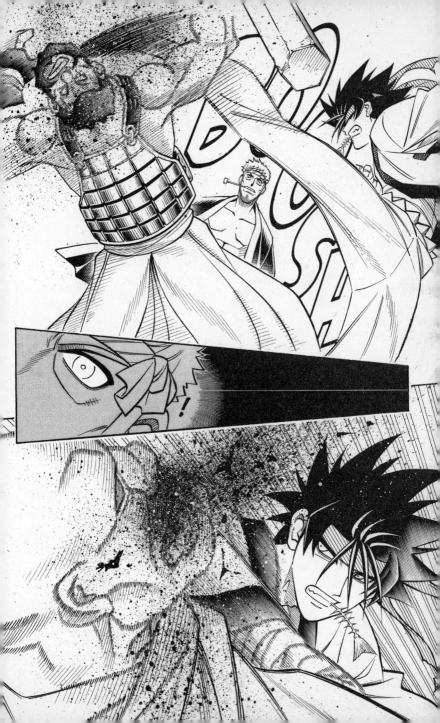

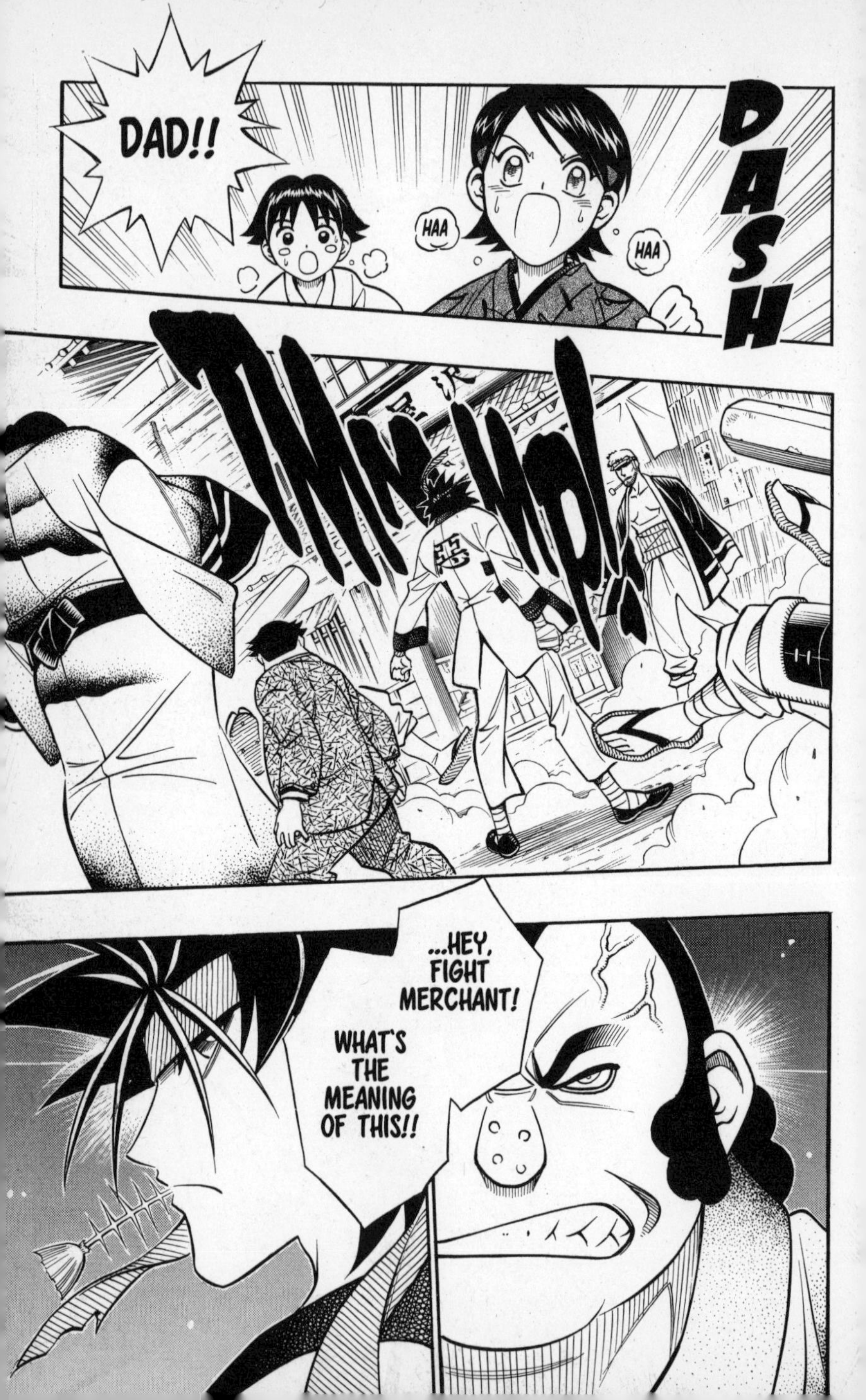
DASH
HAA
HAA
DAD!!
...HEY, FIGHT MERCHANT!
WHAT'S THE MEANING OF THIS!!

Rurouni Kenshin

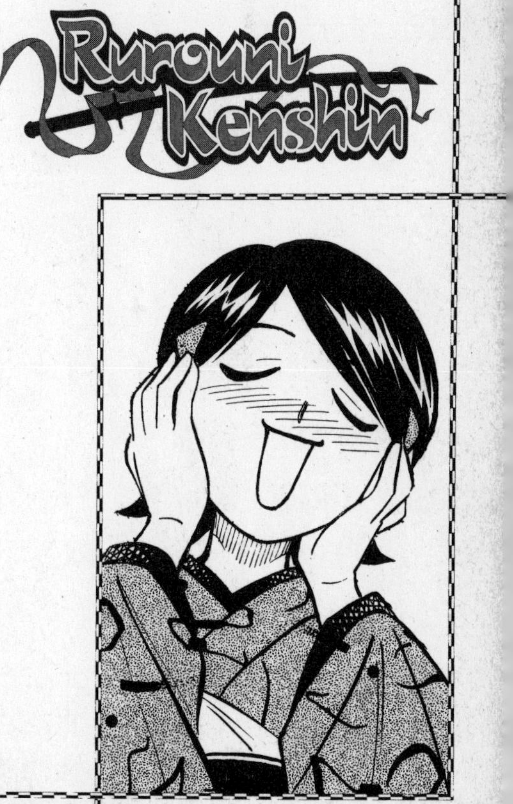

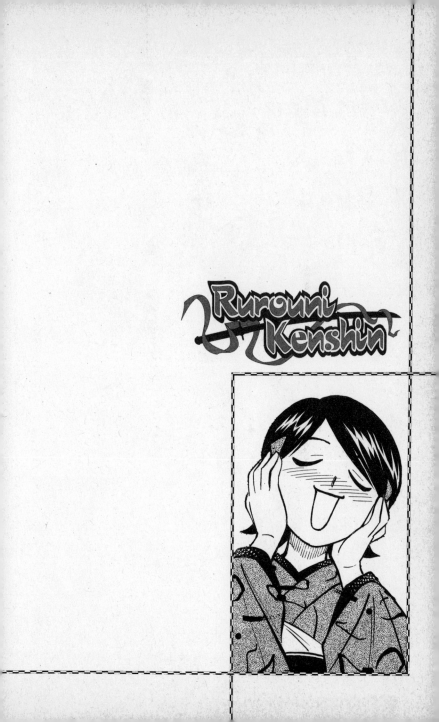

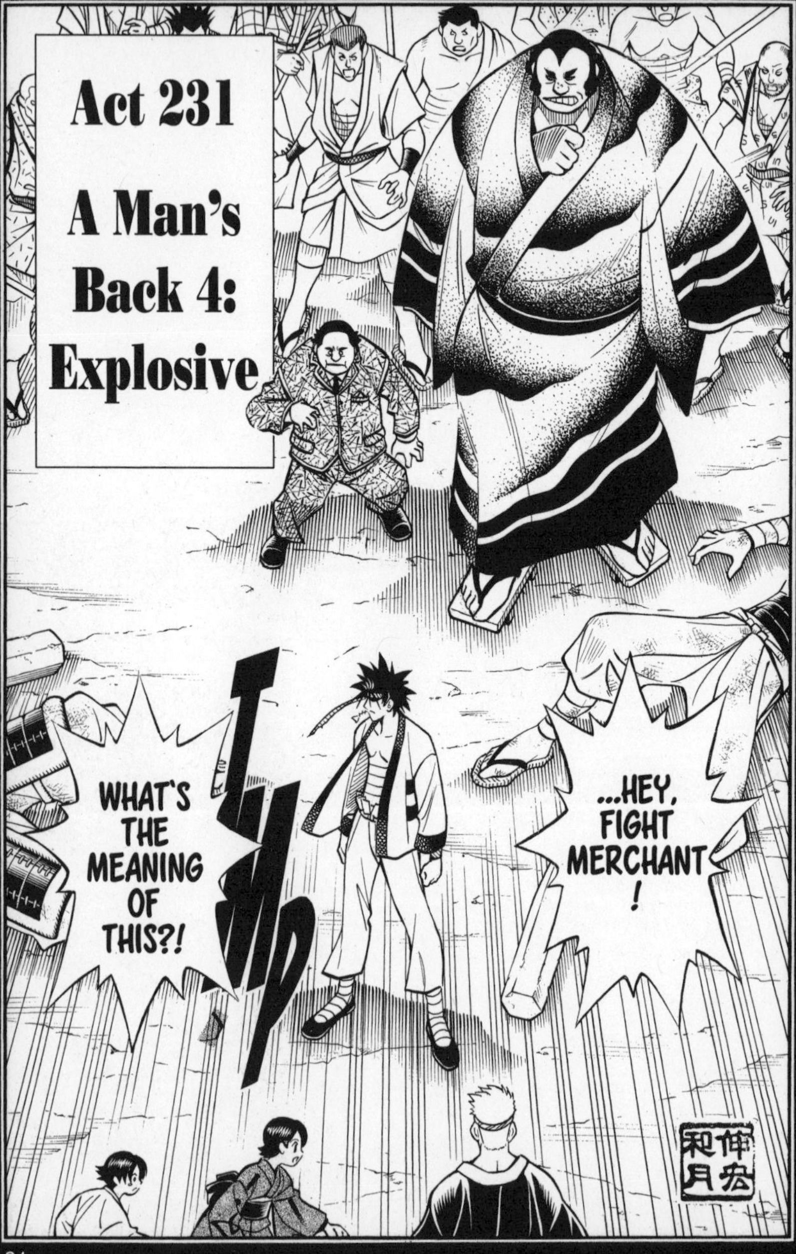
Act 231
A Man's Back 4: Explosive
...HEY, FIGHT MERCHANT!
WHAT'S THE MEANING OF THIS?!

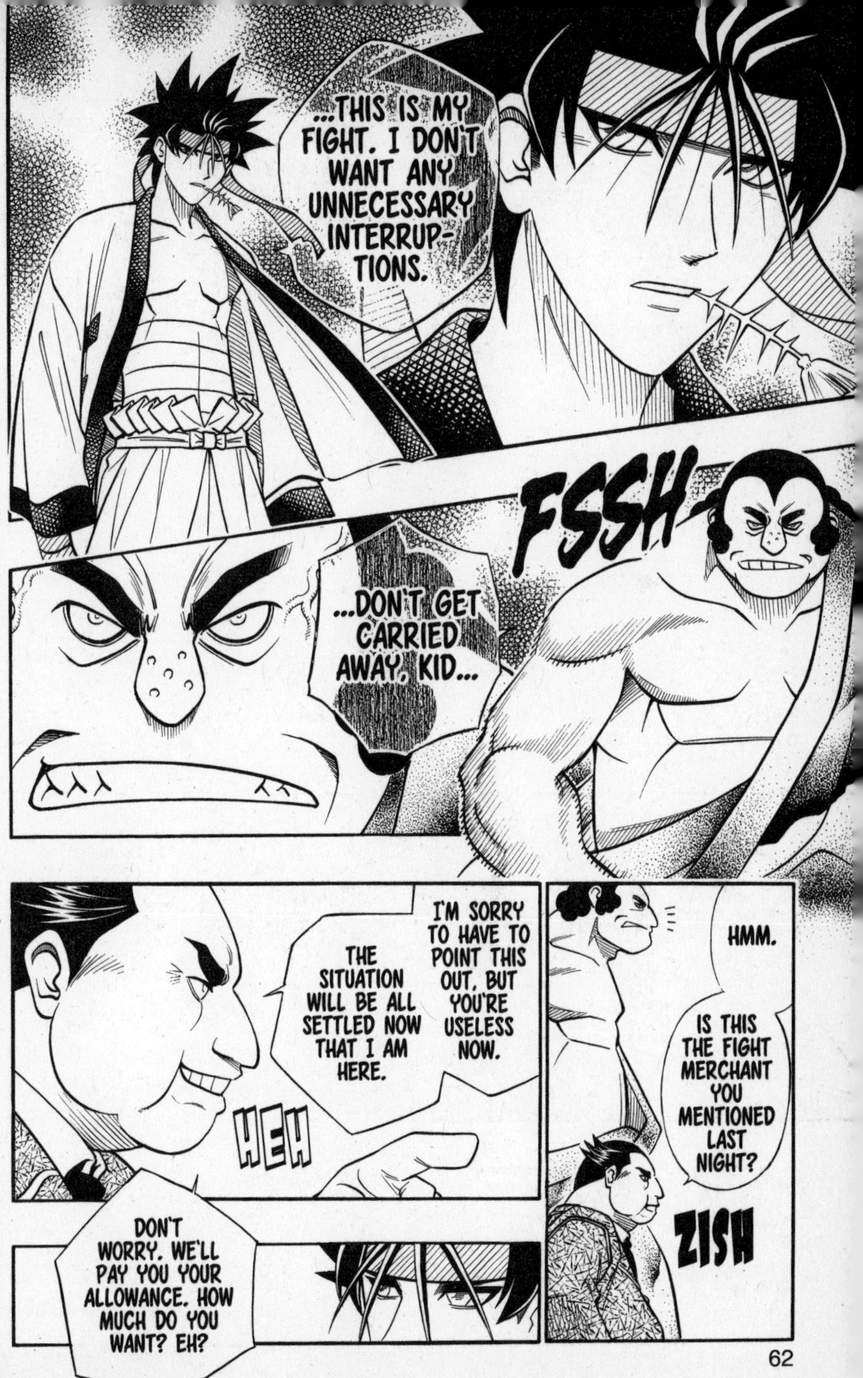
...THIS IS MY FIGHT. I DON'T WANT ANY UNNECESSARY INTERRUP-TIONS.
FSSH
...DON'T GET CARRIED AWAY, KID...
HMM.
IS THIS THE FIGHT MERCHANT YOU MENTIONED LAST NIGHT?
ZISH
I'M SORRY TO HAVE TO POINT THIS OUT, BUT YOU'RE USELESS NOW.
THE SITUATION WILL BE ALL SETTLED NOW THAT I AM HERE.
HEH
DON'T WORRY. WE'LL PAY YOU YOUR ALLOWANCE. HOW MUCH DO YOU WANT? EH?

READ THIS WAY

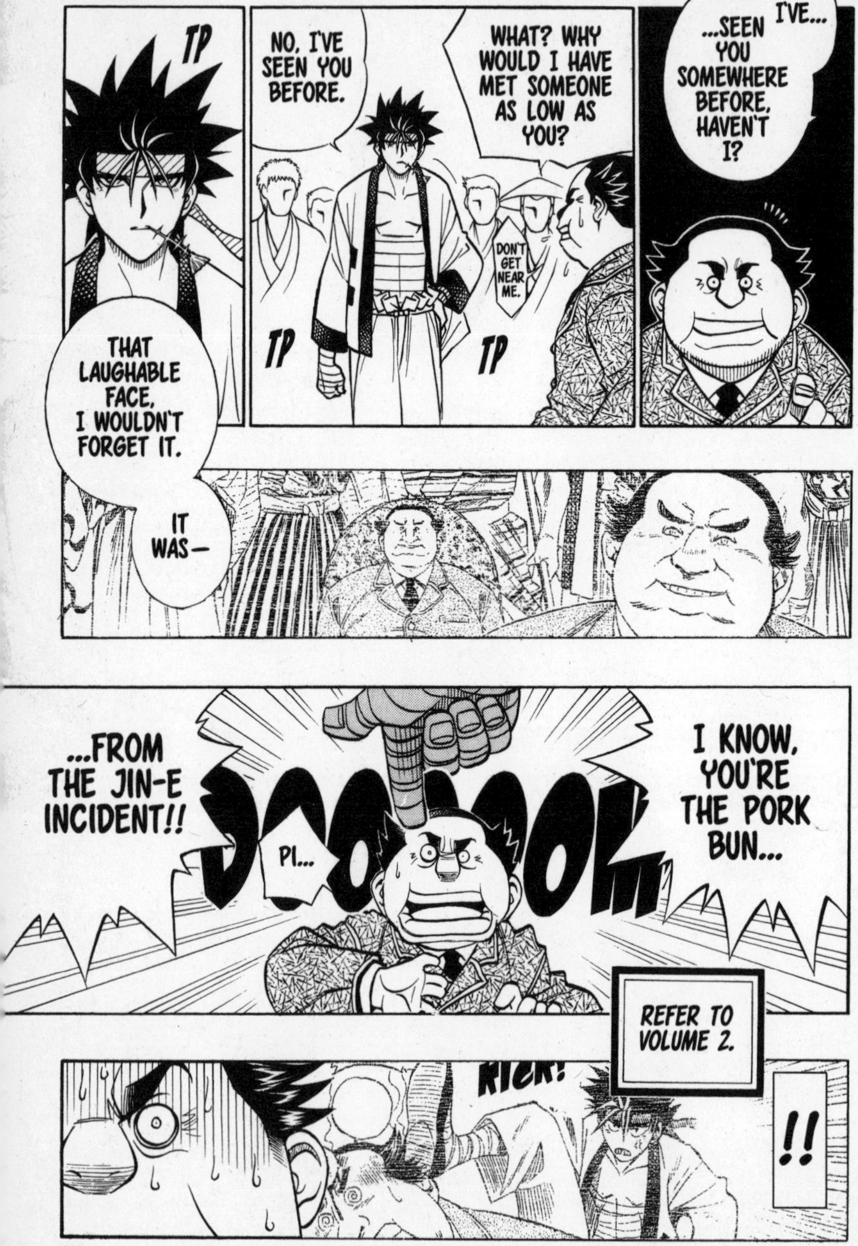
I'VE...
...SEEN YOU SOMEWHERE BEFORE, HAVEN'T I?
WHAT? WHY WOULD I HAVE MET SOMEONE AS LOW AS YOU?
DON'T GET NEAR ME.
NO, I'VE SEEN YOU BEFORE.
TP
TP
TP
THAT LAUGHABLE FACE, I WOULDN'T FORGET IT.
IT WAS—
I KNOW, YOU'RE THE PORK BUN...
PI...
...FROM THE JIN-E INCIDENT!!
REFER TO VOLUME 2.
!!

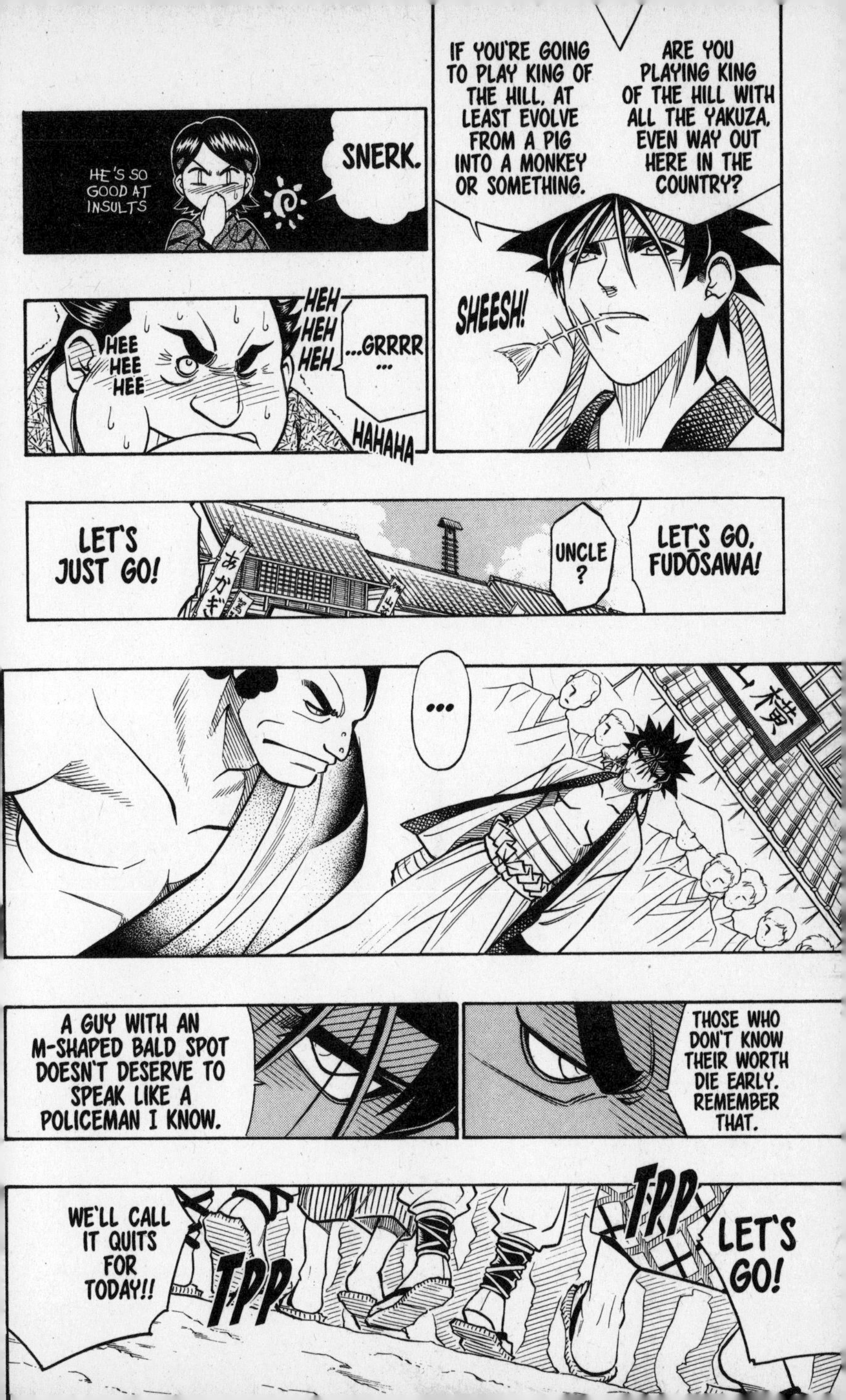
ARE YOU PLAYING KING OF THE HILL WITH ALL THE YAKUZA, EVEN WAY OUT HERE IN THE COUNTRY?
IF YOU'RE GOING TO PLAY KING OF THE HILL, AT LEAST EVOLVE FROM A PIG INTO A MONKEY OR SOMETHING.
SHEESH!
SNERK.
HE'S SO GOOD AT INSULTS
HEH HEH HEH
...GRRRR ...
HEE HEE HEE
HAHAHA
LET'S GO, FUDŌSAWA!
UNCLE ?
LET'S JUST GO!
...
THOSE WHO DON'T KNOW THEIR WORTH DIE EARLY. REMEMBER THAT.
A GUY WITH AN M-SHAPED BALD SPOT DOESN'T DESERVE TO SPEAK LIKE A POLICEMAN I KNOW.
LET'S GO!
TPP
TPP
WE'LL CALL IT QUITS FOR TODAY!!

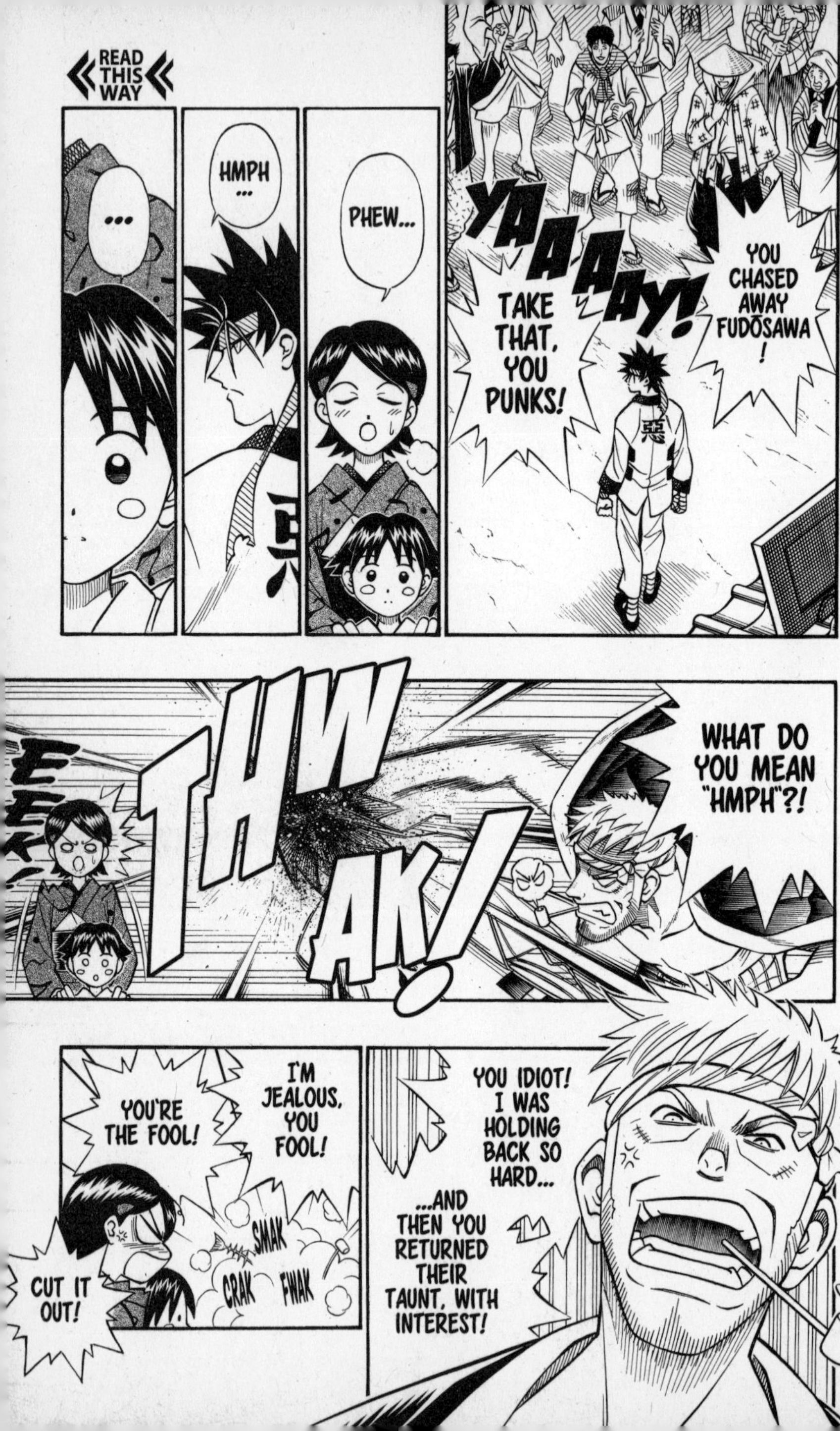

READ THIS WAY
YAAAAY!
YOU CHASED AWAY FUDŌSAWA!
TAKE THAT, YOU PUNKS!
PHEW...
HMPH...
...
WHAT DO YOU MEAN "HMPH"?!
THWAK!
EEEK!
YOU IDIOT! I WAS HOLDING BACK SO HARD...
...AND THEN YOU RETURNED THEIR TAUNT, WITH INTEREST!
I'M JEALOUS, YOU FOOL!
YOU'RE THE FOOL!
SMAK
CRAK
FWAK
CUT IT OUT!

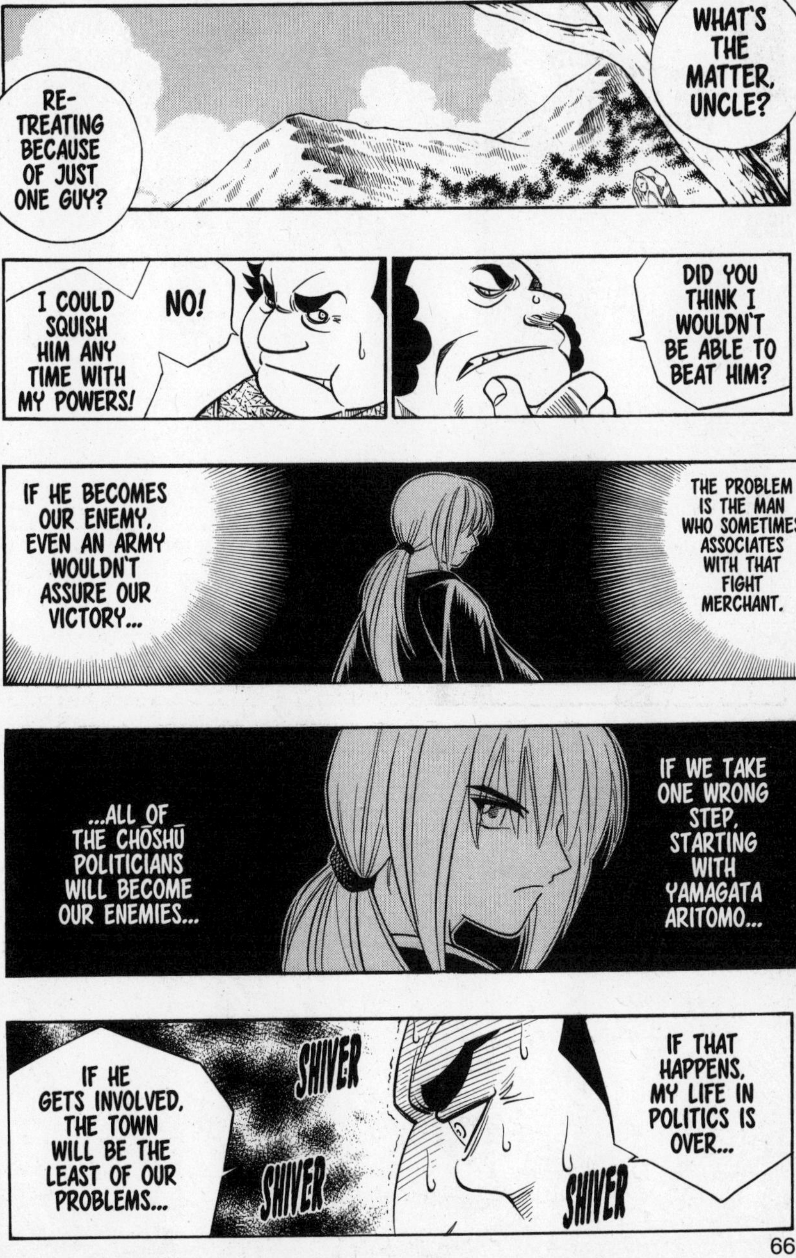
WHAT'S THE MATTER, UNCLE?
RE-TREATING BECAUSE OF JUST ONE GUY?
DID YOU THINK I WOULDN'T BE ABLE TO BEAT HIM?
NO!
I COULD SQUISH HIM ANY TIME WITH MY POWERS!
THE PROBLEM IS THE MAN WHO SOMETIMES ASSOCIATES WITH THAT FIGHT MERCHANT.
IF HE BECOMES OUR ENEMY, EVEN AN ARMY WOULDN'T ASSURE OUR VICTORY...
IF WE TAKE ONE WRONG STEP, STARTING WITH YAMAGATA ARITOMO...
...ALL OF THE CHŌSHŪ POLITICIANS WILL BECOME OUR ENEMIES...
IF THAT HAPPENS, MY LIFE IN POLITICS IS OVER...
SHIVER
SHIVER
SHIVER
IF HE GETS INVOLVED, THE TOWN WILL BE THE LEAST OF OUR PROBLEMS...

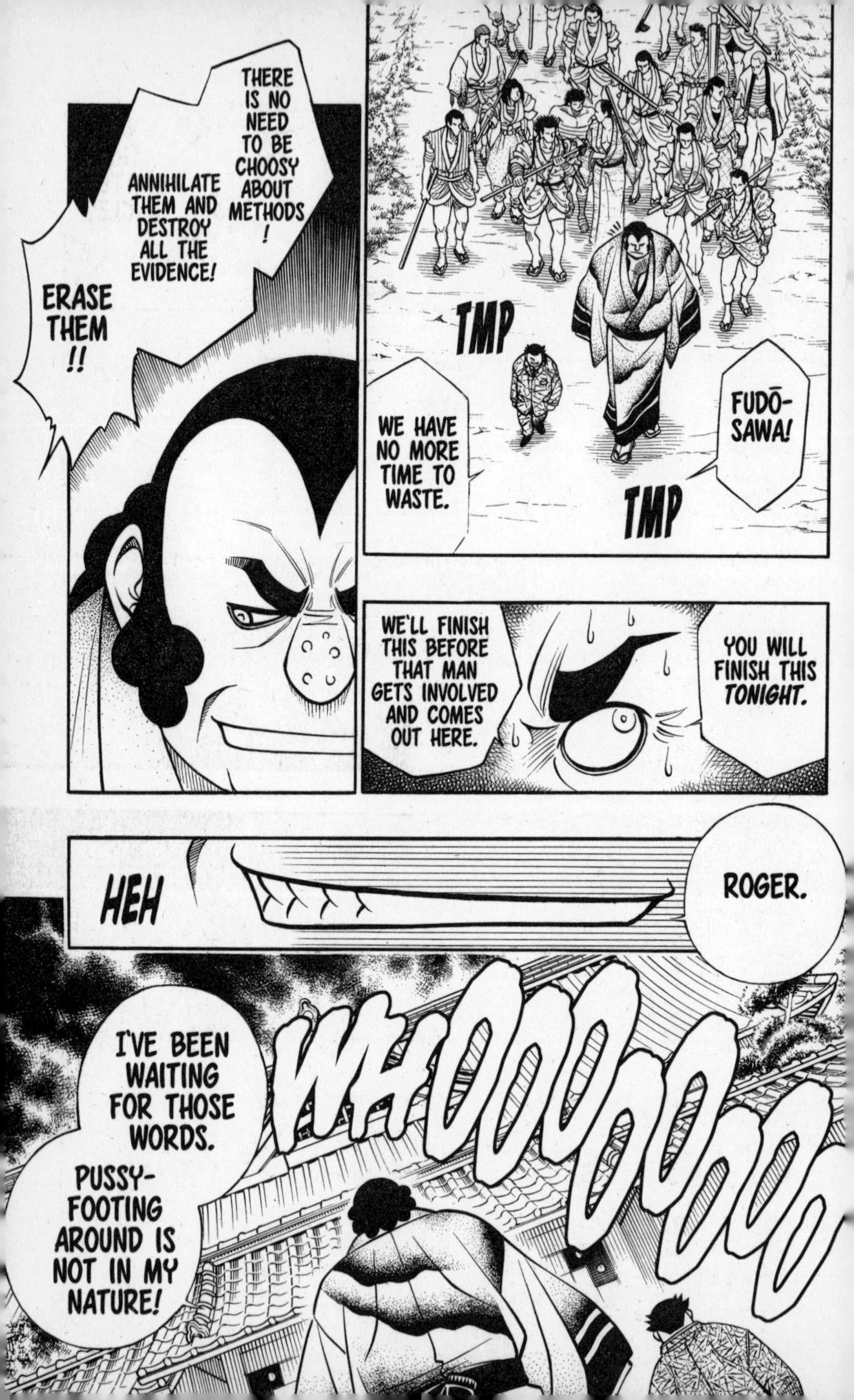
FUDŌ-SAWA!
WE HAVE NO MORE TIME TO WASTE.
TMP
TMP
YOU WILL FINISH THIS *TONIGHT.*
WE'LL FINISH THIS BEFORE THAT MAN GETS INVOLVED AND COMES OUT HERE.
THERE IS NO NEED TO BE CHOOSY ABOUT METHODS!
ANNIHILATE THEM AND DESTROY ALL THE EVIDENCE!
ERASE THEM!!
ROGER.
HEH
WHOOOOOOOOO
I'VE BEEN WAITING FOR THOSE WORDS.
PUSSY-FOOTING AROUND IS NOT IN MY NATURE!

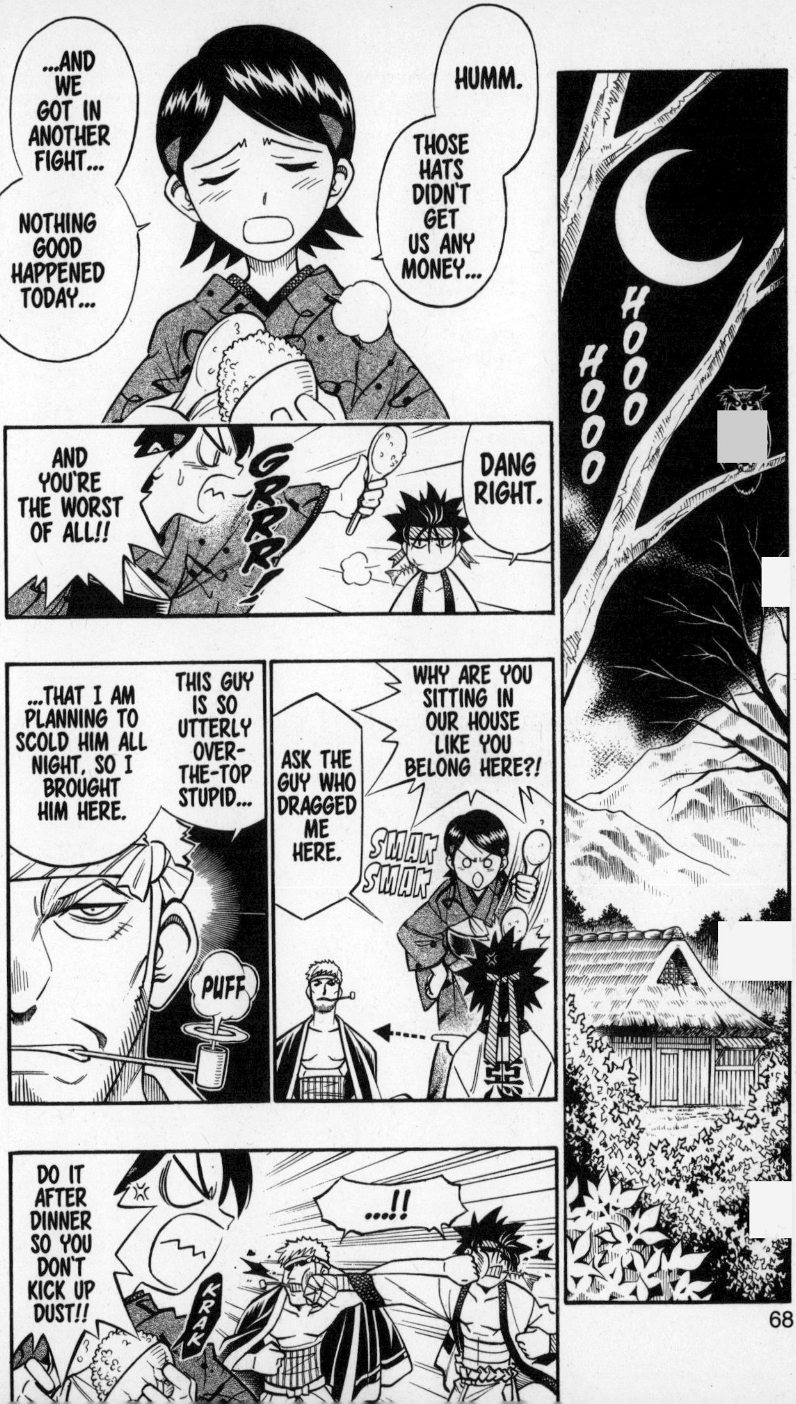

HOOO HOOO
HUMM.
THOSE HATS DIDN'T GET US ANY MONEY...
...AND WE GOT IN ANOTHER FIGHT...
NOTHING GOOD HAPPENED TODAY...
DANG RIGHT.
GRRR!
AND YOU'RE THE WORST OF ALL!!
WHY ARE YOU SITTING IN OUR HOUSE LIKE YOU BELONG HERE?!
SMAK SMAK
ASK THE GUY WHO DRAGGED ME HERE.
THIS GUY IS SO UTTERLY OVER-THE-TOP STUPID...
...THAT I AM PLANNING TO SCOLD HIM ALL NIGHT, SO I BROUGHT HIM HERE.
PUFF
...!!
DO IT AFTER DINNER SO YOU DON'T KICK UP DUST!!
KRAK

READ THIS WAY

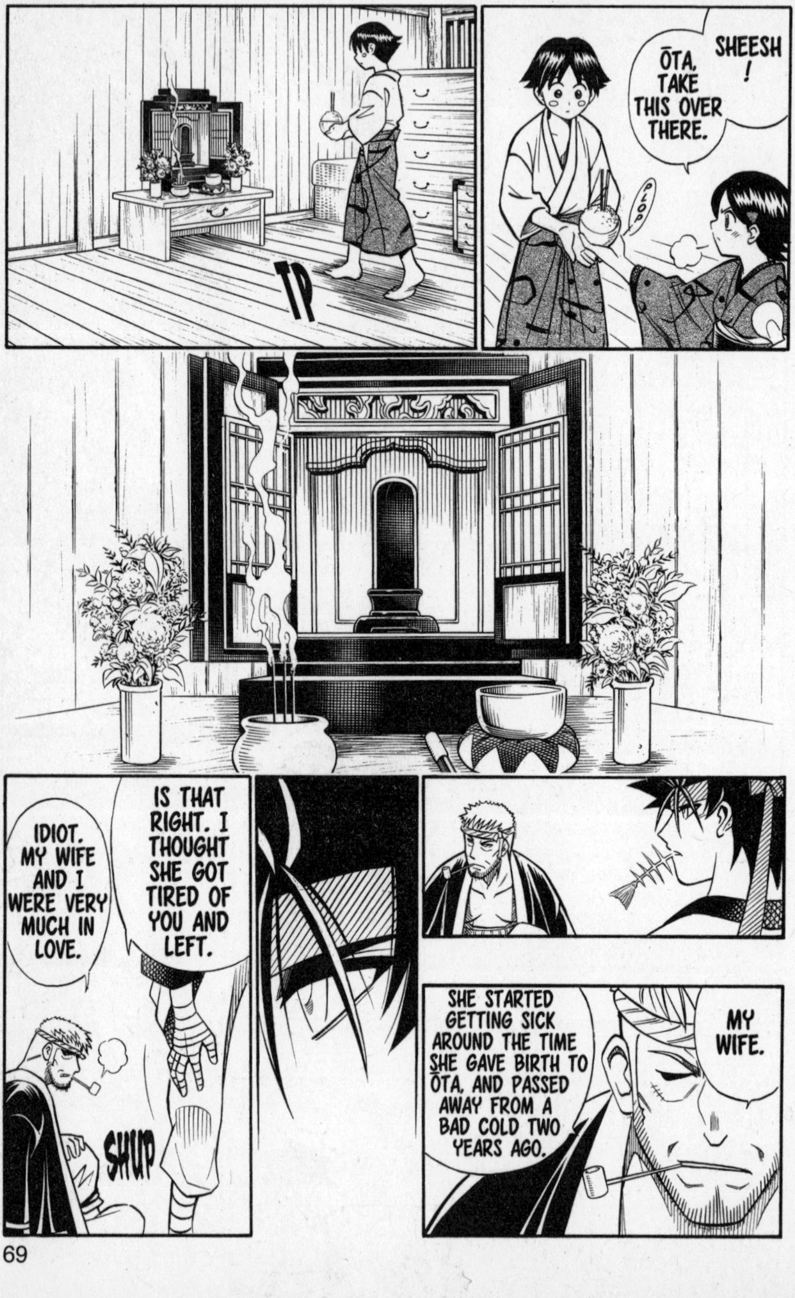
SHEESH!
ŌTA, TAKE THIS OVER THERE.
PLOP
TP
MY WIFE.
SHE STARTED GETTING SICK AROUND THE TIME SHE GAVE BIRTH TO ŌTA, AND PASSED AWAY FROM A BAD COLD TWO YEARS AGO.
IS THAT RIGHT. I THOUGHT SHE GOT TIRED OF YOU AND LEFT.
IDIOT. MY WIFE AND I WERE VERY MUCH IN LOVE.
SHUP

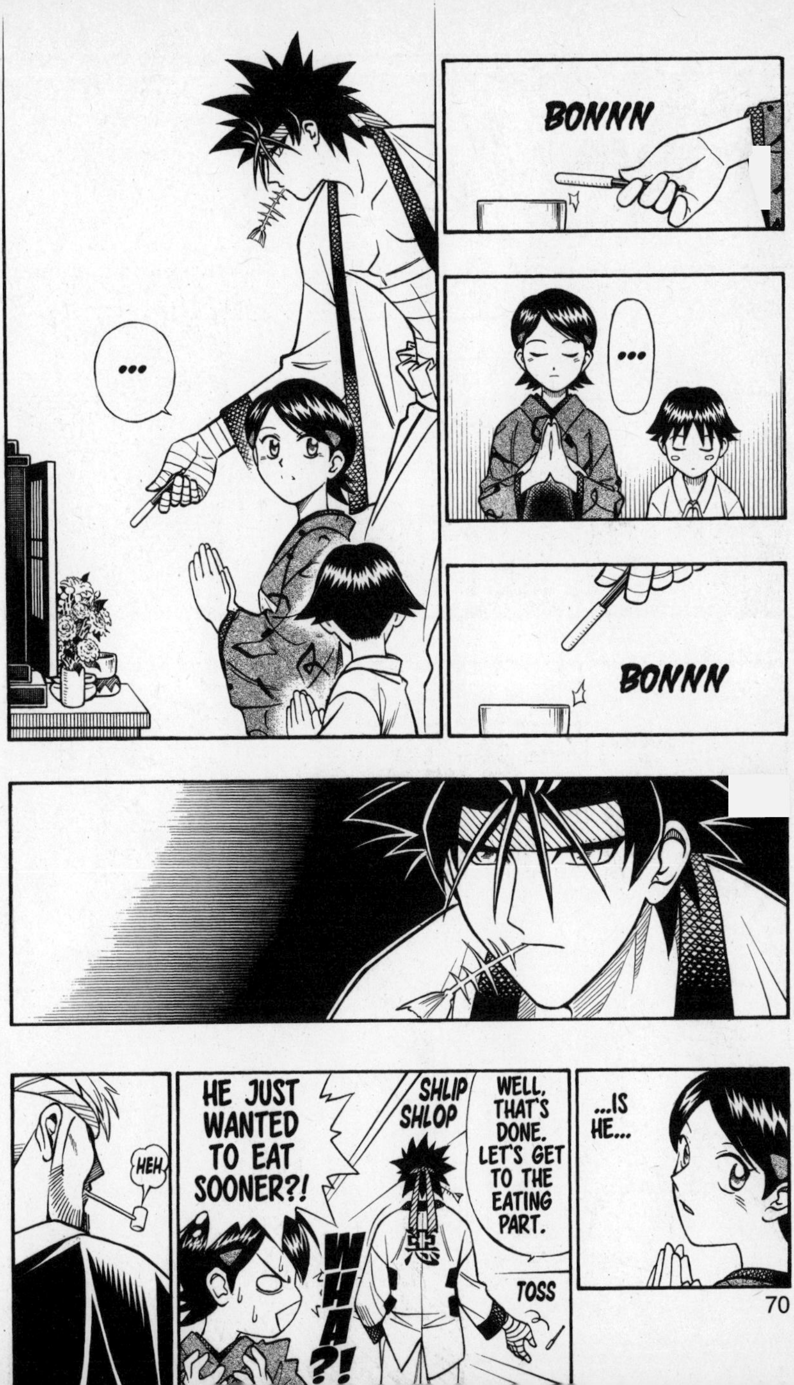
BONNN
...
BONNN
...
...IS HE...
WELL, THAT'S DONE. LET'S GET TO THE EATING PART.
SHLIP SHLOP
TOSS
HE JUST WANTED TO EAT SOONER?!
WHA?!
HEH

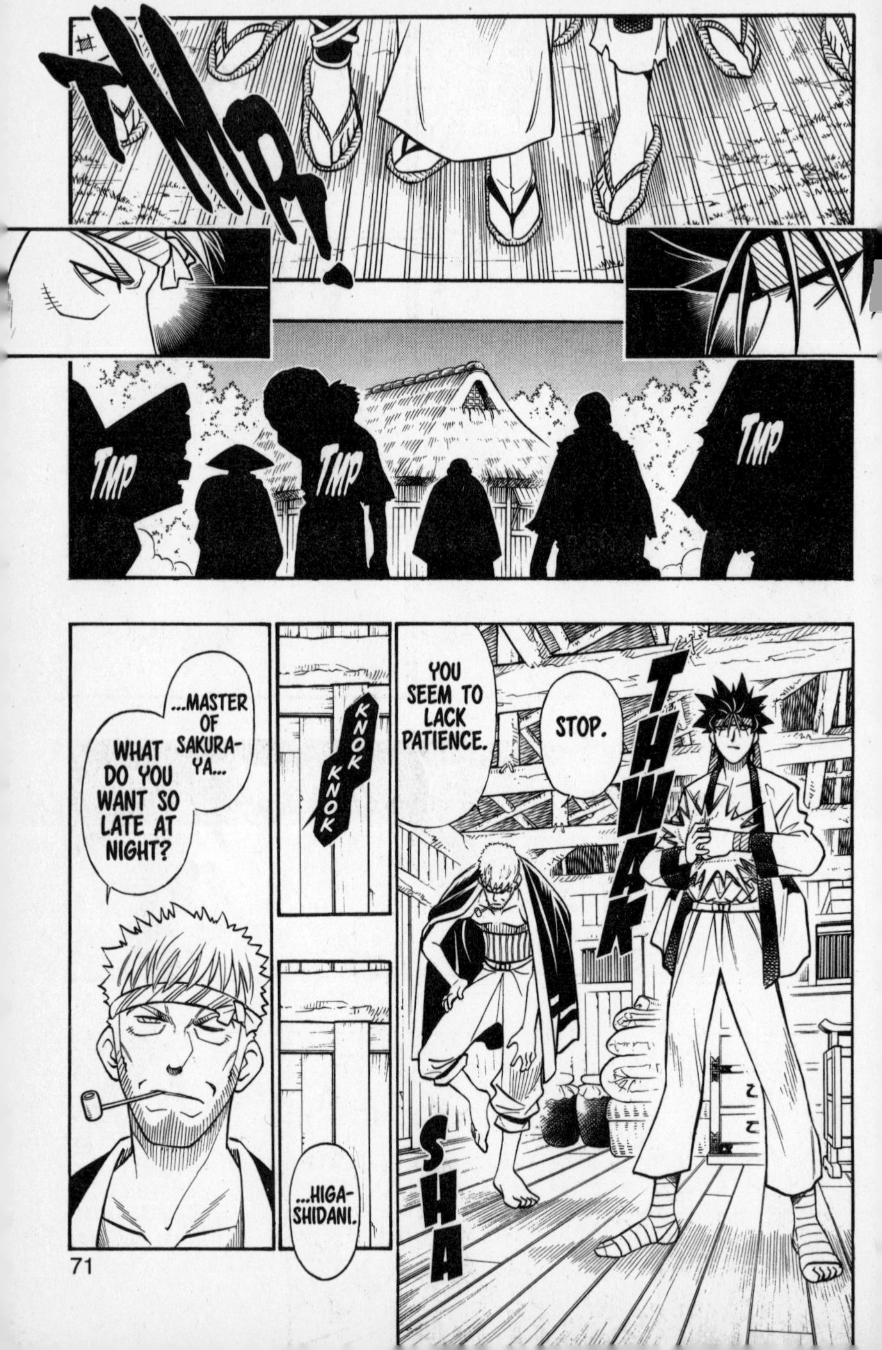
THMP!
TMP
TMP
TMP
THWAK
STOP.
YOU SEEM TO LACK PATIENCE.
SHA
KNOK KNOK KNOK
...HIGA-SHIDANI.
...MASTER OF SAKURA-YA...
WHAT DO YOU WANT SO LATE AT NIGHT?

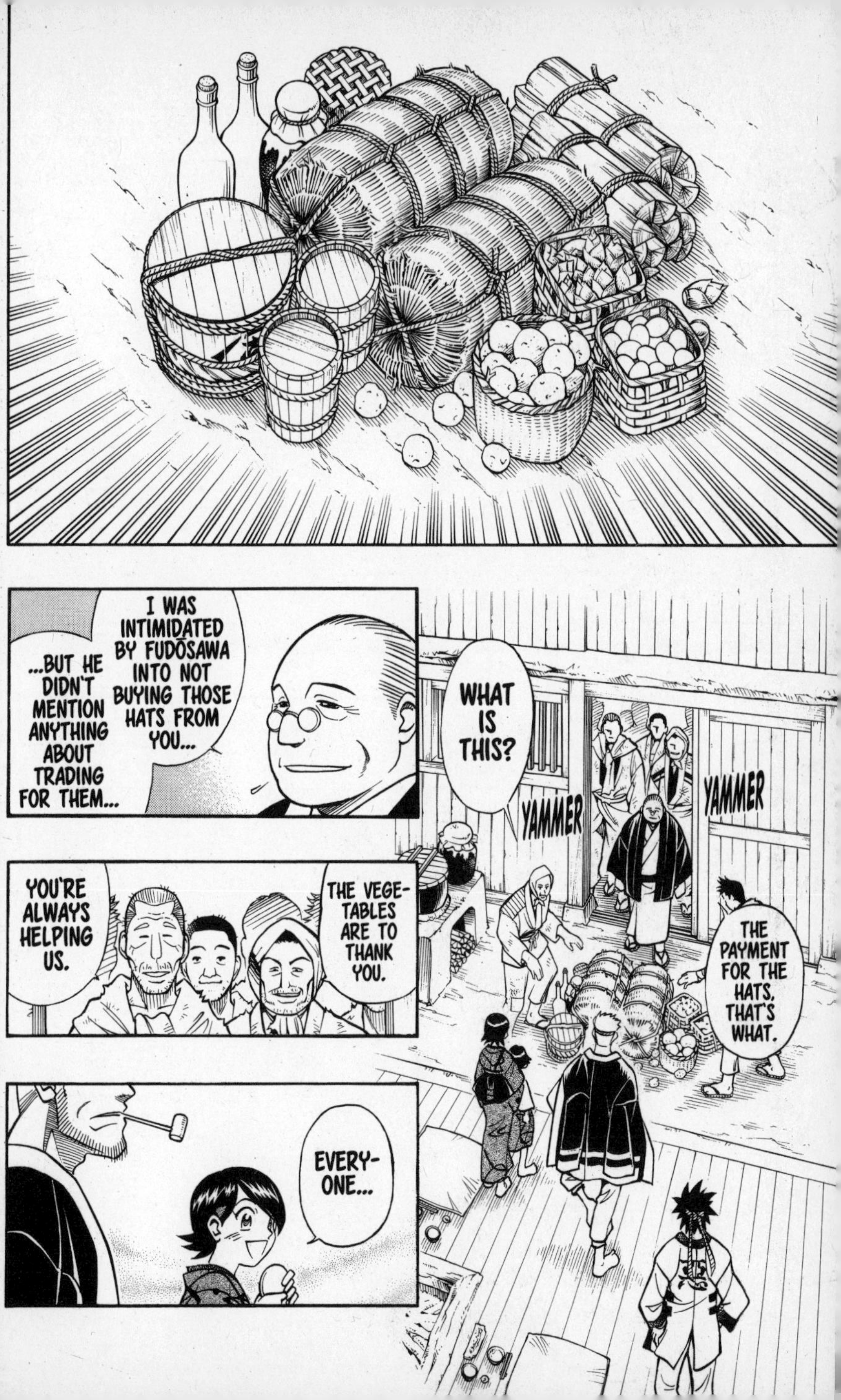
WHAT IS THIS?
YAMMER
YAMMER
THE PAYMENT FOR THE HATS, THAT'S WHAT.
I WAS INTIMIDATED BY FUDŌSAWA INTO NOT BUYING THOSE HATS FROM YOU...
...BUT HE DIDN'T MENTION ANYTHING ABOUT TRADING FOR THEM...
THE VEGE-TABLES ARE TO THANK YOU.
YOU'RE ALWAYS HELPING US.
EVERY-ONE...

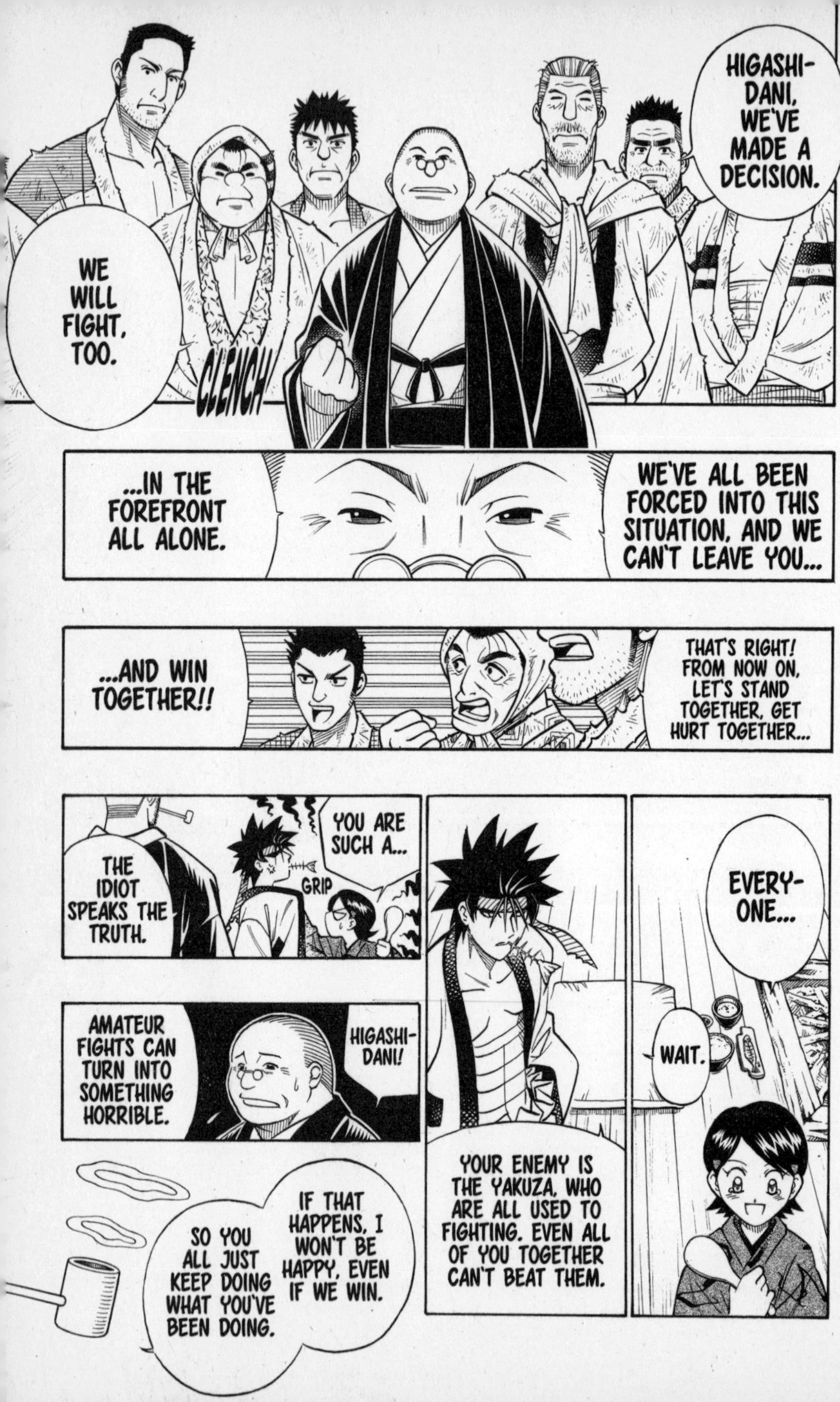

HIGASHIDANI, WE'VE MADE A DECISION.
WE WILL FIGHT, TOO.
CLENCH
WE'VE ALL BEEN FORCED INTO THIS SITUATION, AND WE CAN'T LEAVE YOU...
...IN THE FOREFRONT ALL ALONE.
THAT'S RIGHT! FROM NOW ON, LET'S STAND TOGETHER, GET HURT TOGETHER...
...AND WIN TOGETHER!!
EVERYONE...
WAIT.
YOUR ENEMY IS THE YAKUZA, WHO ARE ALL USED TO FIGHTING. EVEN ALL OF YOU TOGETHER CAN'T BEAT THEM.
YOU ARE SUCH A...
GRIP
THE IDIOT SPEAKS THE TRUTH.
HIGASHIDANI!
AMATEUR FIGHTS CAN TURN INTO SOMETHING HORRIBLE.
IF THAT HAPPENS, I WON'T BE HAPPY, EVEN IF WE WIN.
SO YOU ALL JUST KEEP DOING WHAT YOU'VE BEEN DOING.

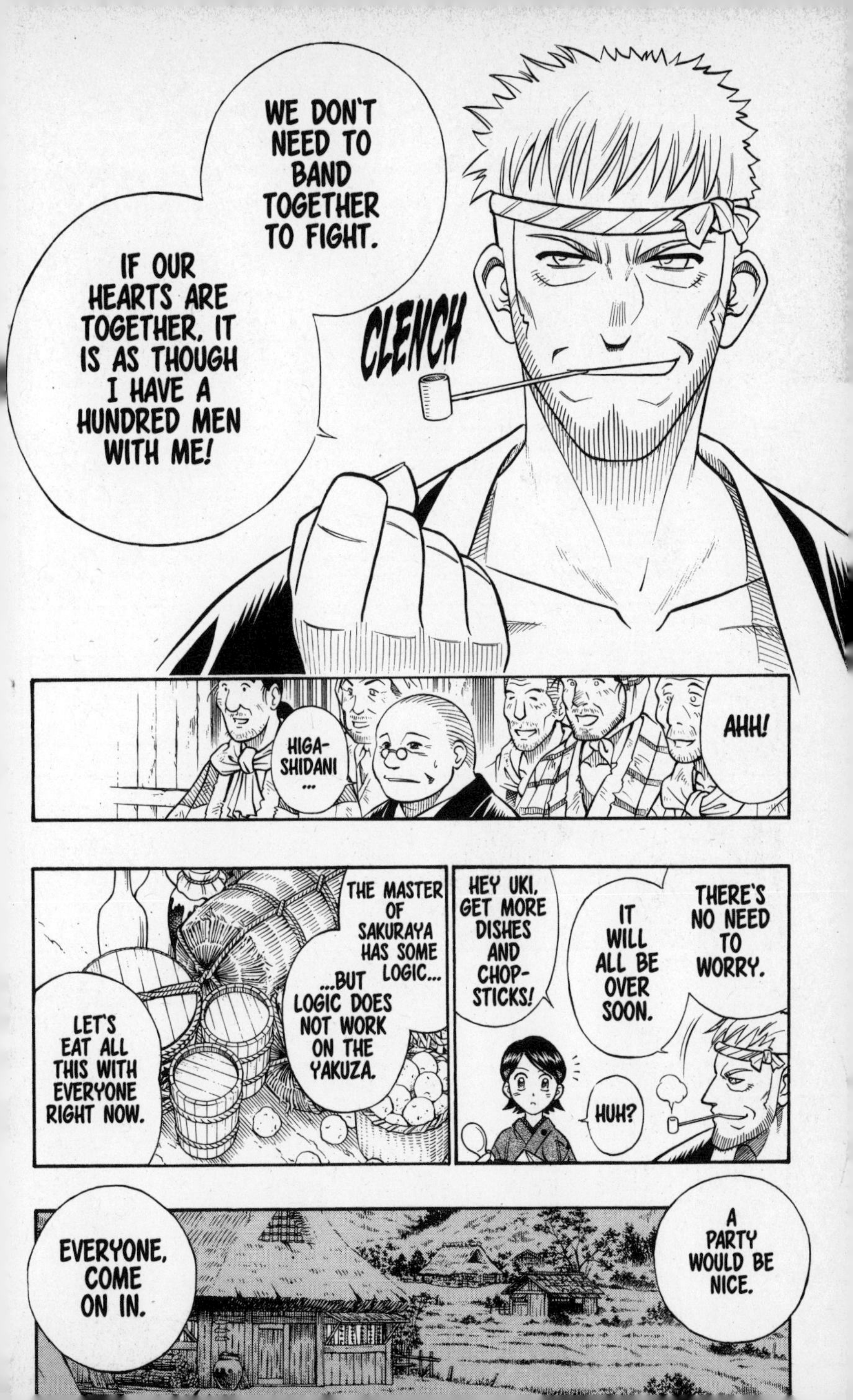
WE DON'T NEED TO BAND TOGETHER TO FIGHT.
IF OUR HEARTS ARE TOGETHER, IT IS AS THOUGH I HAVE A HUNDRED MEN WITH ME!
CLENCH
AHH!
HIGA-SHIDANI...
THERE'S NO NEED TO WORRY.
IT WILL ALL BE OVER SOON.
HEY UKI, GET MORE DISHES AND CHOP-STICKS!
HUH?
THE MASTER OF SAKURAYA HAS SOME LOGIC...
...BUT LOGIC DOES NOT WORK ON THE YAKUZA.
LET'S EAT ALL THIS WITH EVERYONE RIGHT NOW.
A PARTY WOULD BE NICE.
EVERYONE, COME ON IN.

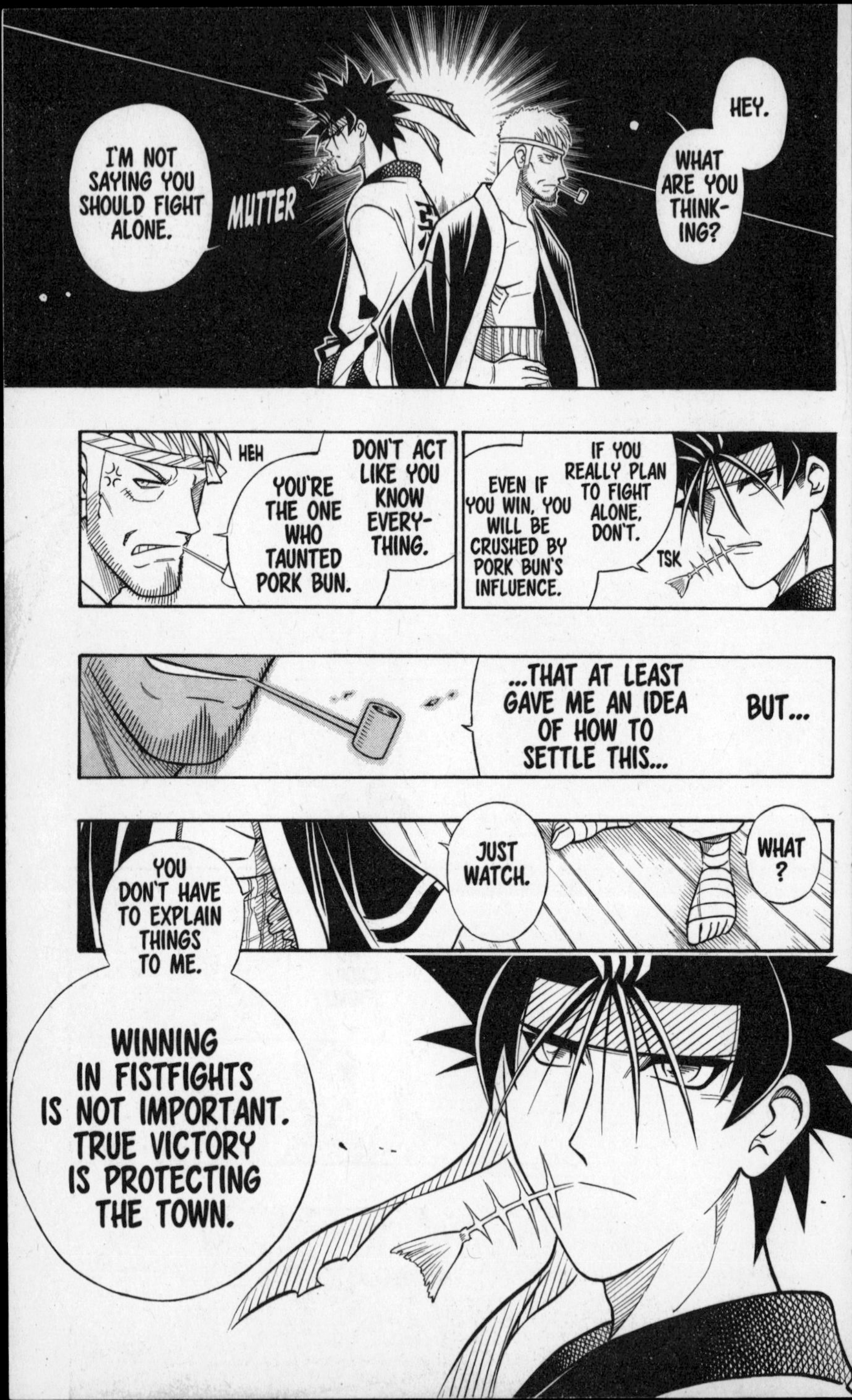
HEY.
WHAT ARE YOU THINK-ING?
I'M NOT SAYING YOU SHOULD FIGHT ALONE.
MUTTER
IF YOU REALLY PLAN TO FIGHT ALONE, DON'T.
EVEN IF YOU WIN, YOU WILL BE CRUSHED BY PORK BUN'S INFLUENCE.
TSK
DON'T ACT LIKE YOU KNOW EVERY-THING.
HEH
YOU'RE THE ONE WHO TAUNTED PORK BUN.
BUT...
...THAT AT LEAST GAVE ME AN IDEA OF HOW TO SETTLE THIS...
WHAT?
JUST WATCH.
YOU DON'T HAVE TO EXPLAIN THINGS TO ME.
WINNING IN FISTFIGHTS IS NOT IMPORTANT. TRUE VICTORY IS PROTECTING THE TOWN.

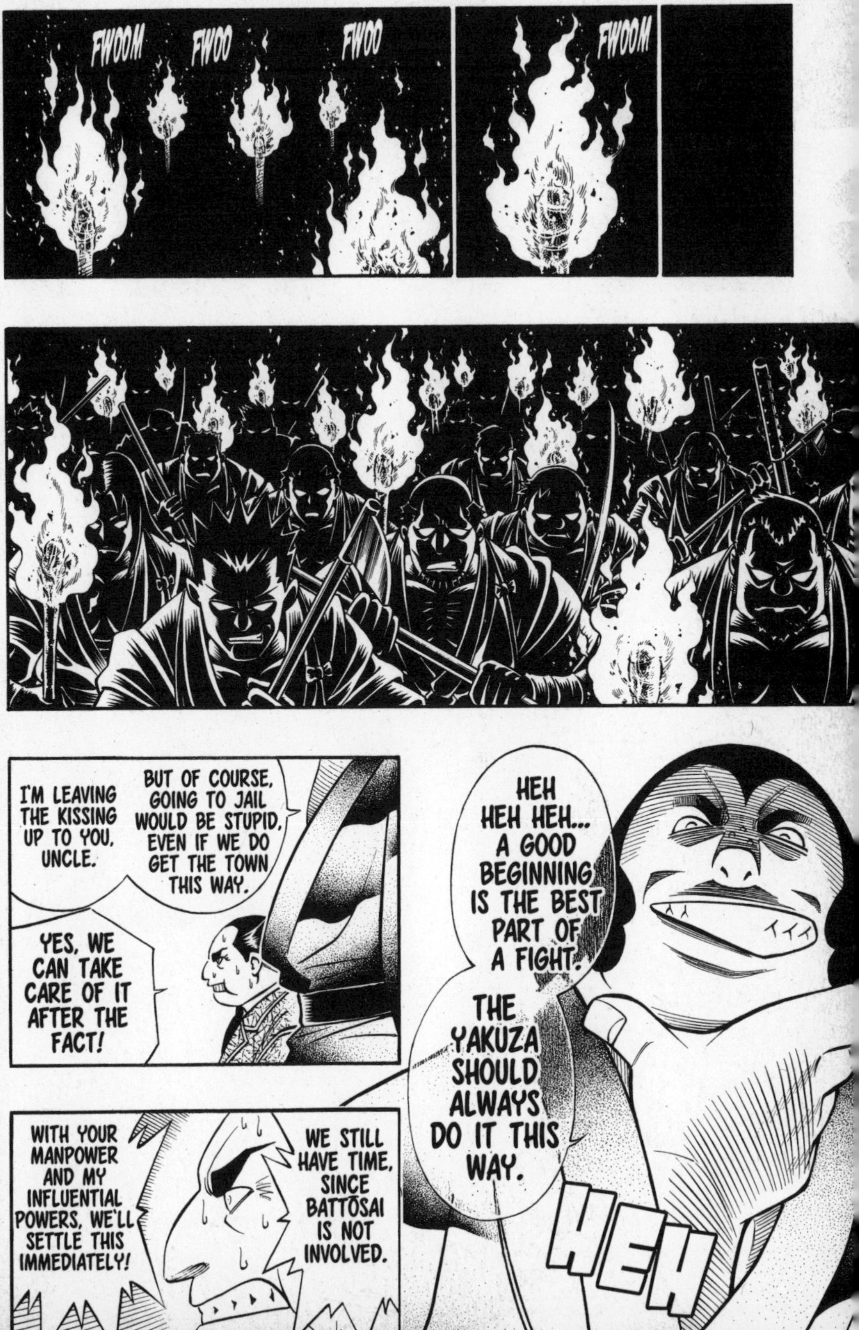
FWOOM
FWOO
FWOO
FWOOM
HEH HEH HEH... A GOOD BEGINNING IS THE BEST PART OF A FIGHT.
THE YAKUZA SHOULD ALWAYS DO IT THIS WAY.
HEH HEH
BUT OF COURSE, GOING TO JAIL WOULD BE STUPID, EVEN IF WE DO GET THE TOWN THIS WAY.
I'M LEAVING THE KISSING UP TO YOU, UNCLE.
YES, WE CAN TAKE CARE OF IT AFTER THE FACT!
WE STILL HAVE TIME, SINCE BATTŌSAI IS NOT INVOLVED.
WITH YOUR MANPOWER AND MY INFLUENTIAL POWERS, WE'LL SETTLE THIS IMMEDIATELY!

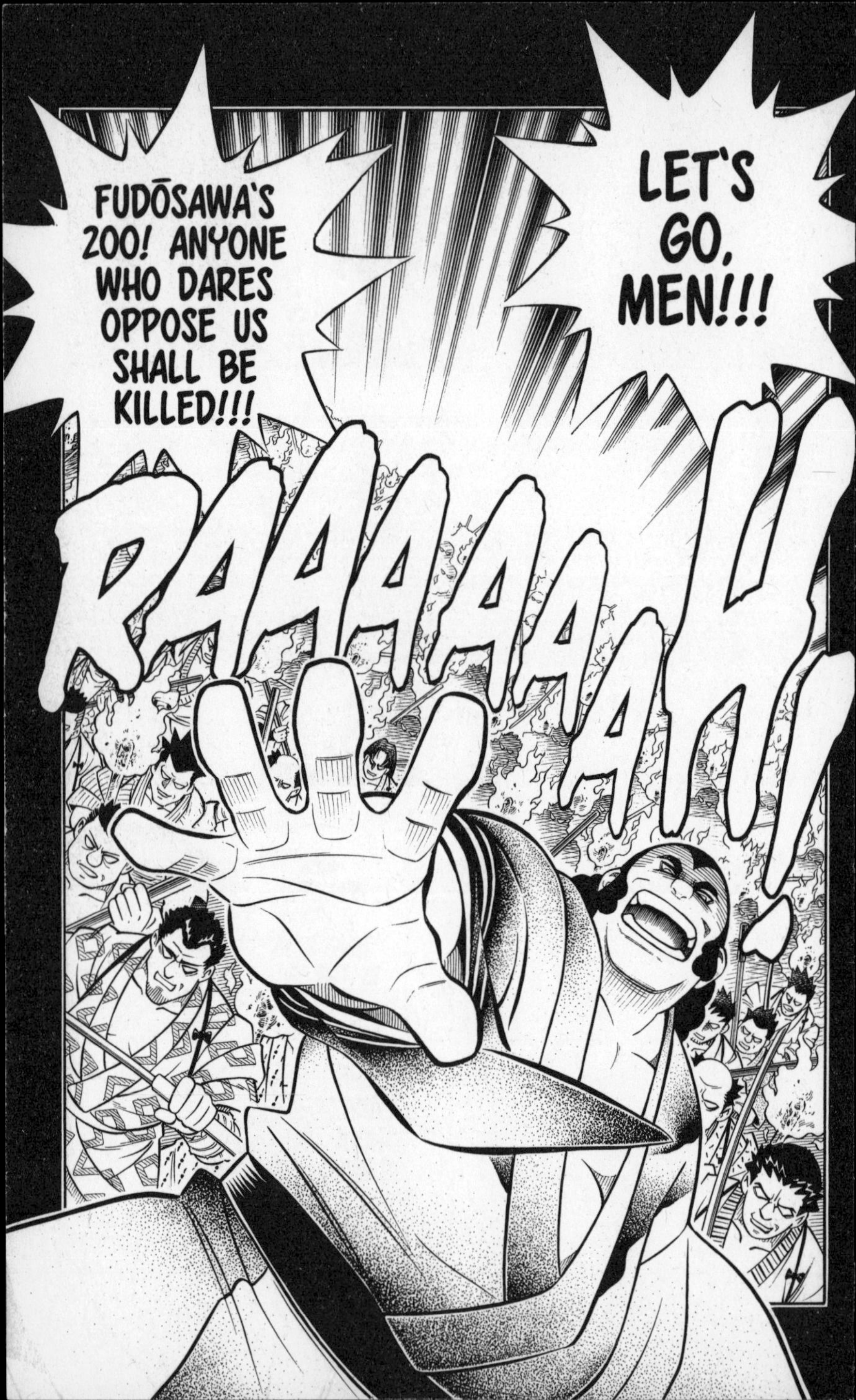
LET'S GO, MEN!!!
FUDŌSAWA'S 200! ANYONE WHO DARES OPPOSE US SHALL BE KILLED!!!
RAAAAAH!!

Rurouni Kenshin

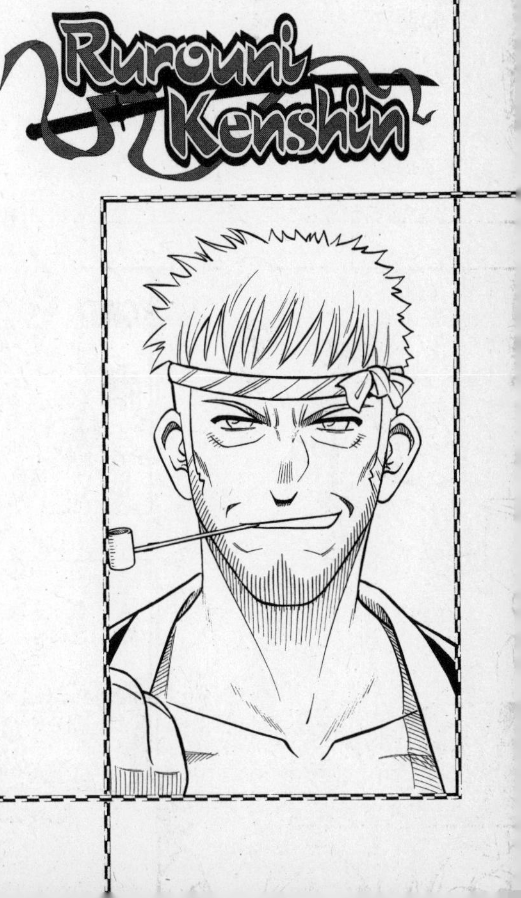

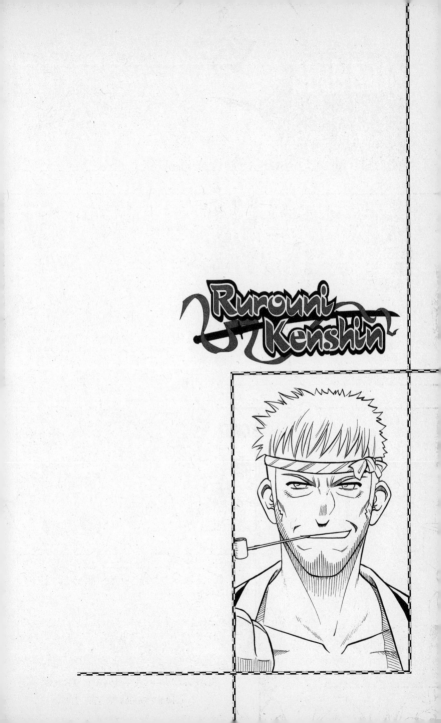

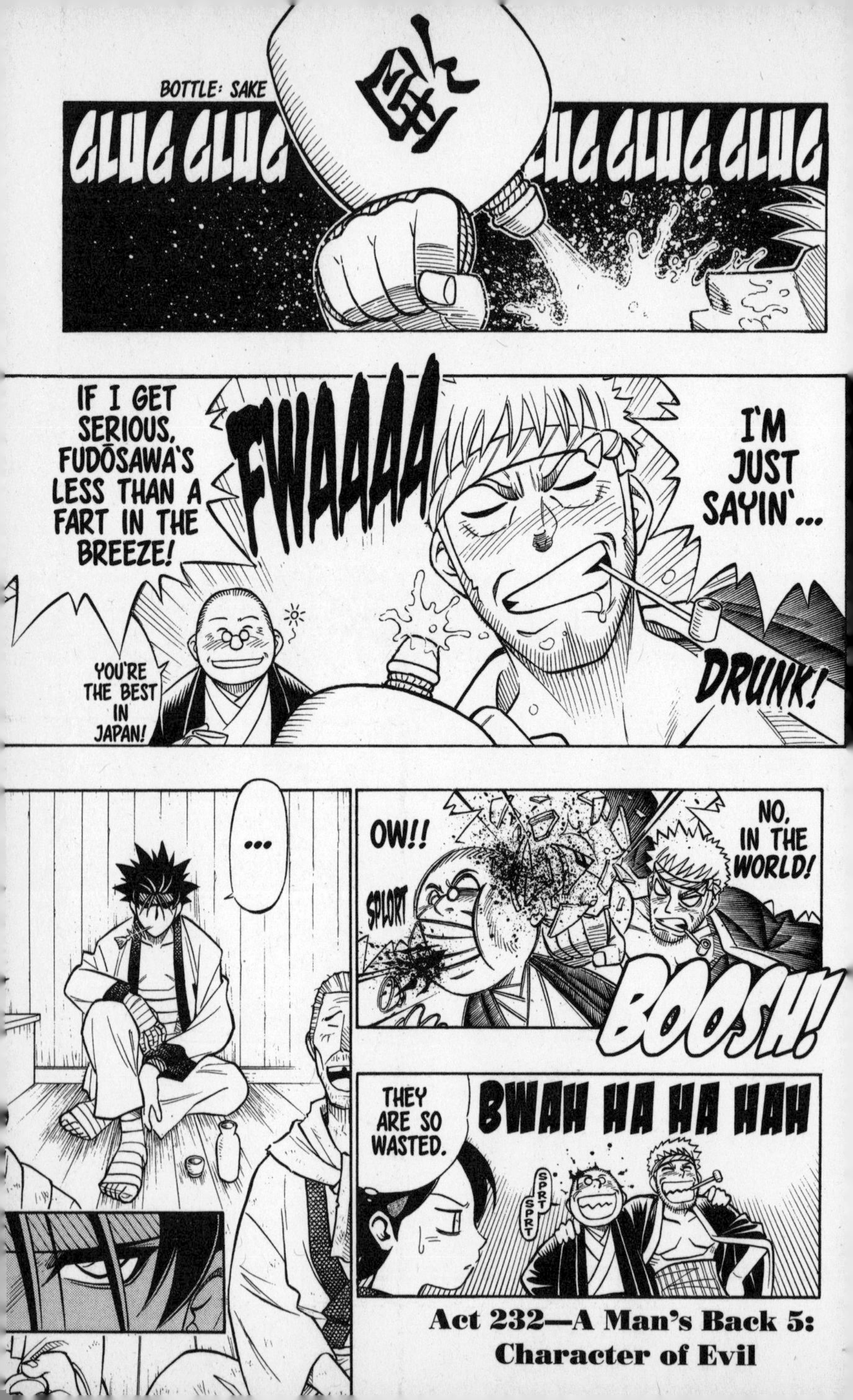
BOTTLE: SAKE
GLUG GLUG GLUG GLUG GLUG
I'M JUST SAYIN'...
DRUNK!
FWAAAA
IF I GET SERIOUS, FUDŌSAWA'S LESS THAN A FART IN THE BREEZE!
YOU'RE THE BEST IN JAPAN!
NO, IN THE WORLD!
BOOSH!
OW!!
SPLORT
BWAH HA HA HAH
THEY ARE SO WASTED.
SPRT SPRT
...

Act 232—A Man's Back 5: Character of Evil

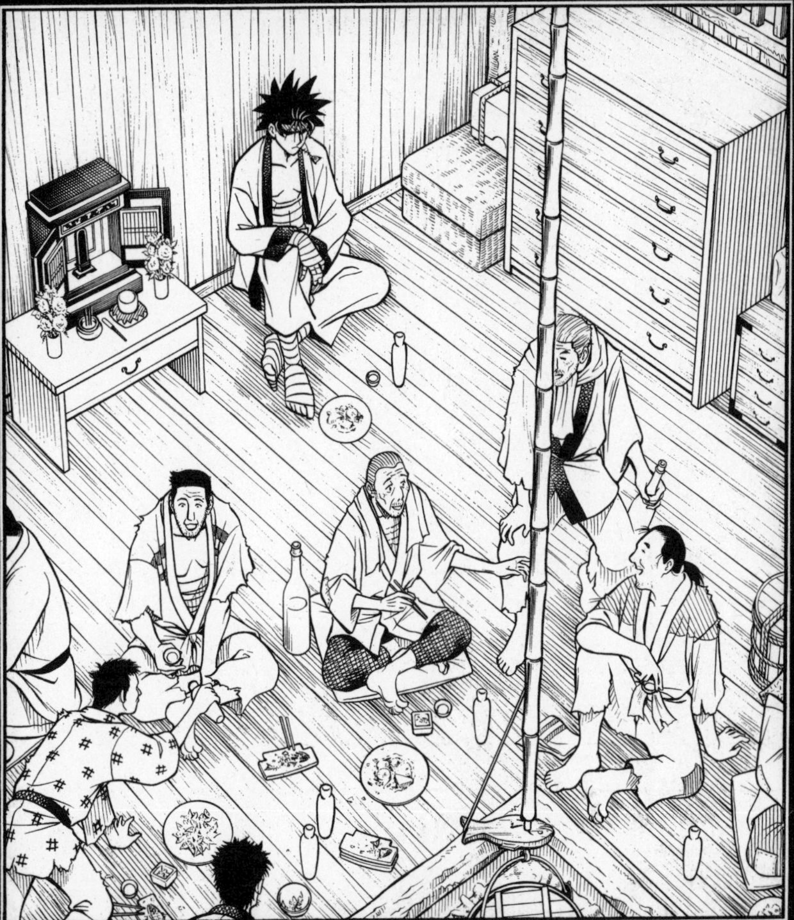

Act 232
A Man's Back 5: Character of Evil

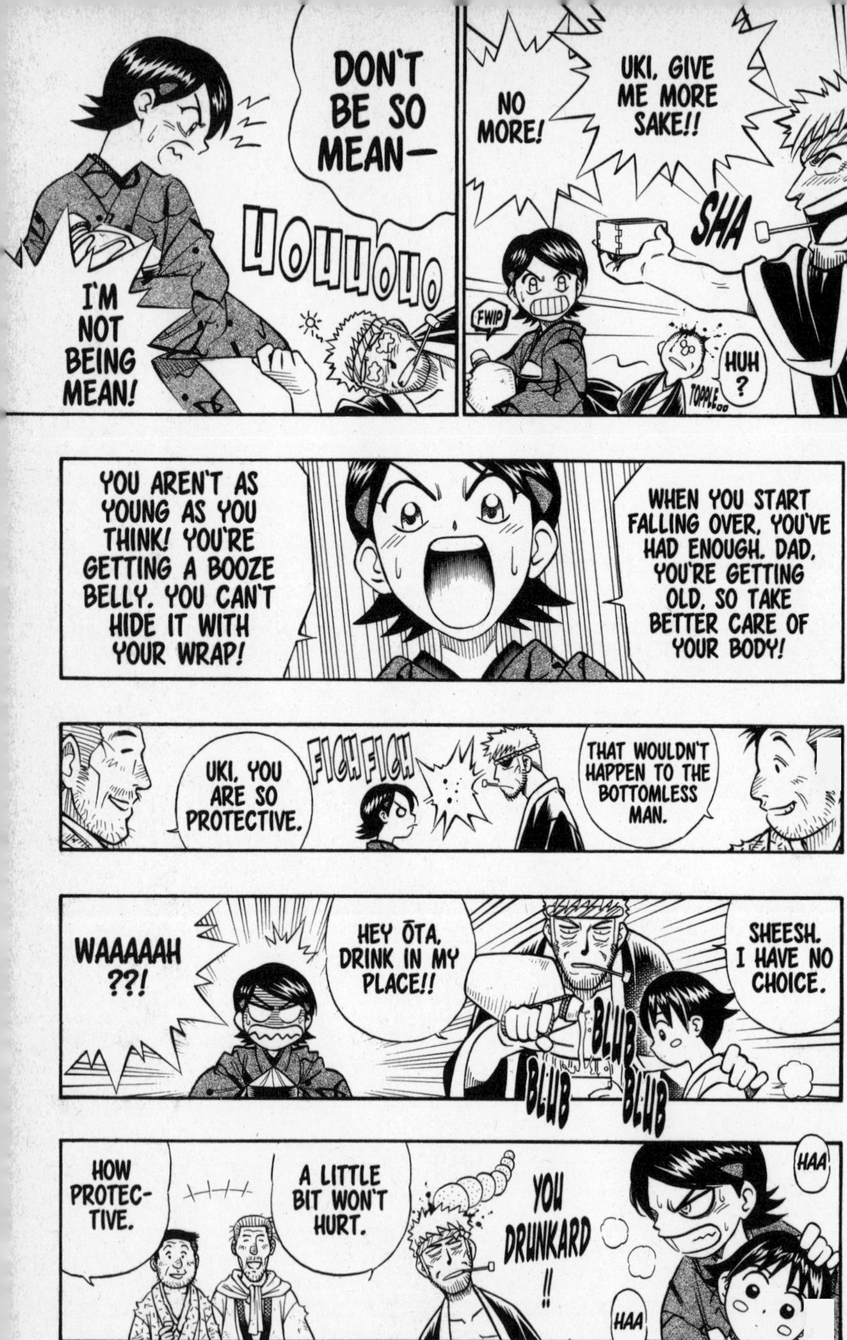
UKI, GIVE ME MORE SAKE!!
SHA
NO MORE!
FWIP
HUH?
TOPPLE..
DON'T BE SO MEAN—
UOHHOHO
I'M NOT BEING MEAN!
WHEN YOU START FALLING OVER, YOU'VE HAD ENOUGH. DAD, YOU'RE GETTING OLD, SO TAKE BETTER CARE OF YOUR BODY!
YOU AREN'T AS YOUNG AS YOU THINK! YOU'RE GETTING A BOOZE BELLY. YOU CAN'T HIDE IT WITH YOUR WRAP!
THAT WOULDN'T HAPPEN TO THE BOTTOMLESS MAN.
FICH FICH
UKI, YOU ARE SO PROTECTIVE.
SHEESH. I HAVE NO CHOICE.
BLUB BLUB BLUB
HEY ŌTA, DRINK IN MY PLACE!!
WAAAAAH ??!
HAA
HAA
YOU DRUNKARD !!
A LITTLE BIT WON'T HURT.
HOW PROTEC-TIVE.

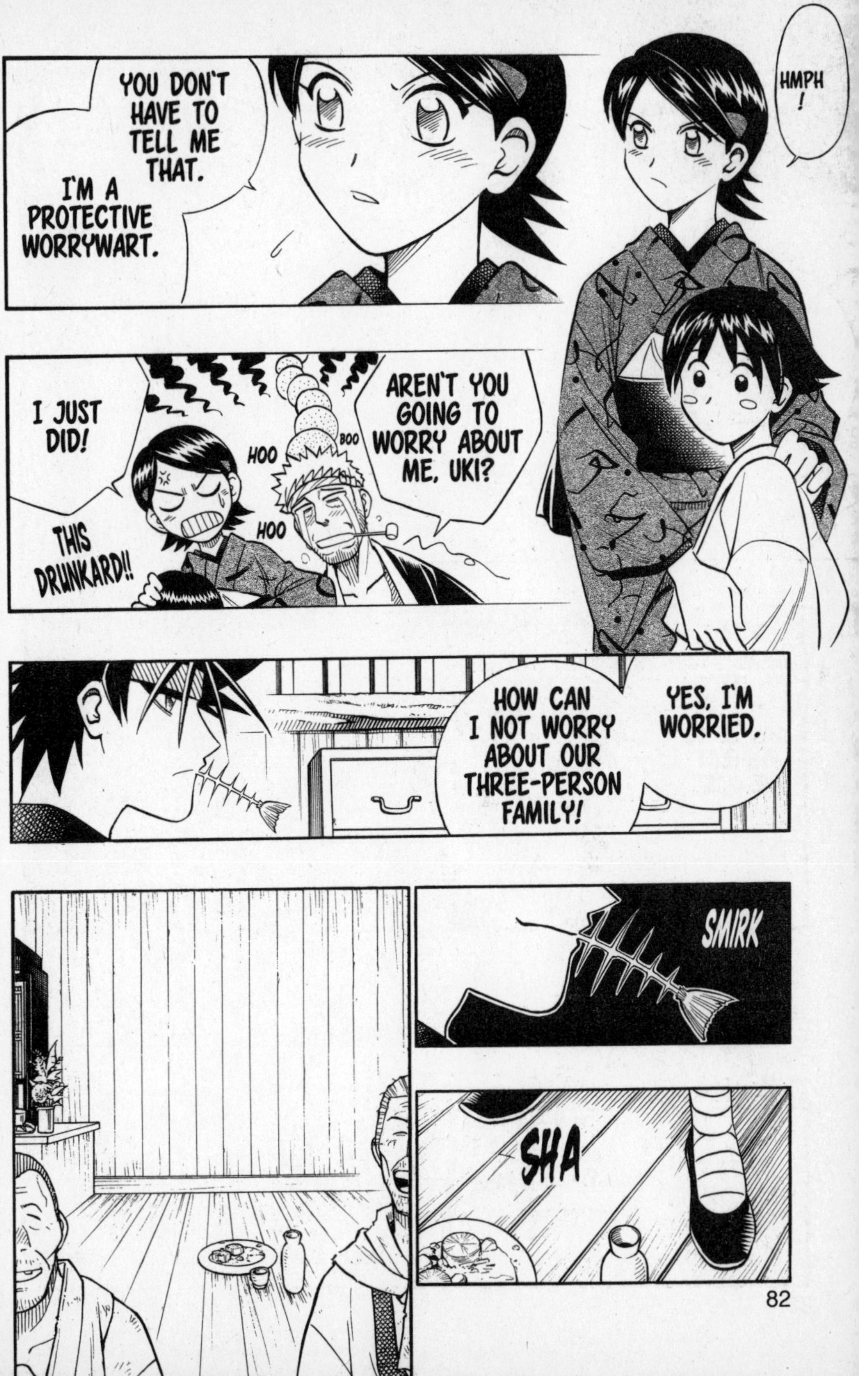
HMPH!
YOU DON'T HAVE TO TELL ME THAT.
I'M A PROTECTIVE WORRYWART.
AREN'T YOU GOING TO WORRY ABOUT ME, UKI?
BOO
HOO
HOO
I JUST DID!
THIS DRUNKARD!!
YES, I'M WORRIED.
HOW CAN I NOT WORRY ABOUT OUR THREE-PERSON FAMILY!
SMIRK
SHA

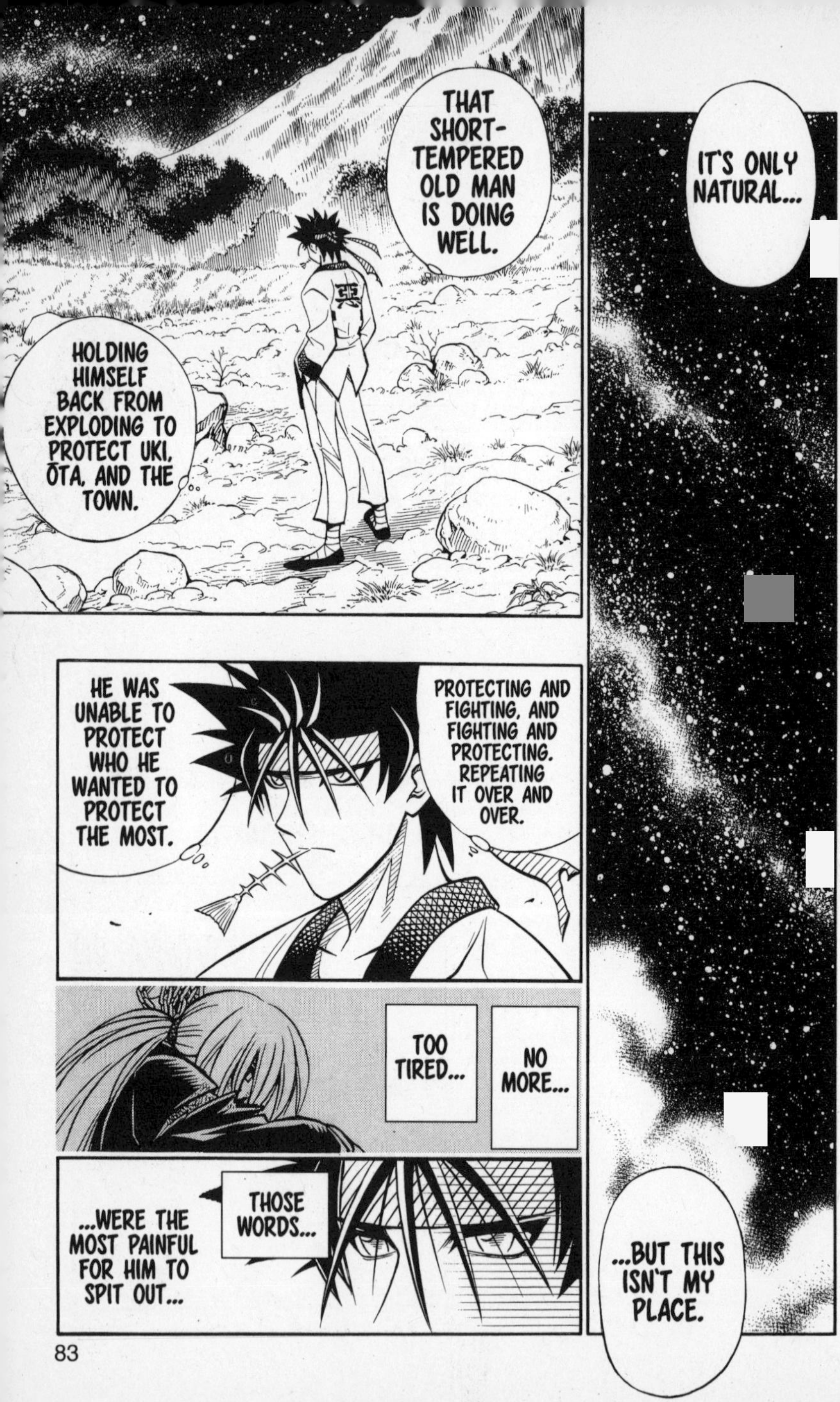
IT'S ONLY NATURAL...
...BUT THIS ISN'T MY PLACE.
THAT SHORT-TEMPERED OLD MAN IS DOING WELL.
HOLDING HIMSELF BACK FROM EXPLODING TO PROTECT UKI, ŌTA, AND THE TOWN.
PROTECTING AND FIGHTING, AND FIGHTING AND PROTECTING. REPEATING IT OVER AND OVER.
HE WAS UNABLE TO PROTECT WHO HE WANTED TO PROTECT THE MOST.
NO MORE...
TOO TIRED...
THOSE WORDS...
...WERE THE MOST PAINFUL FOR HIM TO SPIT OUT...

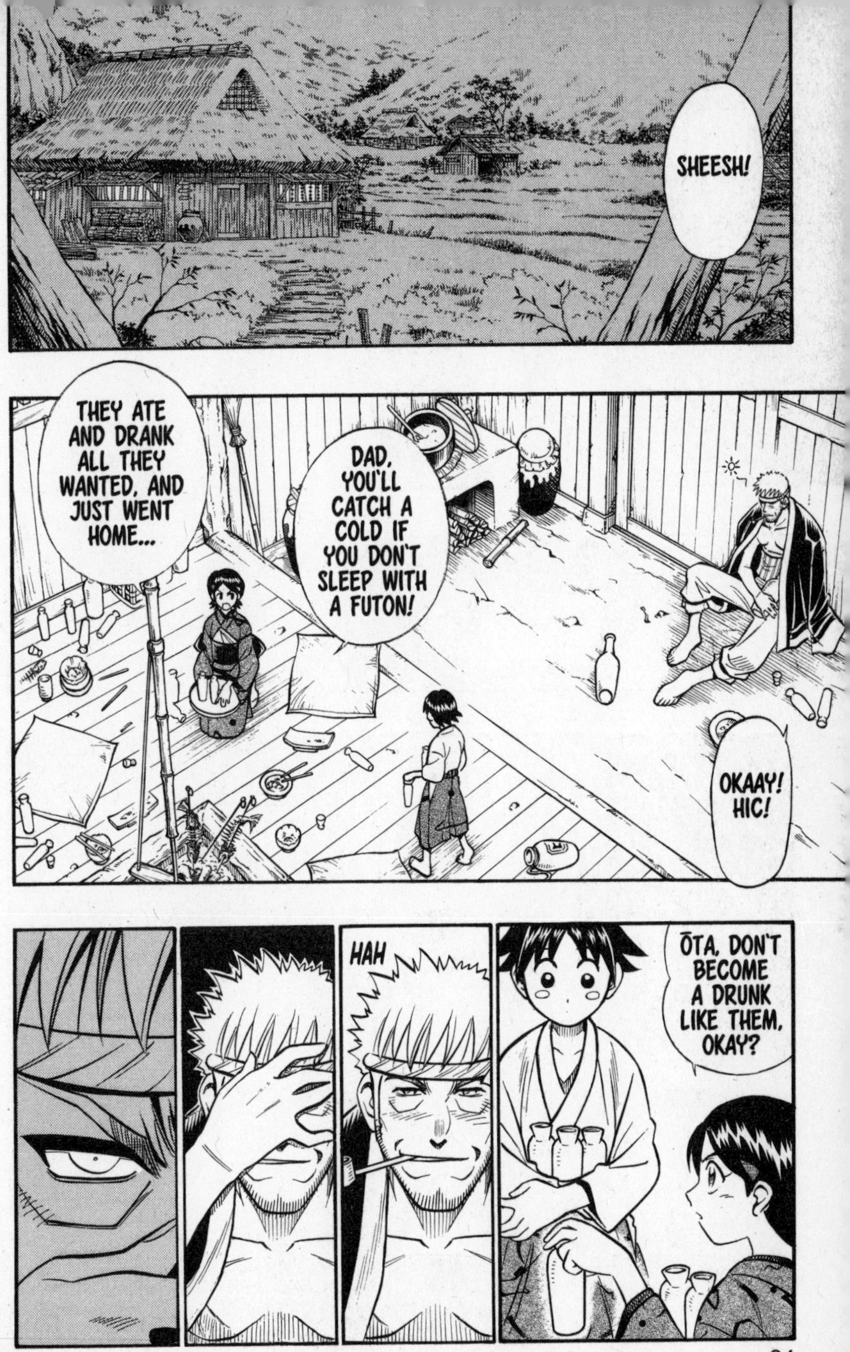
SHEESH!
THEY ATE AND DRANK ALL THEY WANTED, AND JUST WENT HOME...
DAD, YOU'LL CATCH A COLD IF YOU DON'T SLEEP WITH A FUTON!
OKAAY! HIC!
ŌTA, DON'T BECOME A DRUNK LIKE THEM, OKAY?
HAH

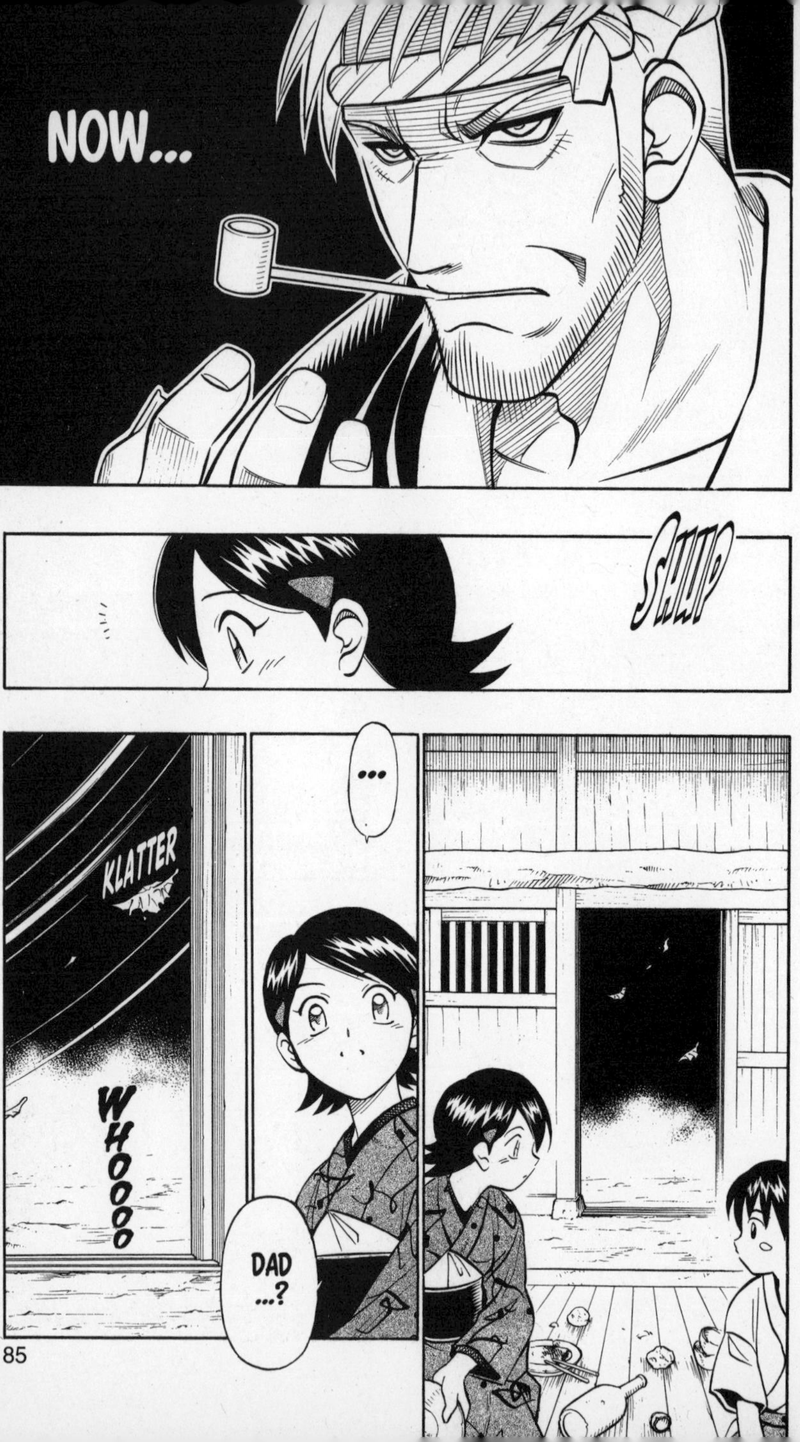
NOW...
SHUP
...
DAD ...?
KLATTER
WHOOOO

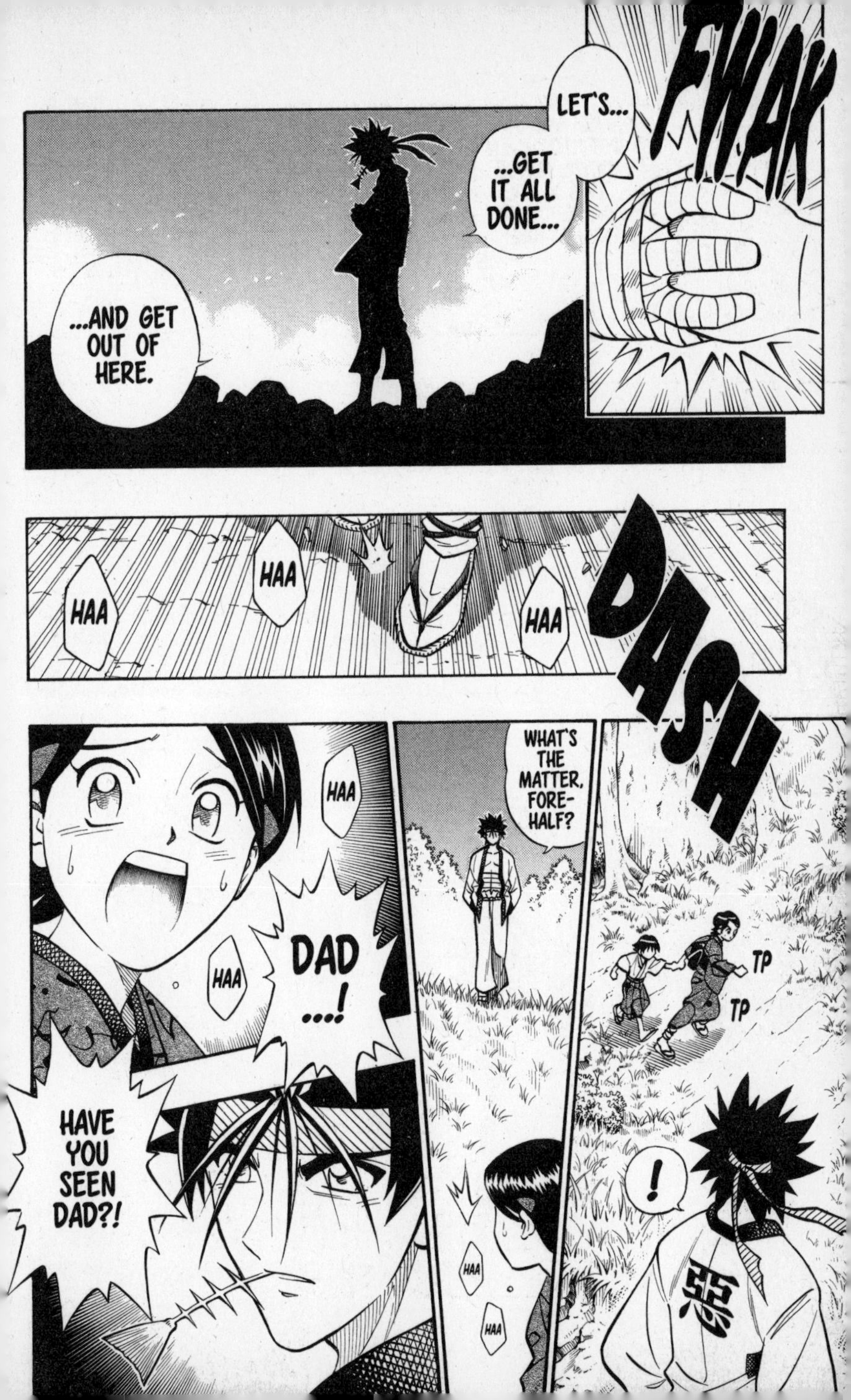
FWAK
LET'S...
...GET IT ALL DONE...
...AND GET OUT OF HERE.
DASH
HAA
HAA
HAA
TP
TP
!
WHAT'S THE MATTER, FORE-HALF?
HAA
HAA
HAA
DAD ...!
HAA
HAVE YOU SEEN DAD?!

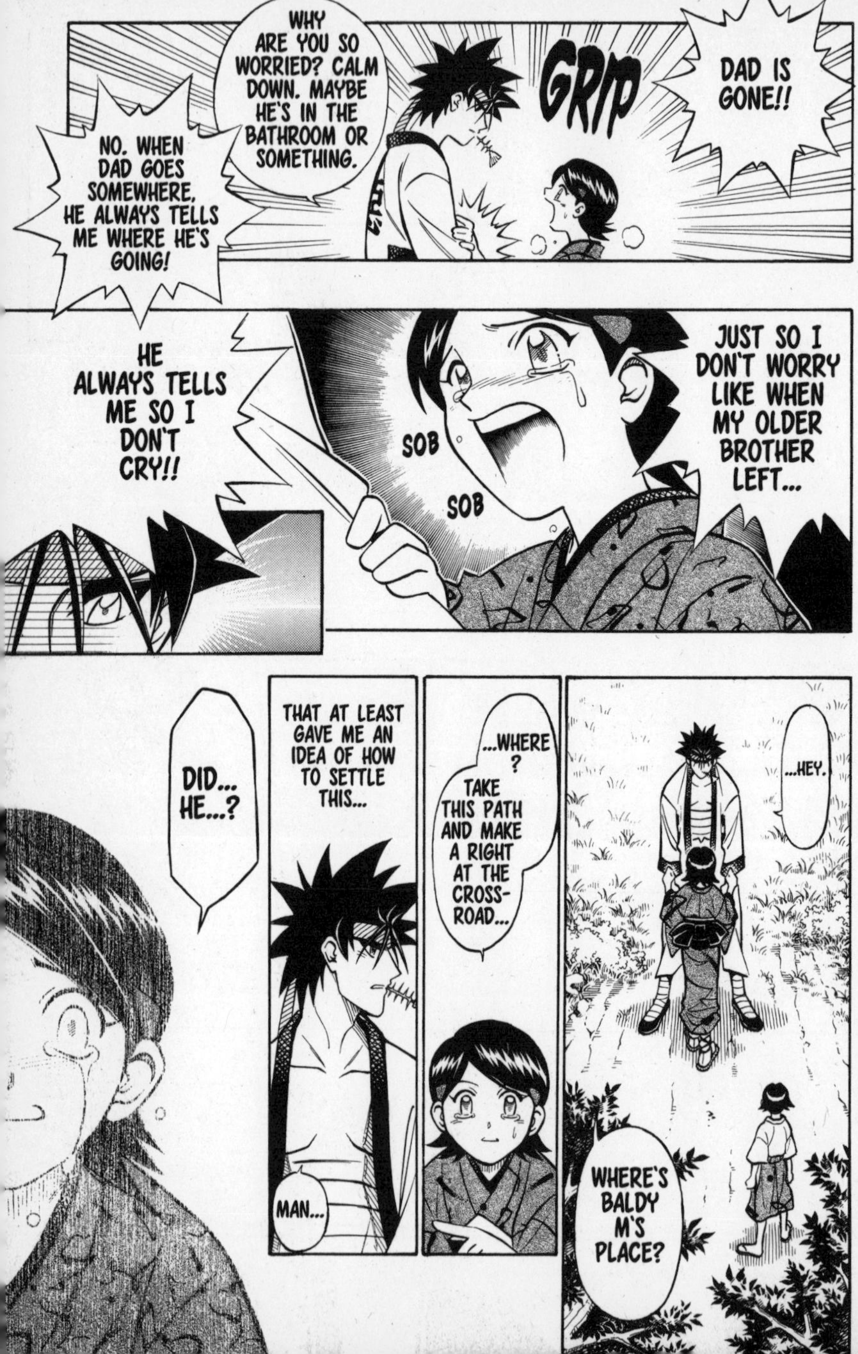
DAD IS GONE!!
GRIP
WHY ARE YOU SO WORRIED? CALM DOWN. MAYBE HE'S IN THE BATHROOM OR SOMETHING.
NO. WHEN DAD GOES SOMEWHERE, HE ALWAYS TELLS ME WHERE HE'S GOING!
JUST SO I DON'T WORRY LIKE WHEN MY OLDER BROTHER LEFT...
SOB
SOB
HE ALWAYS TELLS ME SO I DON'T CRY!!
...HEY.
WHERE'S BALDY M'S PLACE?
...WHERE?
TAKE THIS PATH AND MAKE A RIGHT AT THE CROSS-ROAD...
THAT AT LEAST GAVE ME AN IDEA OF HOW TO SETTLE THIS...
MAN...
DID... HE...?

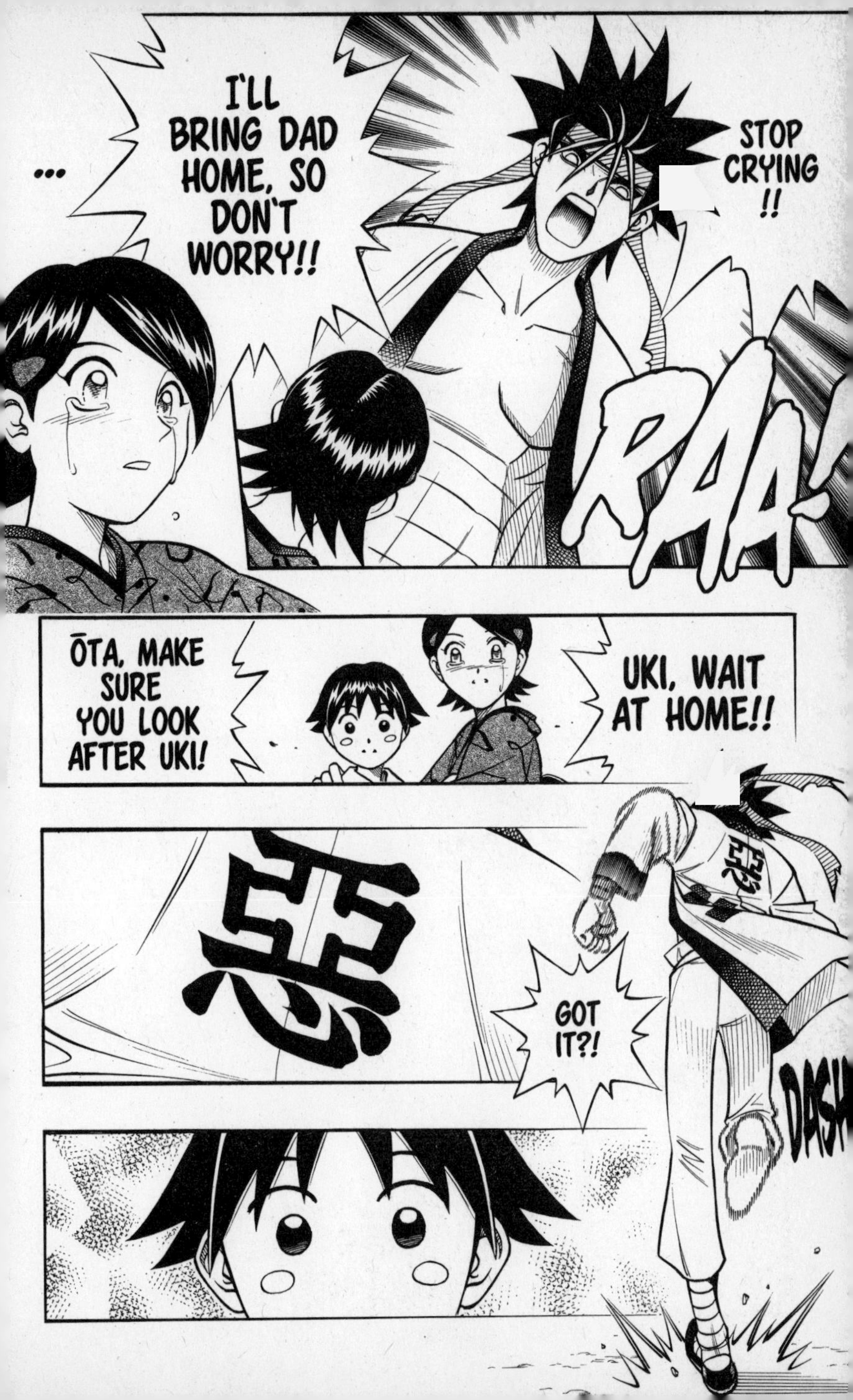

STOP CRYING!!
RAA!
I'LL BRING DAD HOME, SO DON'T WORRY!!
...
UKI, WAIT AT HOME!!
ŌTA, MAKE SURE YOU LOOK AFTER UKI!
DASH
GOT IT?!
悪

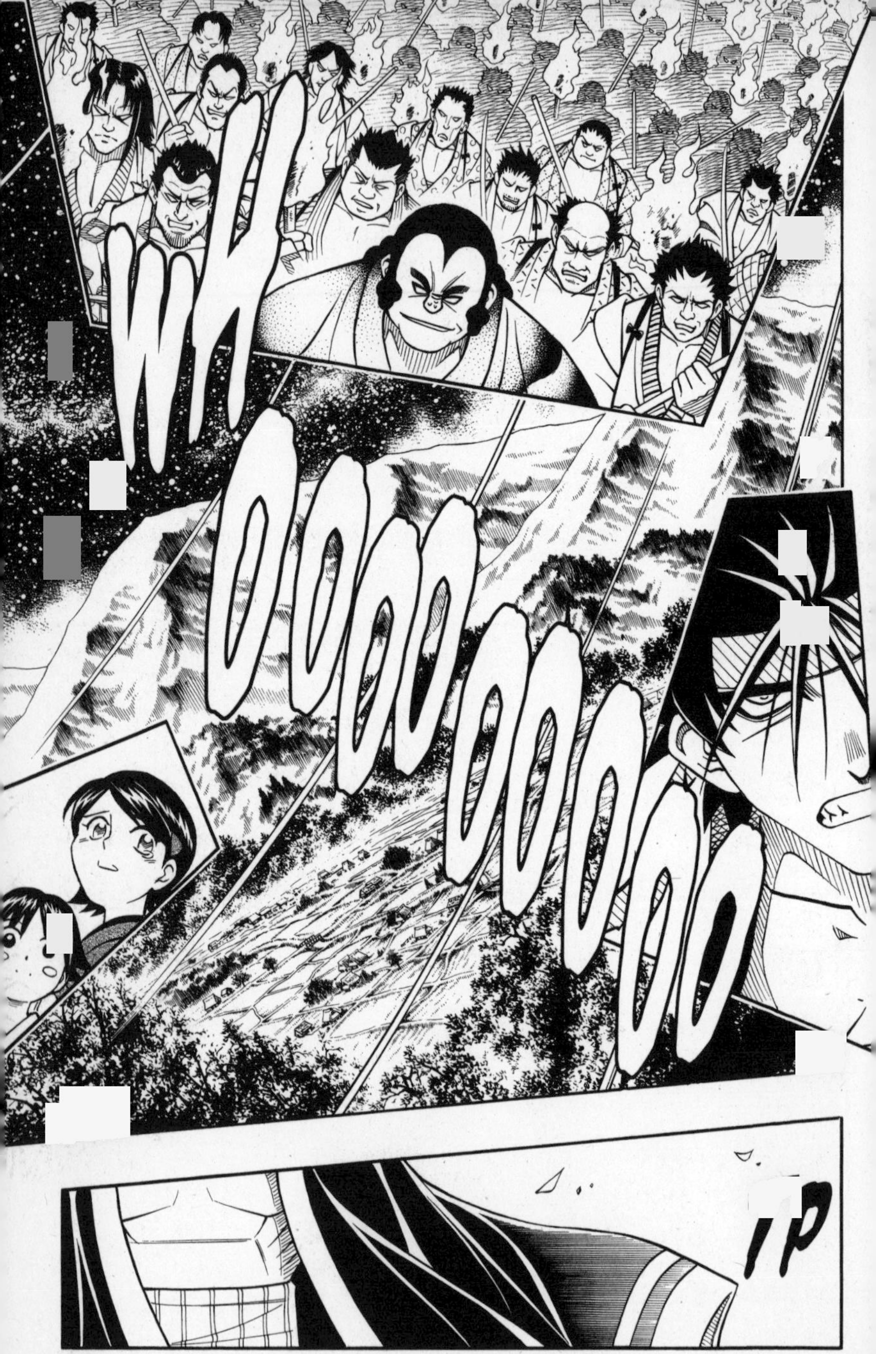
WHOOOOOOOOO
IP

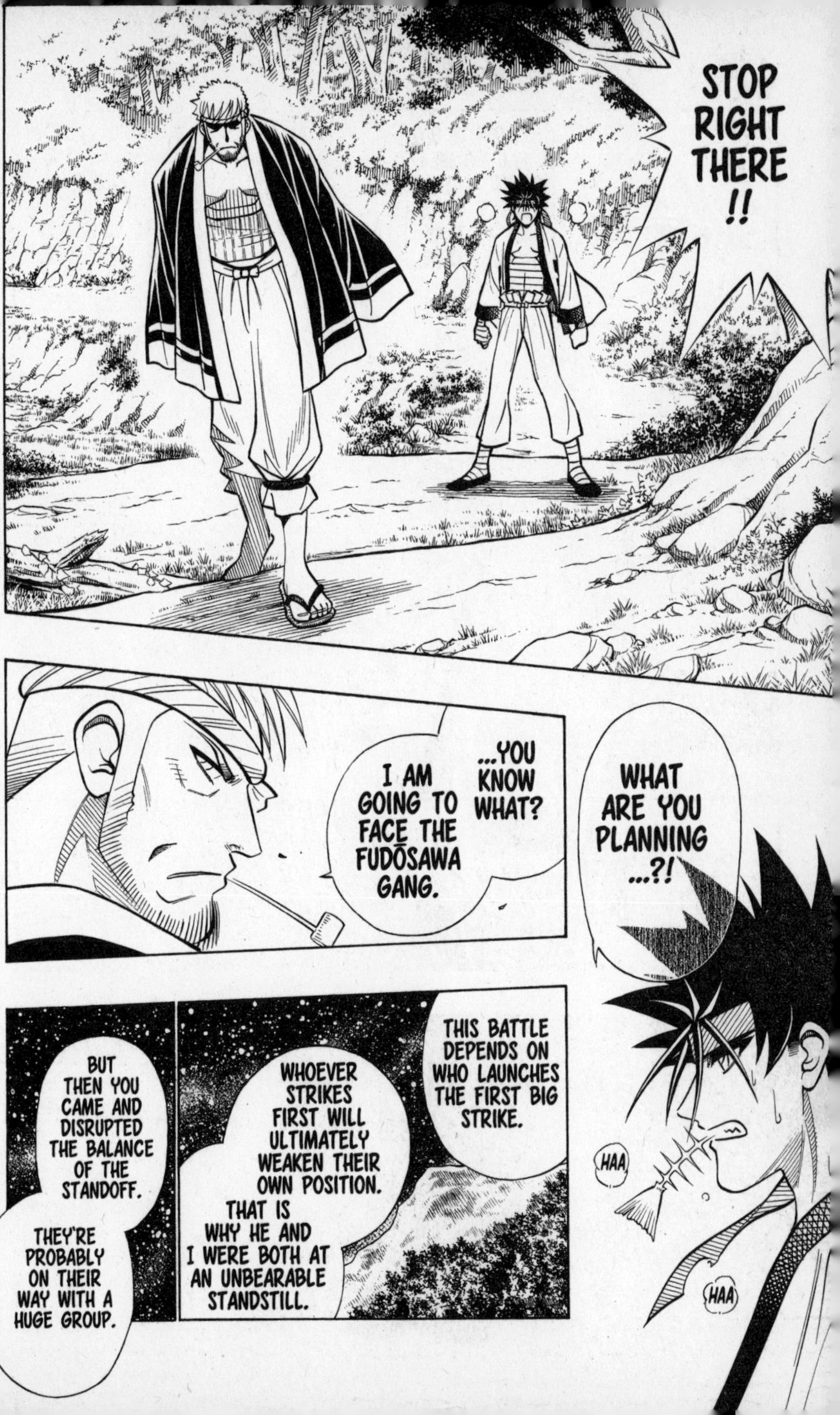
STOP RIGHT THERE!!
WHAT ARE YOU PLANNING...?!
HAA
HAA
...YOU KNOW WHAT?
I AM GOING TO FACE THE FUDŌSAWA GANG.
THIS BATTLE DEPENDS ON WHO LAUNCHES THE FIRST BIG STRIKE.
WHOEVER STRIKES FIRST WILL ULTIMATELY WEAKEN THEIR OWN POSITION.
THAT IS WHY HE AND I WERE BOTH AT AN UNBEARABLE STANDSTILL.
BUT THEN YOU CAME AND DISRUPTED THE BALANCE OF THE STANDOFF.
THEY'RE PROBABLY ON THEIR WAY WITH A HUGE GROUP.

READ THIS WAY

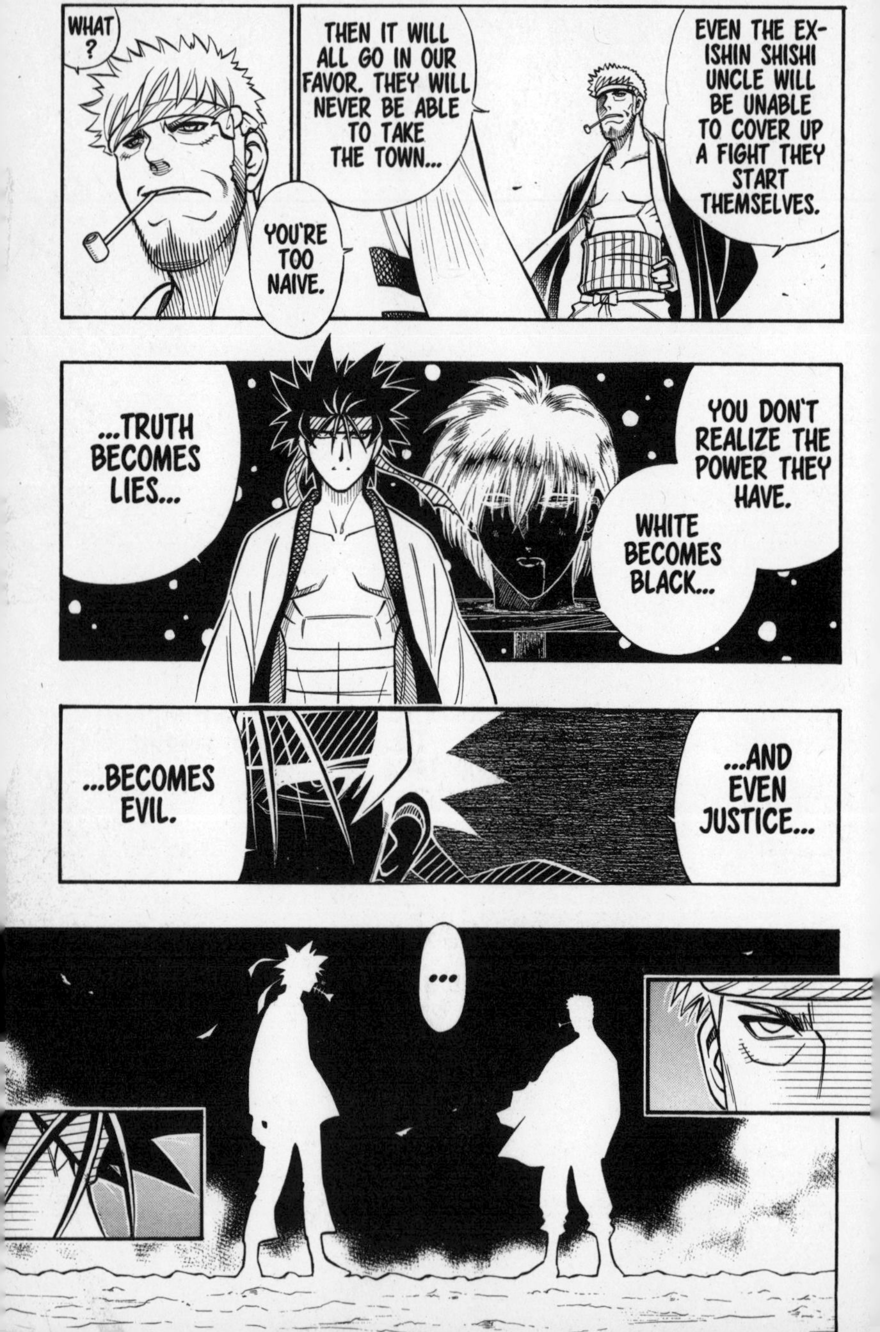
EVEN THE EX-ISHIN SHISHI UNCLE WILL BE UNABLE TO COVER UP A FIGHT THEY START THEMSELVES.
THEN IT WILL ALL GO IN OUR FAVOR. THEY WILL NEVER BE ABLE TO TAKE THE TOWN...
YOU'RE TOO NAIVE.
WHAT?
YOU DON'T REALIZE THE POWER THEY HAVE.
WHITE BECOMES BLACK...
...TRUTH BECOMES LIES...
...AND EVEN JUSTICE...
...BECOMES EVIL.
...

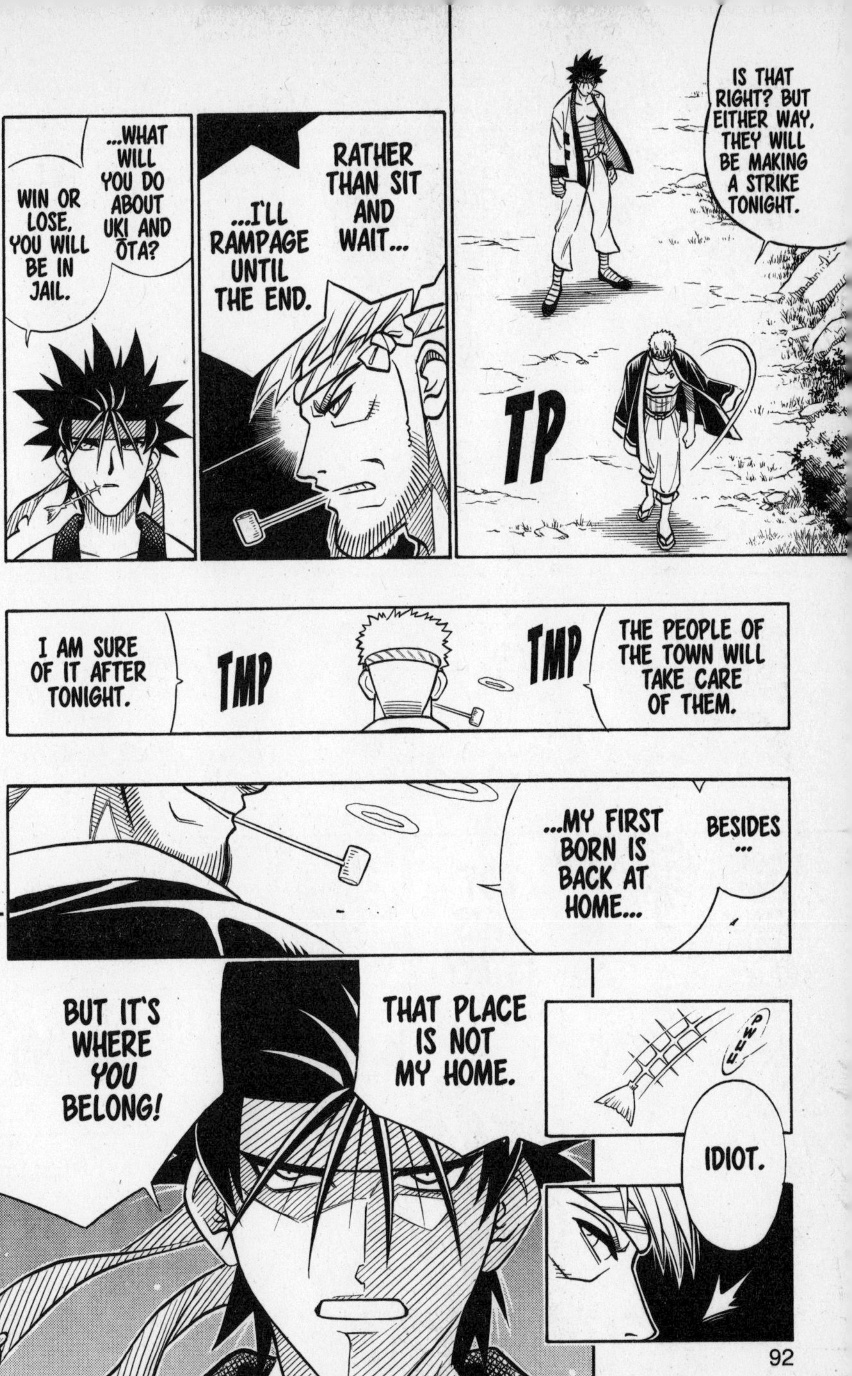
IS THAT RIGHT? BUT EITHER WAY, THEY WILL BE MAKING A STRIKE TONIGHT.
TP
RATHER THAN SIT AND WAIT...
...I'LL RAMPAGE UNTIL THE END.
...WHAT WILL YOU DO ABOUT UKI AND ŌTA?
WIN OR LOSE, YOU WILL BE IN JAIL.
THE PEOPLE OF THE TOWN WILL TAKE CARE OF THEM.
TMP
TMP
I AM SURE OF IT AFTER TONIGHT.
BESIDES...
...MY FIRST BORN IS BACK AT HOME...
IDIOT.
THAT PLACE IS NOT MY HOME.
BUT IT'S WHERE YOU BELONG!

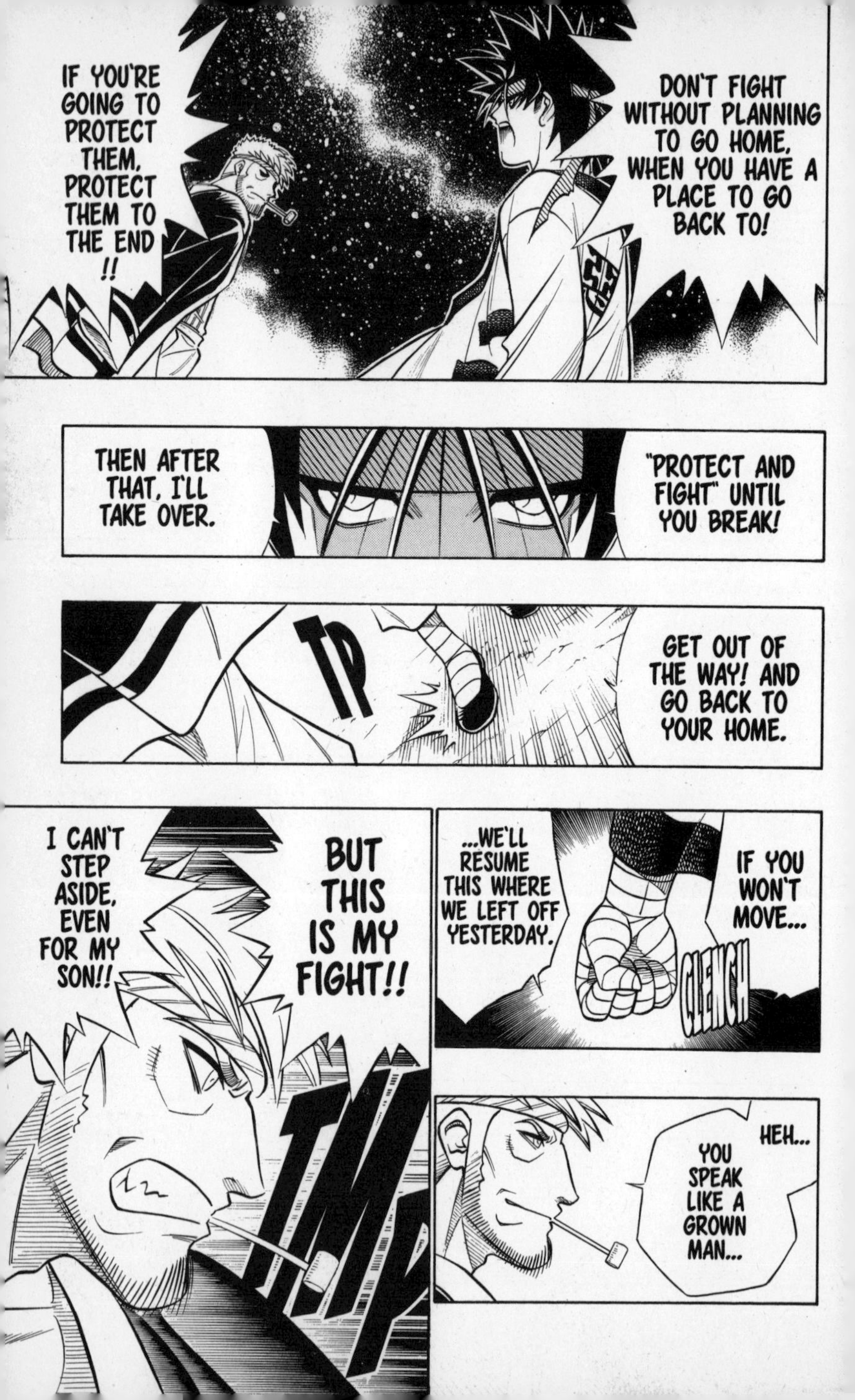

DON'T FIGHT WITHOUT PLANNING TO GO HOME, WHEN YOU HAVE A PLACE TO GO BACK TO!
IF YOU'RE GOING TO PROTECT THEM, PROTECT THEM TO THE END !!
"PROTECT AND FIGHT" UNTIL YOU BREAK!
THEN AFTER THAT, I'LL TAKE OVER.
GET OUT OF THE WAY! AND GO BACK TO YOUR HOME.
TP
IF YOU WON'T MOVE...
...WE'LL RESUME THIS WHERE WE LEFT OFF YESTERDAY.
CLENCH
HEH... YOU SPEAK LIKE A GROWN MAN...
BUT THIS IS MY FIGHT!!
I CAN'T STEP ASIDE, EVEN FOR MY SON!!
TM

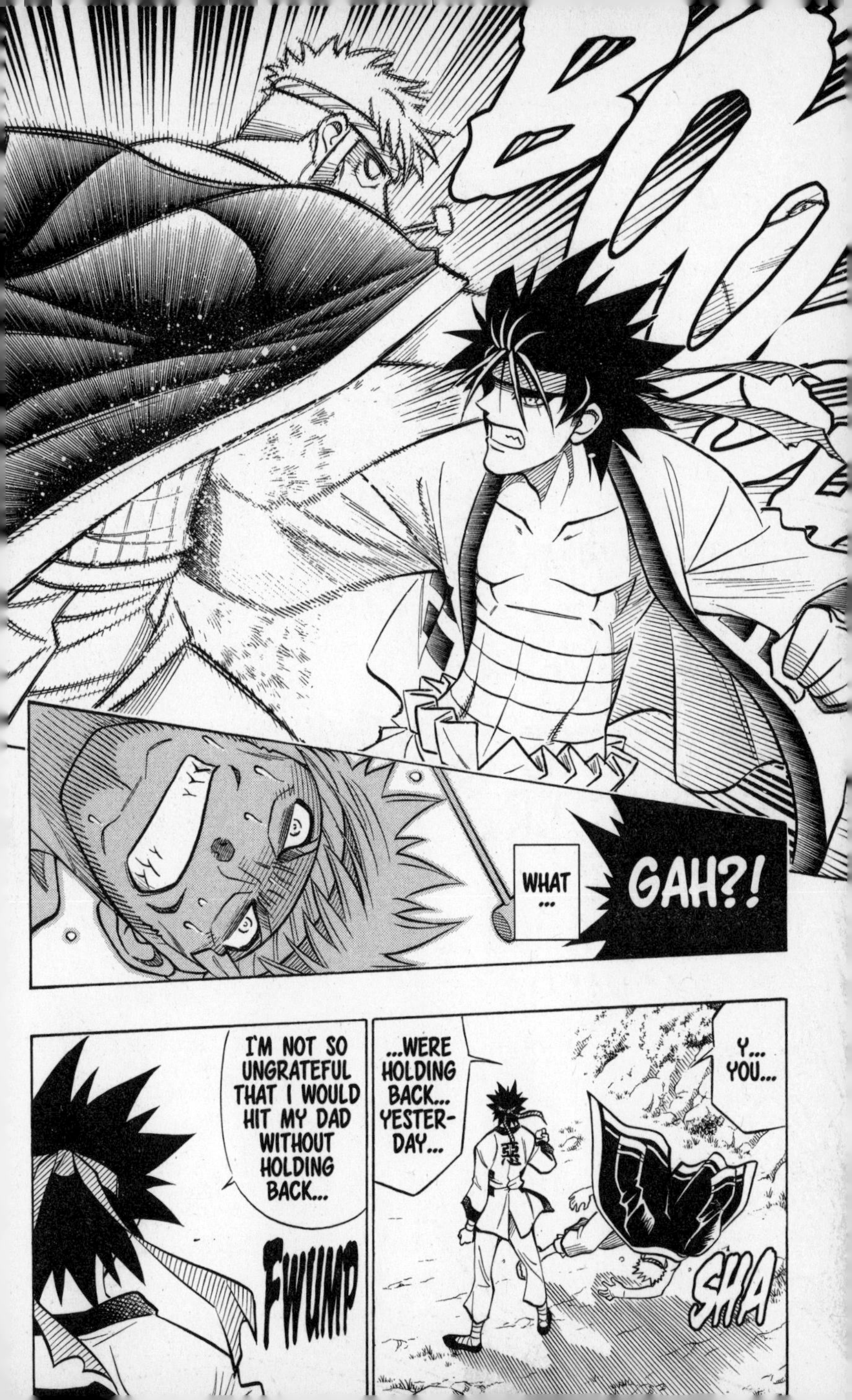
GAH?!
WHAT...
Y... YOU...
...WERE HOLDING BACK... YESTER-DAY...
SHA
I'M NOT SO UNGRATEFUL THAT I WOULD HIT MY DAD WITHOUT HOLDING BACK...
FWUMP

READ THIS WAY

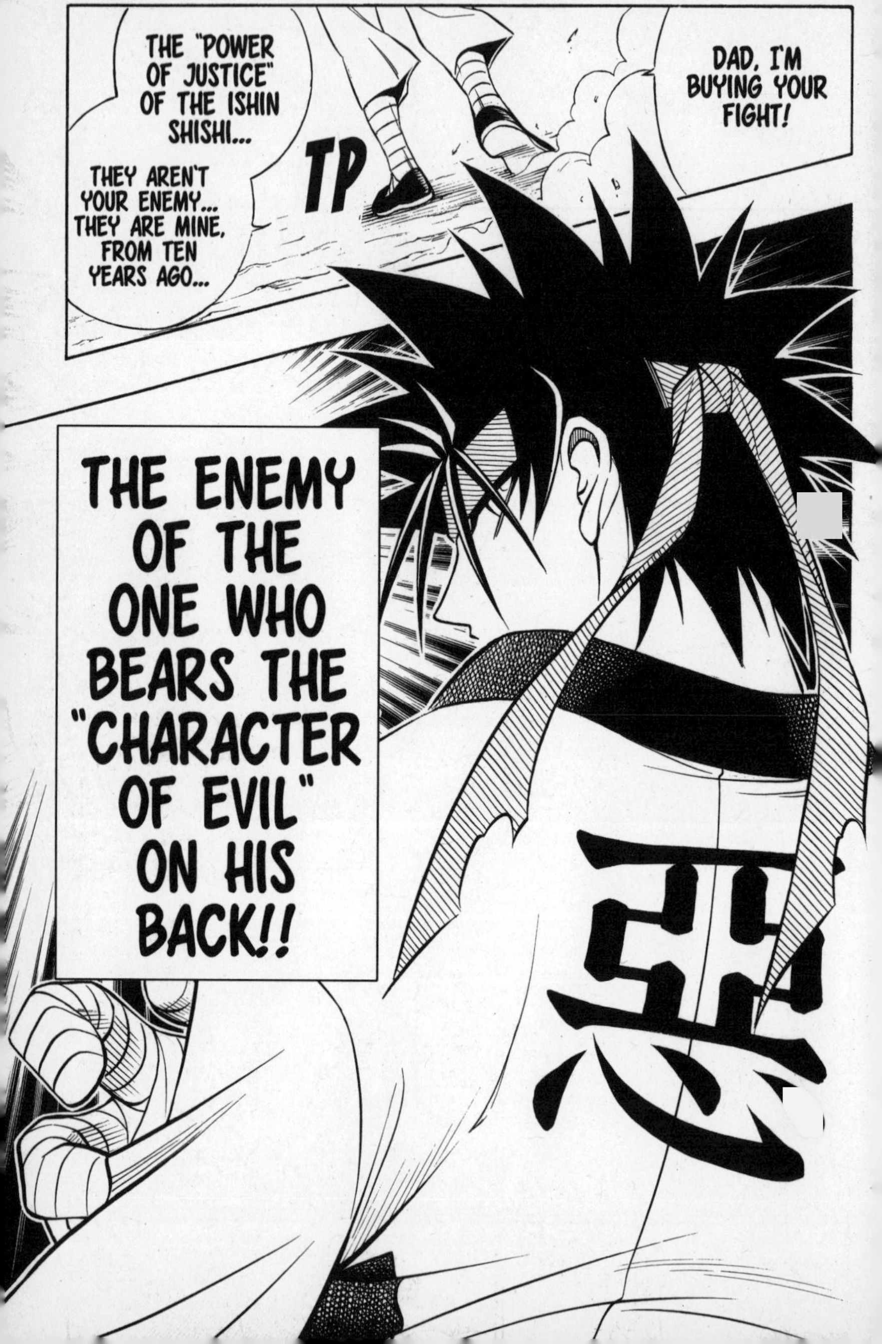

DAD, I'M BUYING YOUR FIGHT!
TP
THE "POWER OF JUSTICE" OF THE ISHIN SHISHI...
THEY AREN'T YOUR ENEMY... THEY ARE MINE, FROM TEN YEARS AGO...
THE ENEMY OF THE ONE WHO BEARS THE "CHARACTER OF EVIL" ON HIS BACK!!

Rurouni Kenshin

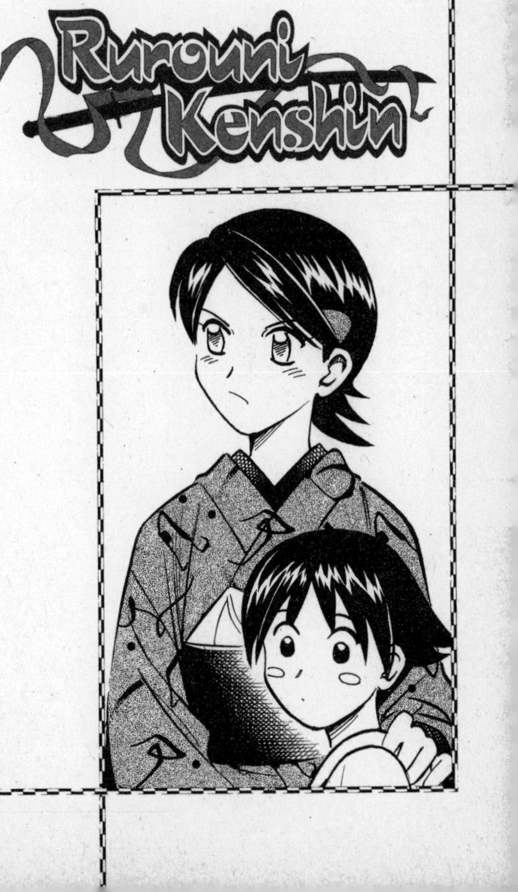

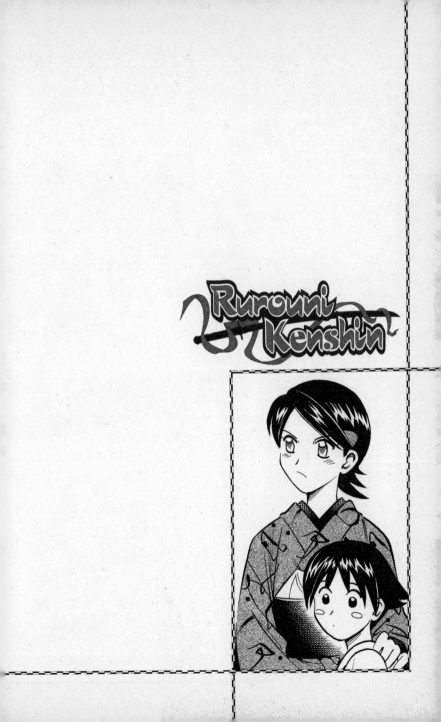

Act 233—A Man's Back 6: Cry of the Mountain

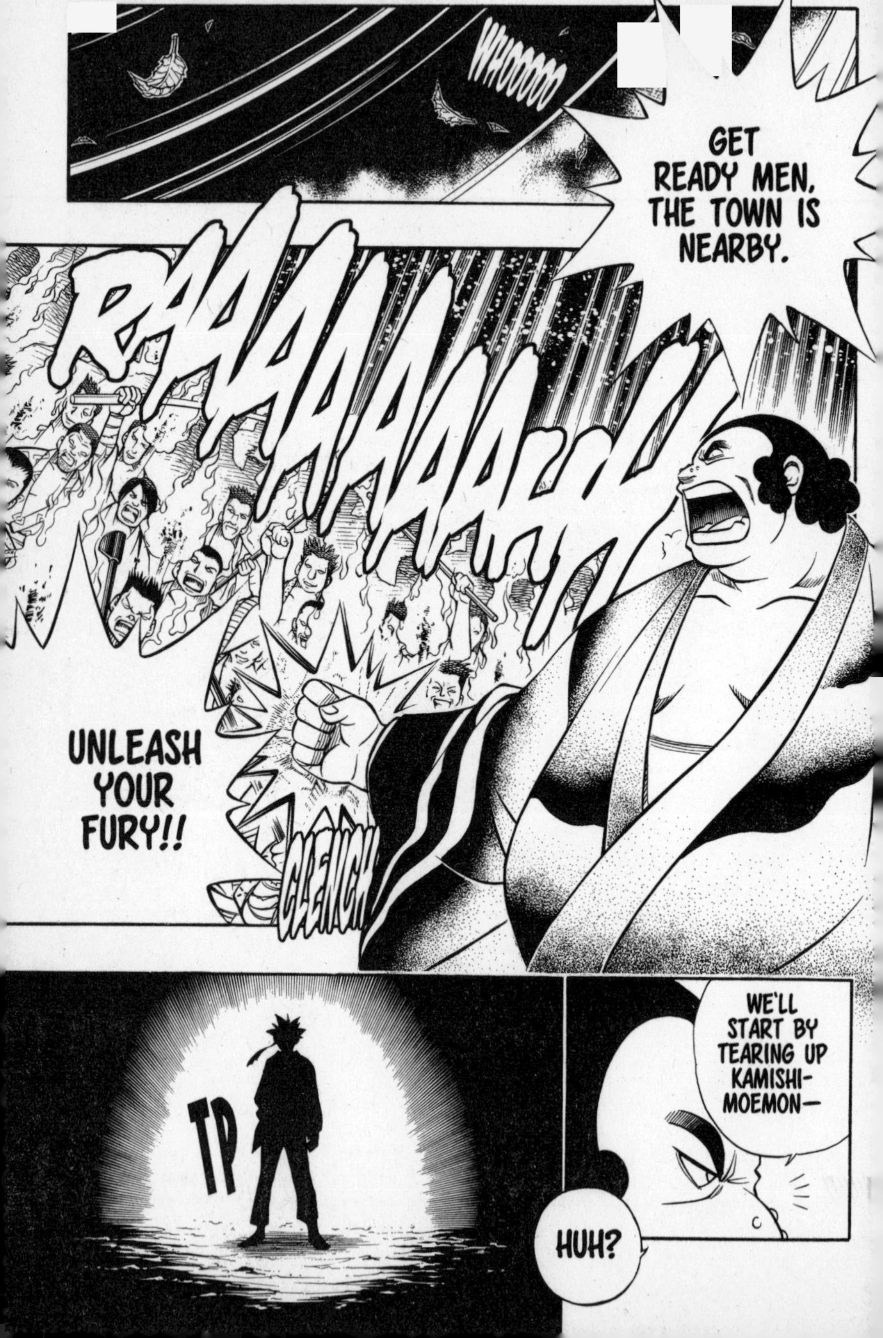
WHOOOOO
GET READY MEN, THE TOWN IS NEARBY.
RAAAAAAAGH!!
UNLEASH YOUR FURY!!
CLENCH
WE'LL START BY TEARING UP KAMISHI-MOEMON—
HUH?
TP

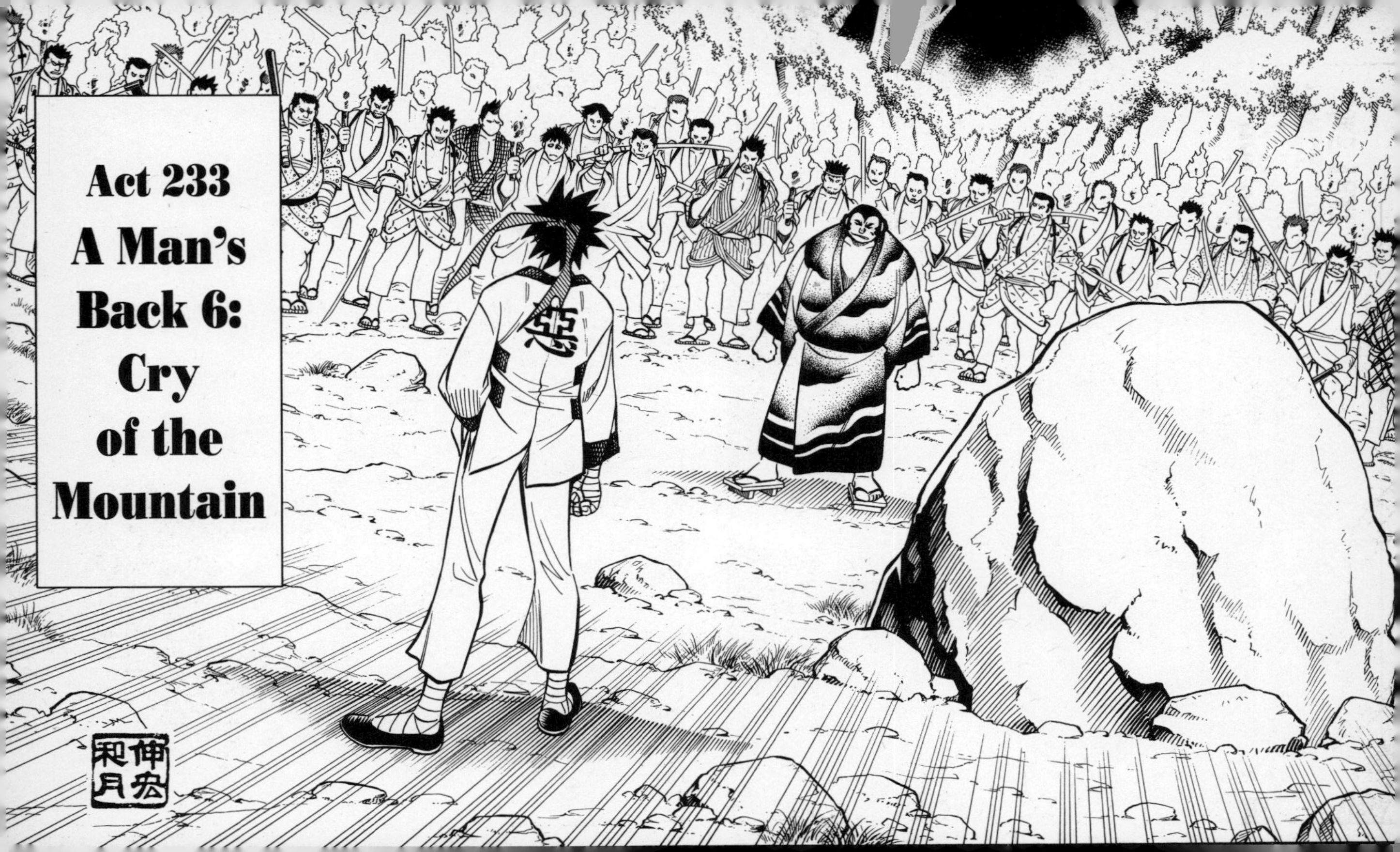
Act 233
A Man's Back 6:
Cry
of the
Mountain
和月伸宏

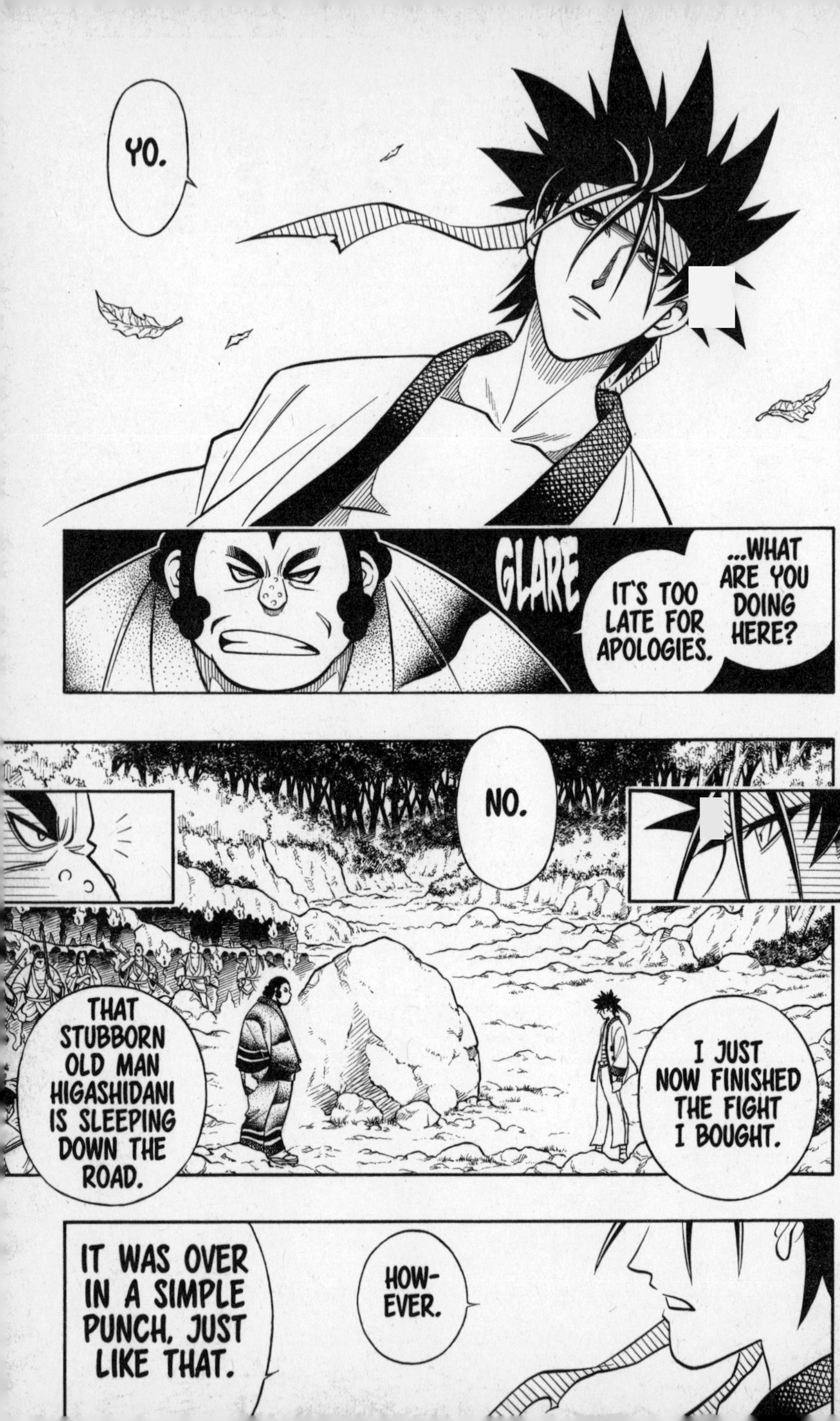
YO.
...WHAT ARE YOU DOING HERE?
IT'S TOO LATE FOR APOLOGIES.
GLARE
NO.
I JUST NOW FINISHED THE FIGHT I BOUGHT.
THAT STUBBORN OLD MAN HIGASHIDANI IS SLEEPING DOWN THE ROAD.
HOW-EVER.
IT WAS OVER IN A SIMPLE PUNCH, JUST LIKE THAT.

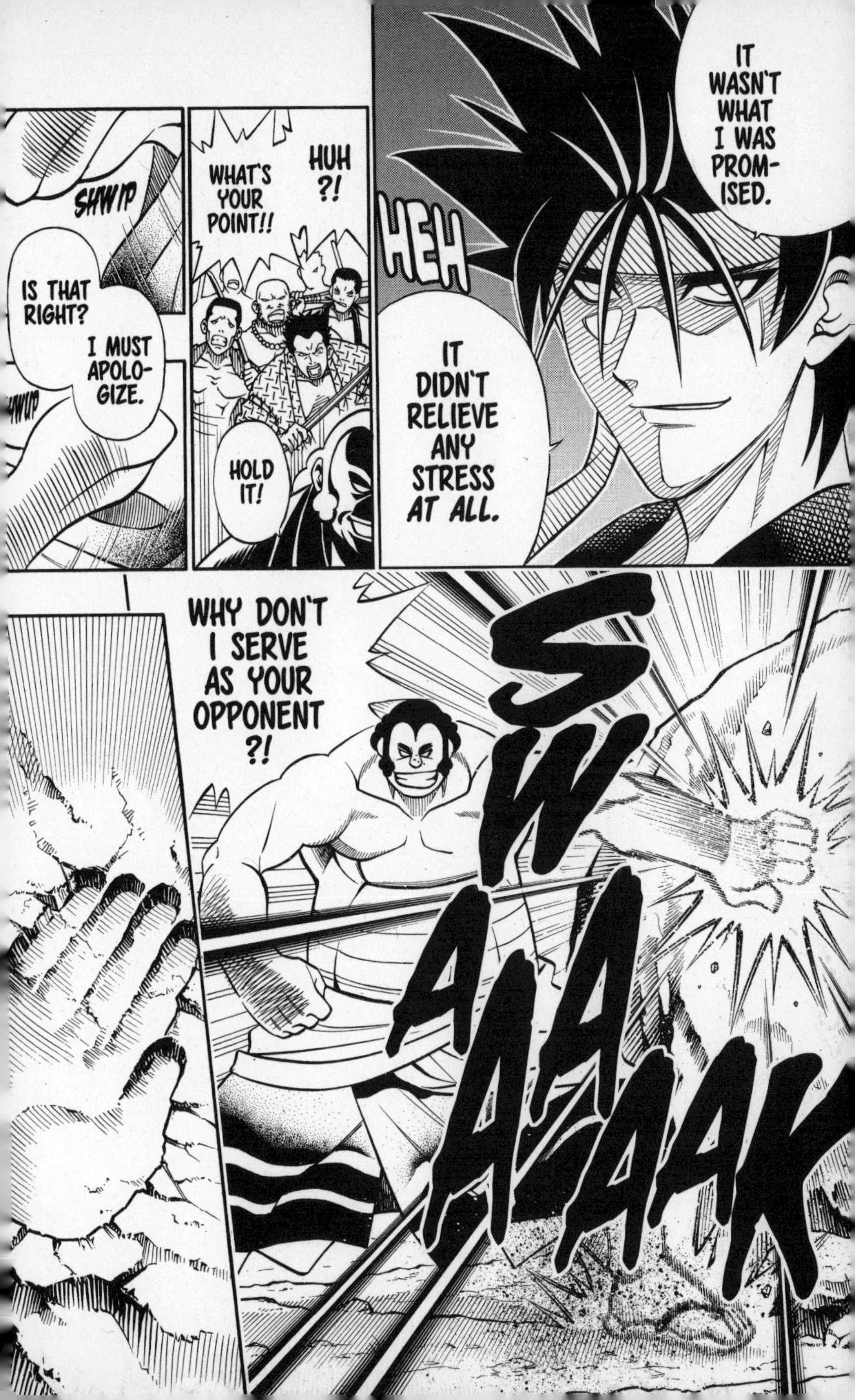
IT WASN'T WHAT I WAS PROMISED.
HEH
IT DIDN'T RELIEVE ANY STRESS AT ALL.
HUH ?!
WHAT'S YOUR POINT!!
HOLD IT!
SHWIP
IS THAT RIGHT?
I MUST APOLOGIZE.
SHWUP
WHY DON'T I SERVE AS YOUR OPPONENT ?!
SWAAAAAK

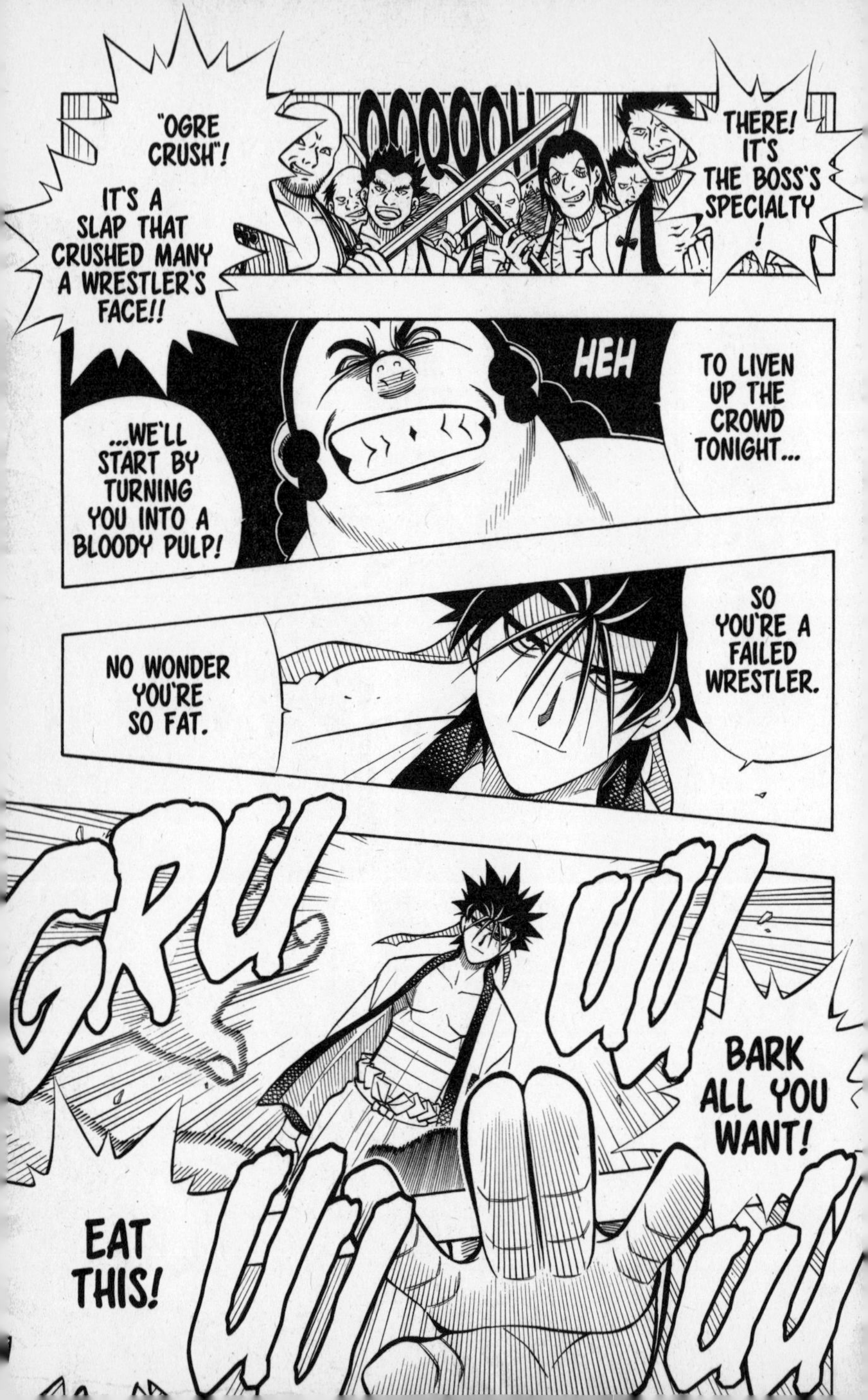
THERE! IT'S THE BOSS'S SPECIALTY!
OOOOOH
"OGRE CRUSH"! IT'S A SLAP THAT CRUSHED MANY A WRESTLER'S FACE!!
TO LIVEN UP THE CROWD TONIGHT...
HEH
...WE'LL START BY TURNING YOU INTO A BLOODY PULP!
SO YOU'RE A FAILED WRESTLER.
NO WONDER YOU'RE SO FAT.
BARK ALL YOU WANT!
GRU UU UUUU
EAT THIS!

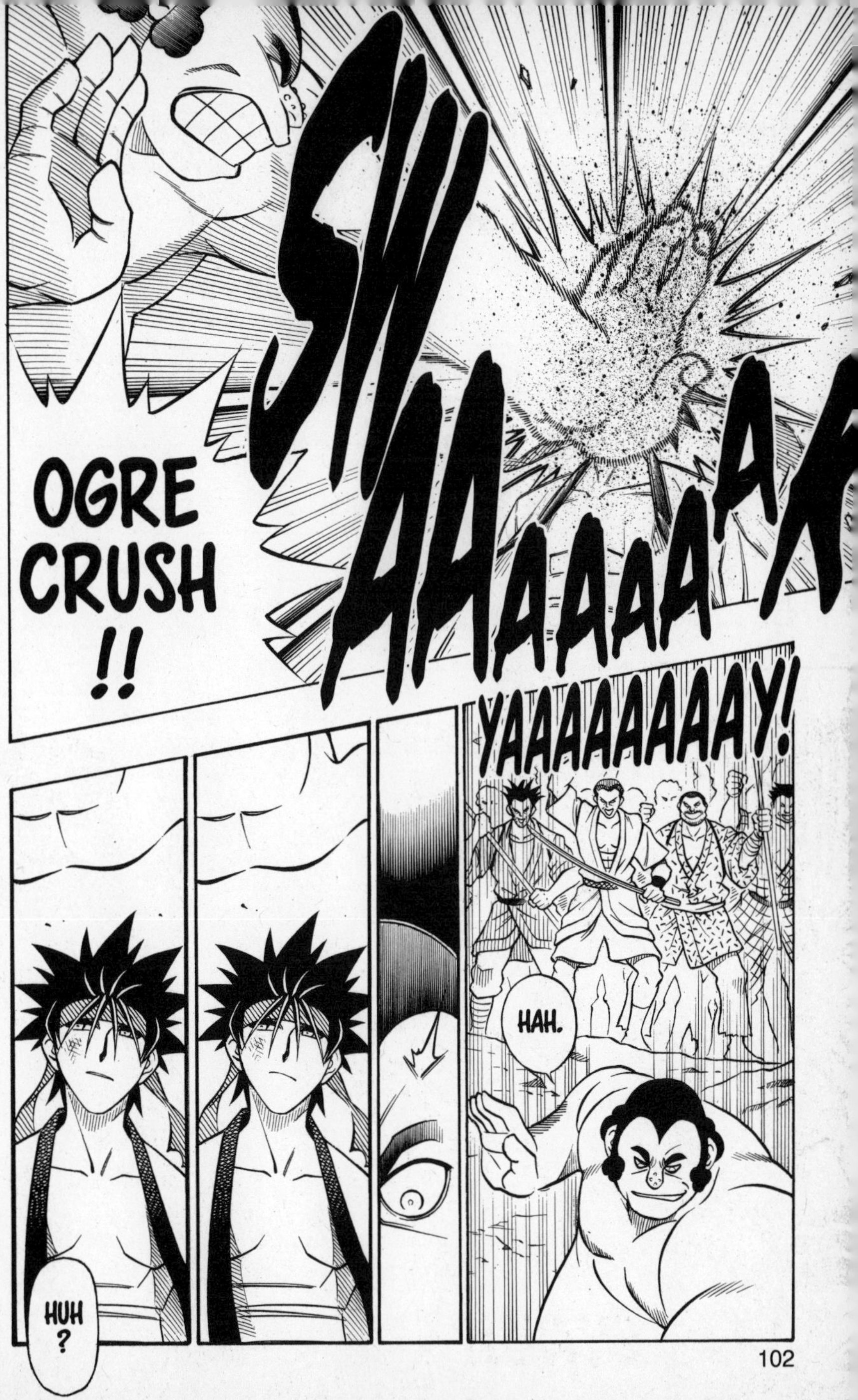
OGRE CRUSH!!
YAAAAAAAAY!
HAH.
HUH?

READ THIS WAY

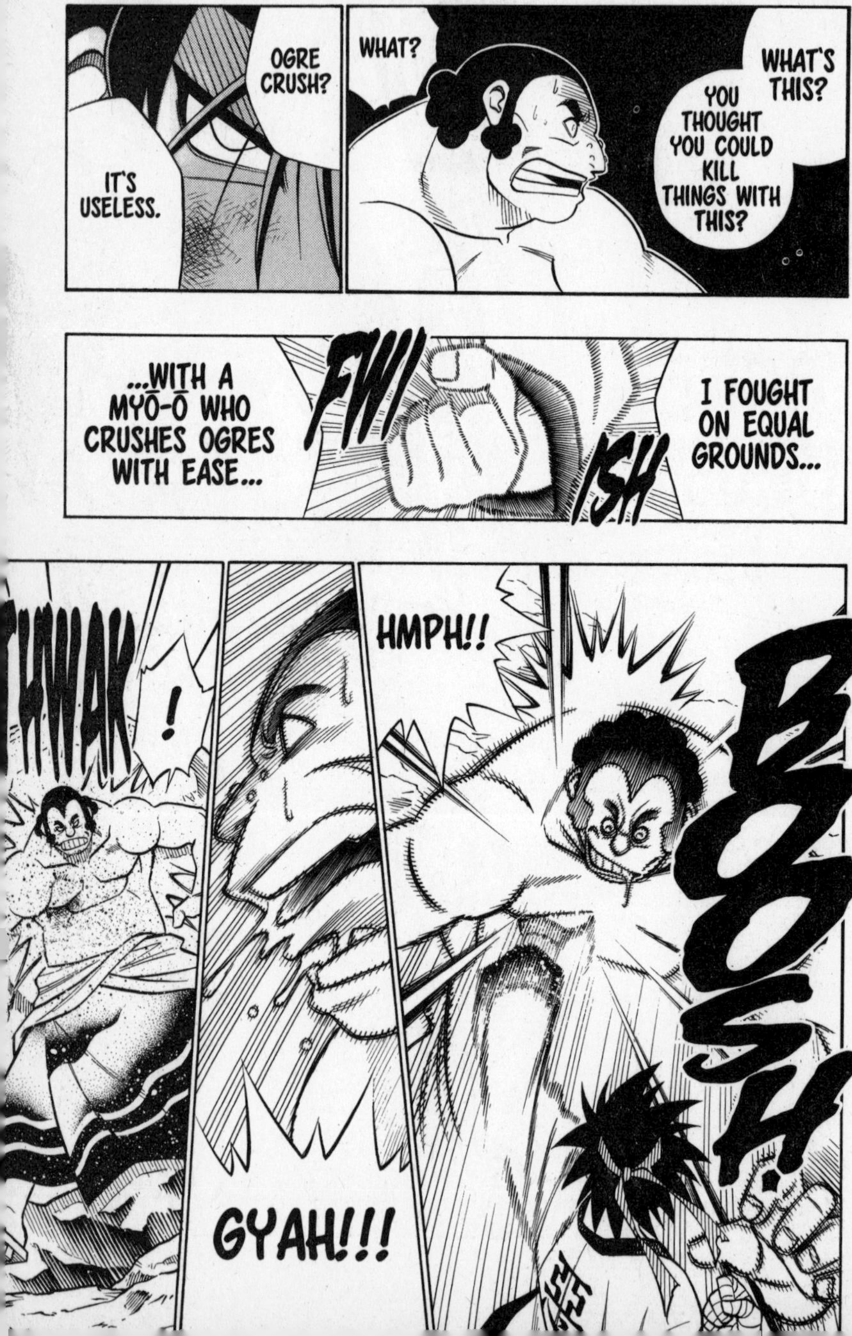
WHAT'S THIS?
YOU THOUGHT YOU COULD KILL THINGS WITH THIS?
WHAT?
OGRE CRUSH?
IT'S USELESS.
I FOUGHT ON EQUAL GROUNDS...
FWISH
...WITH A MYŌ-Ō WHO CRUSHES OGRES WITH EASE...
BOOSH!
HMPH!!
GYAH!!!
!
THWAK

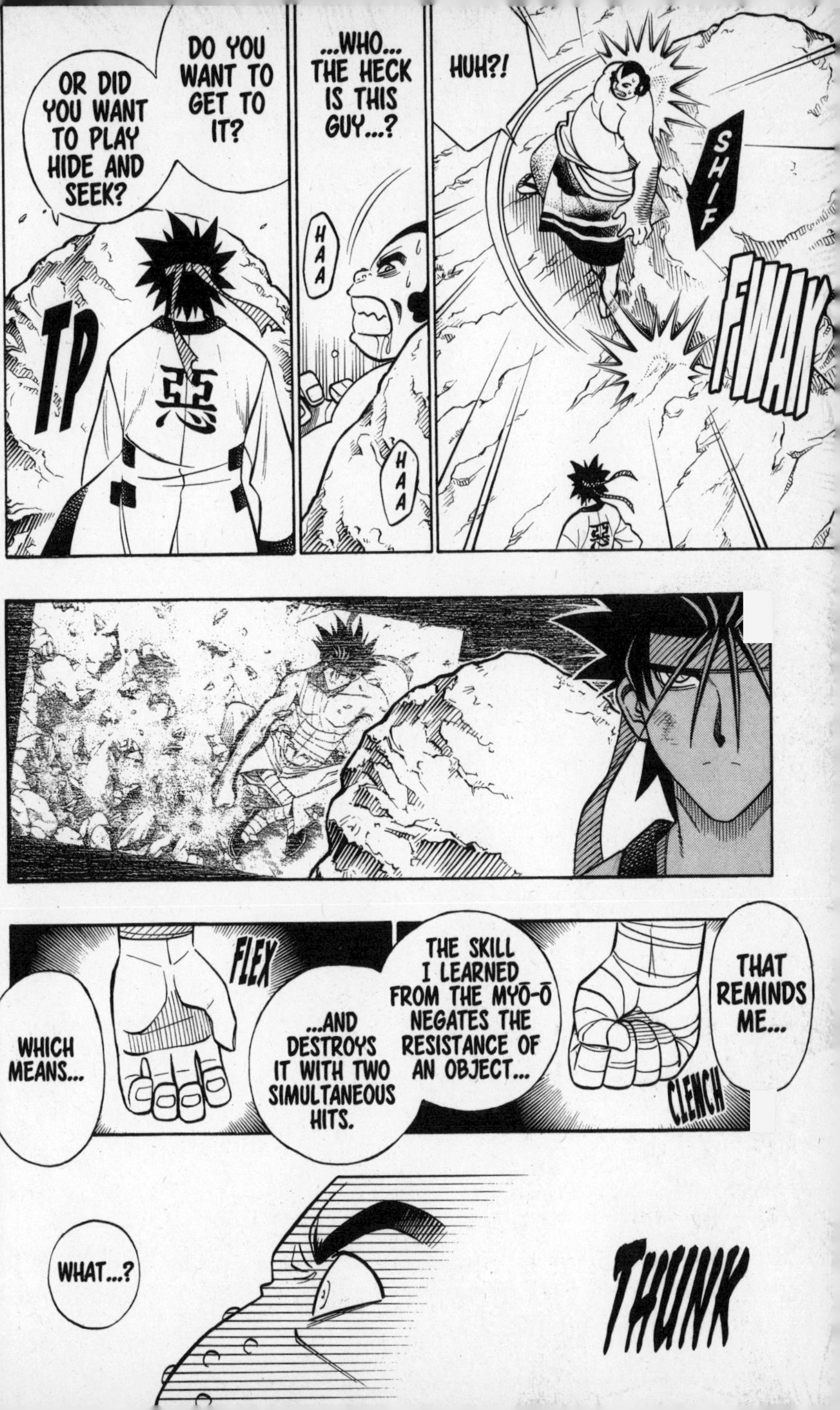
HUH?!
SHIF
FWAK
...WHO... THE HECK IS THIS GUY...?
HAA
HAA
DO YOU WANT TO GET TO IT?
OR DID YOU WANT TO PLAY HIDE AND SEEK?
TP
THAT REMINDS ME...
CLENCH
THE SKILL I LEARNED FROM THE MYŌ-Ō NEGATES THE RESISTANCE OF AN OBJECT...
...AND DESTROYS IT WITH TWO SIMULTANEOUS HITS.
FLEX
WHICH MEANS...
THUNK
WHAT...?

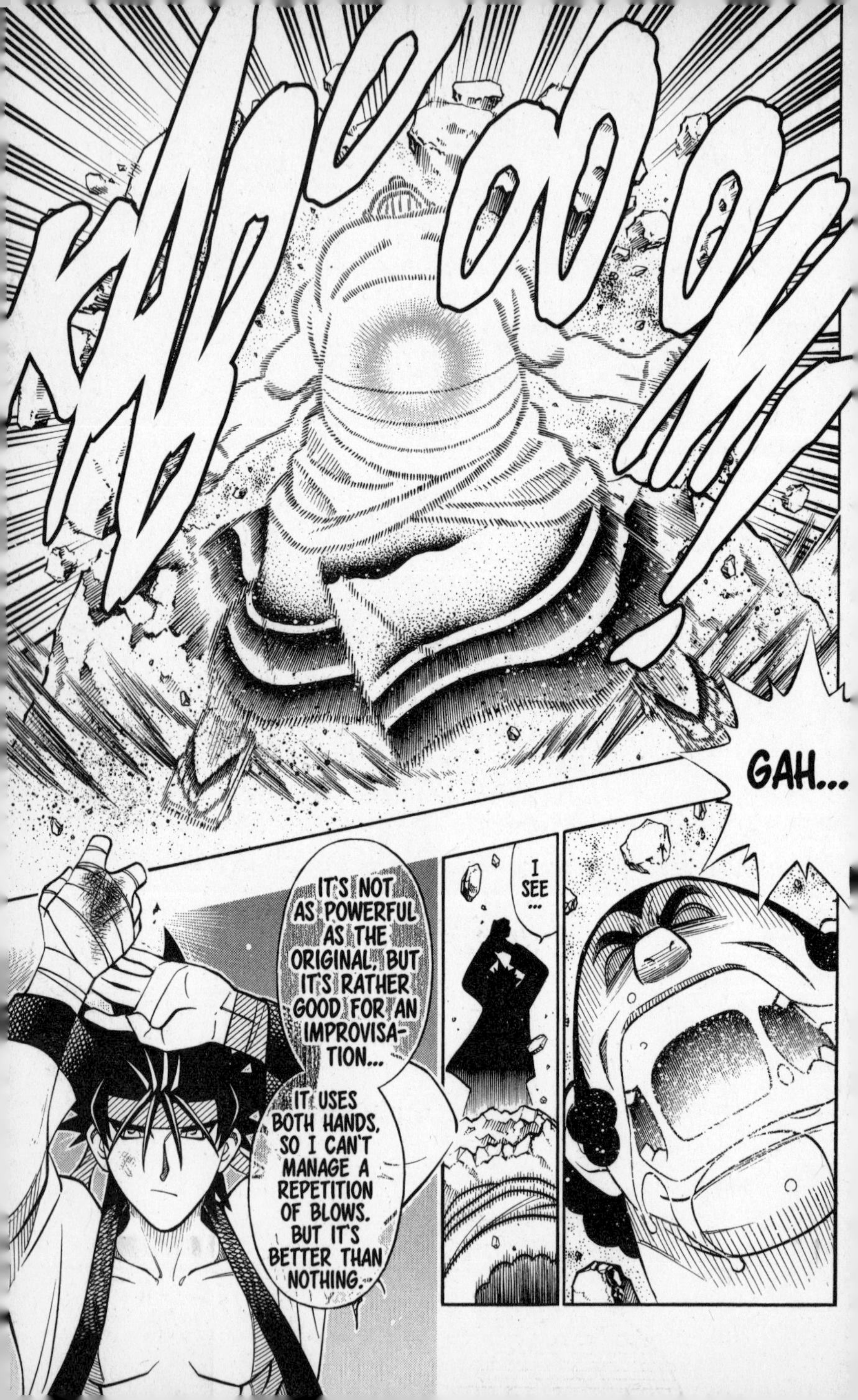
GAH...
I SEE...
IT'S NOT AS POWERFUL AS THE ORIGINAL, BUT IT'S RATHER GOOD FOR AN IMPROVISA-TION...
IT USES BOTH HANDS, SO I CAN'T MANAGE A REPETITION OF BLOWS. BUT IT'S BETTER THAN NOTHING.

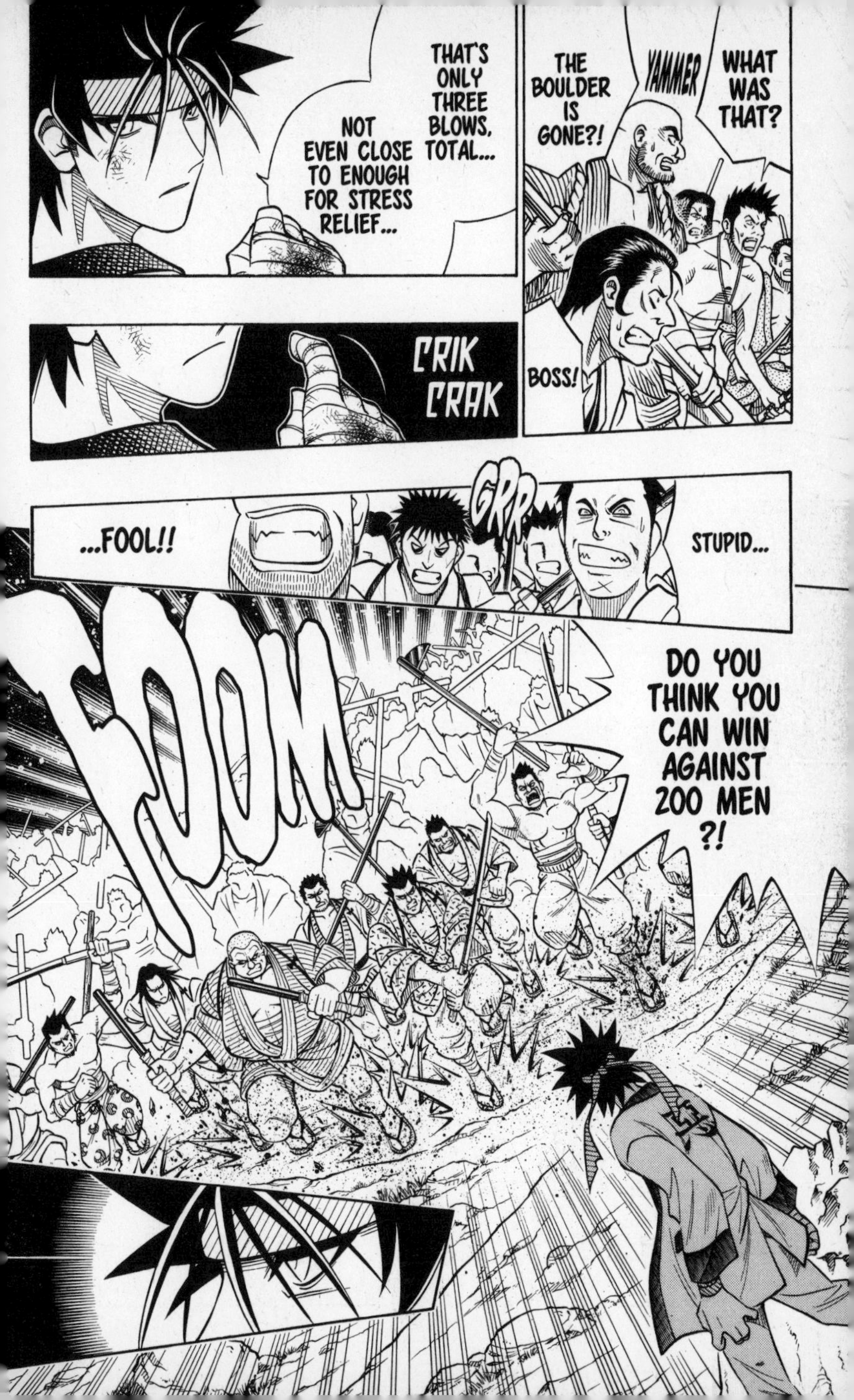
WHAT WAS THAT?
YAMMER
THE BOULDER IS GONE?!
BOSS!
THAT'S ONLY THREE BLOWS, TOTAL...
NOT EVEN CLOSE TO ENOUGH FOR STRESS RELIEF...
CRIK CRAK
STUPID...
GRR
...FOOL!!
DO YOU THINK YOU CAN WIN AGAINST 200 MEN ?!
FOOM

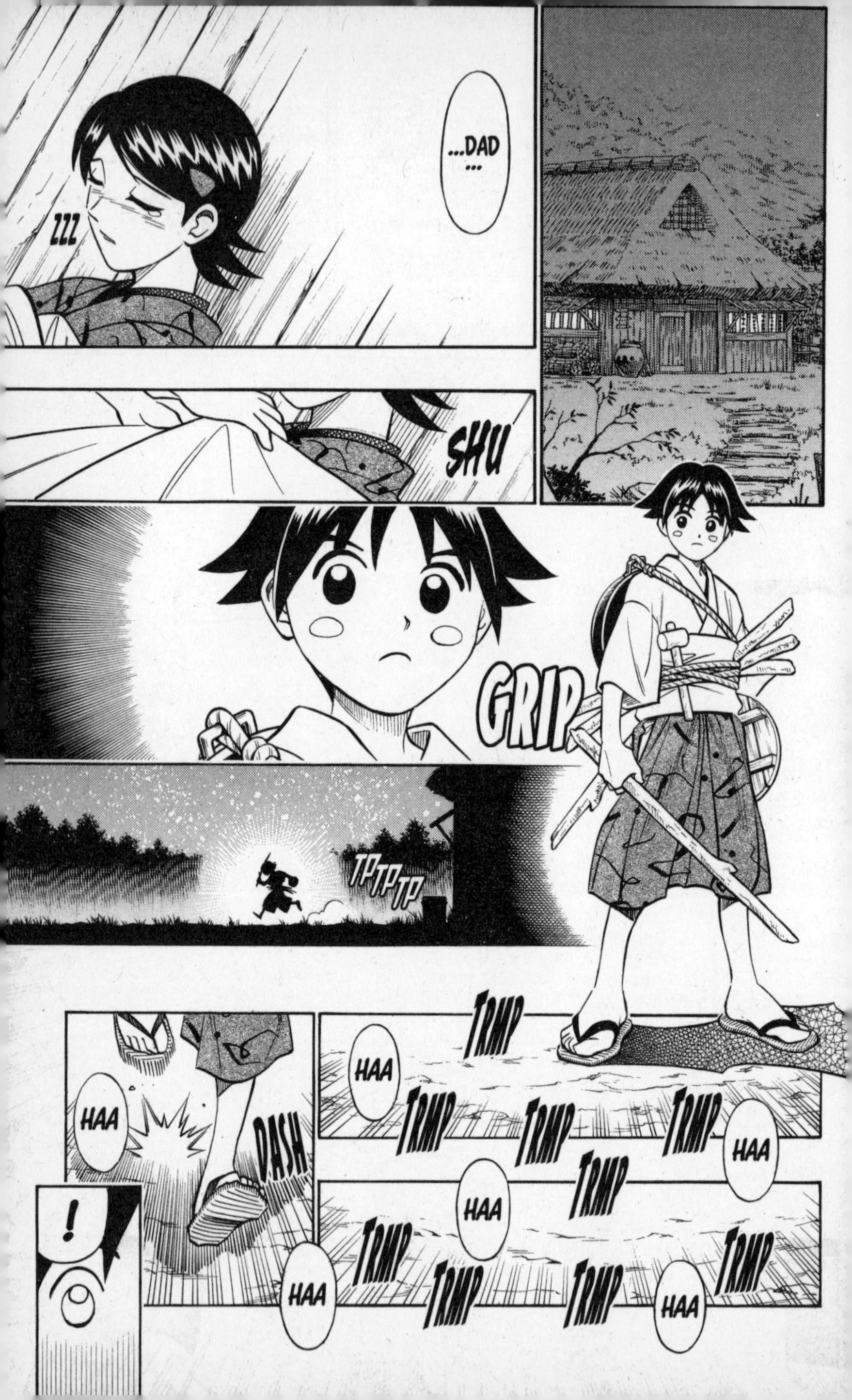
...DAD ...
ZZZ
SHU
GRIP
TPTPTP
TRMP
HAA
TRMP
TRMP
TRMP
HAA
HAA
DASH
TRMP
HAA
TRMP
TRMP
TRMP
TRMP
HAA
HAA
!

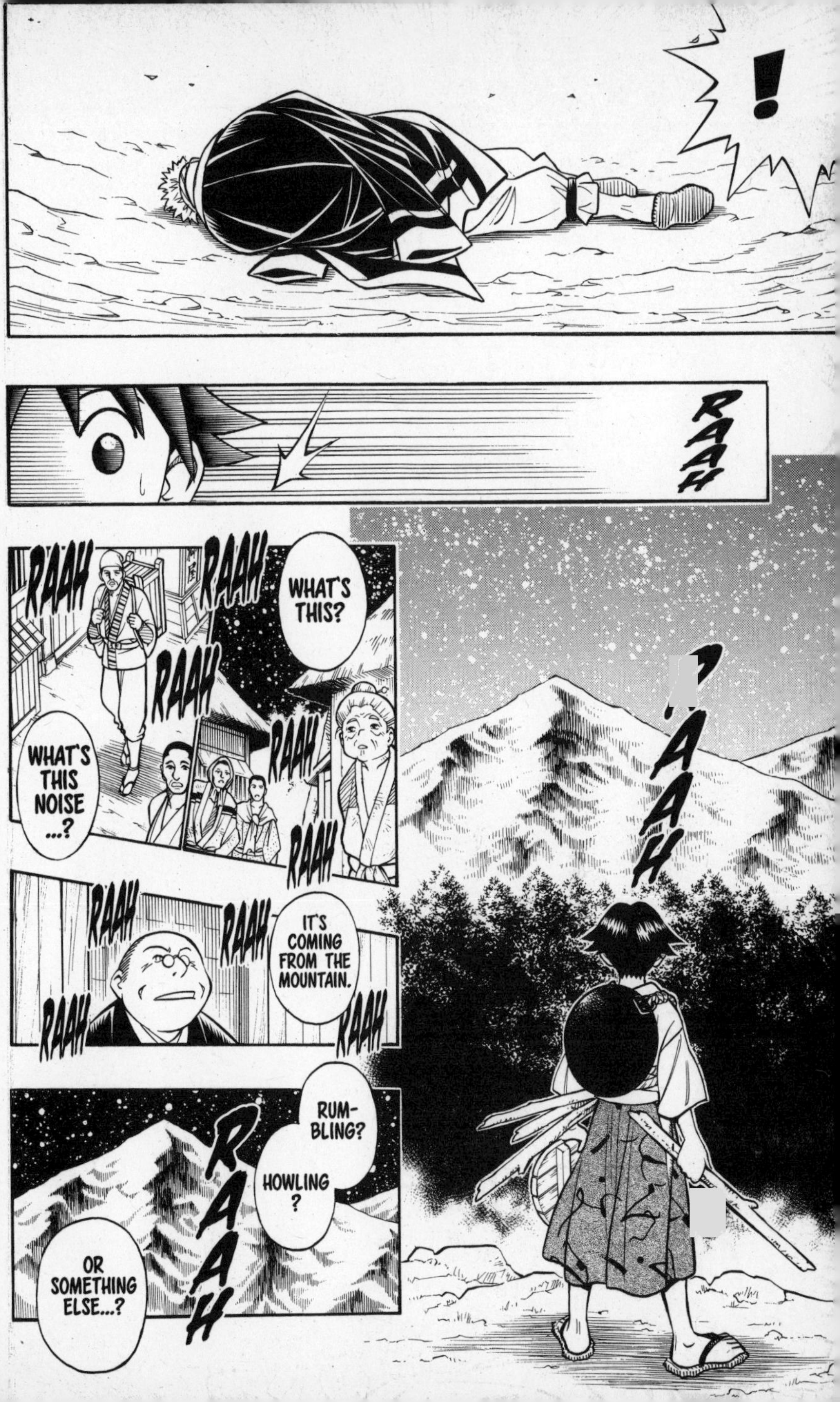
!
RAAH
RAAAH
RAAH
RAAH
WHAT'S THIS?
RAAH
RAAH
RAAH
WHAT'S THIS NOISE ...?
RAAH
RAAH
IT'S COMING FROM THE MOUNTAIN.
RAAH
RAAH
RAAH
RUM-BLING?
HOWLING?
RAAAH
OR SOMETHING ELSE...?

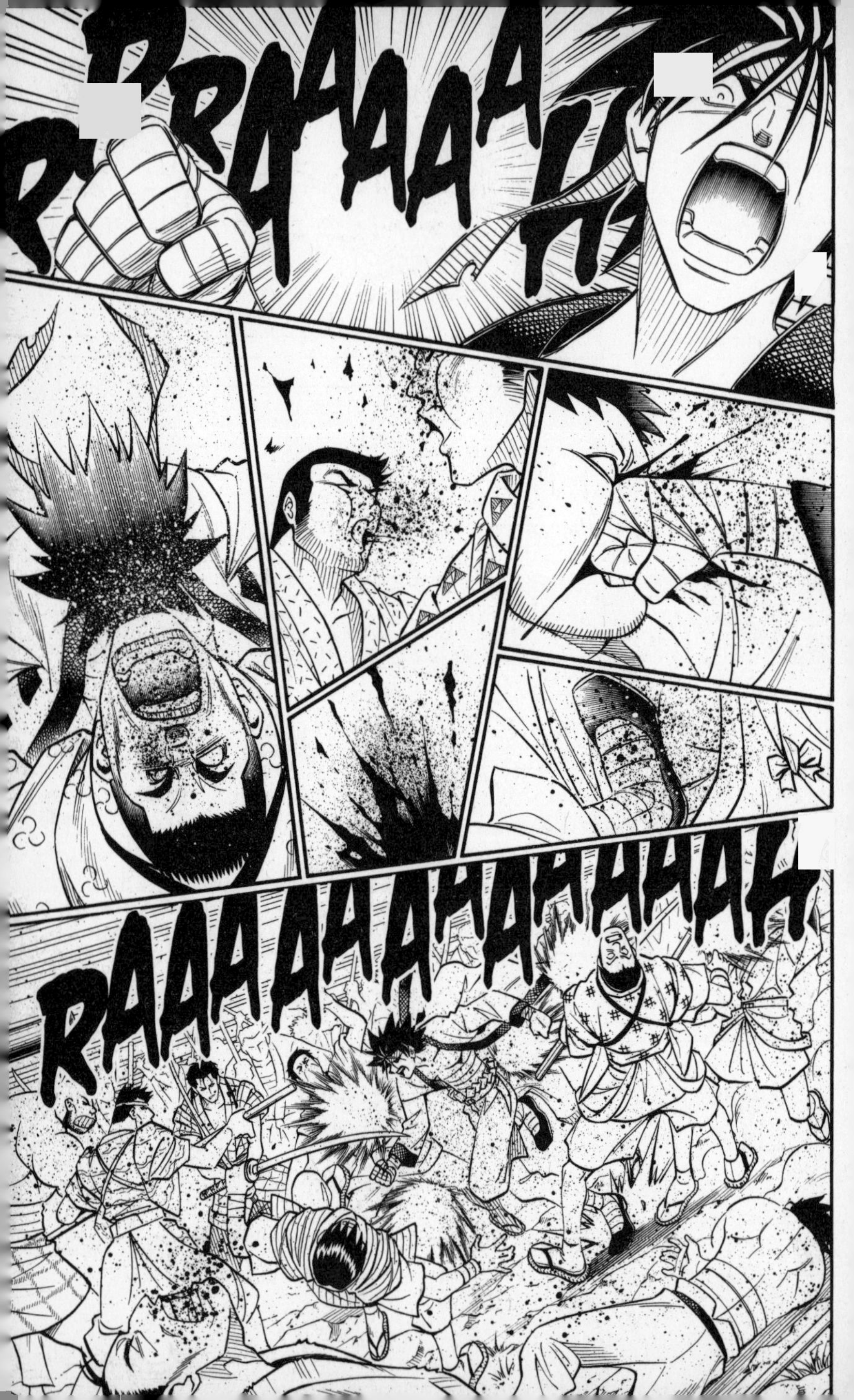
RRAAAAAAAH
RAAAAAAAAAAAAH

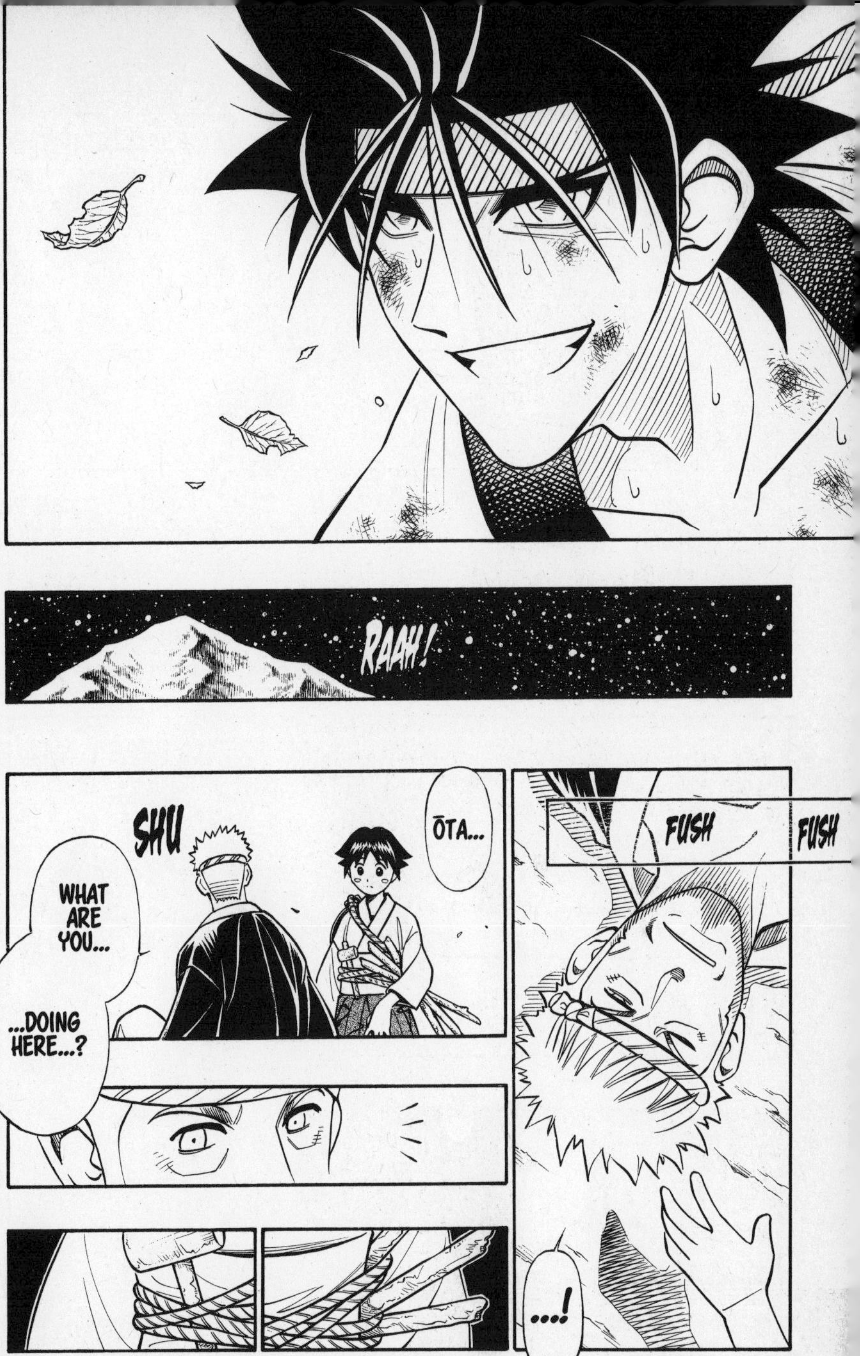
RAAH!
FUSH
FUSH
...!
ŌTA...
SHU
WHAT ARE YOU...
...DOING HERE...?

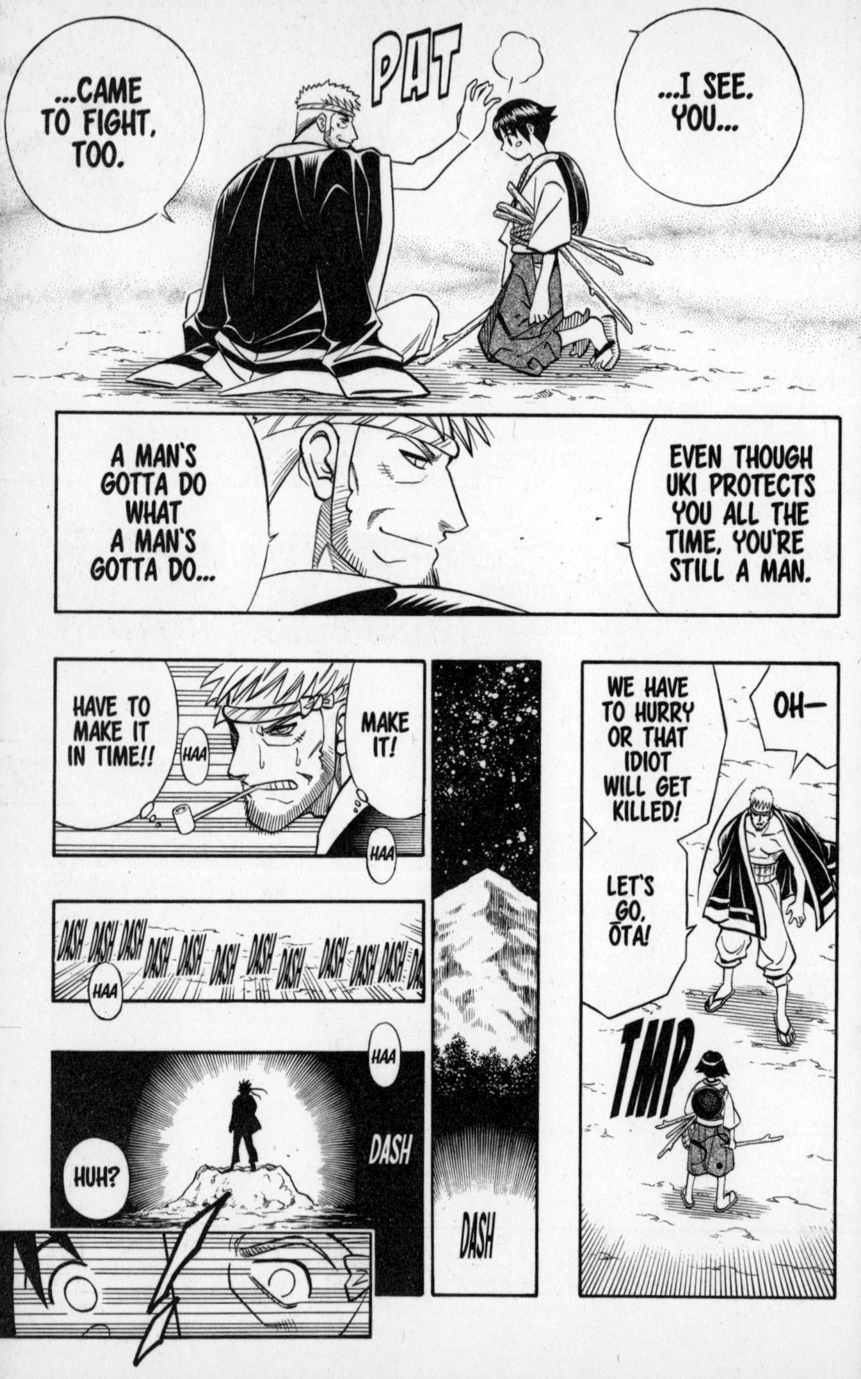
...I SEE. YOU...
PAT
...CAME TO FIGHT, TOO.
EVEN THOUGH UKI PROTECTS YOU ALL THE TIME, YOU'RE STILL A MAN.
A MAN'S GOTTA DO WHAT A MAN'S GOTTA DO...
OH—
WE HAVE TO HURRY OR THAT IDIOT WILL GET KILLED!
LET'S GO, ŌTA!
TMP
DASH
MAKE IT!
HAA
HAVE TO MAKE IT IN TIME!!
HAA
DASH DASH DASH DASH DASH DASH DASH DASH DASH DASH DASH DA
HAA
HAA
DASH
HUH?

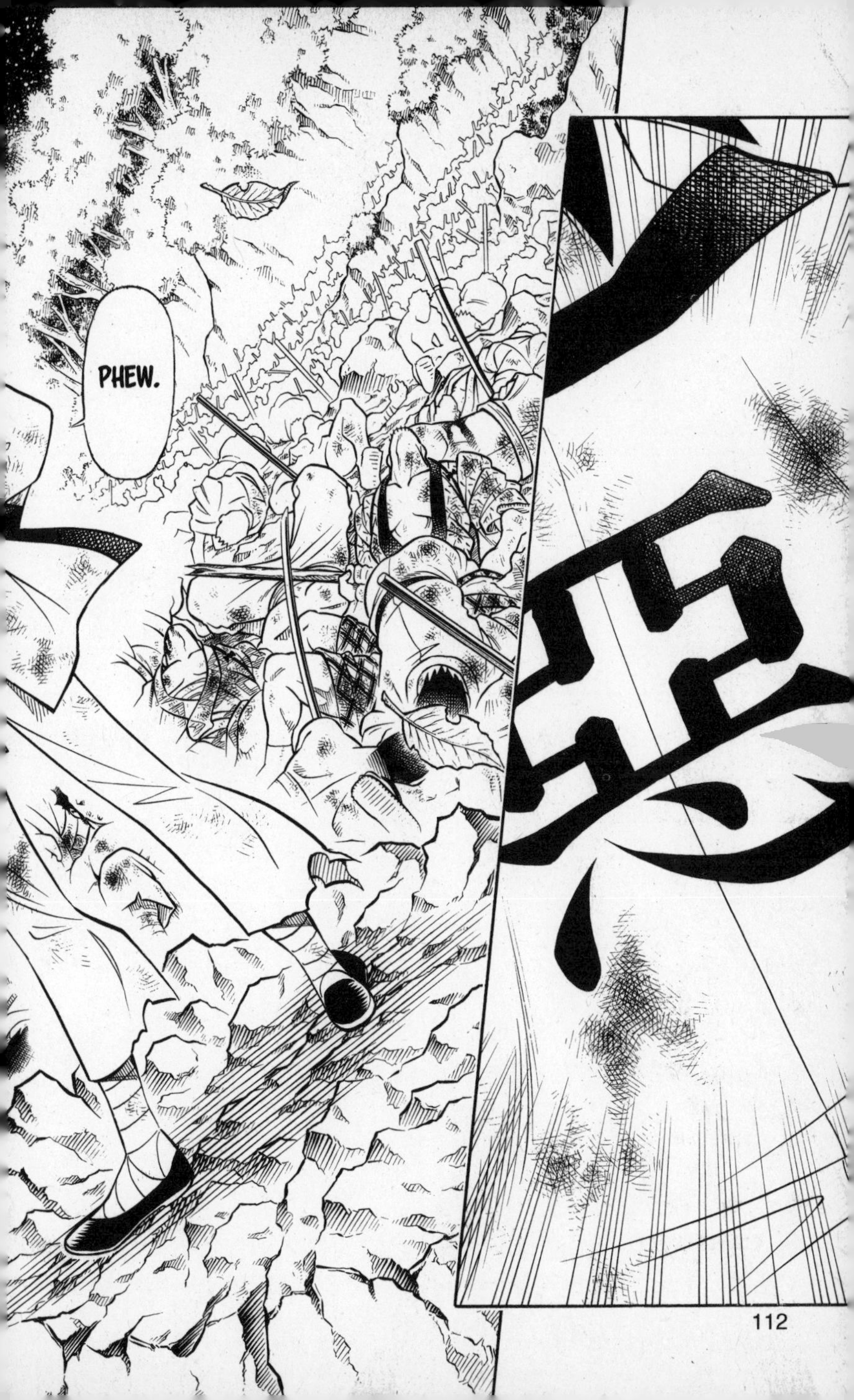
PHEW.

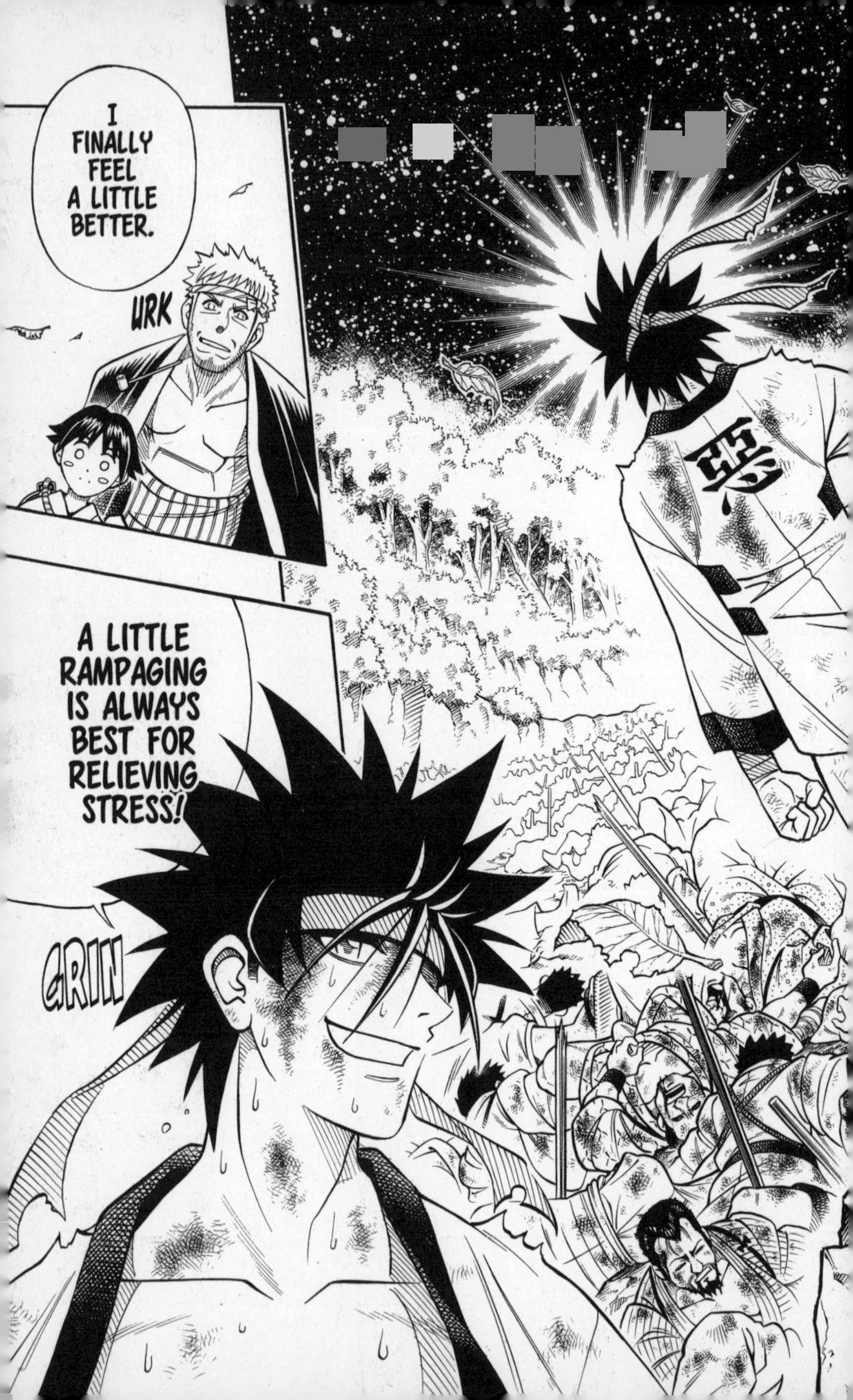
悪
I FINALLY FEEL A LITTLE BETTER.
URK
A LITTLE RAMPAGING IS ALWAYS BEST FOR RELIEVING STRESS!
GRIN

Rurouni Kenshin

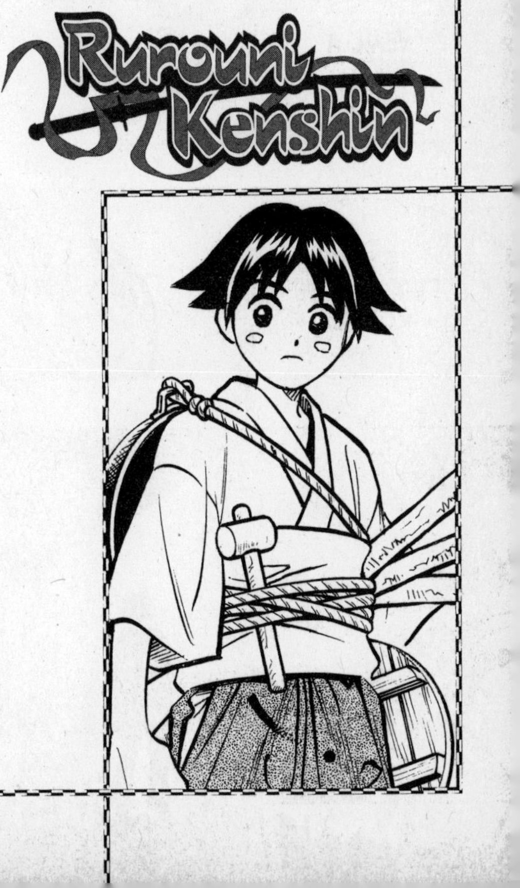

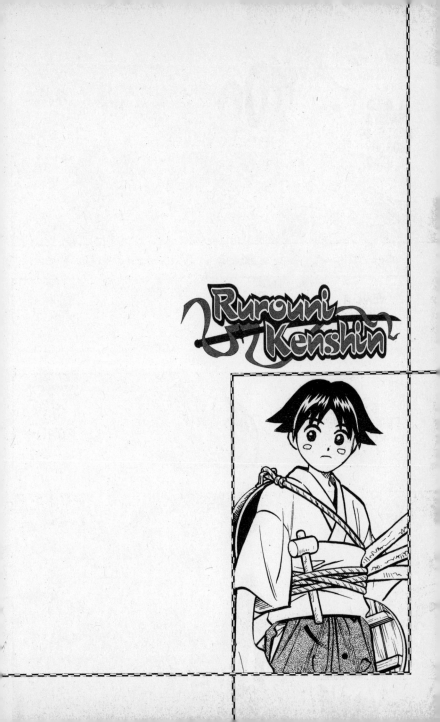

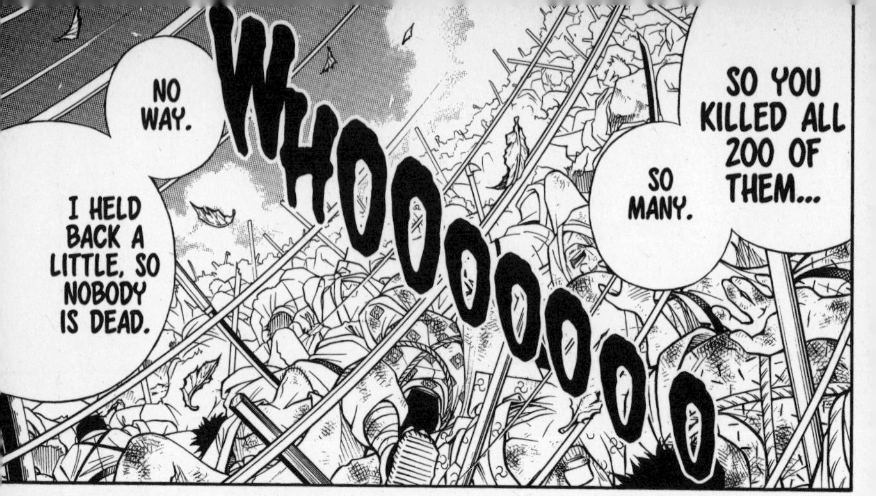
SO YOU KILLED ALL 200 OF THEM...
SO MANY.
WHOOOOOOOOO
NO WAY.
I HELD BACK A LITTLE, SO NOBODY IS DEAD.

Act 234—A Man's Back 7: The Back Tells Tales

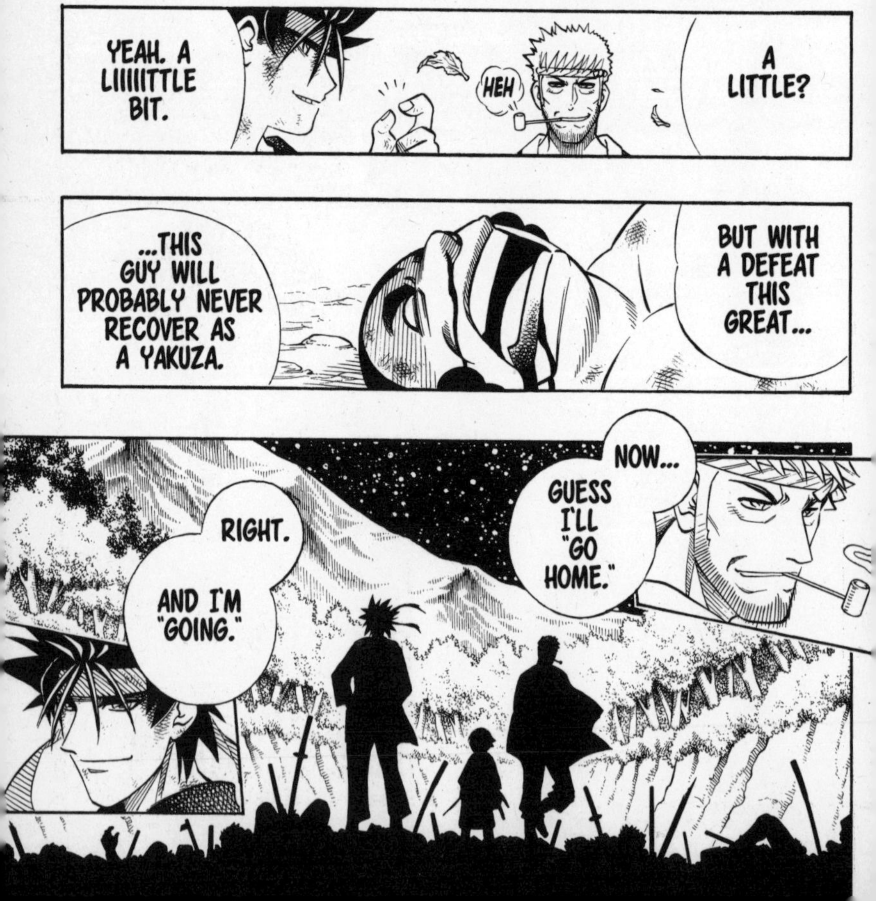
A LITTLE?
HEH
YEAH. A LIIIIITTLE BIT.
BUT WITH A DEFEAT THIS GREAT...
...THIS GUY WILL PROBABLY NEVER RECOVER AS A YAKUZA.
NOW...
GUESS I'LL "GO HOME."
RIGHT.
AND I'M "GOING."

Act 234
A Man's Back 7: The Back Tells Tales

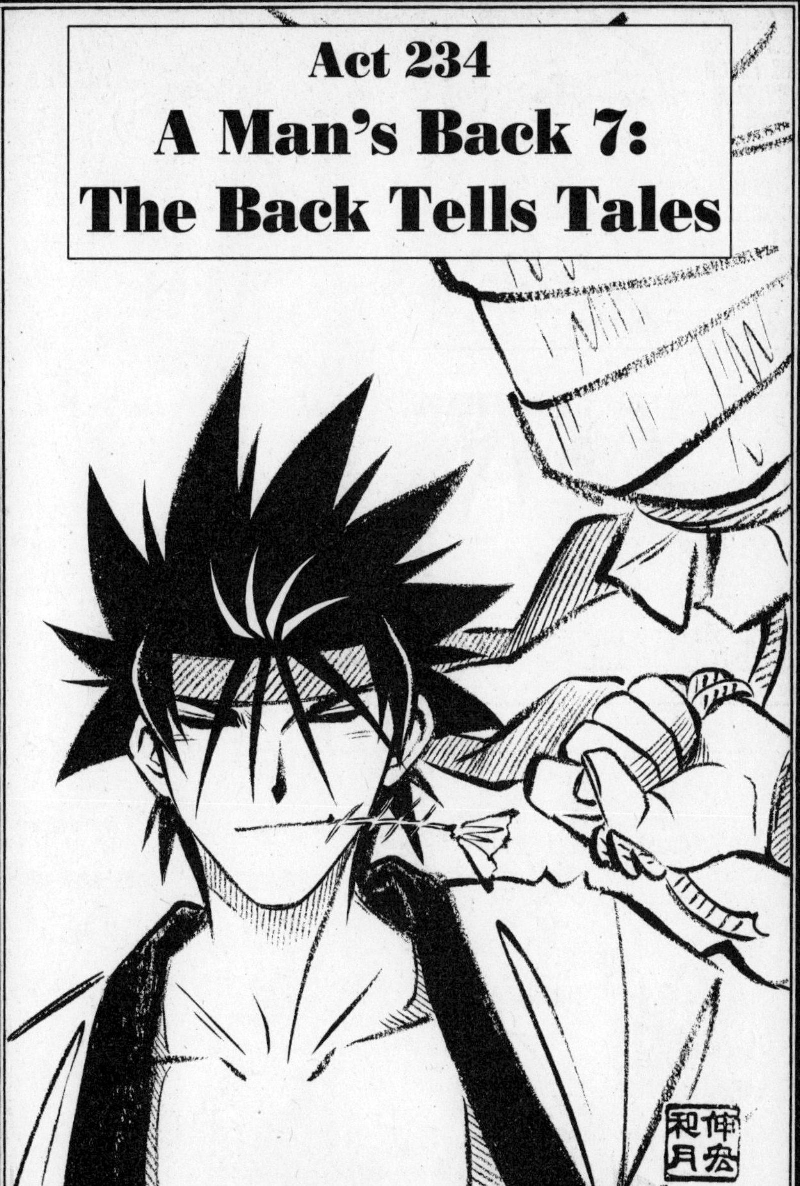

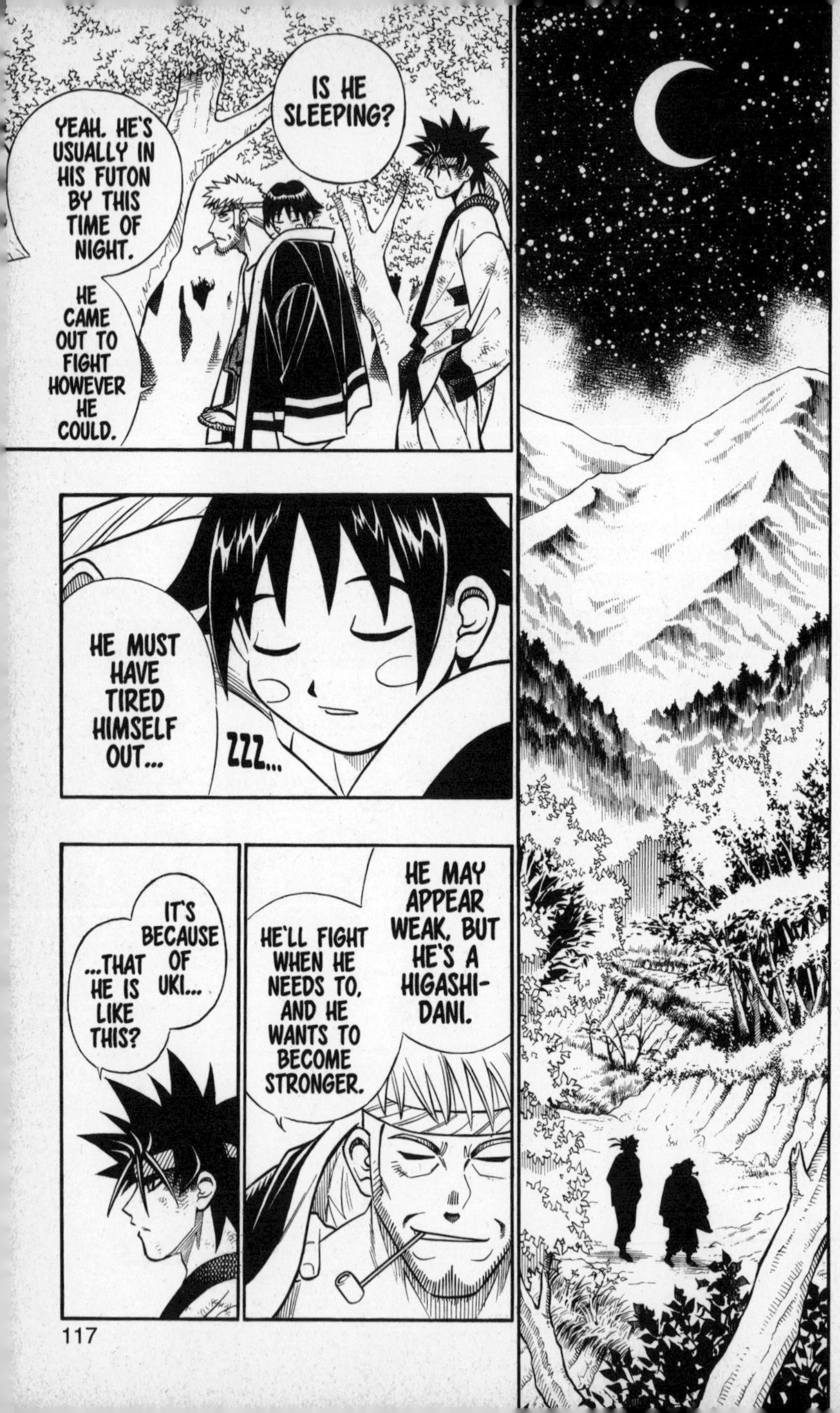
IS HE SLEEPING?
YEAH. HE'S USUALLY IN HIS FUTON BY THIS TIME OF NIGHT.
HE CAME OUT TO FIGHT HOWEVER HE COULD.
HE MUST HAVE TIRED HIMSELF OUT...
ZZZ...
HE MAY APPEAR WEAK, BUT HE'S A HIGASHI-DANI.
HE'LL FIGHT WHEN HE NEEDS TO, AND HE WANTS TO BECOME STRONGER.
IT'S BECAUSE OF UKI...
...THAT HE IS LIKE THIS?

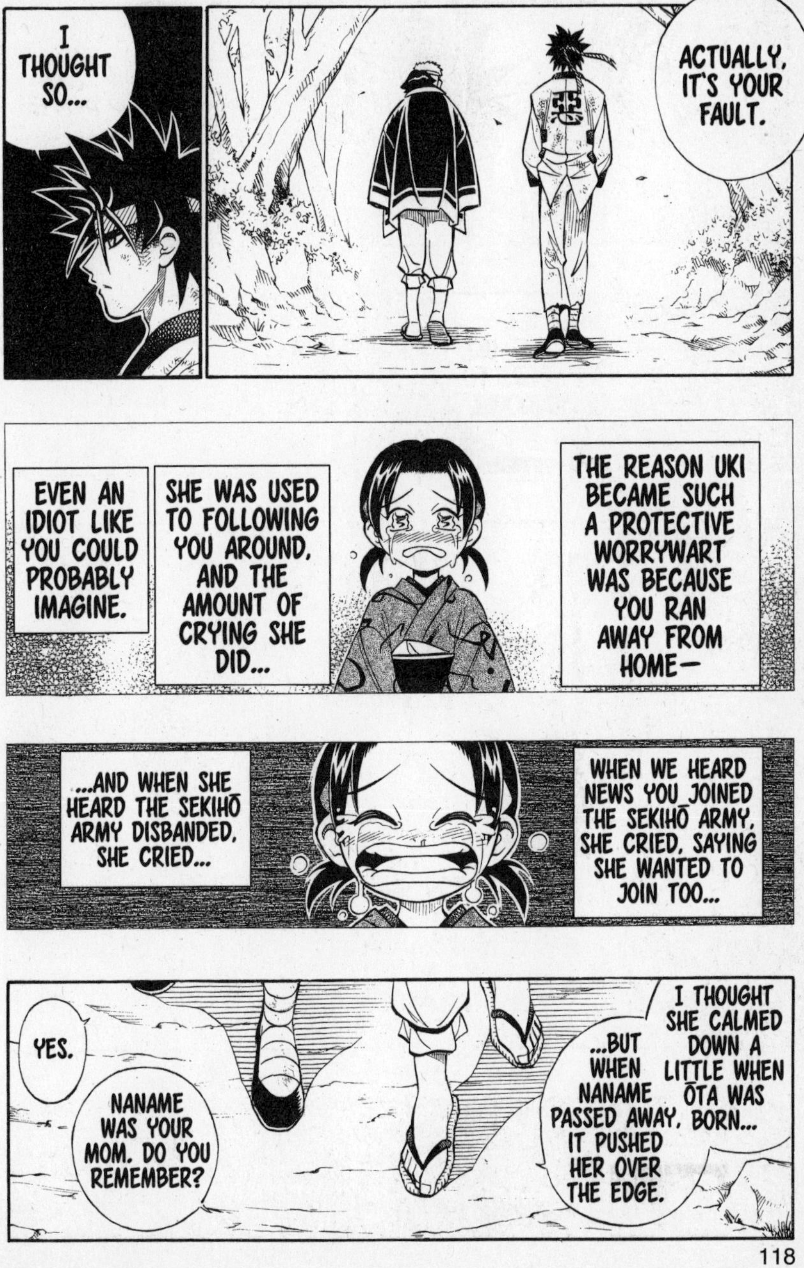
ACTUALLY, IT'S YOUR FAULT.
I THOUGHT SO...
THE REASON UKI BECAME SUCH A PROTECTIVE WORRYWART WAS BECAUSE YOU RAN AWAY FROM HOME—
SHE WAS USED TO FOLLOWING YOU AROUND, AND THE AMOUNT OF CRYING SHE DID...
EVEN AN IDIOT LIKE YOU COULD PROBABLY IMAGINE.
WHEN WE HEARD NEWS YOU JOINED THE SEKIHŌ ARMY, SHE CRIED, SAYING SHE WANTED TO JOIN TOO...
...AND WHEN SHE HEARD THE SEKIHŌ ARMY DISBANDED, SHE CRIED...
I THOUGHT SHE CALMED DOWN A LITTLE WHEN ŌTA WAS BORN...
...BUT WHEN NANAME PASSED AWAY, IT PUSHED HER OVER THE EDGE.
NANAME WAS YOUR MOM. DO YOU REMEMBER?
YES.

READ THIS WAY

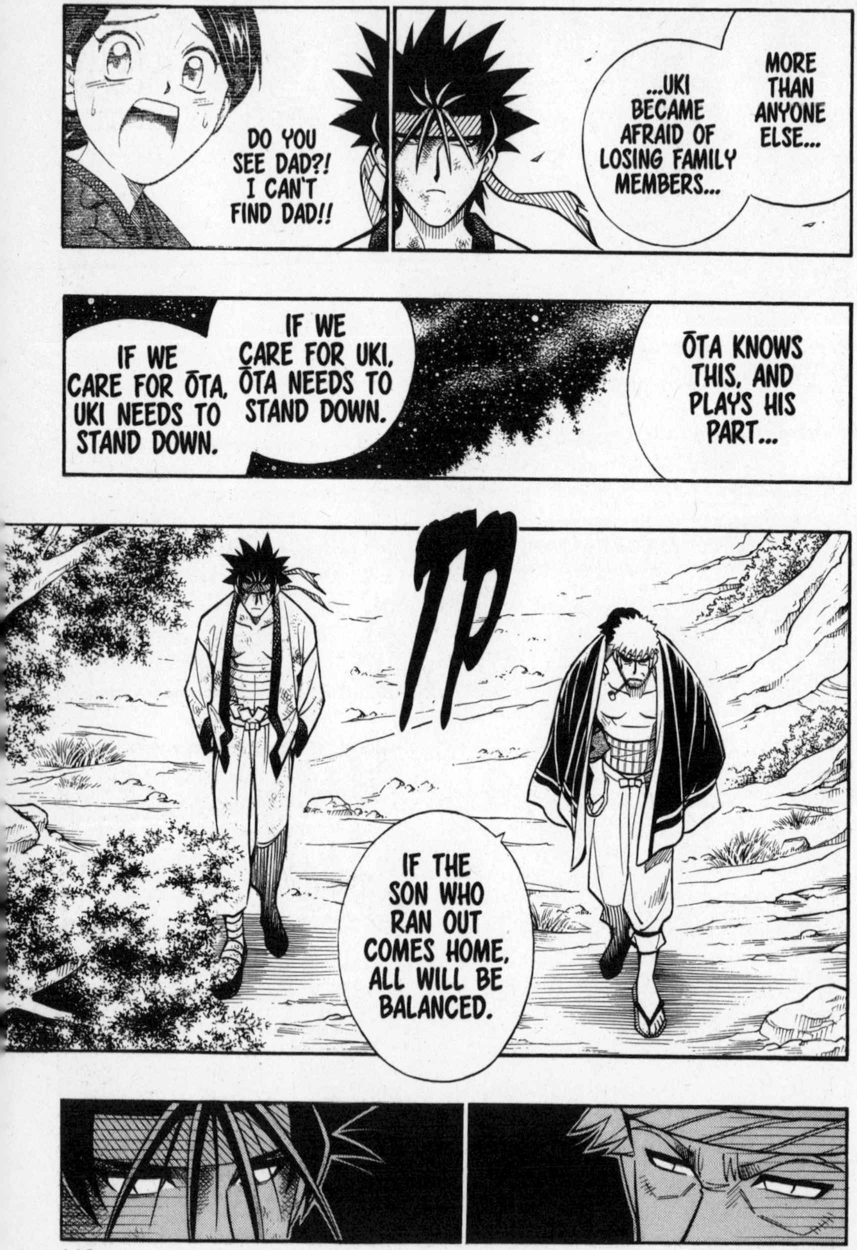
MORE THAN ANYONE ELSE...
...UKI BECAME AFRAID OF LOSING FAMILY MEMBERS...
DO YOU SEE DAD?! I CAN'T FIND DAD!!
ŌTA KNOWS THIS, AND PLAYS HIS PART...
IF WE CARE FOR UKI, ŌTA NEEDS TO STAND DOWN.
IF WE CARE FOR ŌTA, UKI NEEDS TO STAND DOWN.
IF THE SON WHO RAN OUT COMES HOME, ALL WILL BE BALANCED.

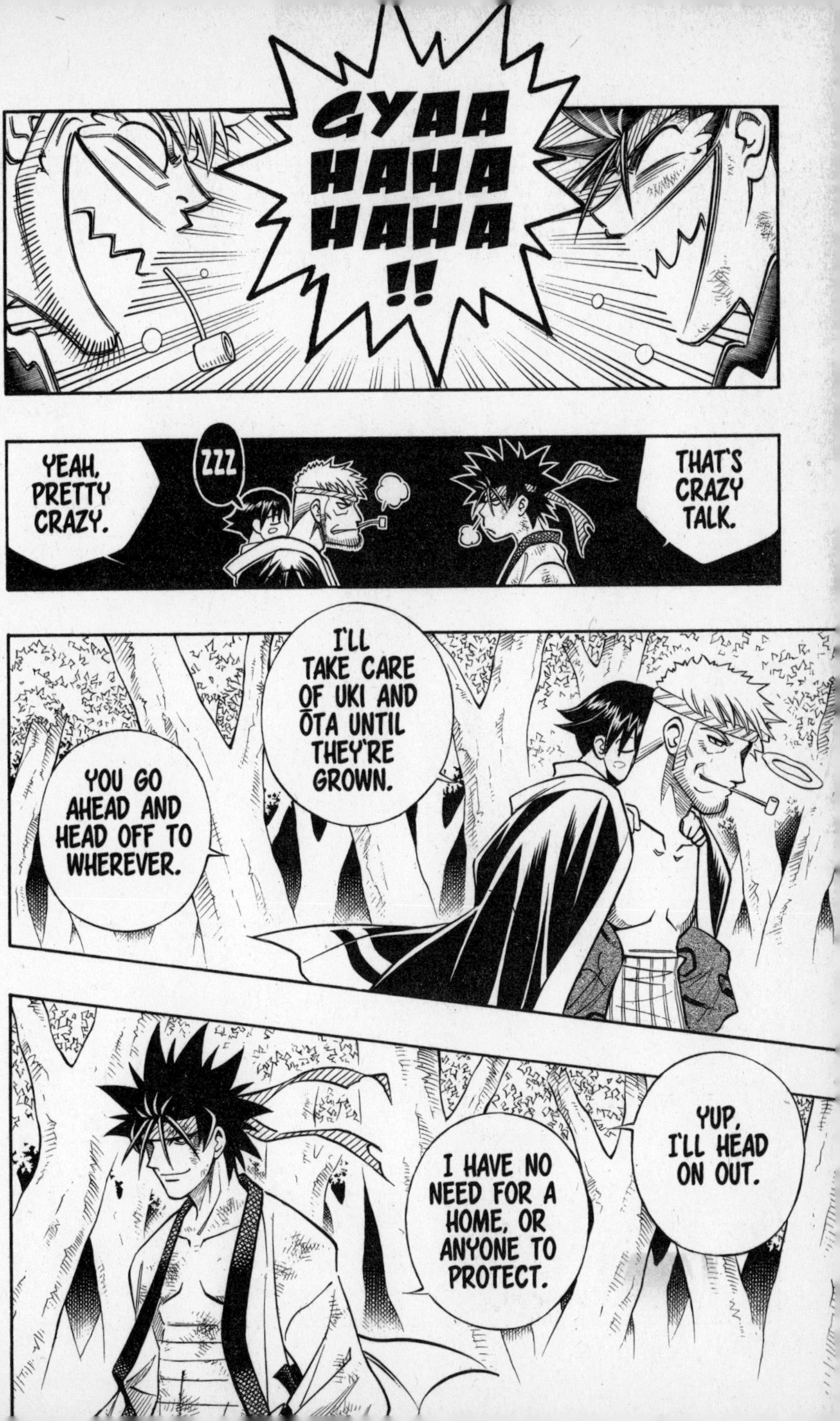
GYAA HAHA HAHA!!
THAT'S CRAZY TALK.
ZZZ
YEAH, PRETTY CRAZY.
I'LL TAKE CARE OF UKI AND ŌTA UNTIL THEY'RE GROWN.
YOU GO AHEAD AND HEAD OFF TO WHEREVER.
YUP, I'LL HEAD ON OUT.
I HAVE NO NEED FOR A HOME, OR ANYONE TO PROTECT.

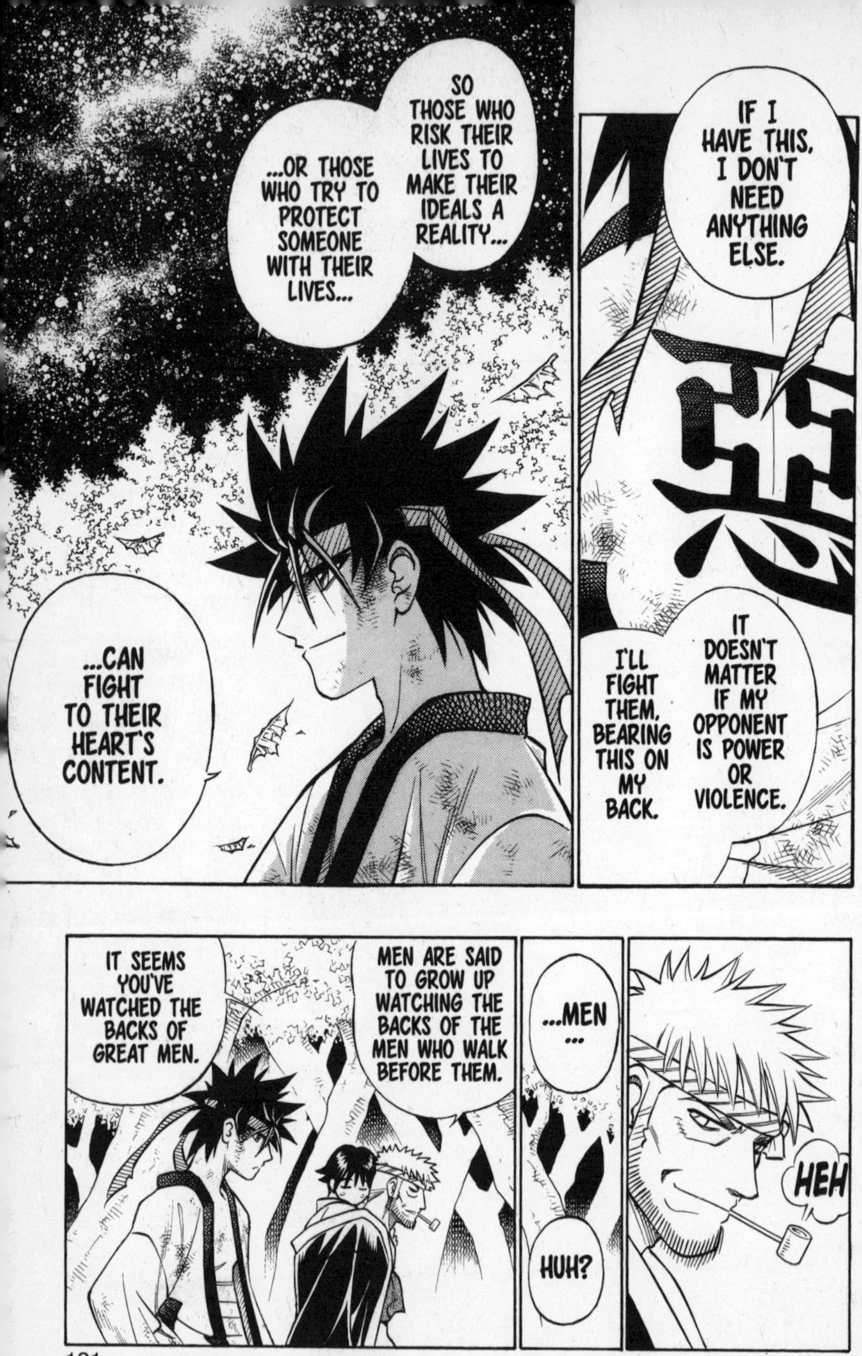
IF I HAVE THIS, I DON'T NEED ANYTHING ELSE.
IT DOESN'T MATTER IF MY OPPONENT IS POWER OR VIOLENCE.
I'LL FIGHT THEM, BEARING THIS ON MY BACK.
SO THOSE WHO RISK THEIR LIVES TO MAKE THEIR IDEALS A REALITY...
...OR THOSE WHO TRY TO PROTECT SOMEONE WITH THEIR LIVES...
...CAN FIGHT TO THEIR HEART'S CONTENT.
HEH
...MEN...
HUH?
MEN ARE SAID TO GROW UP WATCHING THE BACKS OF THE MEN WHO WALK BEFORE THEM.
IT SEEMS YOU'VE WATCHED THE BACKS OF GREAT MEN.

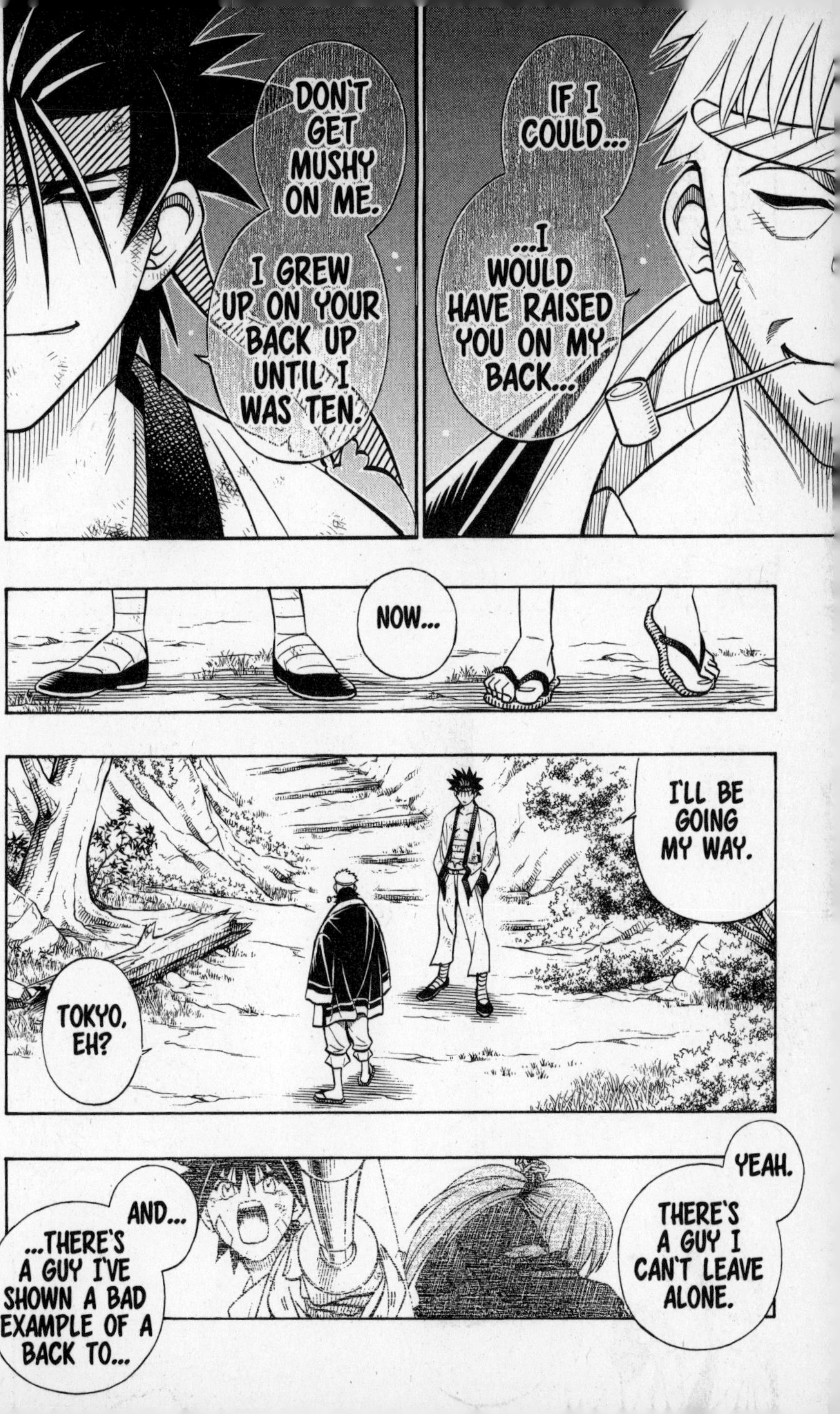
IF I COULD...
...I WOULD HAVE RAISED YOU ON MY BACK...
DON'T GET MUSHY ON ME.
I GREW UP ON YOUR BACK UP UNTIL I WAS TEN.
NOW...
I'LL BE GOING MY WAY.
TOKYO, EH?
YEAH.
THERE'S A GUY I CAN'T LEAVE ALONE.
AND...
...THERE'S A GUY I'VE SHOWN A BAD EXAMPLE OF A BACK TO...

READ THIS WAY

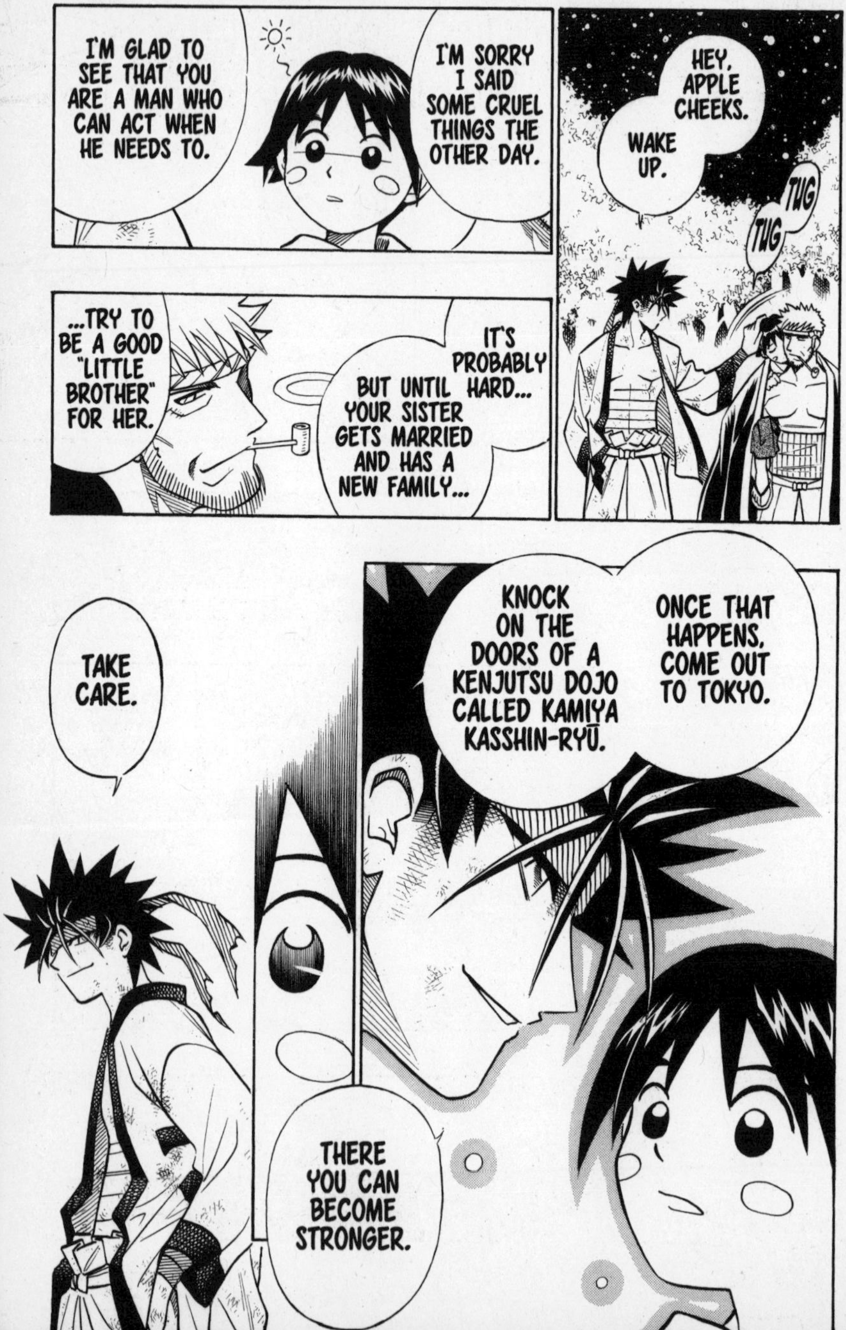
HEY, APPLE CHEEKS.
WAKE UP.
TUG
TUG
I'M SORRY I SAID SOME CRUEL THINGS THE OTHER DAY.
I'M GLAD TO SEE THAT YOU ARE A MAN WHO CAN ACT WHEN HE NEEDS TO.
IT'S PROBABLY HARD... BUT UNTIL YOUR SISTER GETS MARRIED AND HAS A NEW FAMILY...
...TRY TO BE A GOOD "LITTLE BROTHER" FOR HER.
ONCE THAT HAPPENS, COME OUT TO TOKYO.
KNOCK ON THE DOORS OF A KENJUTSU DOJO CALLED KAMIYA KASSHIN-RYŪ.
THERE YOU CAN BECOME STRONGER.
TAKE CARE.

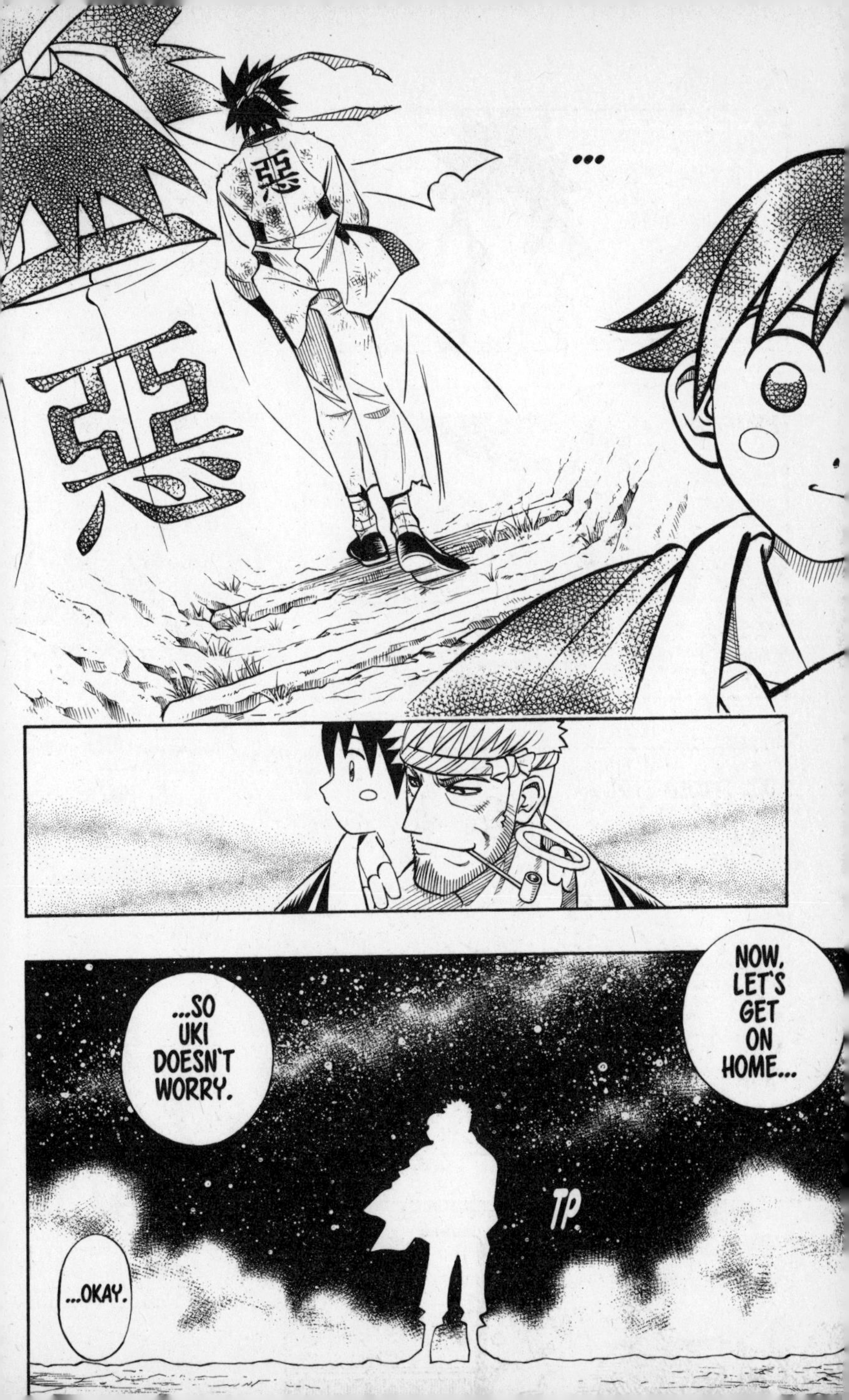

悪
悪
...
NOW, LET'S GET ON HOME...
...SO UKI DOESN'T WORRY.
TP
...OKAY.

READ THIS WAY

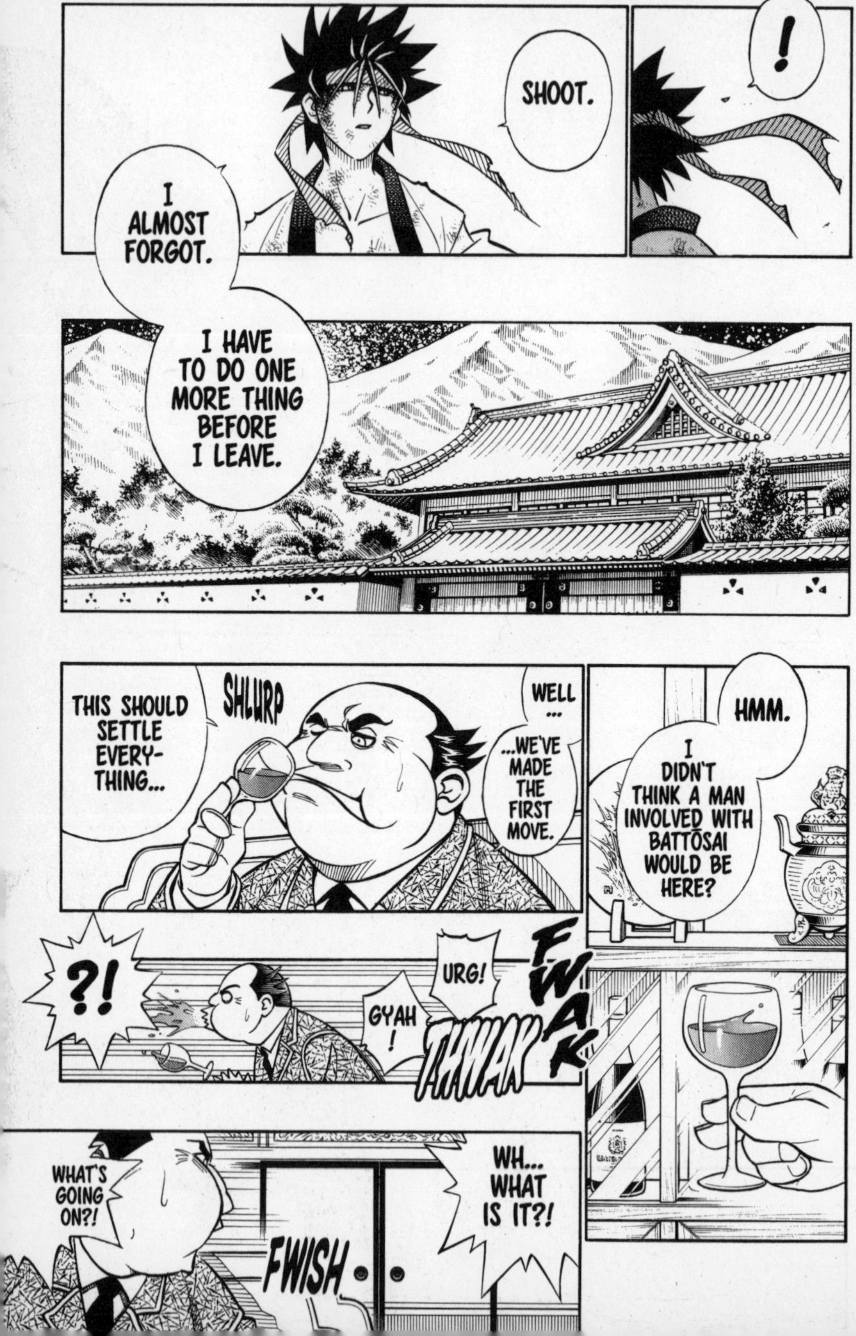
!
SHOOT.
I ALMOST FORGOT.
I HAVE TO DO ONE MORE THING BEFORE I LEAVE.
HMM.
I DIDN'T THINK A MAN INVOLVED WITH BATTŌSAI WOULD BE HERE?
WELL ... ...WE'VE MADE THE FIRST MOVE.
SHLURP
THIS SHOULD SETTLE EVERYTHING...
FWAK
THWAK
URG!
GYAH!
?!
WH... WHAT IS IT?!
FWISH
WHAT'S GOING ON?!

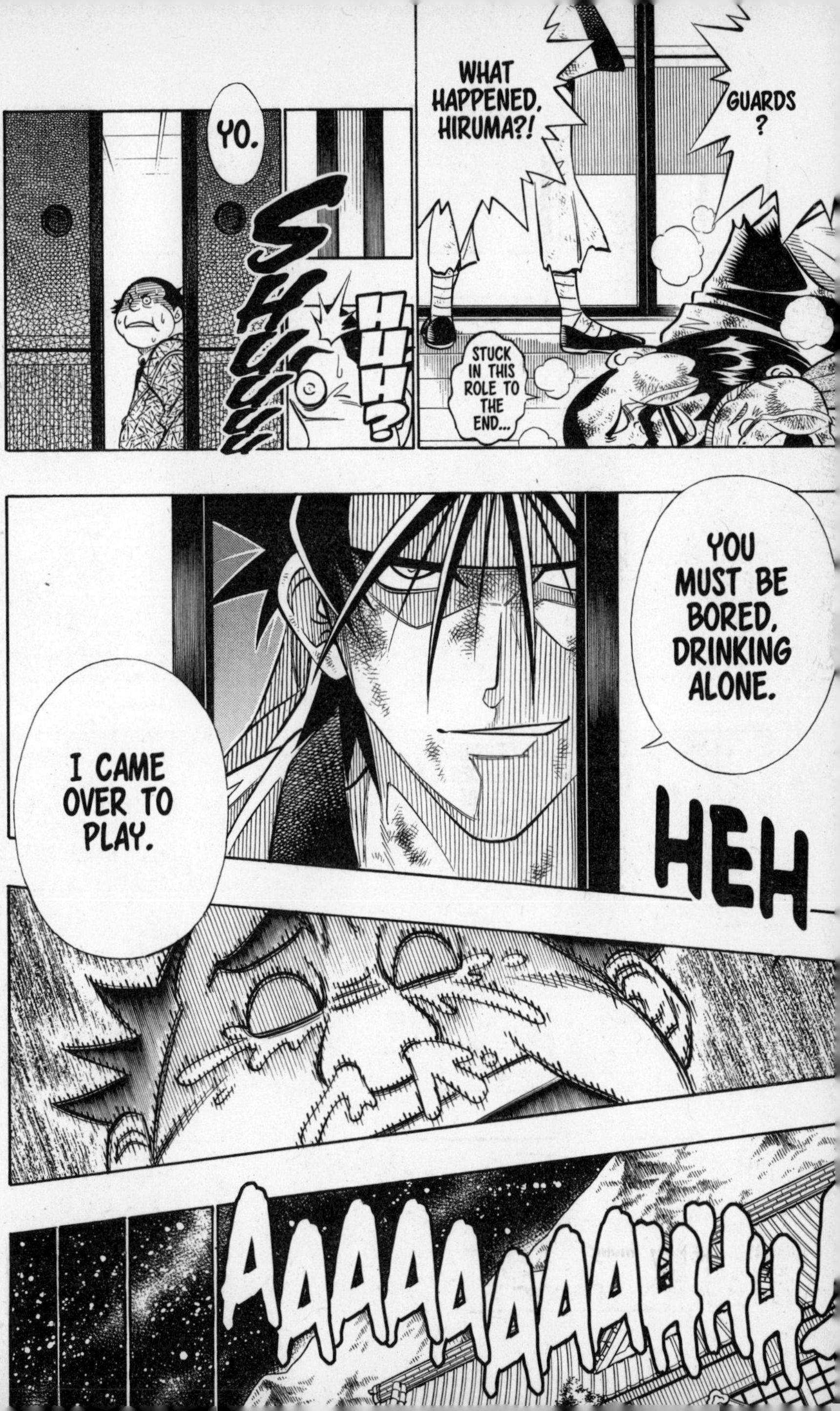
GUARDS ?
WHAT HAPPENED, HIRUMA?!
STUCK IN THIS ROLE TO THE END...
HUH?
SHUUUUU
YO.
YOU MUST BE BORED, DRINKING ALONE.
HEH
I CAME OVER TO PLAY.
AAAAAAAAHH!

READ THIS WAY

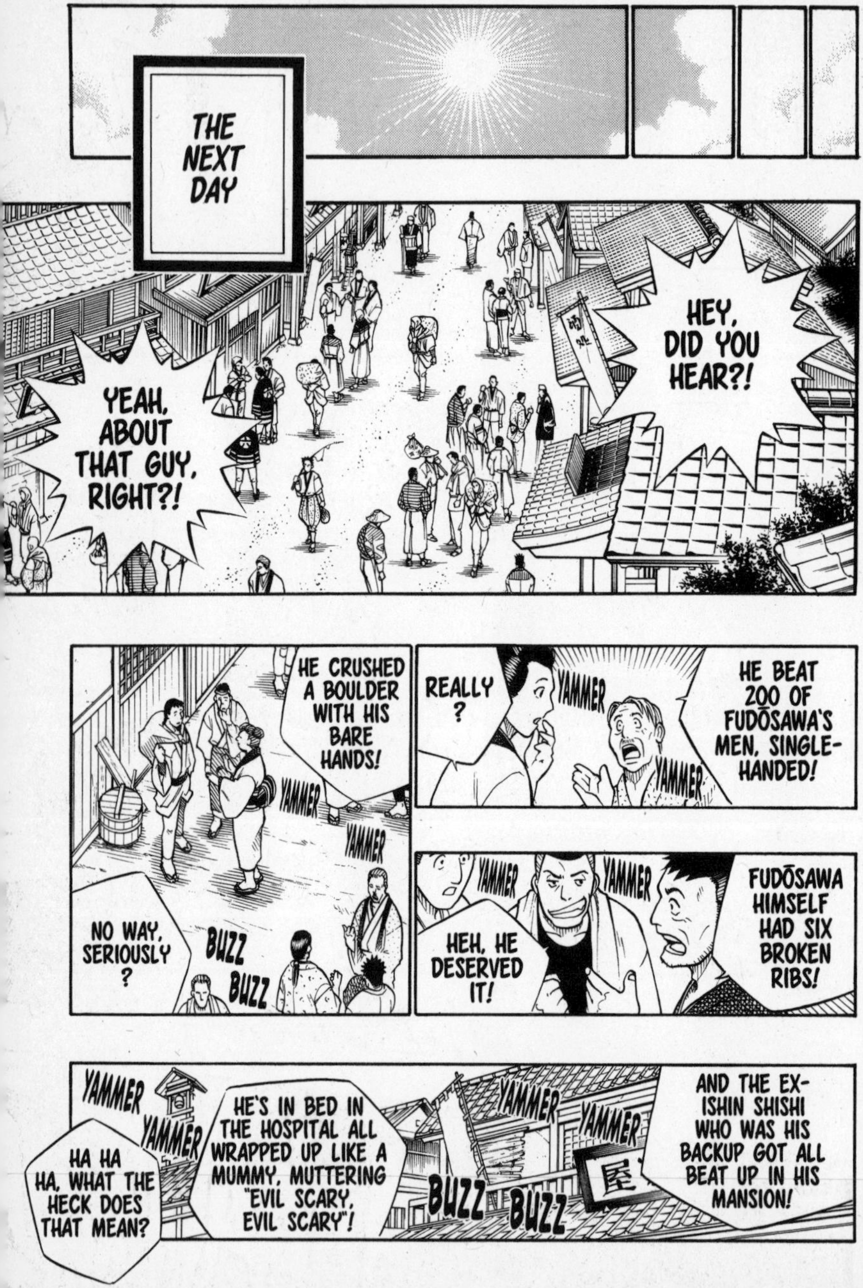
THE NEXT DAY
HEY, DID YOU HEAR?!
YEAH, ABOUT THAT GUY, RIGHT?!
HE BEAT 200 OF FUDŌSAWA'S MEN, SINGLE-HANDED!
YAMMER
YAMMER
REALLY?
FUDŌSAWA HIMSELF HAD SIX BROKEN RIBS!
YAMMER
YAMMER
HEH, HE DESERVED IT!
HE CRUSHED A BOULDER WITH HIS BARE HANDS!
YAMMER
YAMMER
NO WAY, SERIOUSLY?
BUZZ
BUZZ
AND THE EX-ISHIN SHISHI WHO WAS HIS BACKUP GOT ALL BEAT UP IN HIS MANSION!
YAMMER
YAMMER
BUZZ
BUZZ
HE'S IN BED IN THE HOSPITAL ALL WRAPPED UP LIKE A MUMMY, MUTTERING "EVIL SCARY, EVIL SCARY"!
YAMMER
YAMMER
HA HA HA, WHAT THE HECK DOES THAT MEAN?

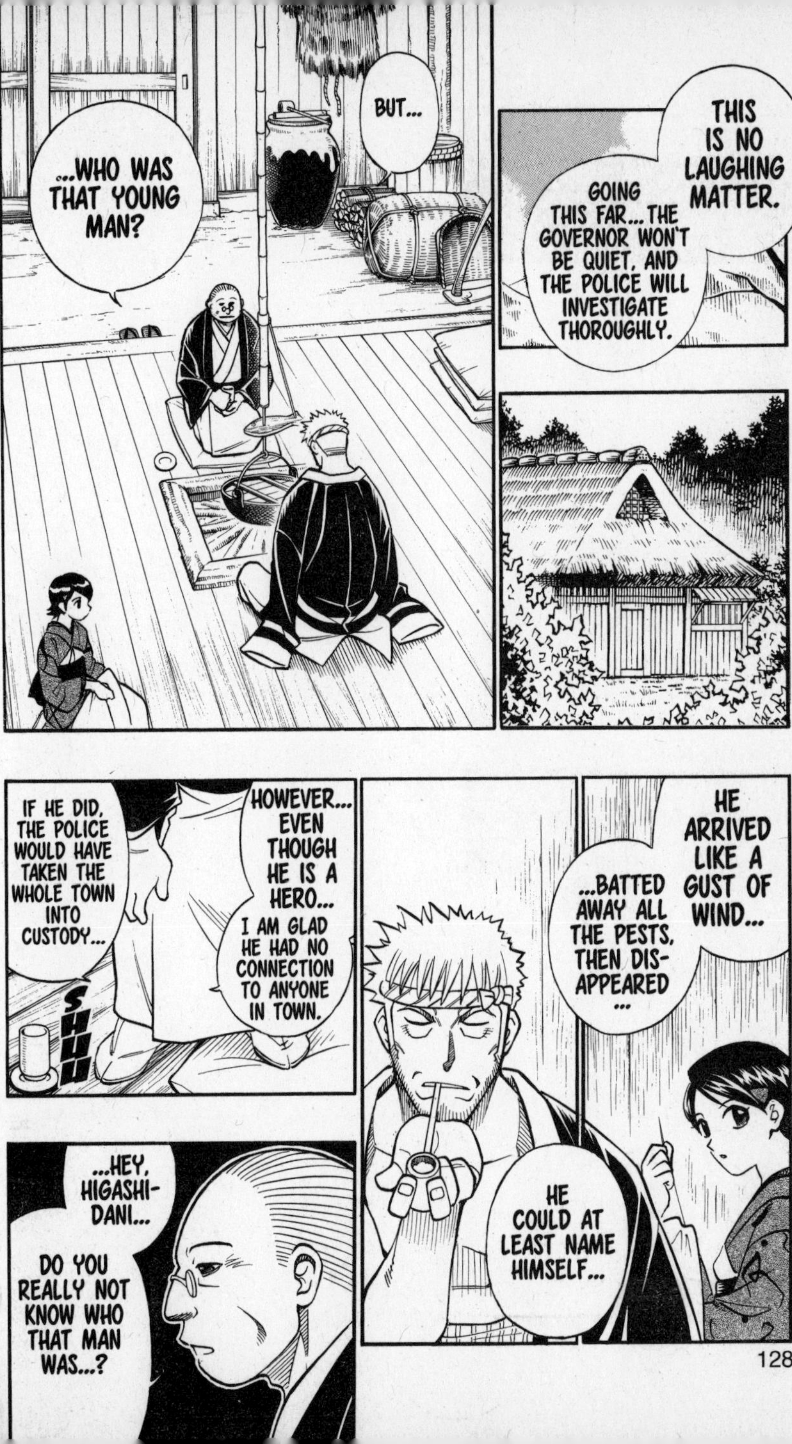
THIS IS NO LAUGHING MATTER.
GOING THIS FAR... THE GOVERNOR WON'T BE QUIET, AND THE POLICE WILL INVESTIGATE THOROUGHLY.
BUT...
...WHO WAS THAT YOUNG MAN?
HE ARRIVED LIKE A GUST OF WIND...
...BATTED AWAY ALL THE PESTS, THEN DIS-APPEARED ...
HE COULD AT LEAST NAME HIMSELF...
HOWEVER... EVEN THOUGH HE IS A HERO... I AM GLAD HE HAD NO CONNECTION TO ANYONE IN TOWN.
IF HE DID, THE POLICE WOULD HAVE TAKEN THE WHOLE TOWN INTO CUSTODY...
SHUU
...HEY, HIGASHI-DANI...
DO YOU REALLY NOT KNOW WHO THAT MAN WAS...?

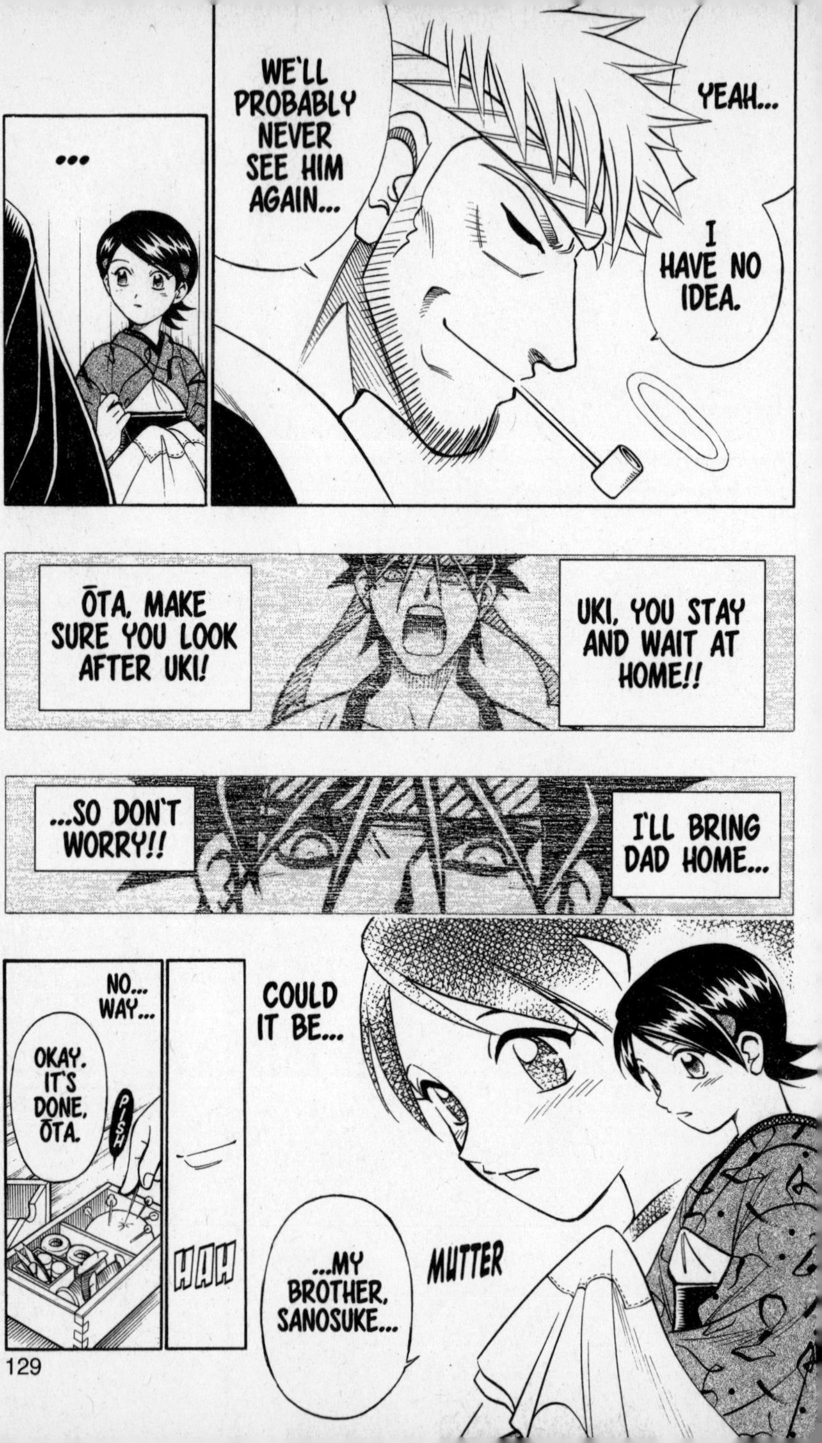

WE'LL PROBABLY NEVER SEE HIM AGAIN...
YEAH...
I HAVE NO IDEA.
...
UKI, YOU STAY AND WAIT AT HOME!!
ŌTA, MAKE SURE YOU LOOK AFTER UKI!
I'LL BRING DAD HOME...
...SO DON'T WORRY!!
COULD IT BE...
MUTTER
...MY BROTHER, SANOSUKE...
HAH
NO... WAY...
OKAY. IT'S DONE, ŌTA.
PISH

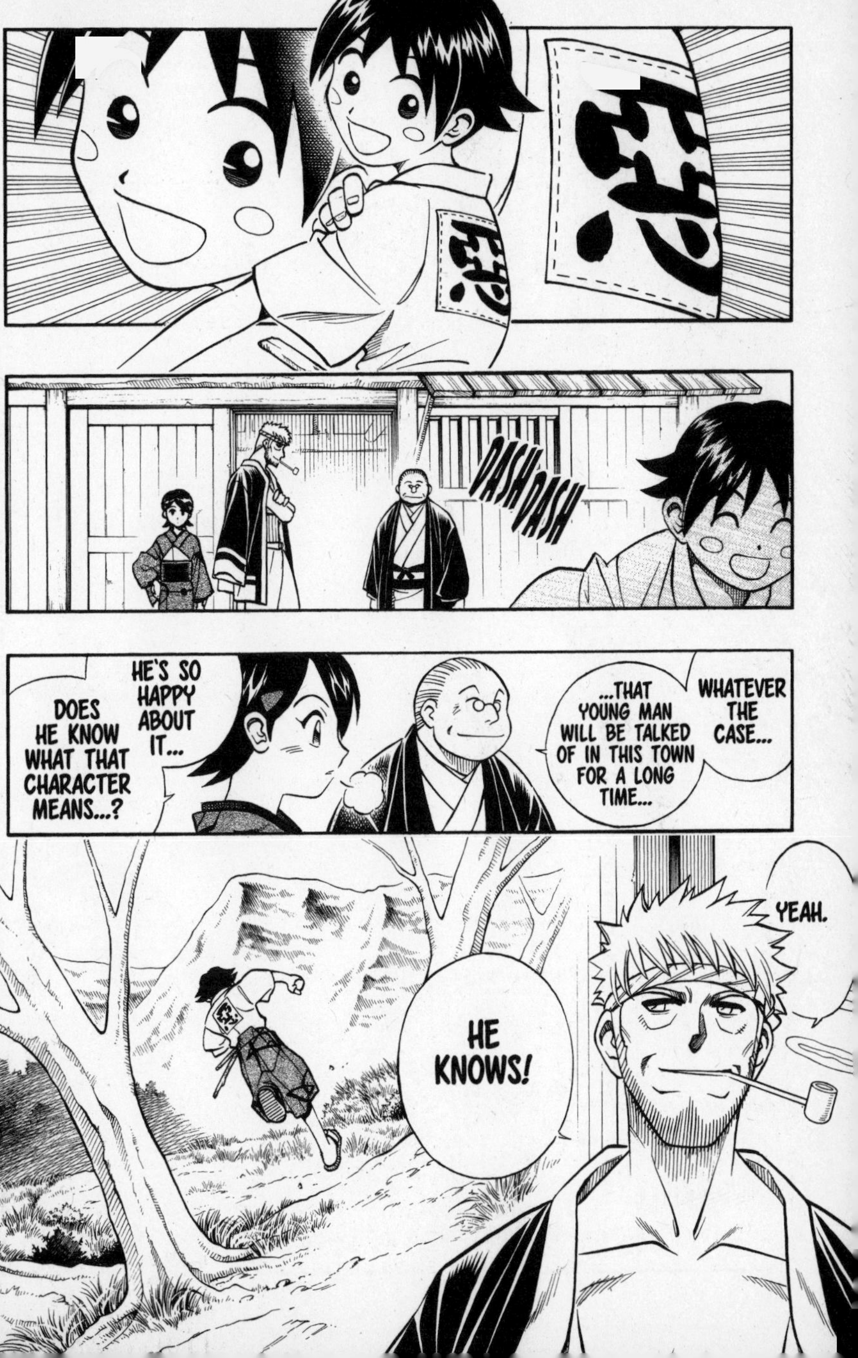
DASH DASH
WHATEVER THE CASE...
...THAT YOUNG MAN WILL BE TALKED OF IN THIS TOWN FOR A LONG TIME...
HE'S SO HAPPY ABOUT IT...
DOES HE KNOW WHAT THAT CHARACTER MEANS...?
YEAH.
HE KNOWS!

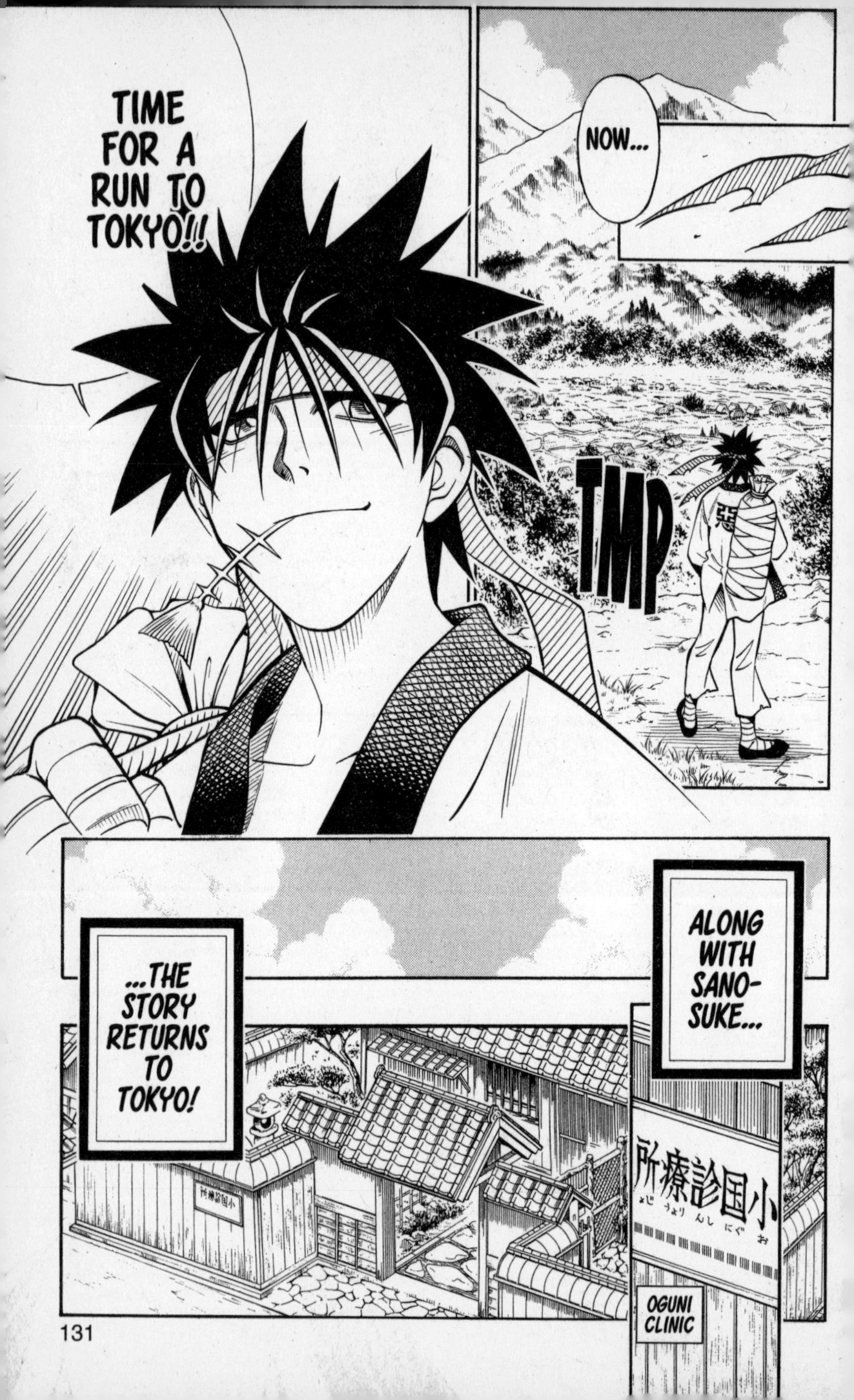
NOW...
TMP
TIME FOR A RUN TO TOKYO!!!
ALONG WITH SANO-SUKE...
...THE STORY RETURNS TO TOKYO!
小国診療所
おぐにしんりょうじょ
OGUNI CLINIC

The Secret Life of Characters (50)

—Higashidani Family—

I've always had an idea of what Sanosuke's family might be like, and the Higashidani family is formed along those lines. The father, Kamishimoemon, is just what Sanosuke will be like when he's older. The sister, Uki, is a very lively person and very protective. The youngest brother, Ōta, is the exact opposite of Sanosuke, a weak little boy. These basic characteristics, with some storyline added, turned them into what they are now. But to be honest, this story is a little unsatisfactory. Under the keywords of "a man's back," Sanosuke was supposed to return to his origin, realize his life was on a different path from Kenshin's, and continue on his own way. However, I struggled a lot with the storyline for Kenshin before this, using up my energy, and wasn't able to concentrate on this storyline. The story had a lot of unnecessary parts included, and lost its focus on Sanosuke. The plan for four episodes turned into seven. When I think back, I should have concentrated on either Uki or Ōta, made it a three person family, and not been caught up on the four person family.

But the Higashidani family was fun to illustrate, so it's fine. A family is something I'd like to keep challenging myself with, so I'll hone my skills and take another shot at it.

There are no real models in terms of design. Kamishimoemon was refined from an aged Sanosuke that appeared in one of the ideas for the final episode for *Ruro-Ken*. Uki is just a modern, easy to draw type. But she also comes from the idea that Sanosuke's sister must have pointy hair, which made me add the pointy hair at the back. Ōta is a typical Watsuki image of a weak, country boy, with the circle marks on the cheeks. Overall, I was aiming for a design that wouldn't take long to draw out, but this was rather difficult. Things gradually changed as I kept drawing them, but I ended up feeling like I needed to go out and look at real people and learn a bit more. Building a design out of elements taken from pictures and images seems to have its limits.

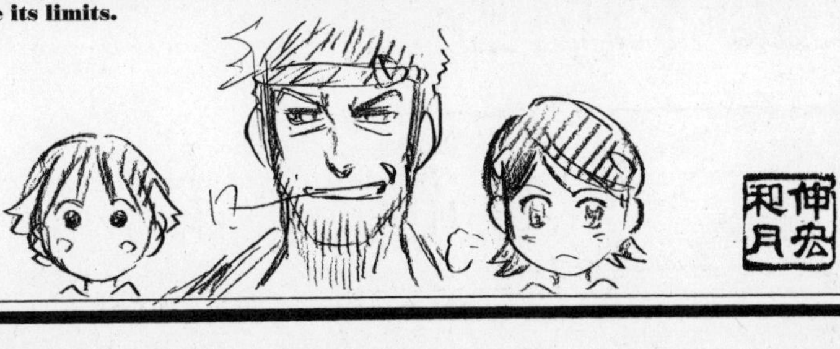
伸宏
和月

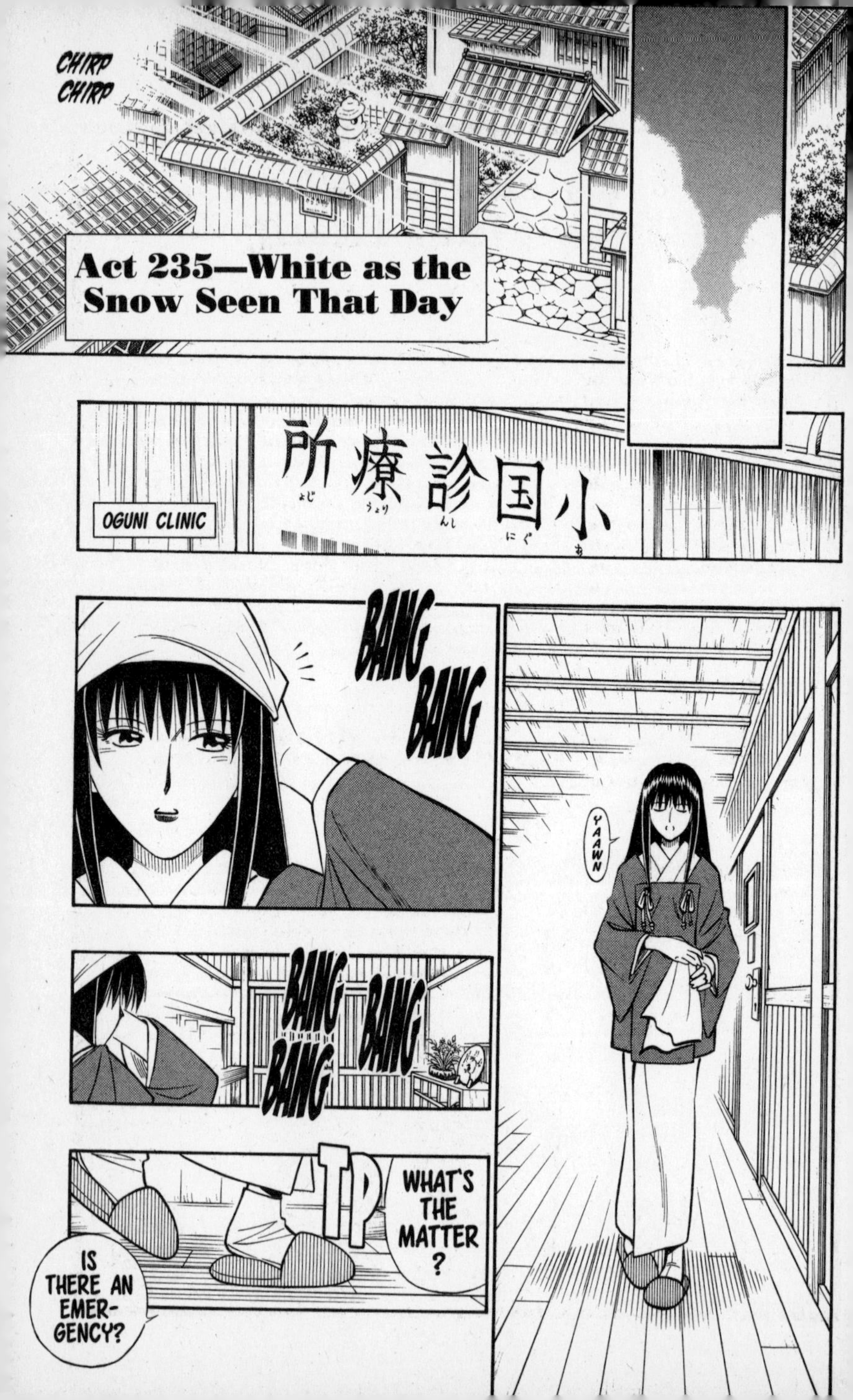
CHIRP
CHIRP
Act 235—White as the Snow Seen That Day
小国診療所
OGUNI CLINIC
YAAAWN
BANG BANG
BANG BANG BANG BANG
TP
WHAT'S THE MATTER?
IS THERE AN EMERGENCY?

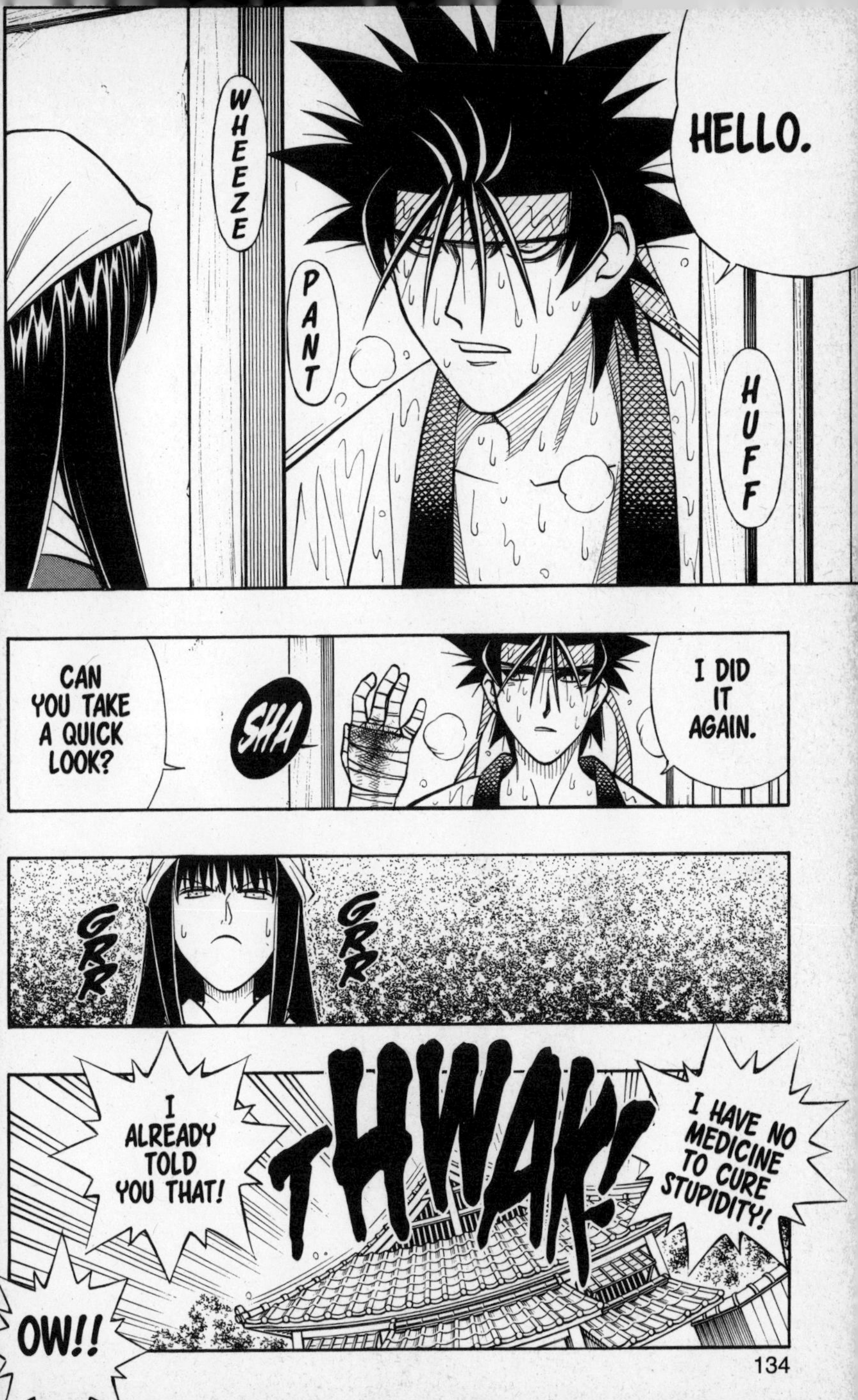
HELLO.
HUFF
WHEEZE
PANT
I DID IT AGAIN.
SHA
CAN YOU TAKE A QUICK LOOK?
GRR
GRR
I HAVE NO MEDICINE TO CURE STUPIDITY!
THWAK!
I ALREADY TOLD YOU THAT!
OW!!

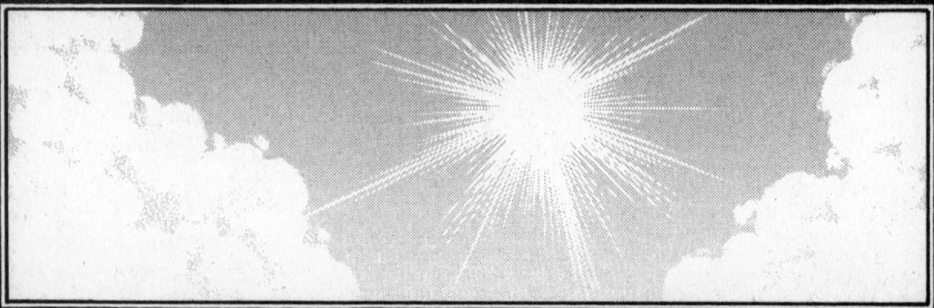

Act 235

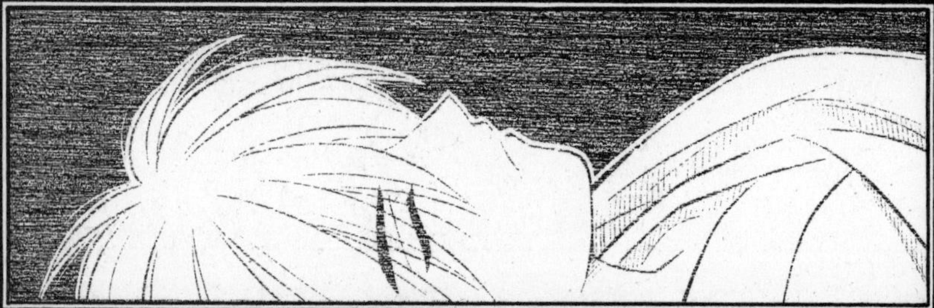

White as the Snow Seen That Day

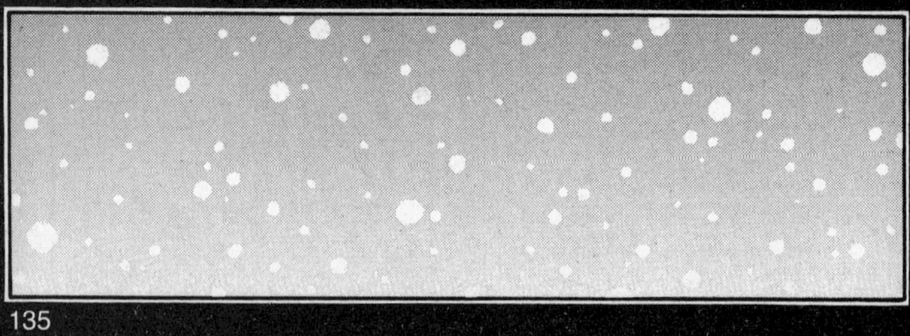

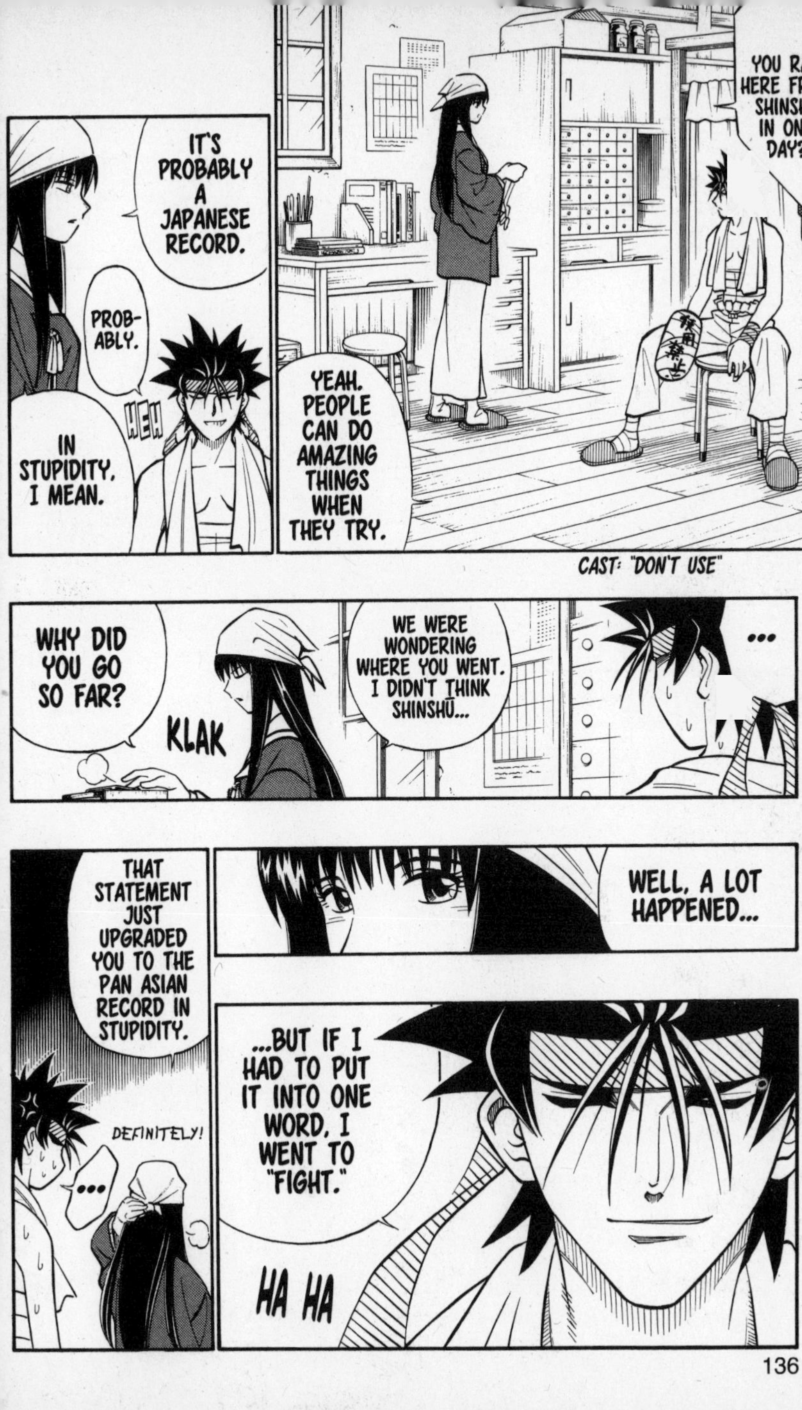
YOU RAN HERE FROM SHINSHŪ IN ONE DAY?
YEAH. PEOPLE CAN DO AMAZING THINGS WHEN THEY TRY.
IT'S PROBABLY A JAPANESE RECORD.
PROB-ABLY.
HEH
IN STUPIDITY, I MEAN.
CAST: "DON'T USE"
...
WE WERE WONDERING WHERE YOU WENT. I DIDN'T THINK SHINSHŪ...
WHY DID YOU GO SO FAR?
KLAK
WELL, A LOT HAPPENED...
...BUT IF I HAD TO PUT IT INTO ONE WORD, I WENT TO "FIGHT."
HA HA
THAT STATEMENT JUST UPGRADED YOU TO THE PAN ASIAN RECORD IN STUPIDITY.
...
DEFINITELY!

READ THIS WAY

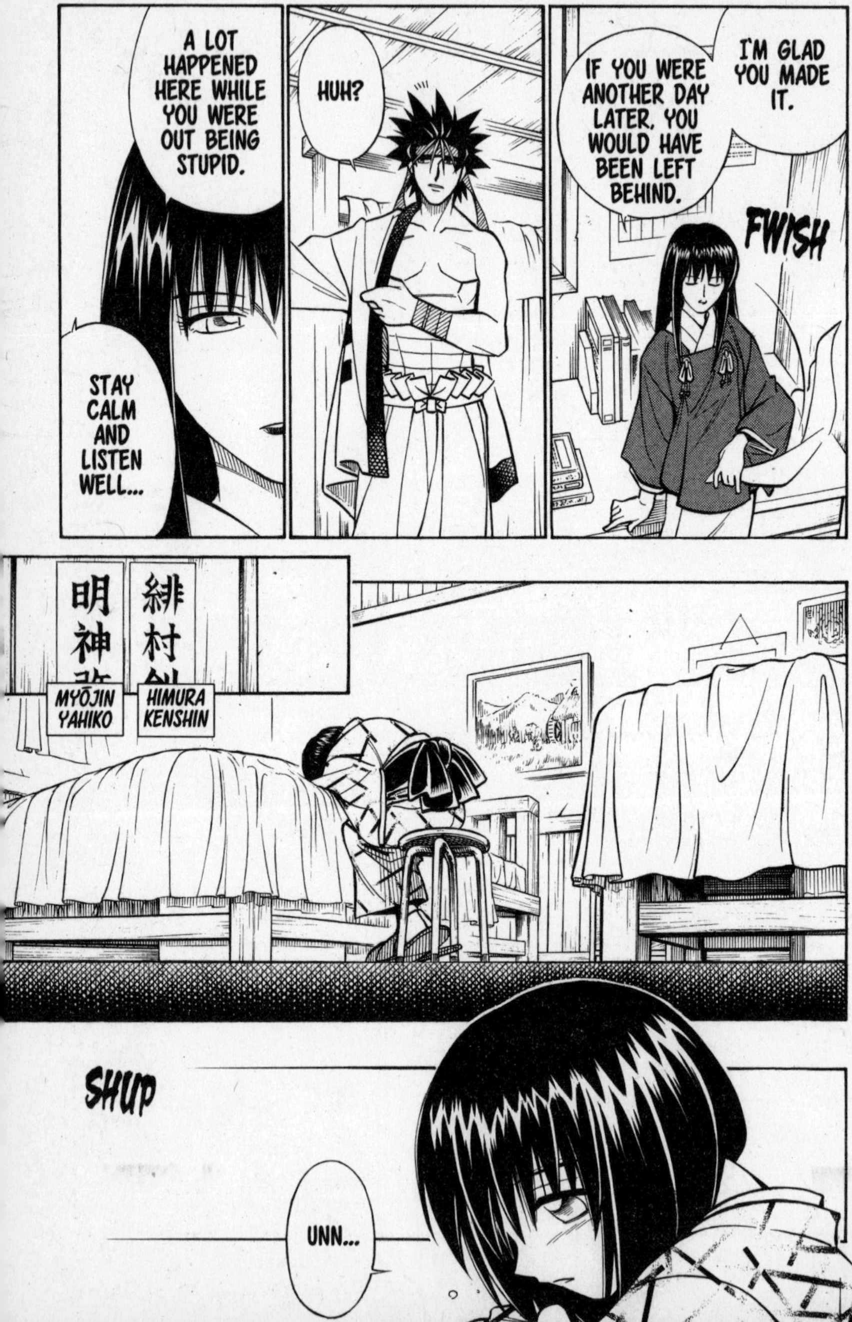
I'M GLAD YOU MADE IT.
IF YOU WERE ANOTHER DAY LATER, YOU WOULD HAVE BEEN LEFT BEHIND.
FWISH
HUH?
A LOT HAPPENED HERE WHILE YOU WERE OUT BEING STUPID.
STAY CALM AND LISTEN WELL...
緋村
HIMURA KENSHIN
明神
MYŌJIN YAHIKO
SHUP
UNN...

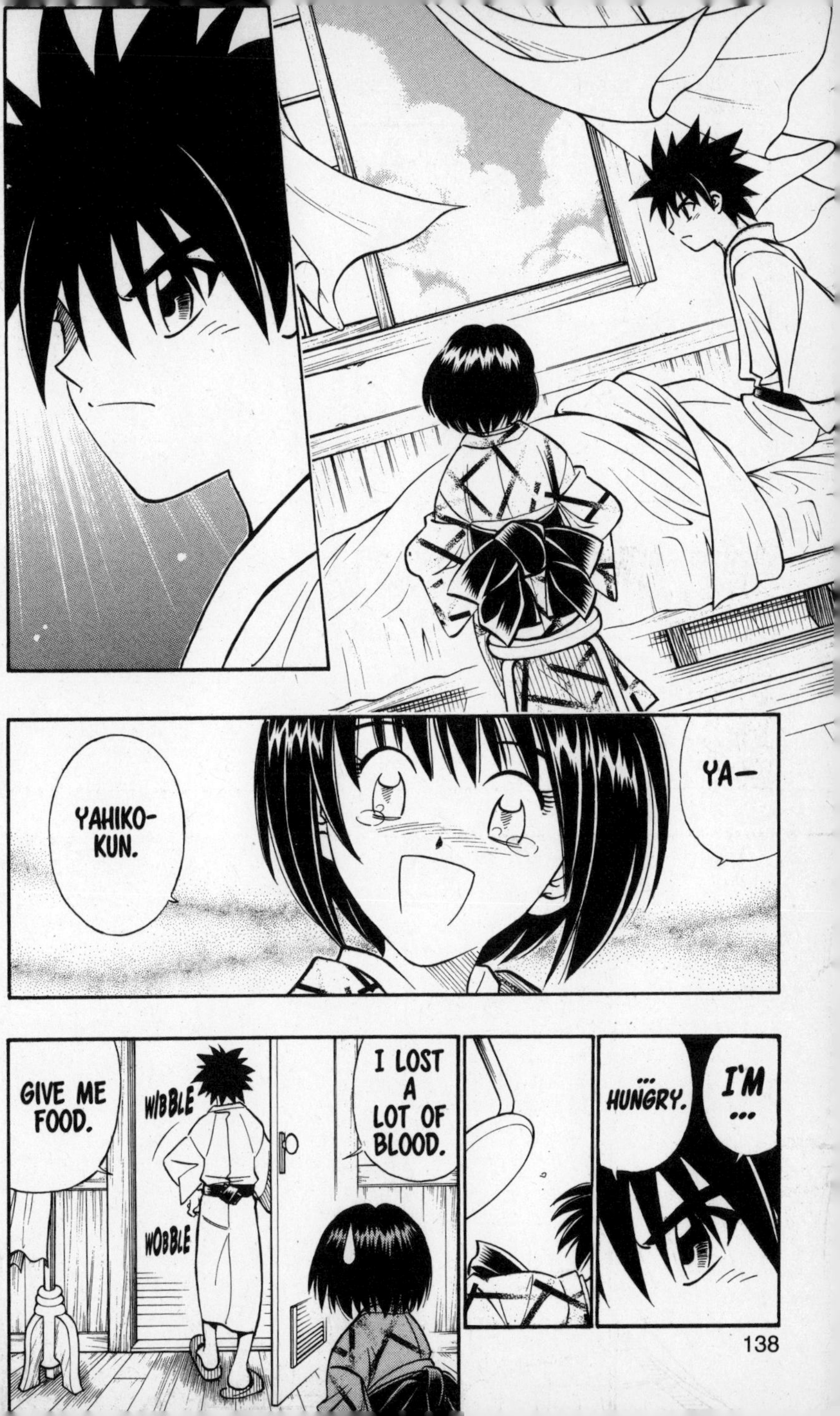
YA—
YAHIKO-KUN.
I'M ...
... HUNGRY.
I LOST A LOT OF BLOOD.
WIBBLE
GIVE ME FOOD.
WOBBLE

READ THIS WAY

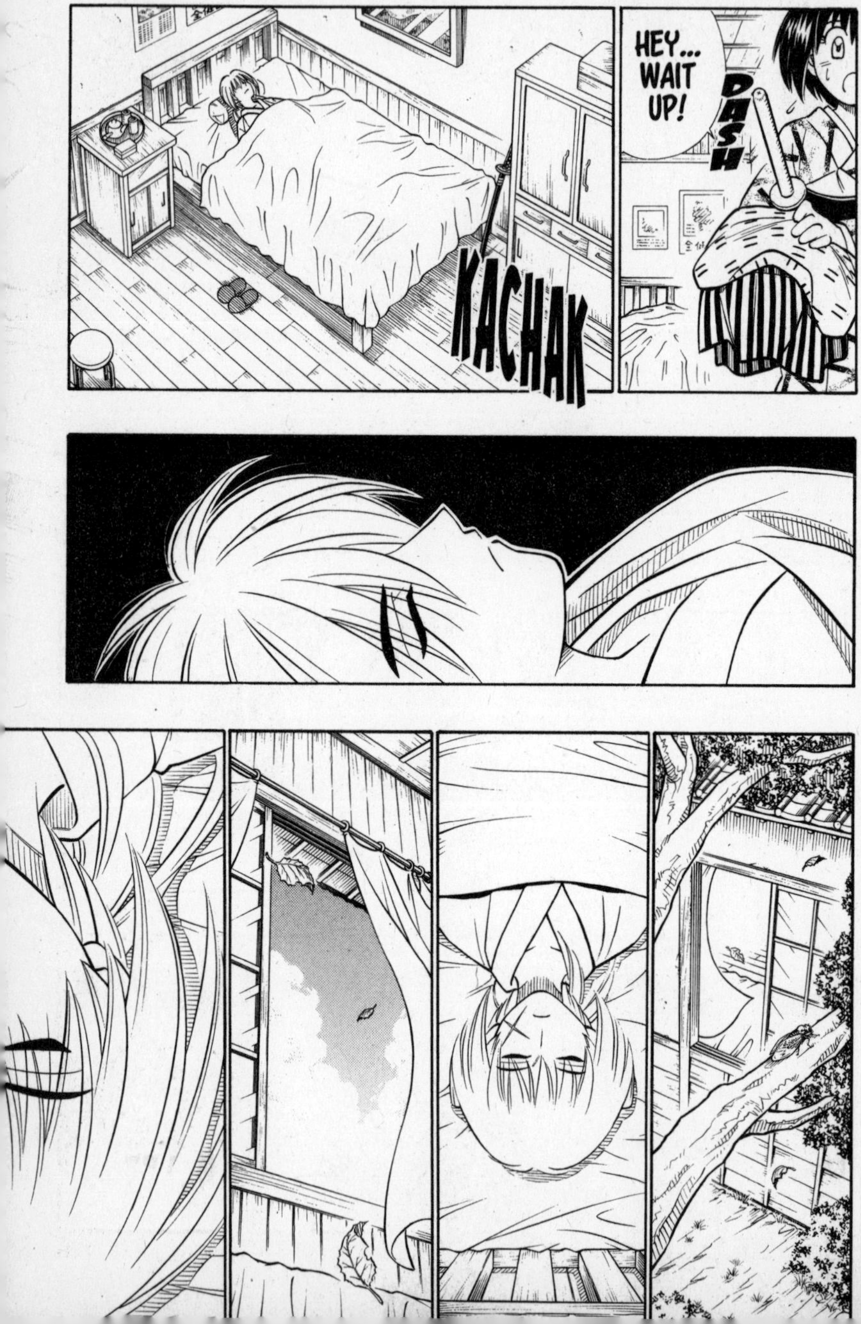
HEY... WAIT UP!
DASH
KACHAK

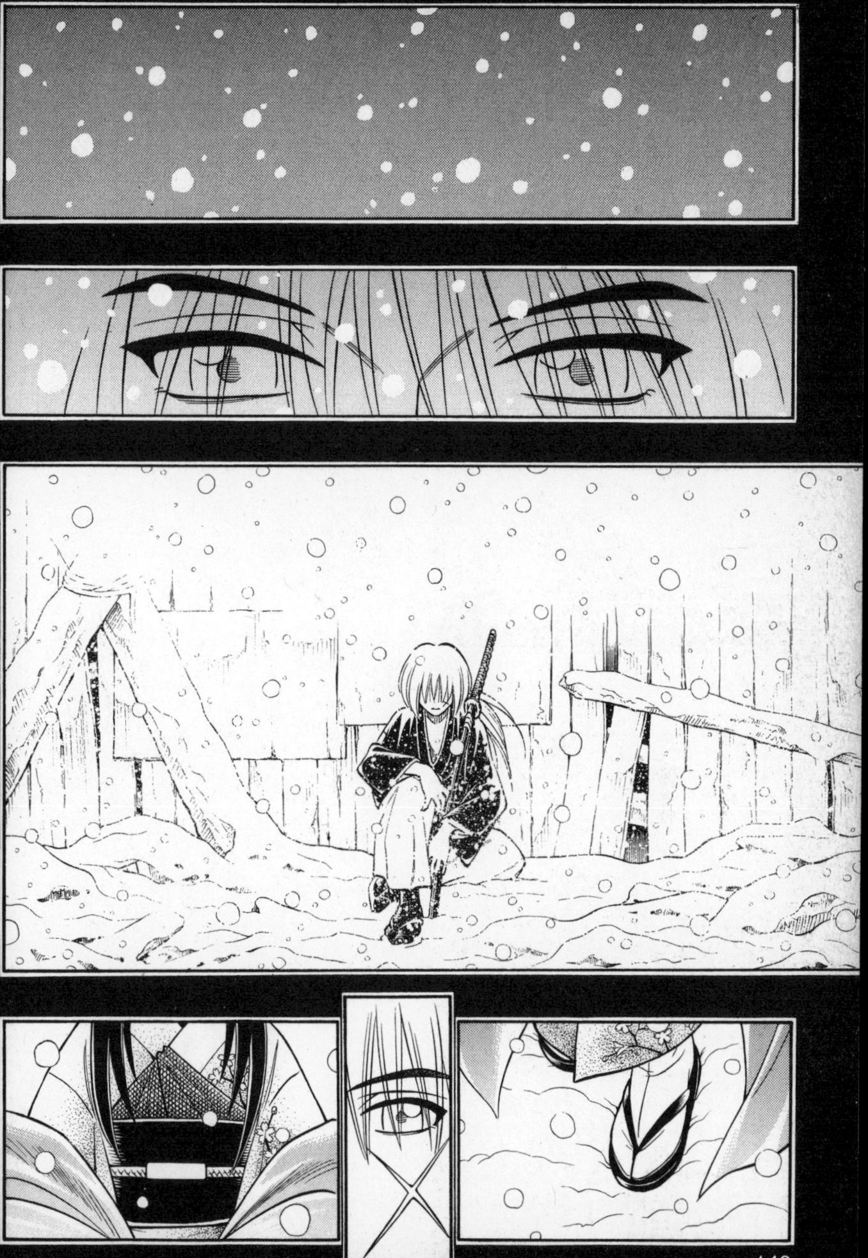

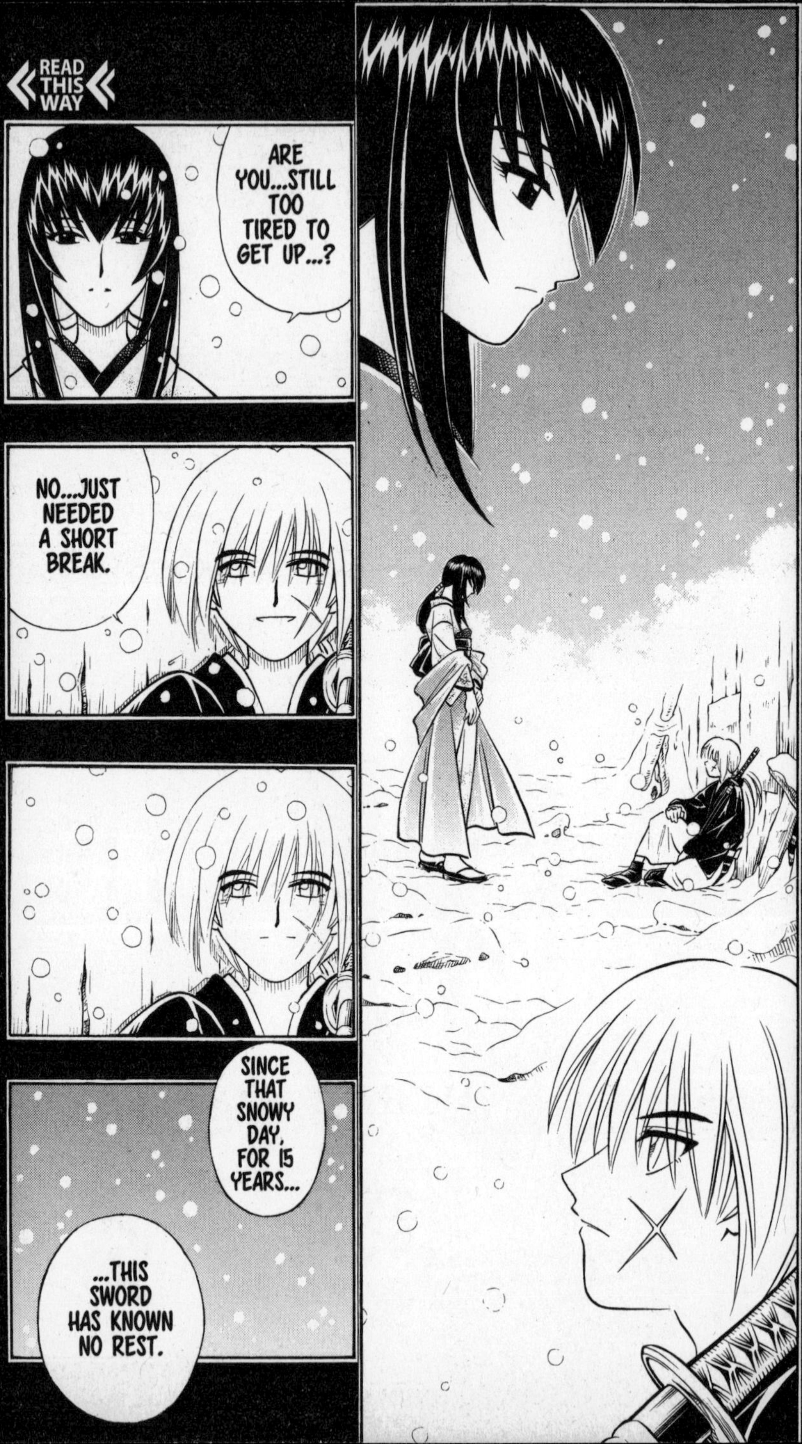
READ THIS WAY
ARE YOU...STILL TOO TIRED TO GET UP...?
NO...JUST NEEDED A SHORT BREAK.
SINCE THAT SNOWY DAY, FOR 15 YEARS...
...THIS SWORD HAS KNOWN NO REST.

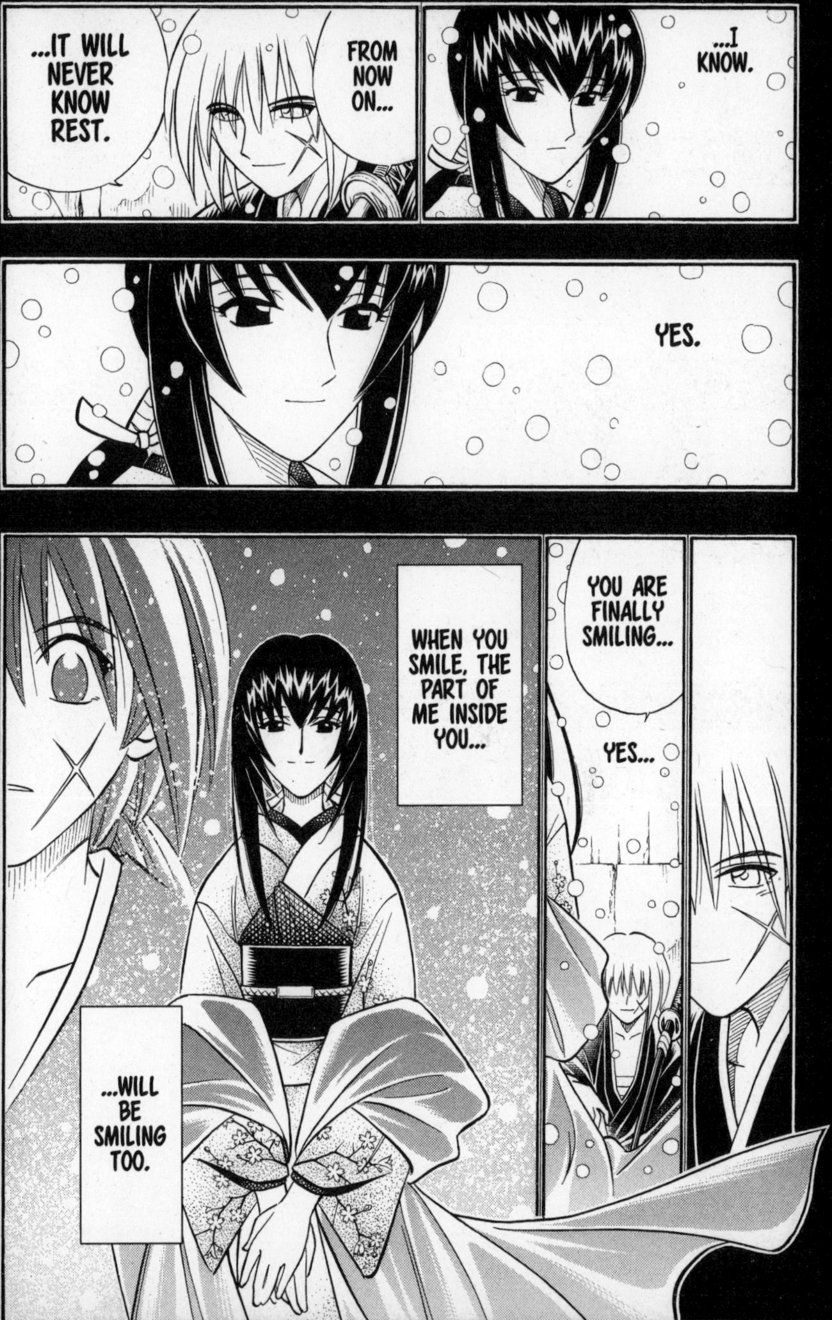
...I KNOW.
FROM NOW ON...
...IT WILL NEVER KNOW REST.
YES.
YOU ARE FINALLY SMILING...
YES...
WHEN YOU SMILE, THE PART OF ME INSIDE YOU...
...WILL BE SMILING TOO.

READ THIS WAY

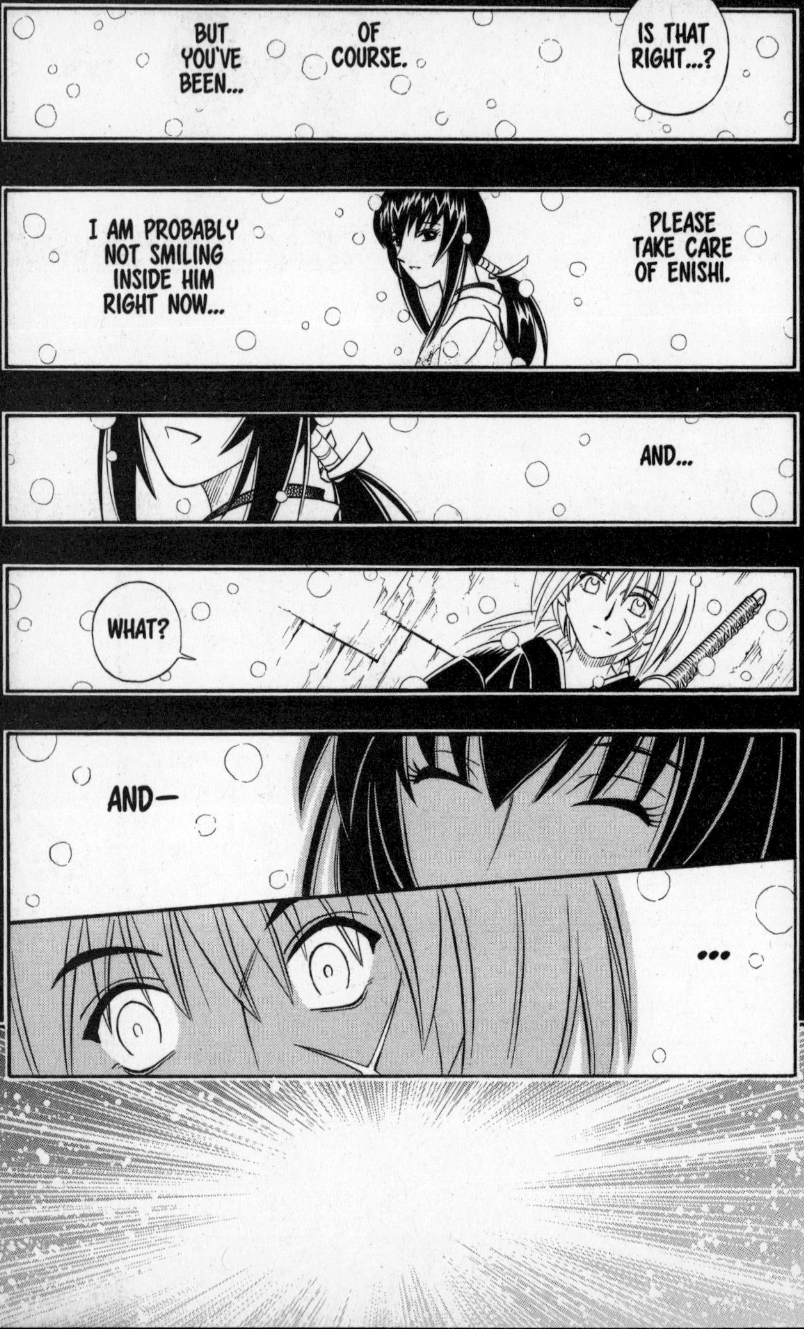
IS THAT RIGHT...?
OF COURSE.
BUT YOU'VE BEEN...
PLEASE TAKE CARE OF ENISHI.
I AM PROBABLY NOT SMILING INSIDE HIM RIGHT NOW...
AND...
WHAT?
AND—
...

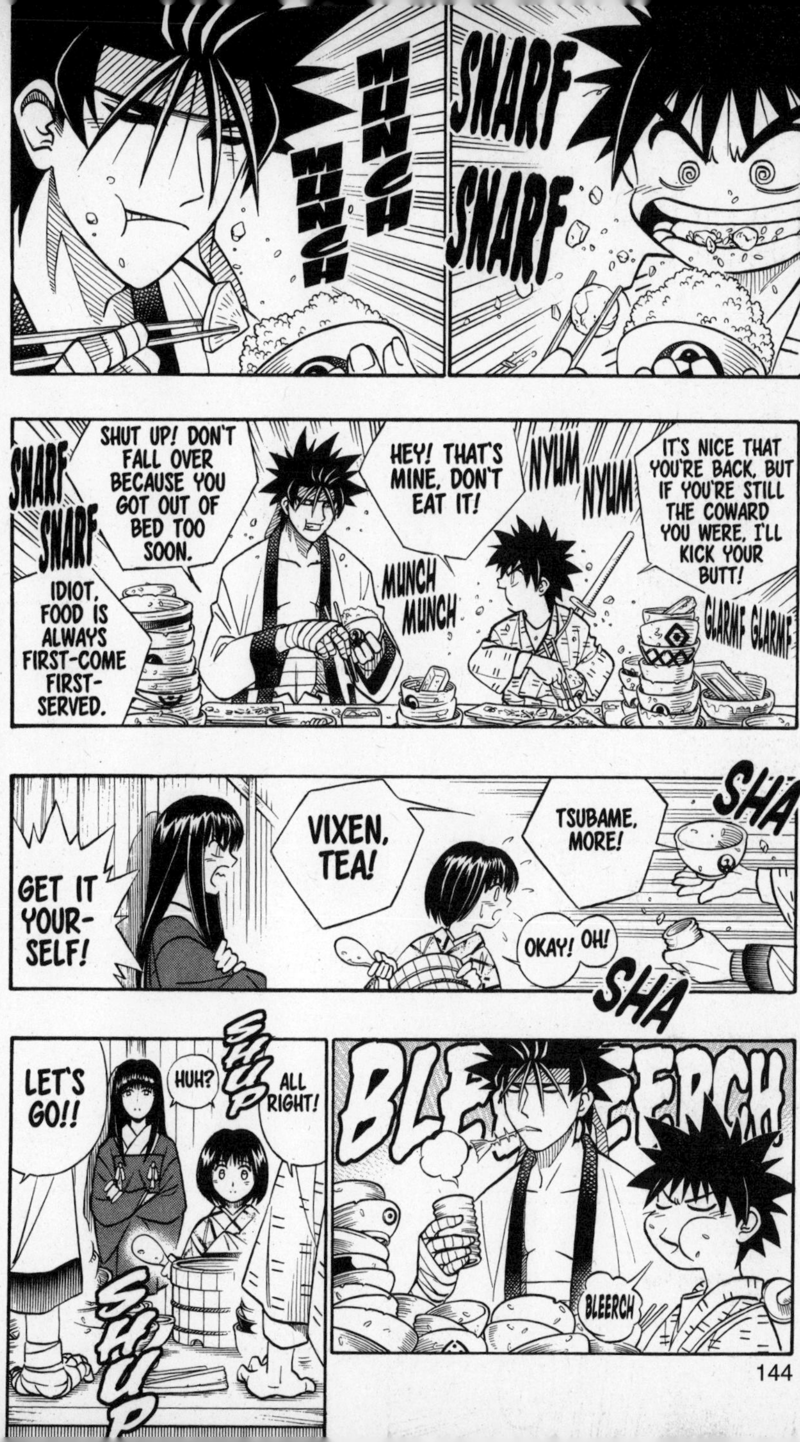
SNARF
SNARF
MUNCH
MUNCH
IT'S NICE THAT YOU'RE BACK, BUT IF YOU'RE STILL THE COWARD YOU WERE, I'LL KICK YOUR BUTT!
GLARMF GLARMF
NYUM
NYUM
HEY! THAT'S MINE, DON'T EAT IT!
MUNCH MUNCH
SHUT UP! DON'T FALL OVER BECAUSE YOU GOT OUT OF BED TOO SOON.
SNARF
SNARF
IDIOT, FOOD IS ALWAYS FIRST-COME FIRST-SERVED.
SHA
TSUBAME, MORE!
OKAY! OH!
SHA
VIXEN, TEA!
GET IT YOURSELF!
BLEEERCH
BLEERCH
ALL RIGHT!
SHUP
HUH?
LET'S GO!!
SHUP

READ THIS WAY

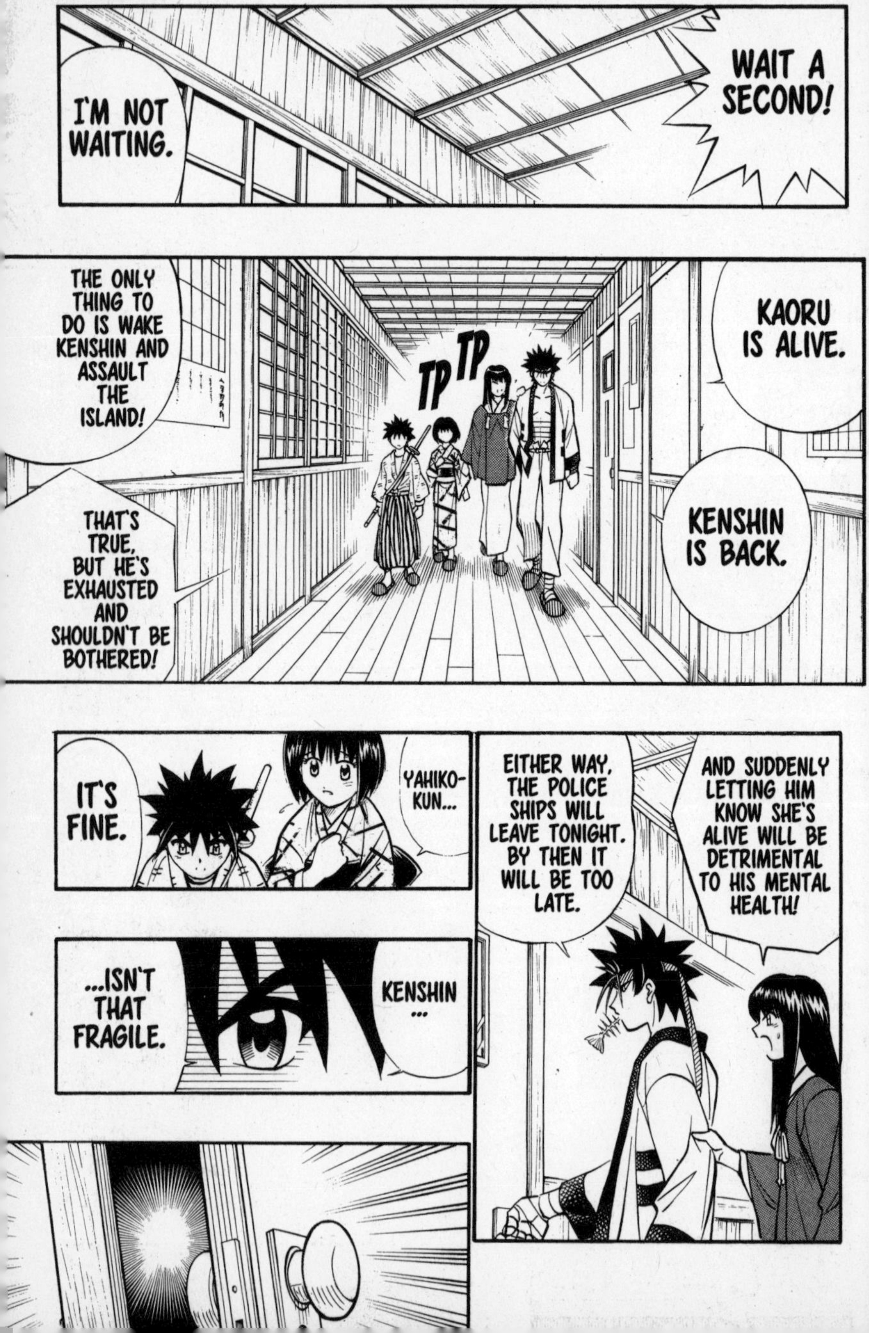
WAIT A SECOND!
I'M NOT WAITING.
TP TP
KAORU IS ALIVE.
KENSHIN IS BACK.
THE ONLY THING TO DO IS WAKE KENSHIN AND ASSAULT THE ISLAND!
THAT'S TRUE, BUT HE'S EXHAUSTED AND SHOULDN'T BE BOTHERED!
AND SUDDENLY LETTING HIM KNOW SHE'S ALIVE WILL BE DETRIMENTAL TO HIS MENTAL HEALTH!
EITHER WAY, THE POLICE SHIPS WILL LEAVE TONIGHT. BY THEN IT WILL BE TOO LATE.
YAHIKO-KUN...
IT'S FINE.
KENSHIN...
...ISN'T THAT FRAGILE.

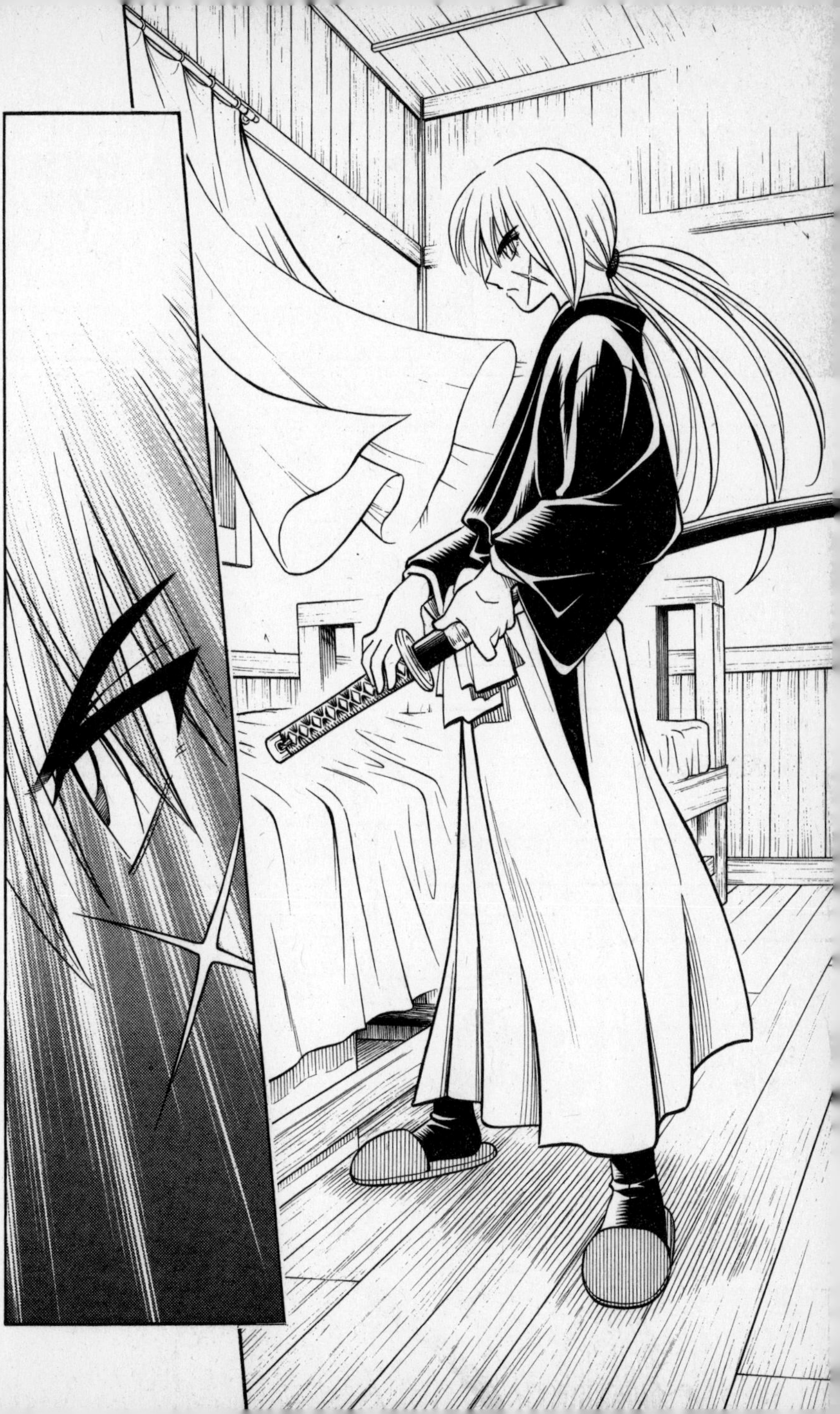

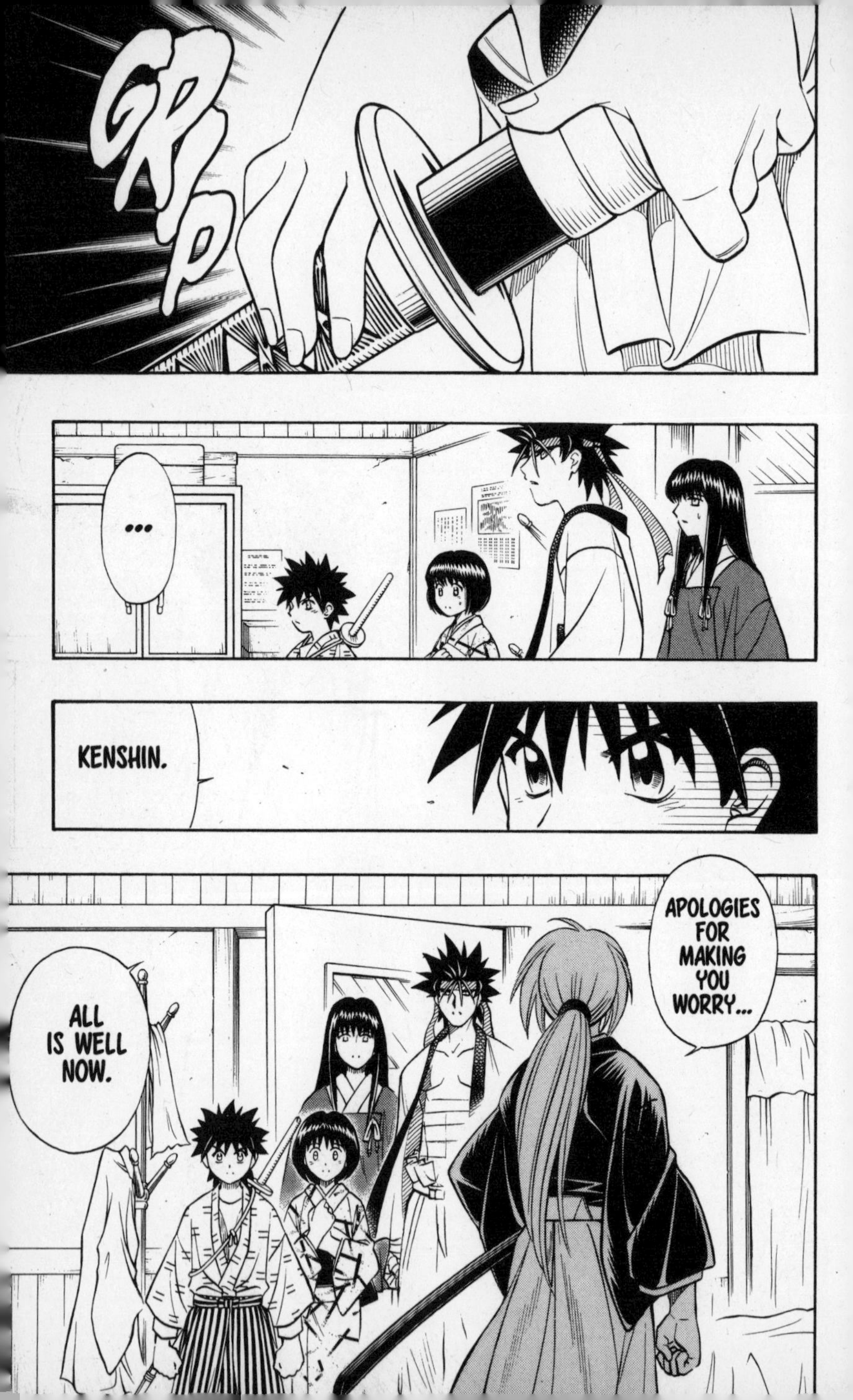
GRIP
...
KENSHIN.
APOLOGIES FOR MAKING YOU WORRY...
ALL IS WELL NOW.

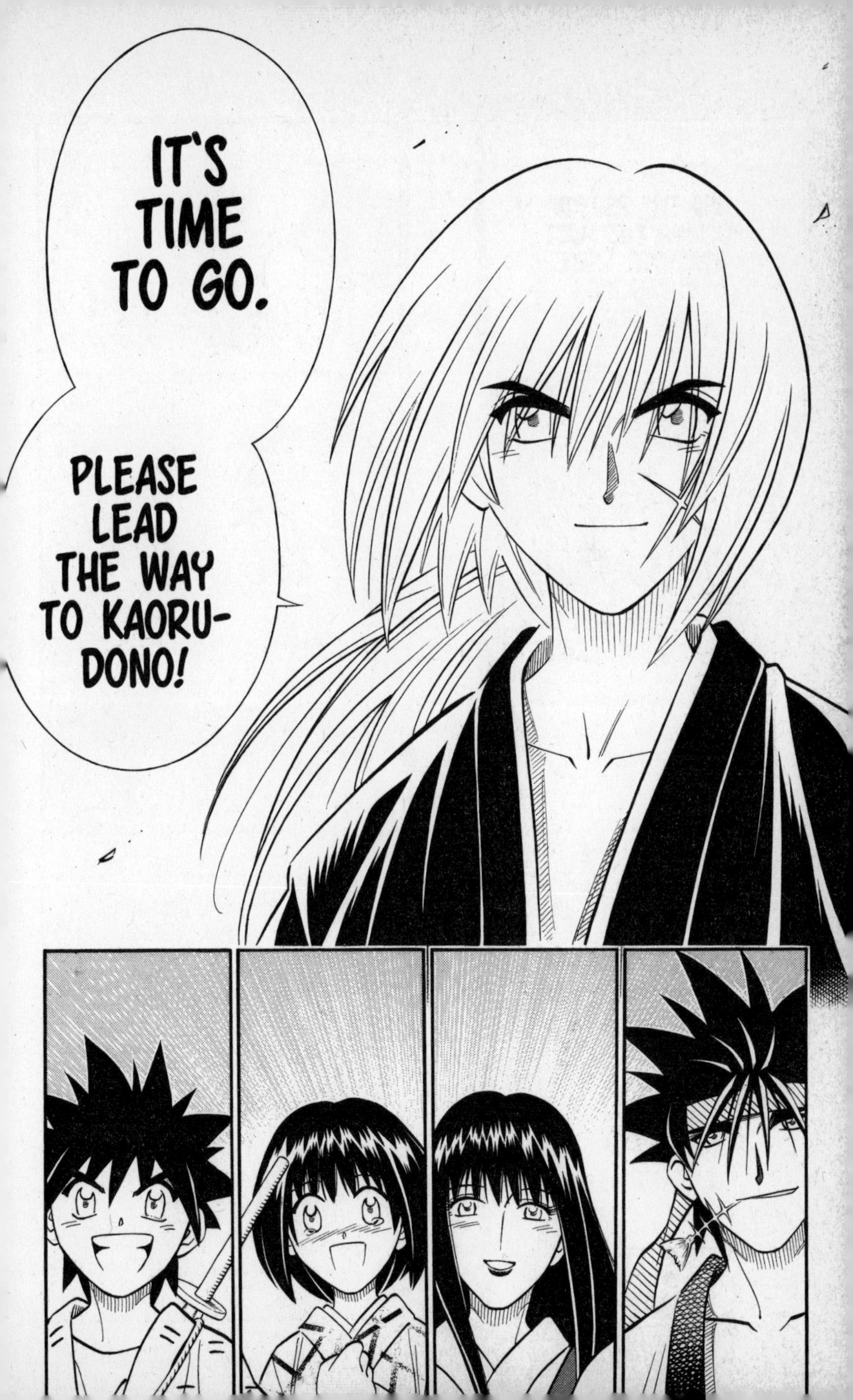
IT'S TIME TO GO.
PLEASE LEAD THE WAY TO KAORU-DONO!

READ THIS WAY

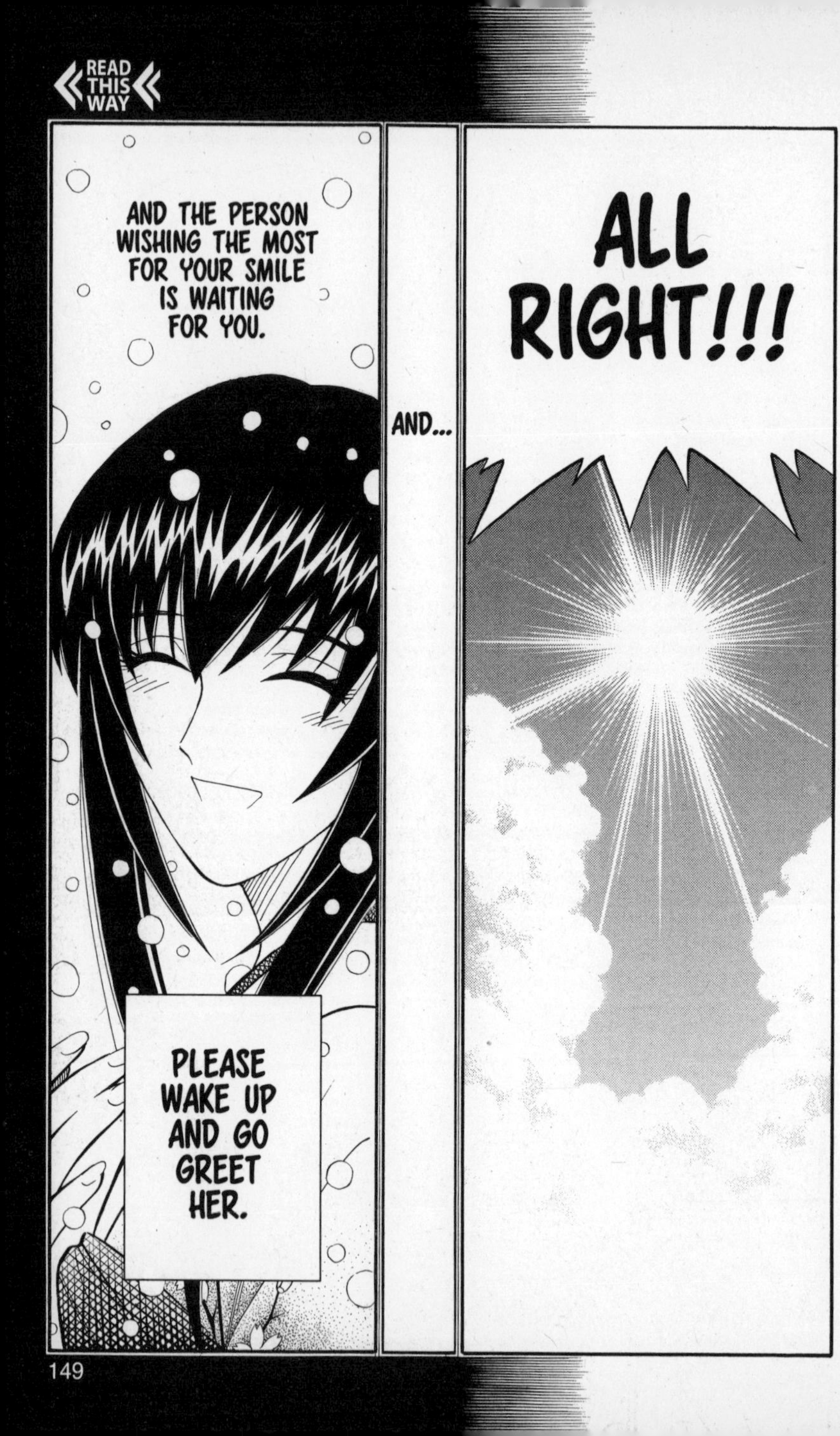
ALL RIGHT!!!
AND...
AND THE PERSON WISHING THE MOST FOR YOUR SMILE IS WAITING FOR YOU.
PLEASE WAKE UP AND GO GREET HER.

"FREE TALK"〈PART I〉

Yes, it is here. This corner named "FREE TALK" is actually a record of how a manga artist breaks down in five years of fierce work. It is titled "A record! How a wretch is made." Long time no see, this is Watsuki.

Now, let's go ahead and go into feature number one of this corner—figure talk. Action figures are so-so, as usual. The conclusion of *X-Men* (Toy Biz) has gradually been showing its effects. It seems that the Japanese translation of the comics were discontinued around the same time, making the whole thing worse. There are some interesting things like the sports series and such, but for Watsuki, *X-Men* was the best... In contrast to the early summer warmth, autumn gusts are blowing inside my heart.

Not to fill that gap, but the "Gachapon" is at the peak of its fever. *Gundam, SD Gundam* (BANDAI), *To Heart, Samurai Spirits* (Yujin), etc. have been collected one after another. For Watsuki, who has collected a box full of the *Ultraman* monster erasers, the act of turning the handle of the "Gachapon" machine is a moment of happiness and excitement right there. Back then, it was 20 yen each, and now it is 10 times that, at 200 yen each! But the economic power of an adult covers this. However, a grown man of about 180 cm with an unshaven beard, curled over in excitement in front of these machines, is embarrassing enough. So I go to the toy stores right at opening or right before closing. Gacha gacha.

Feature two of this corner—the games. I have been playing the two titles I mentioned before (in vol. 25) in between work. First is *Rising Zan* (UEP Systems, PS), a 3D gun action game. A samurai gunman protagonist hustles around, slashing and shooting villains with super-wrong views of Japanese culture. It's a hopelessly moronic game! So moronic I love it!! The dramatization and names aimed for laughs are so catchy. Due to my unfamiliarity with 3D games, I haven't been able to advance much, but the refreshing nature of the hustling and manly law breaking events of mashing every button are so fun. I recommend it to adults who understand that at times the word stupid is said with the highest level of love.

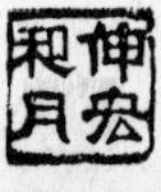

伸宏
和月

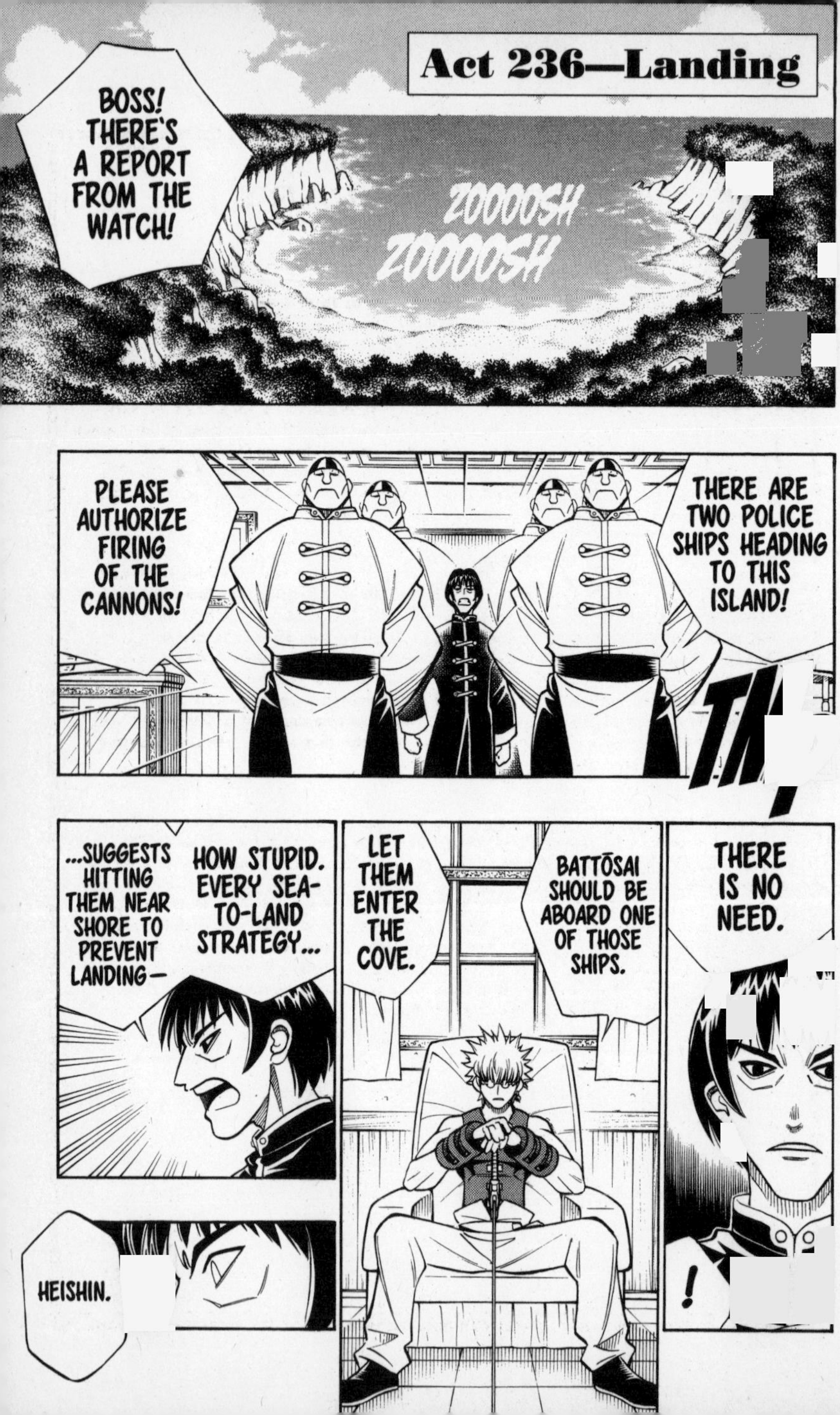
Act 236—Landing
BOSS! THERE'S A REPORT FROM THE WATCH!
ZOOOOSH ZOOOOOSH
THERE ARE TWO POLICE SHIPS HEADING TO THIS ISLAND!
PLEASE AUTHORIZE FIRING OF THE CANNONS!
THERE IS NO NEED.
!
BATTŌSAI SHOULD BE ABOARD ONE OF THOSE SHIPS.
LET THEM ENTER THE COVE.
HOW STUPID. EVERY SEA-TO-LAND STRATEGY...
...SUGGESTS HITTING THEM NEAR SHORE TO PREVENT LANDING—
HEISHIN.

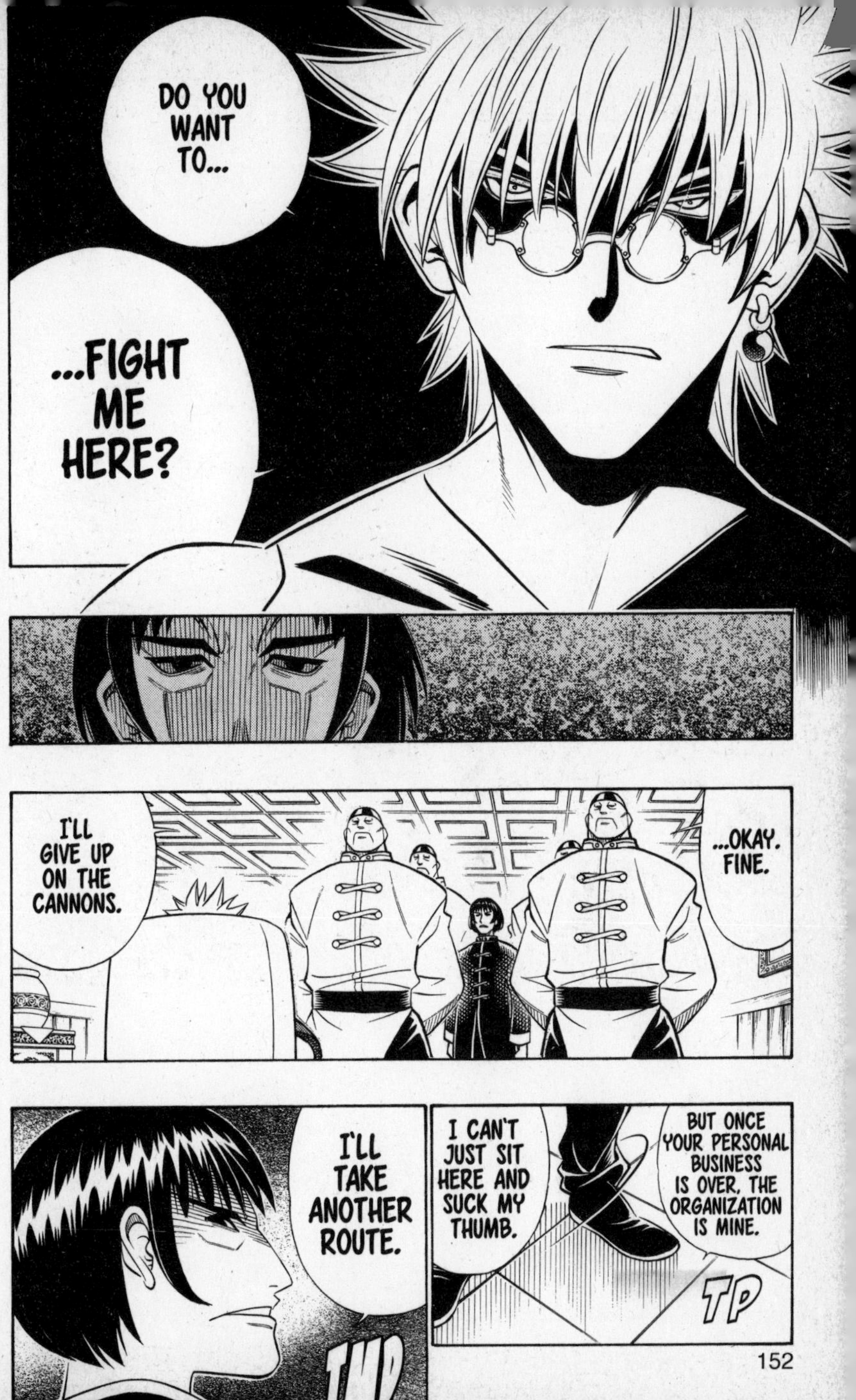
DO YOU WANT TO...
...FIGHT ME HERE?
...OKAY. FINE.
I'LL GIVE UP ON THE CANNONS.
BUT ONCE YOUR PERSONAL BUSINESS IS OVER, THE ORGANIZATION IS MINE.
I CAN'T JUST SIT HERE AND SUCK MY THUMB.
TP
I'LL TAKE ANOTHER ROUTE.
THMP

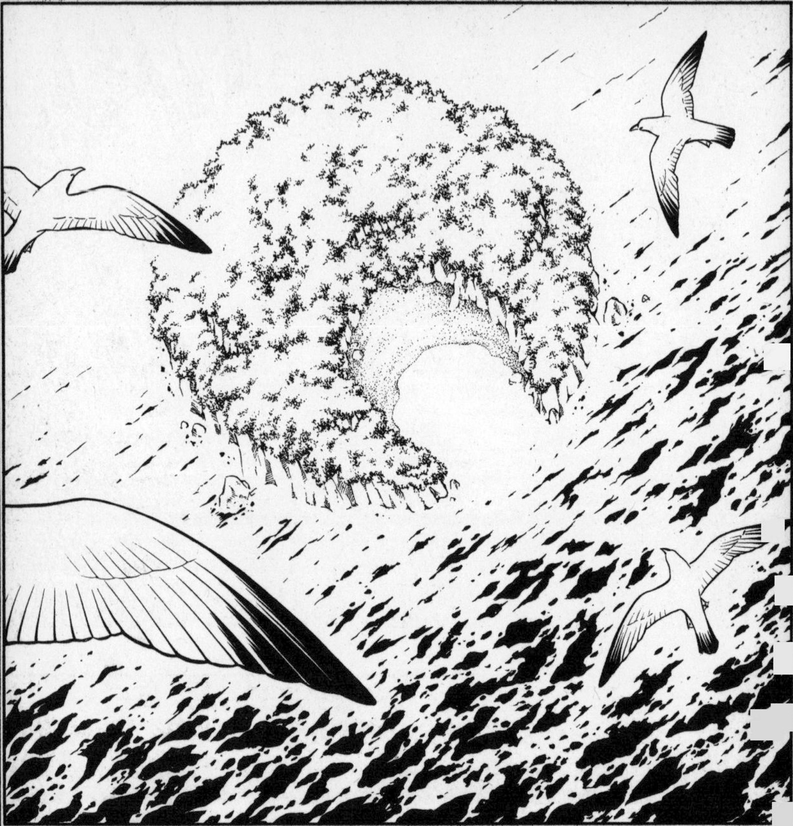

Act 236
Landing

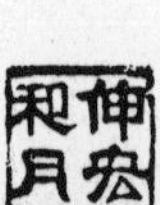
伸宏
和月

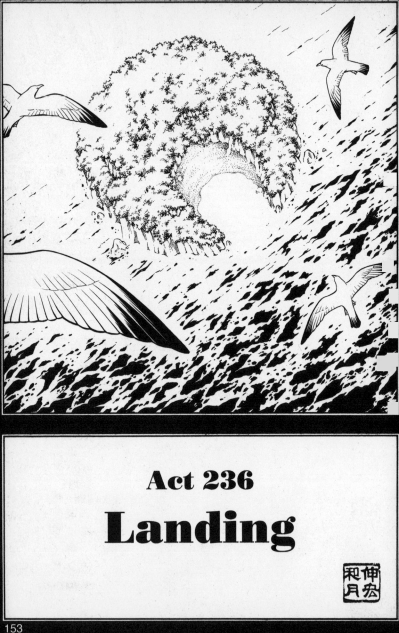

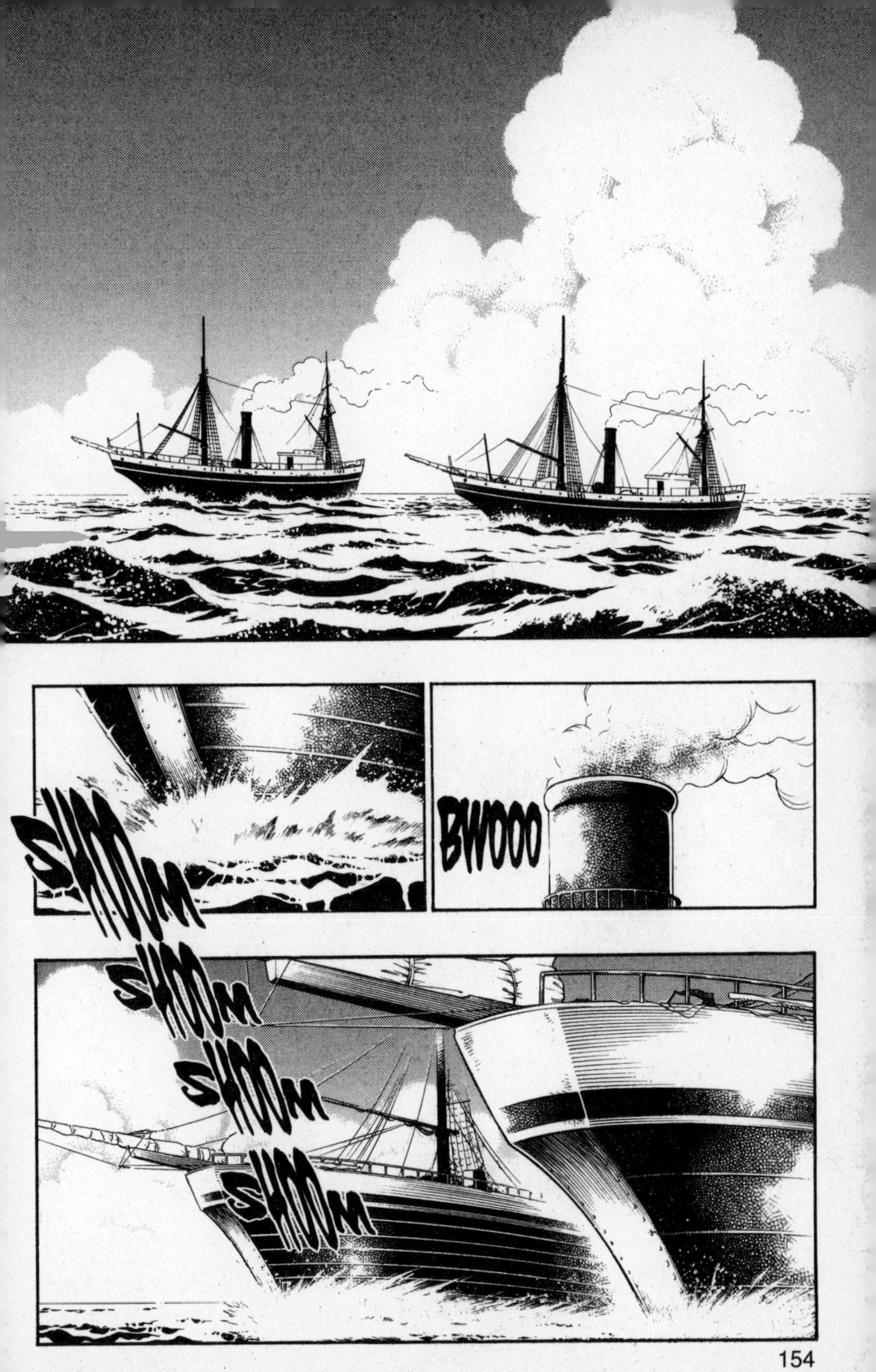
BWOOO
SHOOM
SHOOM
SHOOM
SHOOM

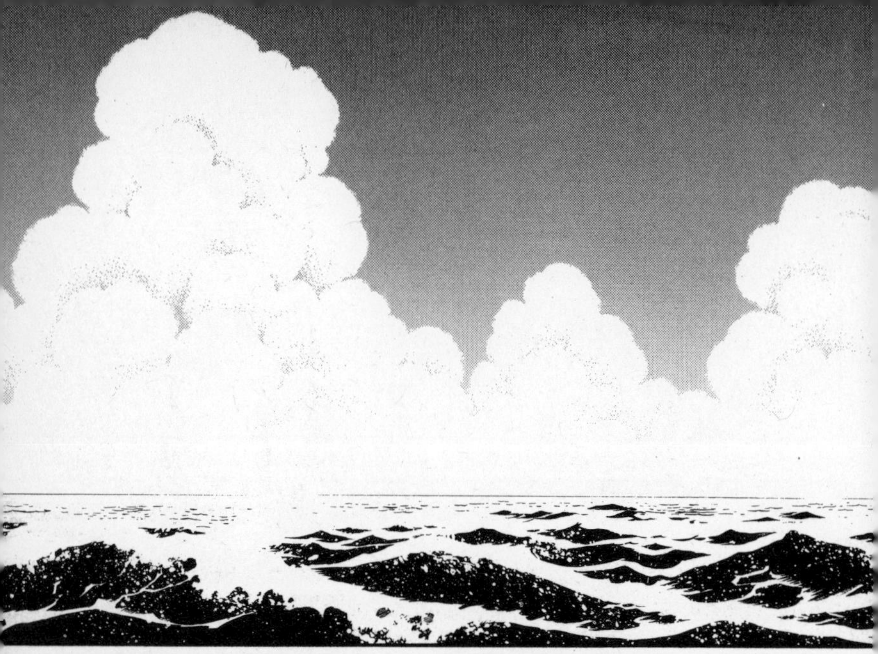

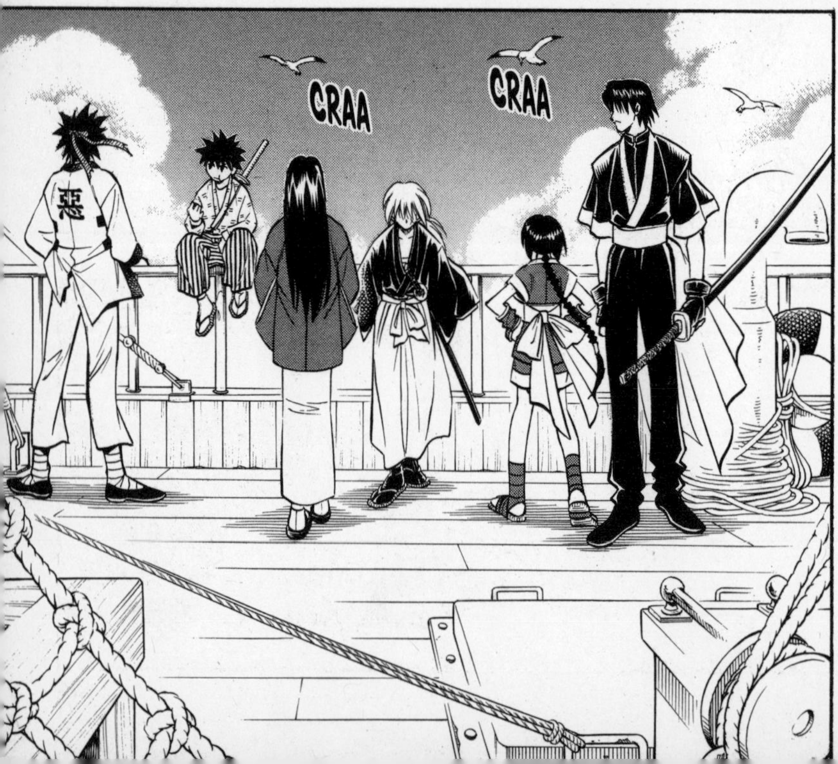
CRAA
CRAA

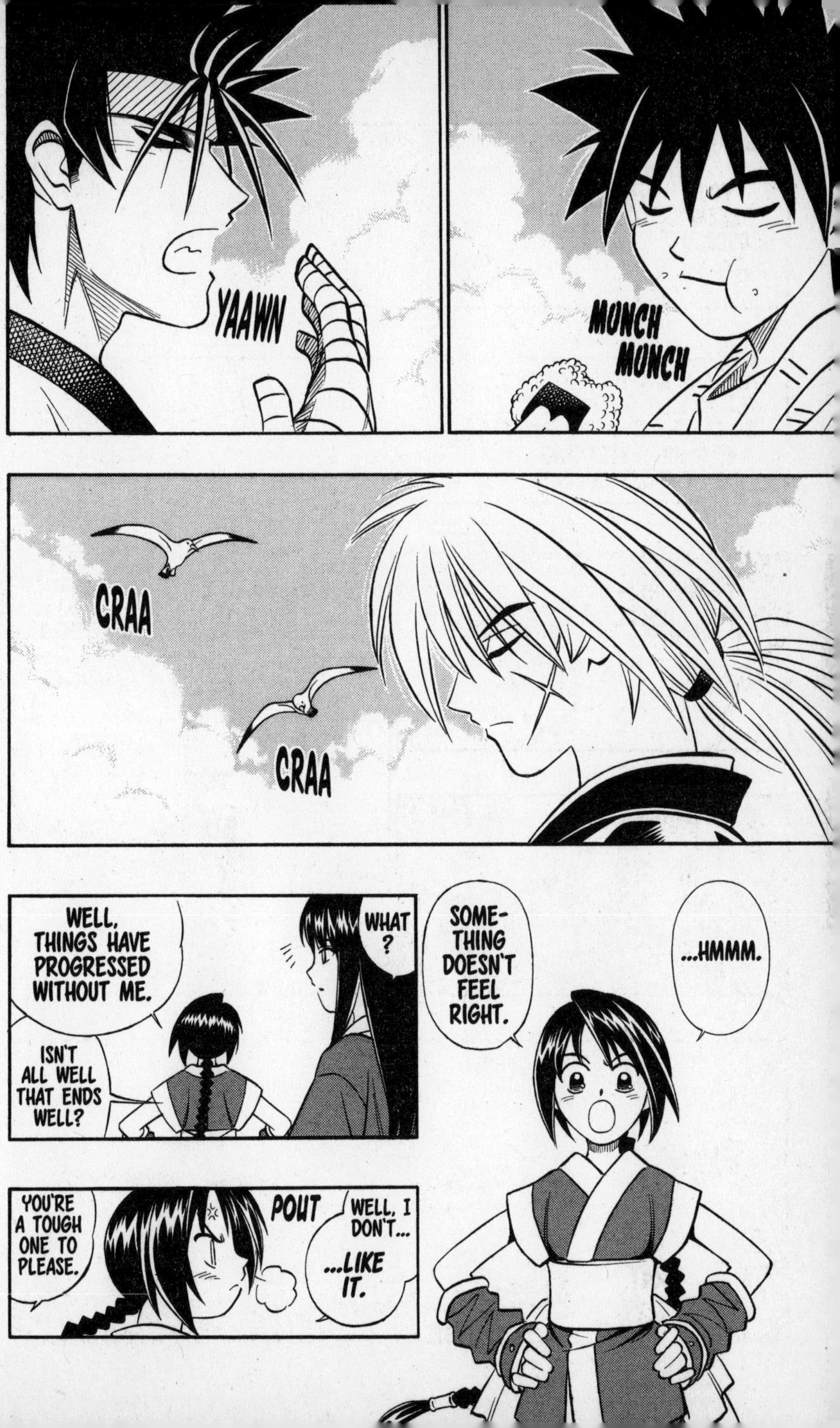
MUNCH MUNCH
YAAWN
CRAA
CRAA
...HMMM.
SOME-THING DOESN'T FEEL RIGHT.
WHAT?
WELL, THINGS HAVE PROGRESSED WITHOUT ME.
ISN'T ALL WELL THAT ENDS WELL?
WELL, I DON'T...
...LIKE IT.
POUT
YOU'RE A TOUGH ONE TO PLEASE.

READ THIS WAY

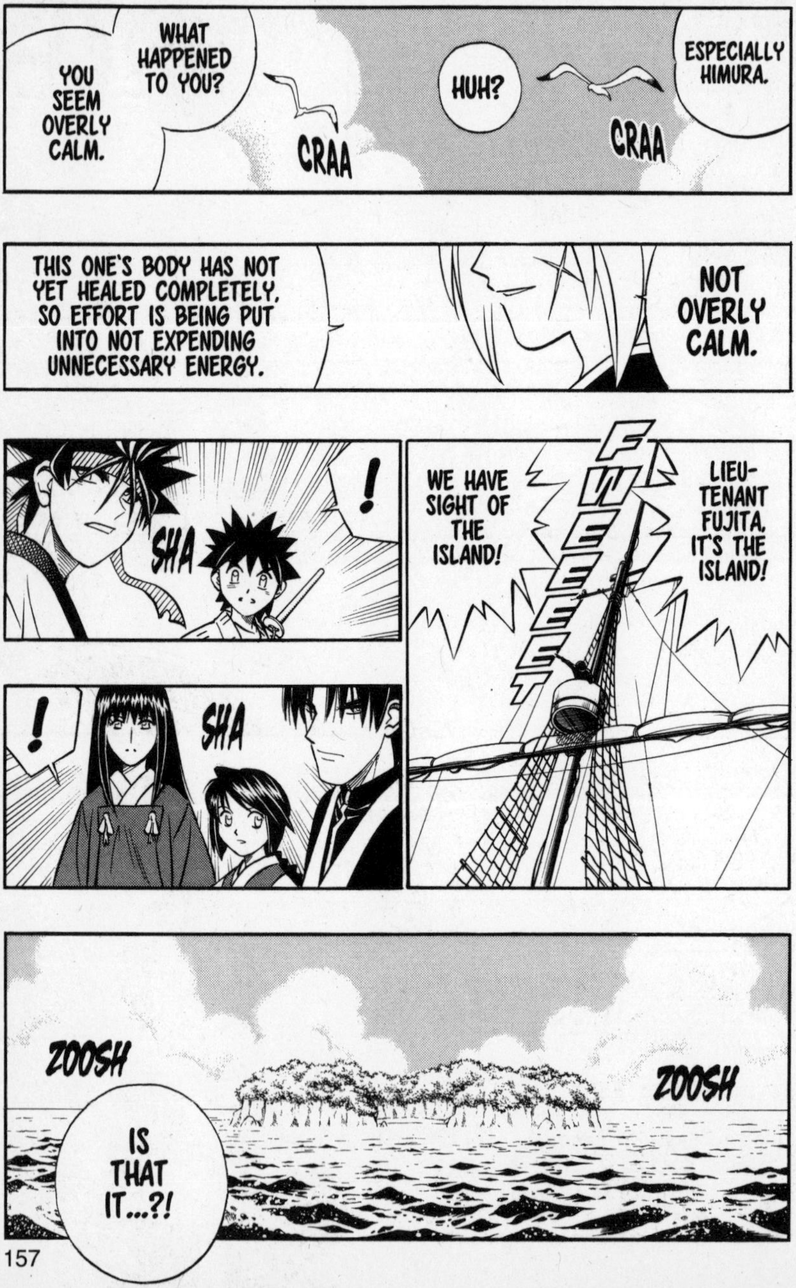

ESPECIALLY HIMURA.
CRAA
HUH?
CRAA
WHAT HAPPENED TO YOU?
YOU SEEM OVERLY CALM.
NOT OVERLY CALM.
THIS ONE'S BODY HAS NOT YET HEALED COMPLETELY, SO EFFORT IS BEING PUT INTO NOT EXPENDING UNNECESSARY ENERGY.
LIEU-TENANT FUJITA, IT'S THE ISLAND!
FWEEEEET
WE HAVE SIGHT OF THE ISLAND!
!
SHA
SHA
!
ZOOSH
ZOOSH
IS THAT IT...?!

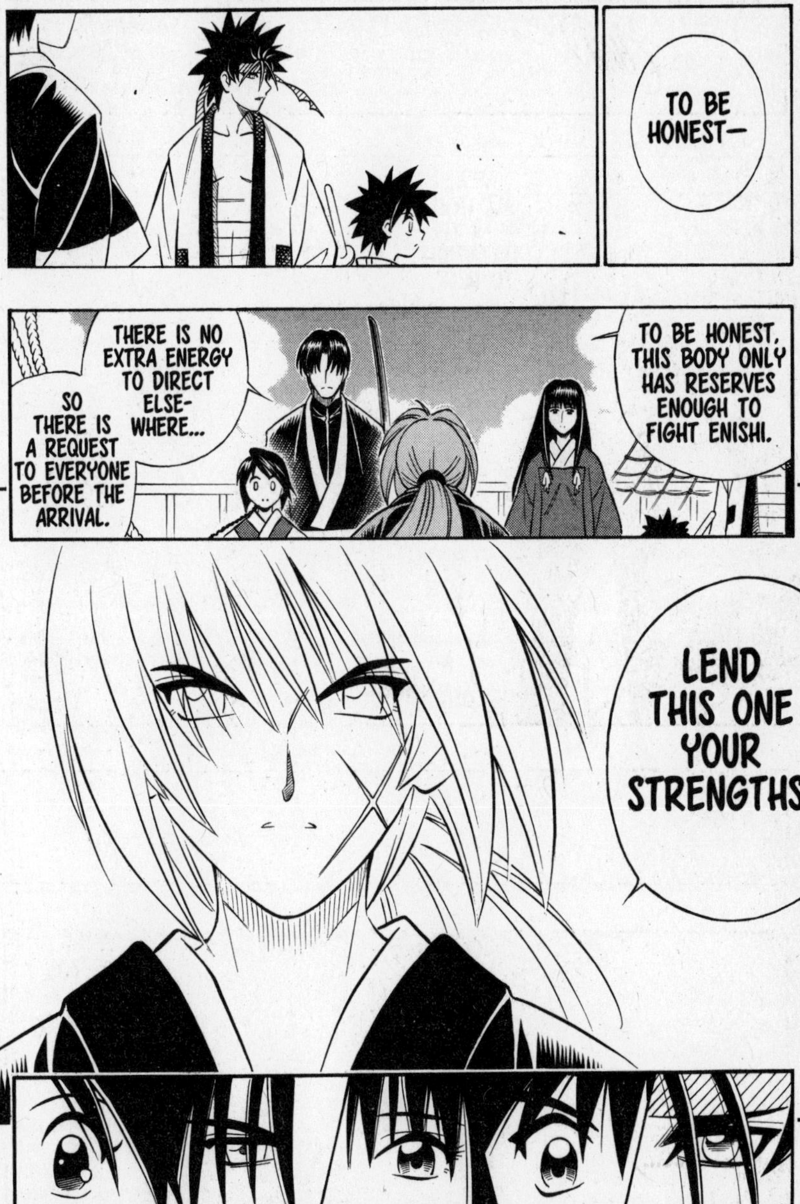
TO BE HONEST—
TO BE HONEST, THIS BODY ONLY HAS RESERVES ENOUGH TO FIGHT ENISHI.
THERE IS NO EXTRA ENERGY TO DIRECT ELSE-WHERE...
SO THERE IS A REQUEST TO EVERYONE BEFORE THE ARRIVAL.
LEND THIS ONE YOUR STRENGTHS.

READ THIS WAY

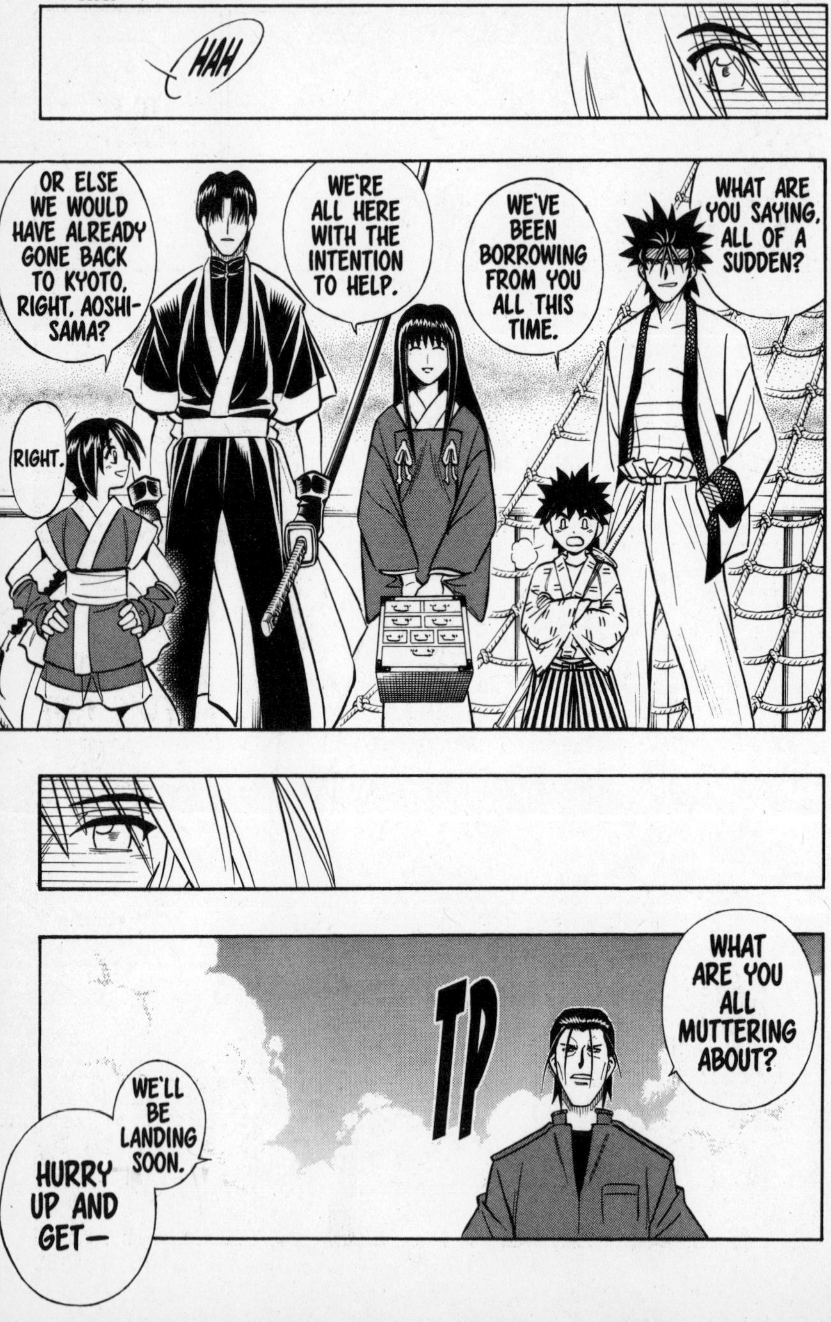
HAH
WHAT ARE YOU SAYING, ALL OF A SUDDEN?
WE'VE BEEN BORROWING FROM YOU ALL THIS TIME.
WE'RE ALL HERE WITH THE INTENTION TO HELP.
OR ELSE WE WOULD HAVE ALREADY GONE BACK TO KYOTO, RIGHT, AOSHI-SAMA?
RIGHT.
WHAT ARE YOU ALL MUTTERING ABOUT?
TP
WE'LL BE LANDING SOON.
HURRY UP AND GET—

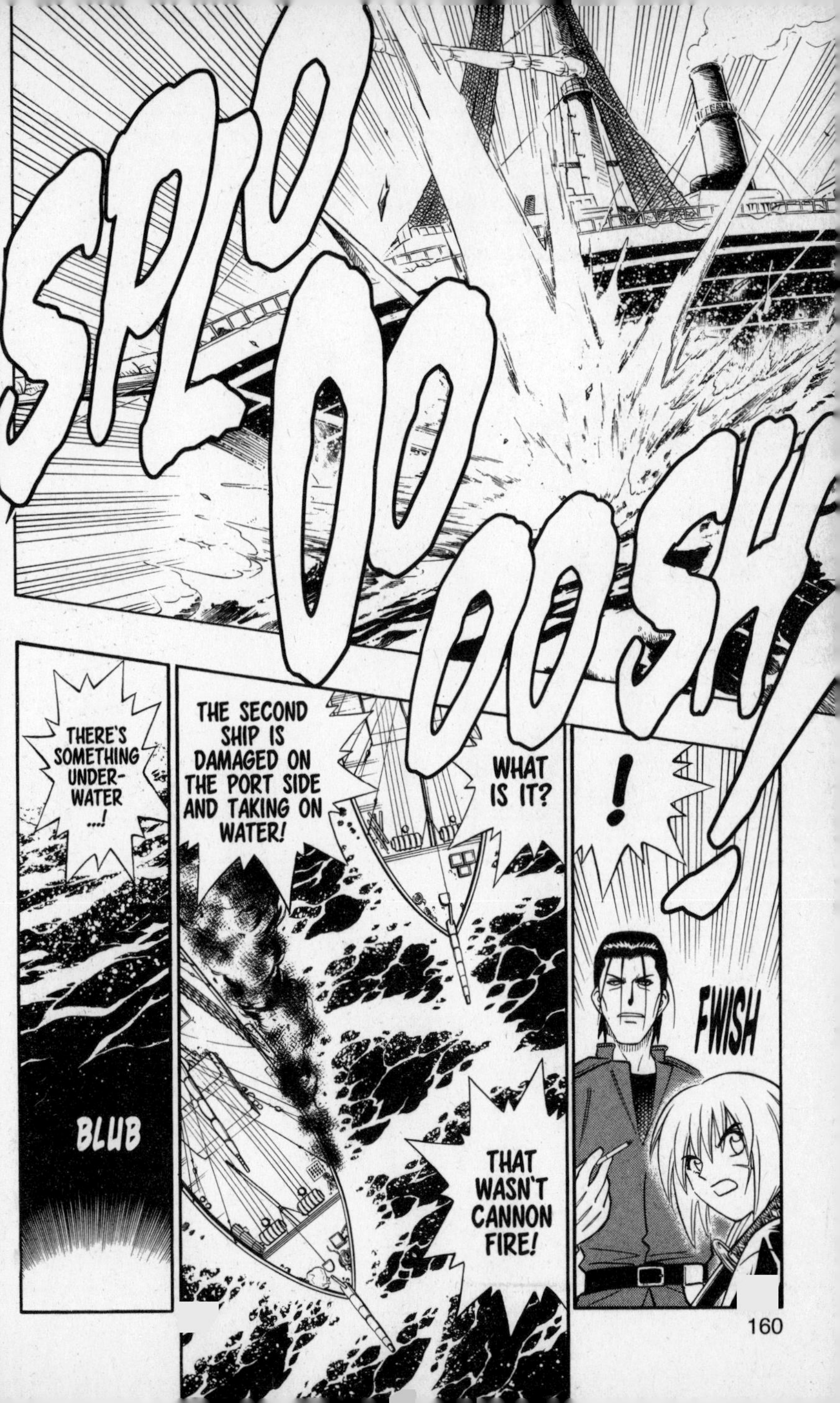
SPLOOOOOSH!
!
FWISH
WHAT IS IT?
THE SECOND SHIP IS DAMAGED ON THE PORT SIDE AND TAKING ON WATER!
THAT WASN'T CANNON FIRE!
THERE'S SOMETHING UNDER-WATER ...!
BLUB

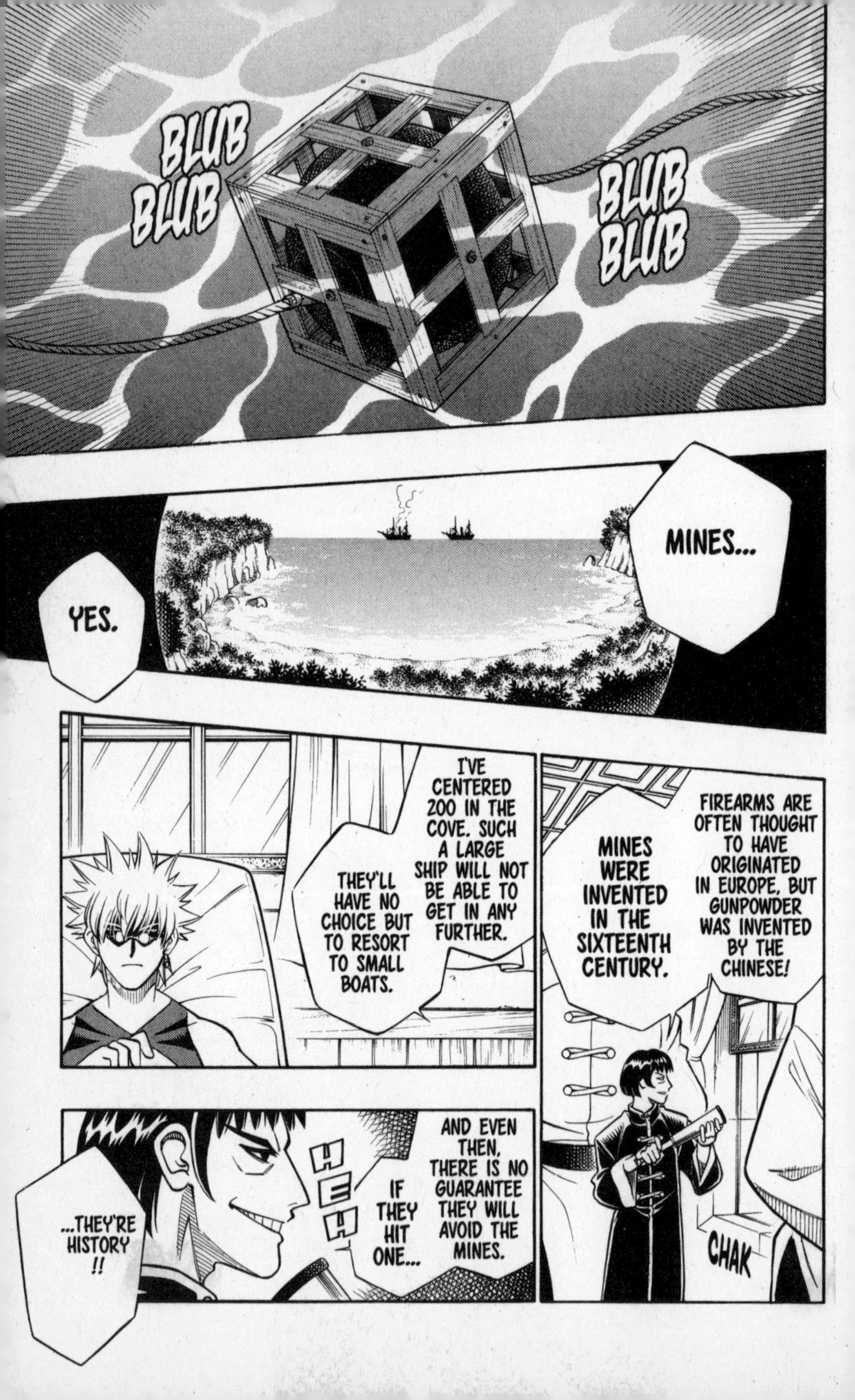
BLUB BLUB
BLUB BLUB
MINES...
YES.
FIREARMS ARE OFTEN THOUGHT TO HAVE ORIGINATED IN EUROPE, BUT GUNPOWDER WAS INVENTED BY THE CHINESE!
MINES WERE INVENTED IN THE SIXTEENTH CENTURY.
CHAK
I'VE CENTERED ZOO IN THE COVE. SUCH A LARGE SHIP WILL NOT BE ABLE TO GET IN ANY FURTHER.
THEY'LL HAVE NO CHOICE BUT TO RESORT TO SMALL BOATS.
AND EVEN THEN, THERE IS NO GUARANTEE THEY WILL AVOID THE MINES.
IF THEY HIT ONE...
HEH
...THEY'RE HISTORY !!

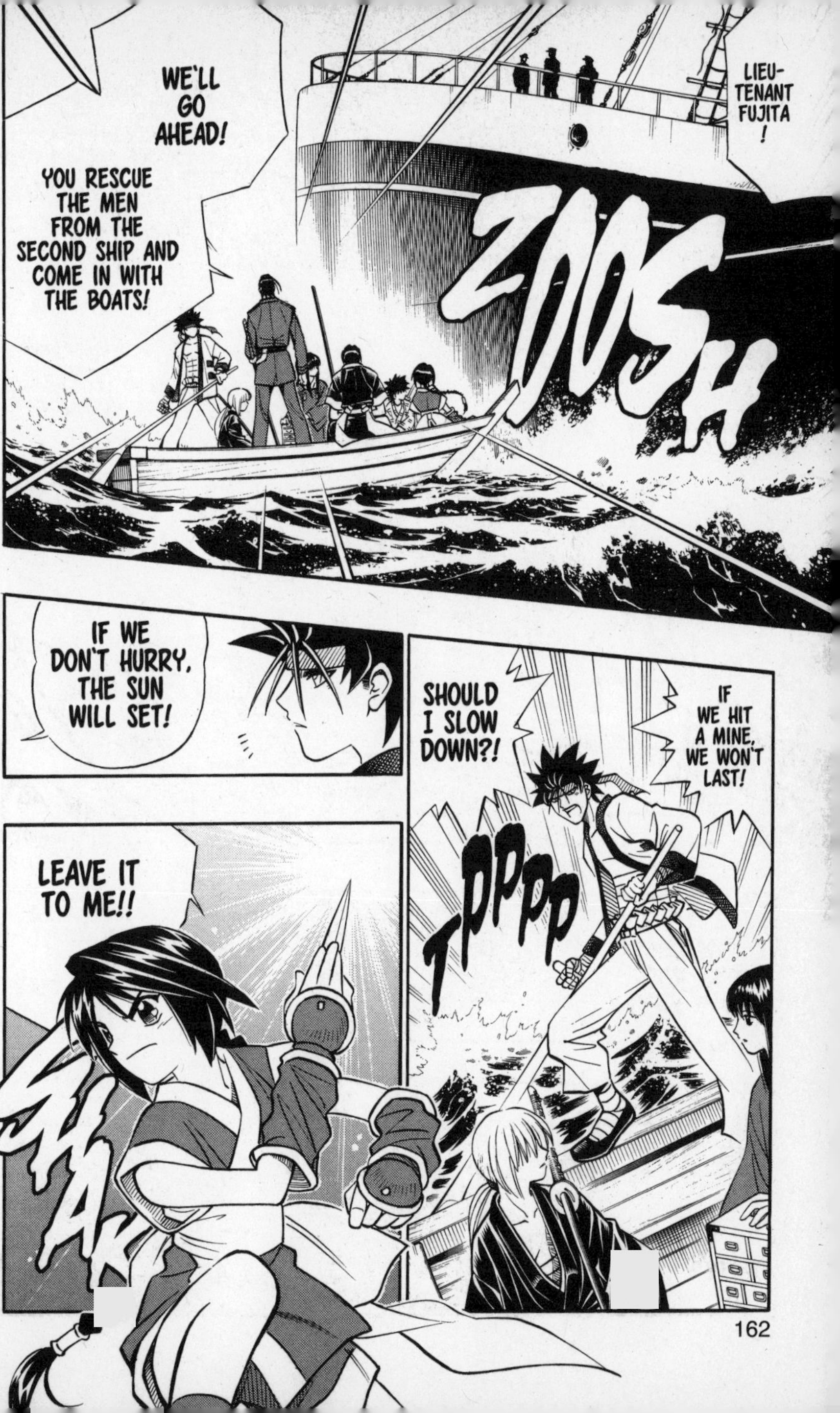
LIEUTENANT FUJITA!
WE'LL GO AHEAD!
YOU RESCUE THE MEN FROM THE SECOND SHIP AND COME IN WITH THE BOATS!
ZOOSH
IF WE HIT A MINE, WE WON'T LAST!
SHOULD I SLOW DOWN?!
TPPPP
IF WE DON'T HURRY, THE SUN WILL SET!
LEAVE IT TO ME!!

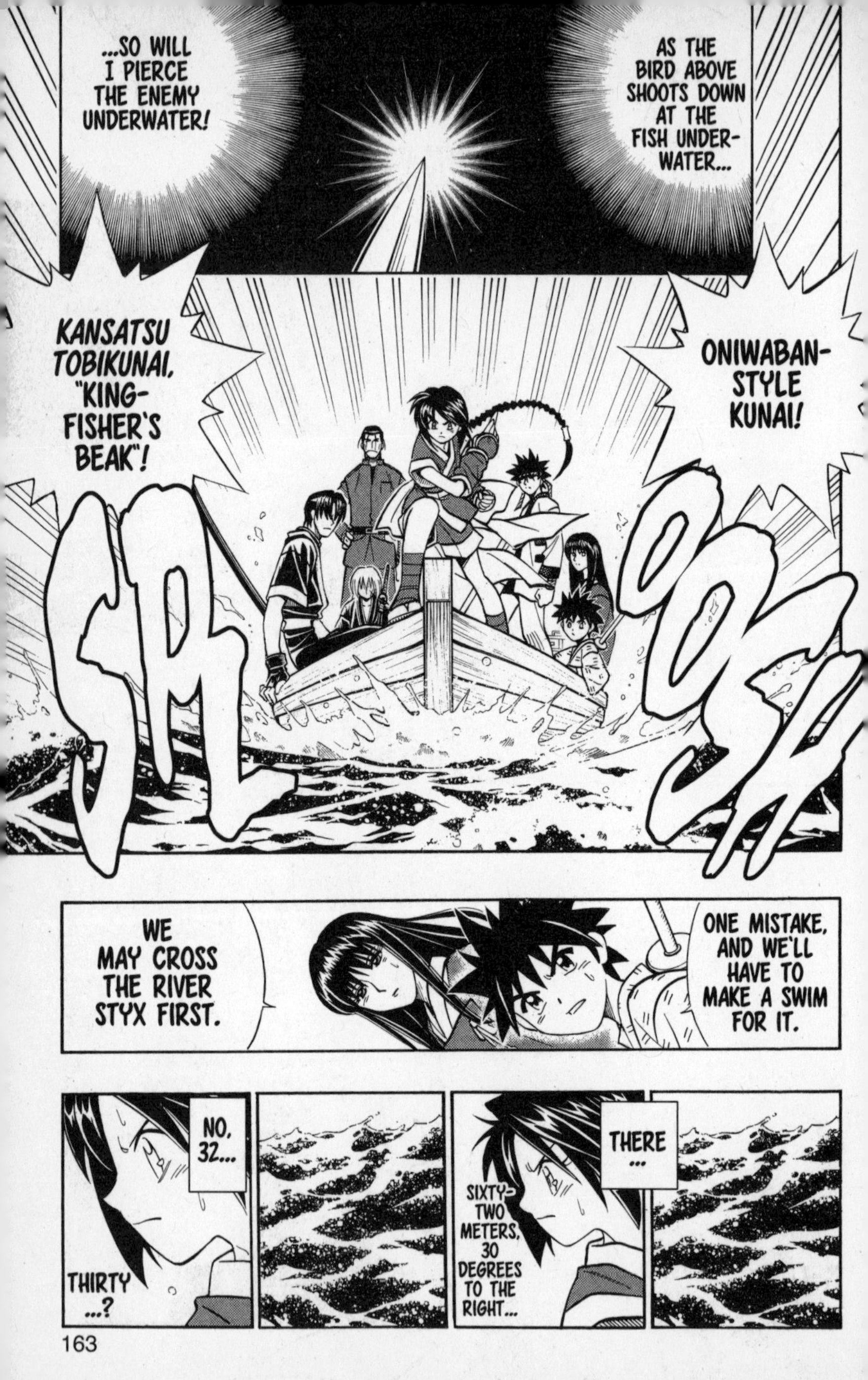
AS THE BIRD ABOVE SHOOTS DOWN AT THE FISH UNDER-WATER...
...SO WILL I PIERCE THE ENEMY UNDERWATER!
ONIWABAN-STYLE KUNAI!
KANSATSU TOBIKUNAI, "KING-FISHER'S BEAK"!
ONE MISTAKE, AND WE'LL HAVE TO MAKE A SWIM FOR IT.
WE MAY CROSS THE RIVER STYX FIRST.
THERE...
SIXTY-TWO METERS, 30 DEGREES TO THE RIGHT...
NO, 32...
THIRTY...?

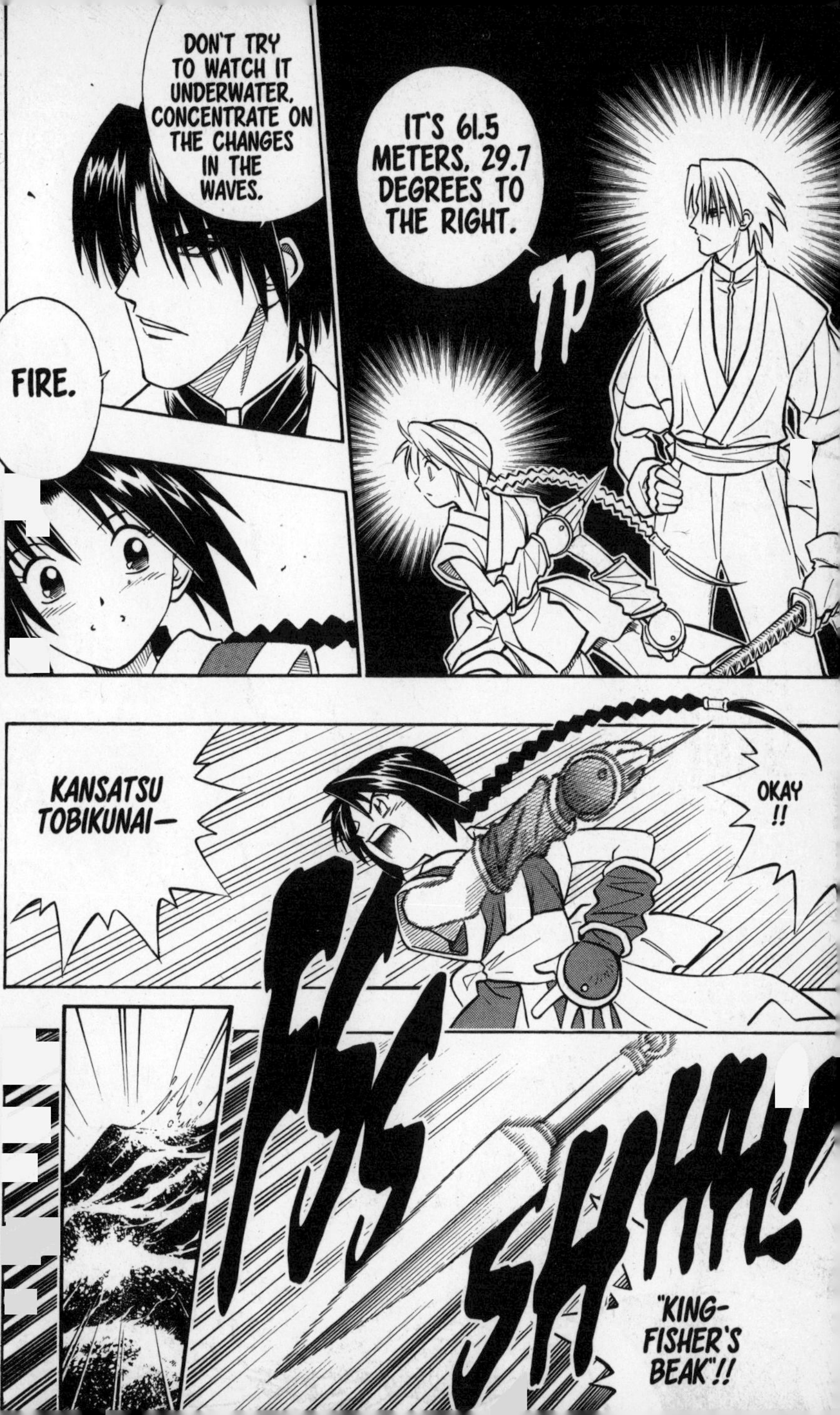
IT'S 61.5 METERS, 29.7 DEGREES TO THE RIGHT.
TP
DON'T TRY TO WATCH IT UNDERWATER, CONCENTRATE ON THE CHANGES IN THE WAVES.
FIRE.
OKAY !!
KANSATSU TOBIKUNAI—
"KING-FISHER'S BEAK"!!

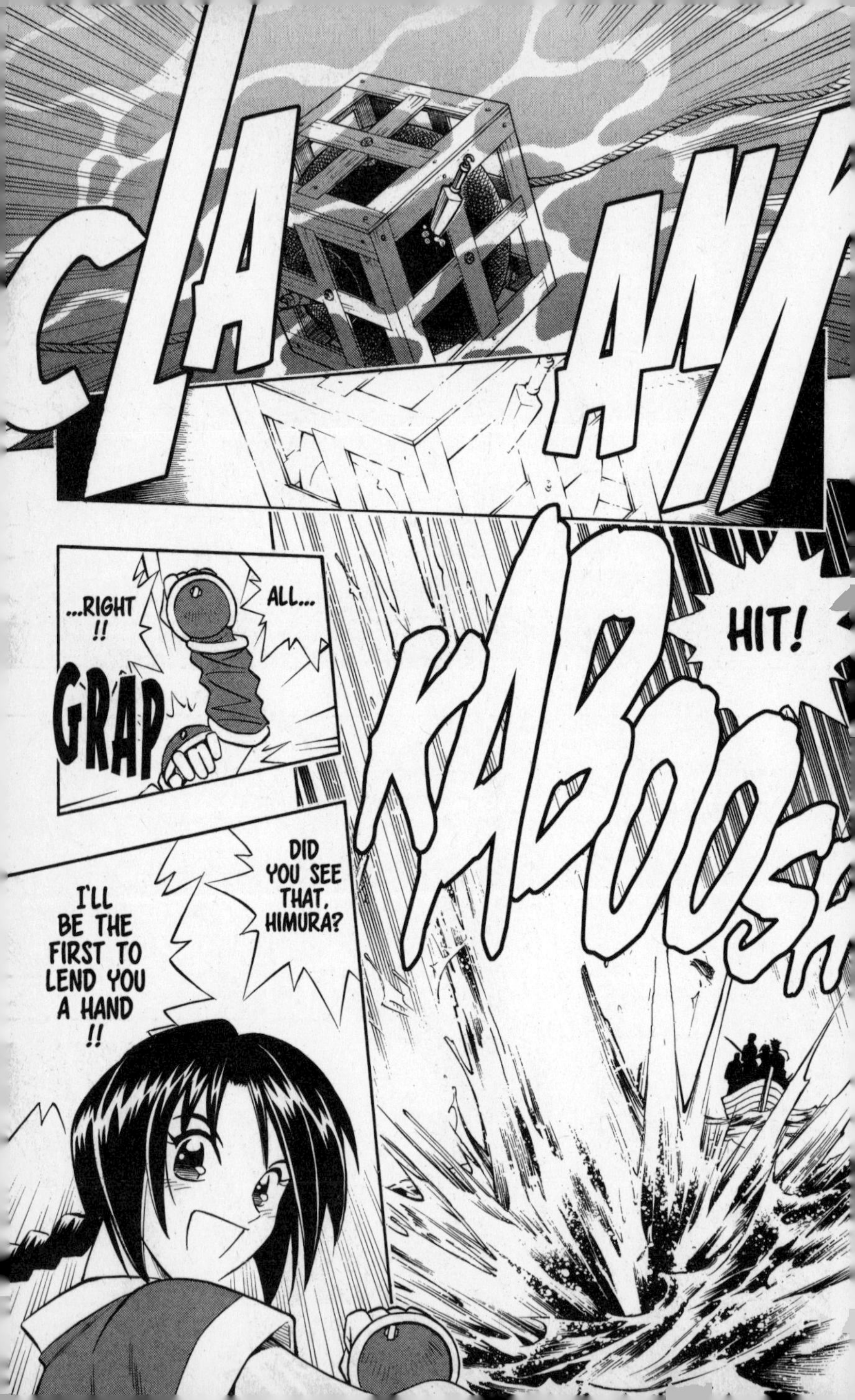
CLAAN
KABOOS
HIT!
ALL...
...RIGHT !!
GRAP
DID YOU SEE THAT, HIMURA?
I'LL BE THE FIRST TO LEND YOU A HAND !!

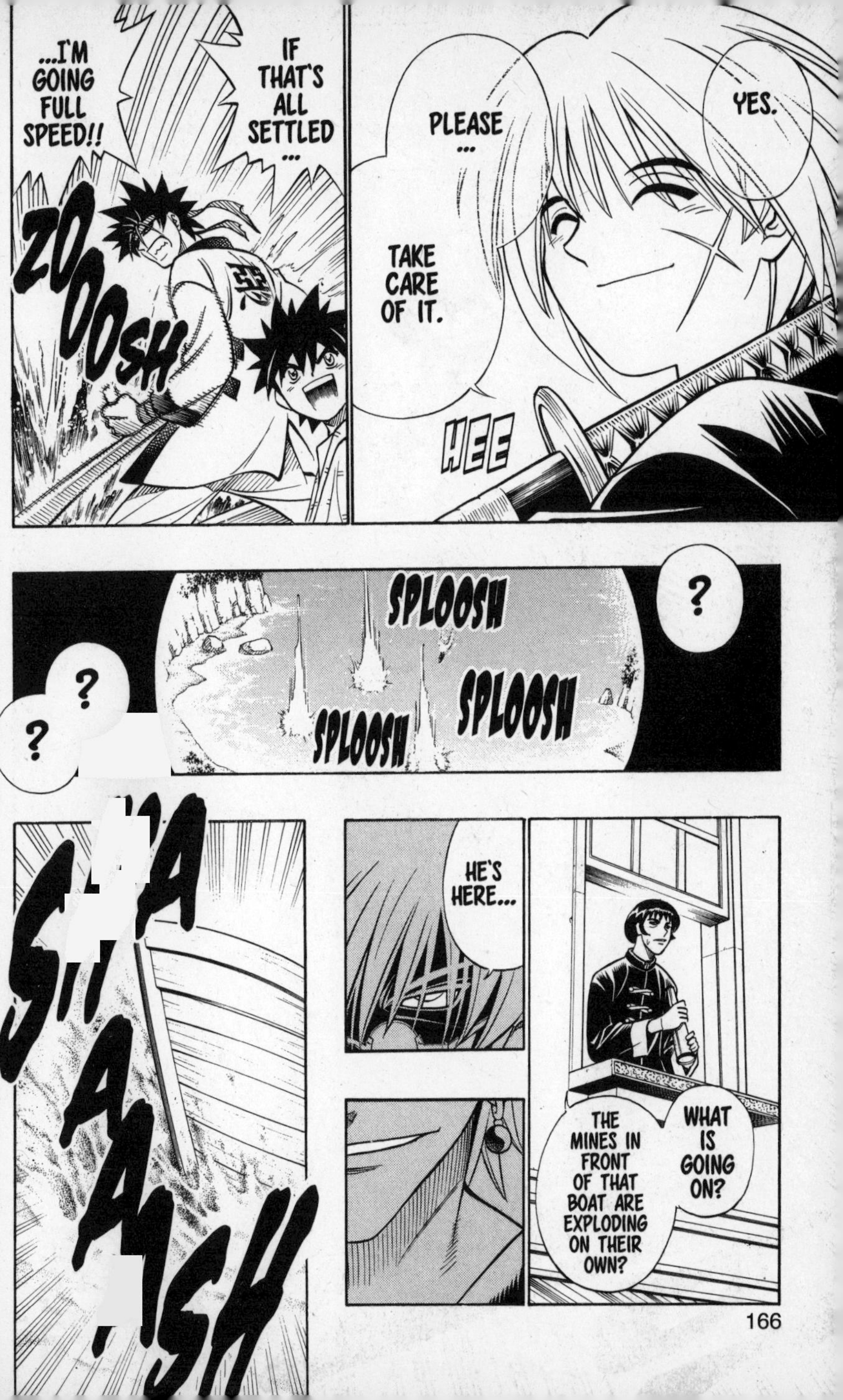
YES.
PLEASE... TAKE CARE OF IT.
HEE
IF THAT'S ALL SETTLED...
...I'M GOING FULL SPEED!!
ZOOOOSH
?
SPLOOSH
SPLOOSH
SPLOOSH
?
?
WHAT IS GOING ON?
THE MINES IN FRONT OF THAT BOAT ARE EXPLODING ON THEIR OWN?
HE'S HERE...

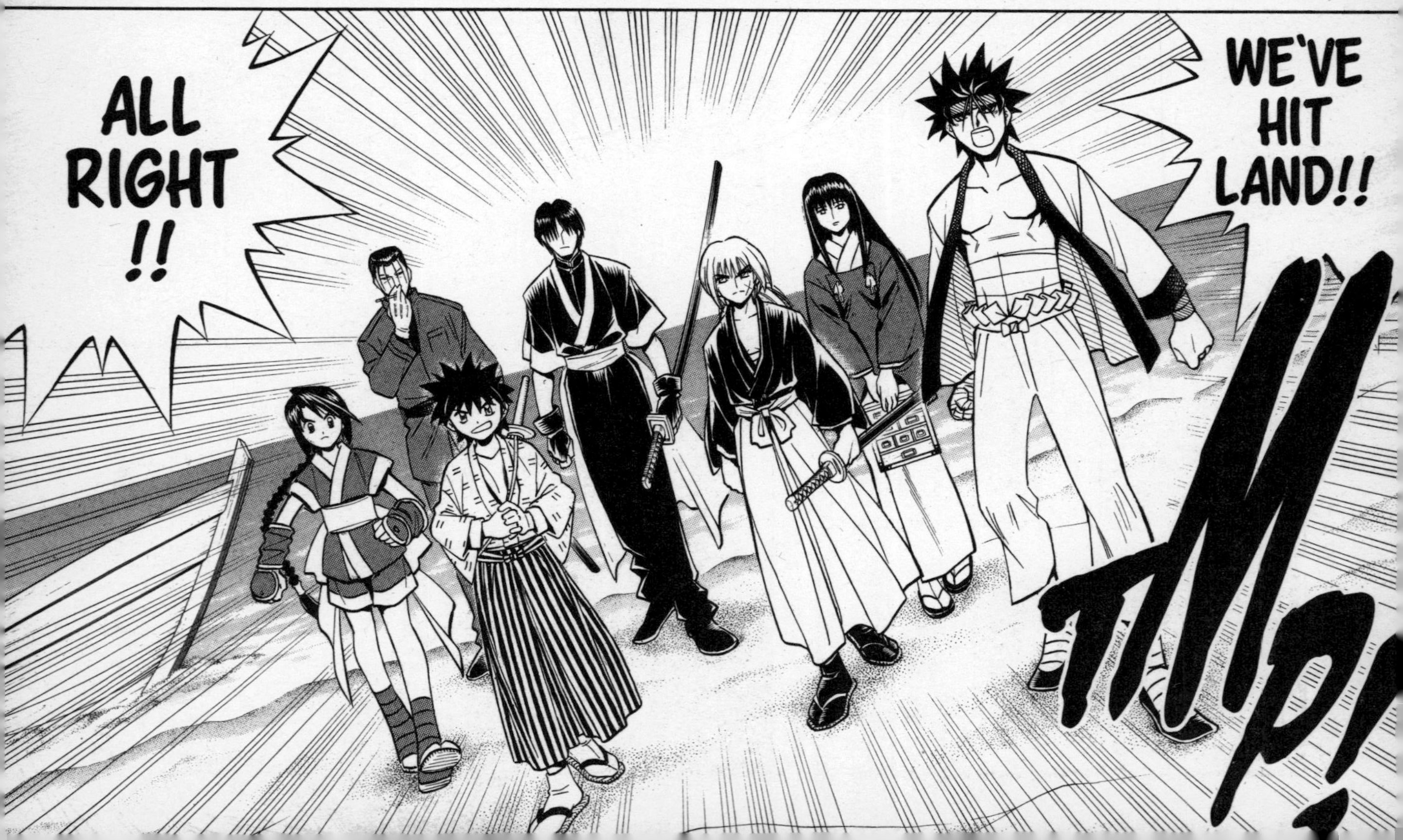
WE'VE HIT LAND!!
TMP!
ALL RIGHT!!

"FREE TALK" 〈PART II〉

The second game may have been evident to you when I mentioned it was a girly game being released around the same time as the last manga volume, but it is *To Heart* (Aquaplus, PS). I may get comments from the people in the forefront of the otaku world like "What, finally? Watsuki is not too good." I'm finally getting to it. *To Heart* (Leaf, PC) was a huge topic in the semi-annual greatest otaku festival held in this certain city. But since it was a PC game AND a love comedy, it was so far off my radar as a manga artist that I thought, "this has nothing to do with me." When it moved onto the PS console, I decided to play it due to the recommendations of my friends. This is the first girly game I've played (I have never played *Sakura Taisen* by Red Company. In the past, Okina had been seen singing a parody song of that theme song, but this is because I bought the soundtrack after an assistant recommended it to me with the words "the music is really good." I was interested in the lore and such, but I never got to play it). Maybe because of that, *To Heart* is a lot of fun. Watsuki suffers a critical hit! From the lessons I learned from *Eva* and *Samu-Supi*, I won't ever get totally hooked as a manga artist, but I am enjoying it as a semi-otaku. At this point, my favorite heroine is Kamigishi Akari. From the left over "Gachapon," a Watsuki's special customized Akari (Akari 2 head + Akari 1 torso + Kotone 2 or Rio's legs and waist put together with flexible eraser, allowing easy exchange! Akari 2 head + Maid Multi Black version is nice also) has been made and is displayed on my desk. This was a while ago, but Tsubame called Yahiko, "Yahiko-*chan*"... Bad sign. It might be affecting me on many levels...

Hooked on "Gachapon," hooked on *Rising Zan*, and hooked on *To Heart*. I am such a wretch as a member of society, I couldn't complain if I was put to the guillotine. But as a manga artist, I am working hard to deserve some respect. Manga is easily sitting on the throne of my heart as the champion. Figures and games always come second. I would like to run right through the upcoming crossroad, and go on to the next step. I will see you in the next volume.

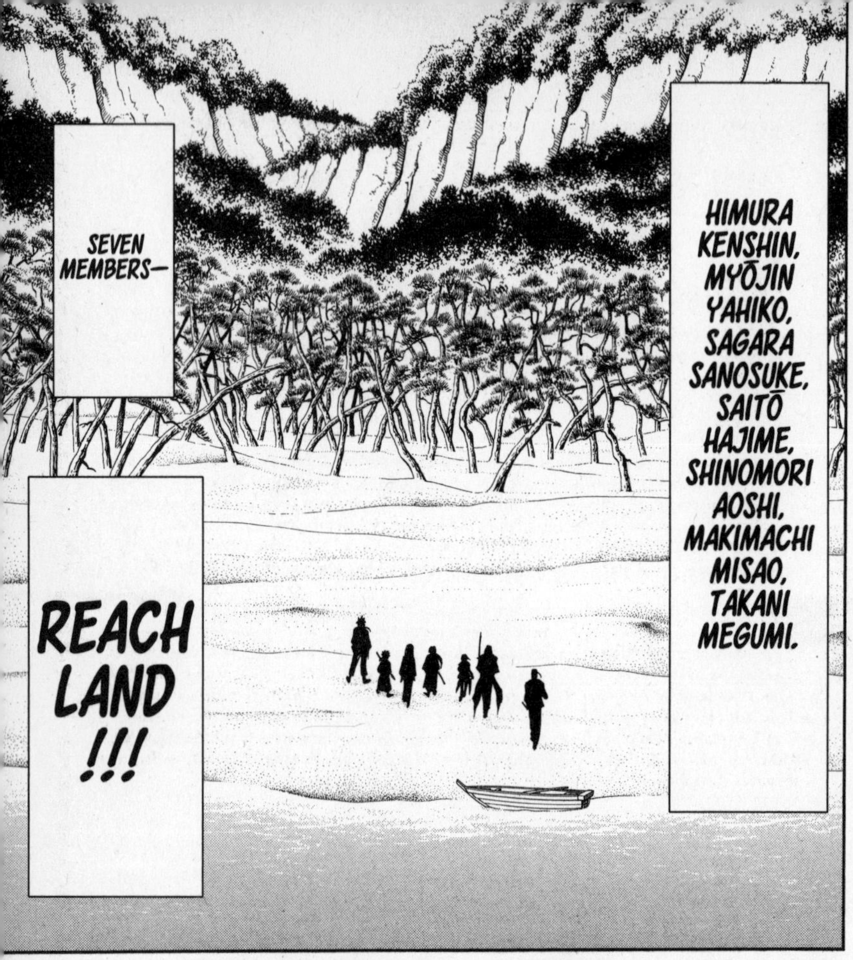
HIMURA KENSHIN, MYŌJIN YAHIKO, SAGARA SANOSUKE, SAITŌ HAJIME, SHINOMORI AOSHI, MAKIMACHI MISAO, TAKANI MEGUMI.
SEVEN MEMBERS—
REACH LAND !!!

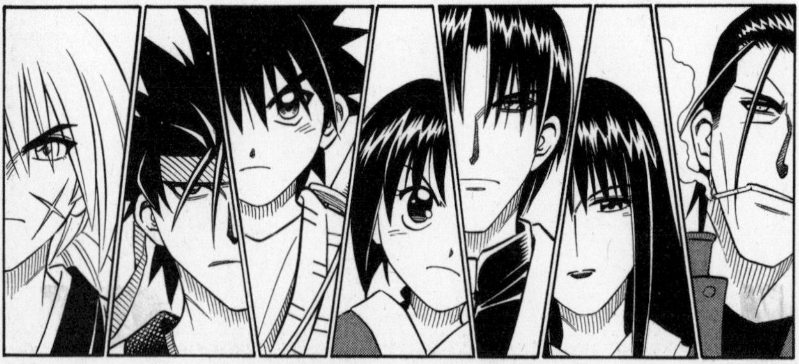

Act 237—Quarrel

Who is Kenshin's biggest rival?? Survey results!

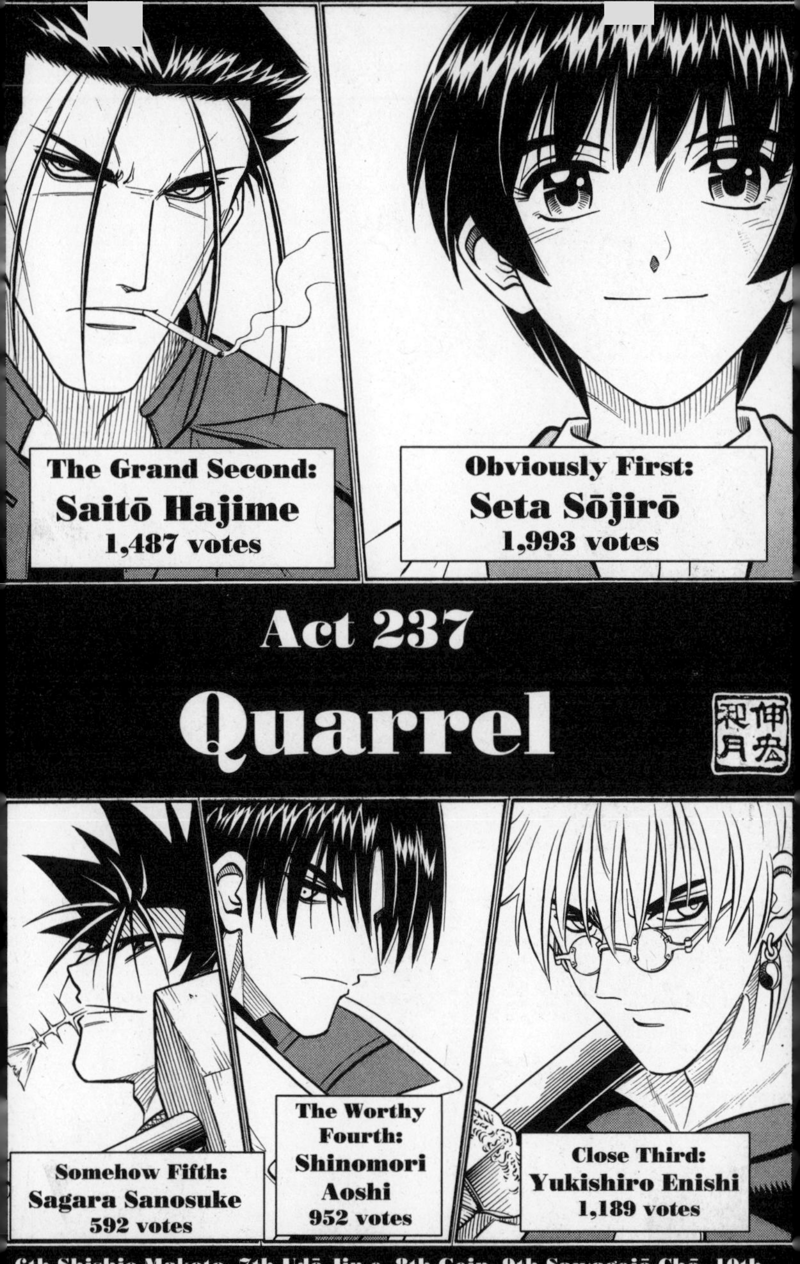

Obviously First:
Seta Sōjirō
1,993 votes
The Grand Second:
Saitō Hajime
1,487 votes
Act 237
Quarrel
Close Third:
Yukishiro Enishi
1,189 votes
The Worthy Fourth:
Shinomori Aoshi
952 votes
Somehow Fifth:
Sagara Sanosuke
592 votes

6th Shishio Makoto, 7th Udō Jin-e, 8th Gein, 9th Sawagejō Chō, 10th Kujiranami Hyōgo. Thank you for your cooperation!

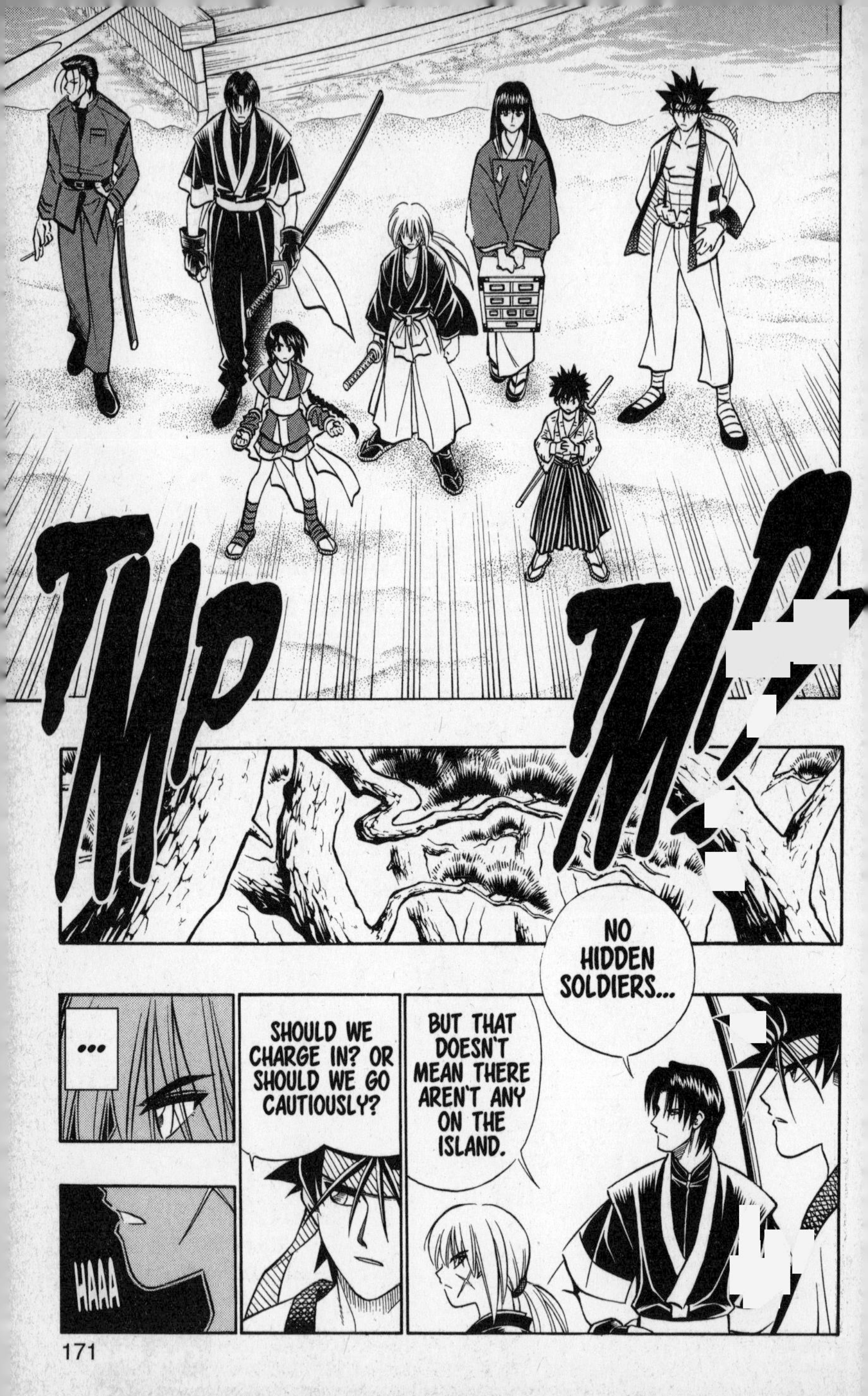
TMP
NO HIDDEN SOLDIERS...
BUT THAT DOESN'T MEAN THERE AREN'T ANY ON THE ISLAND.
SHOULD WE CHARGE IN? OR SHOULD WE GO CAUTIOUSLY?
...
HAAA

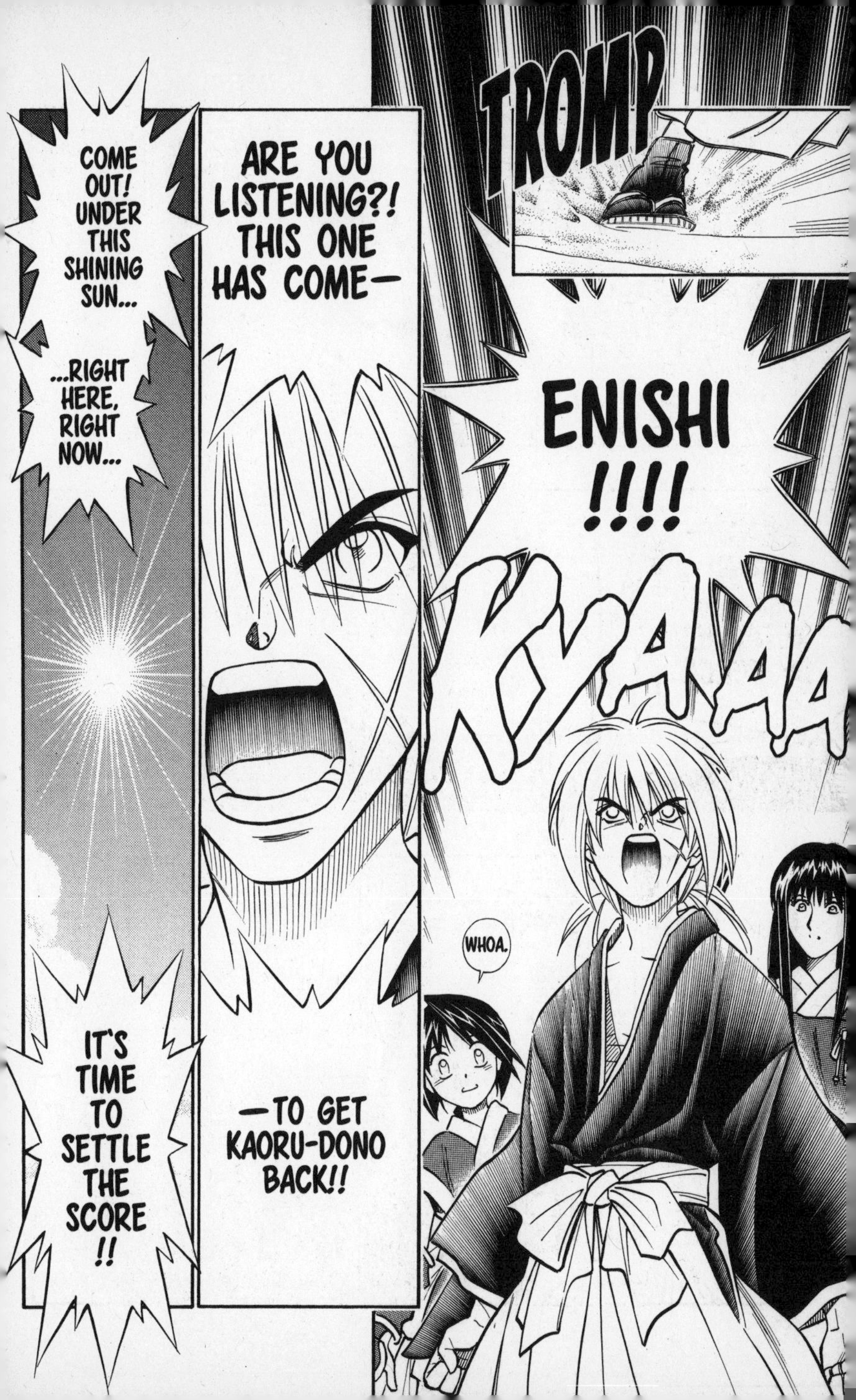
TROMP
ENISHI!!!!
KYAAA
WHOA.
ARE YOU LISTENING?! THIS ONE HAS COME—
—TO GET KAORU-DONO BACK!!
COME OUT! UNDER THIS SHINING SUN...
...RIGHT HERE, RIGHT NOW...
IT'S TIME TO SETTLE THE SCORE!!

READ THIS WAY

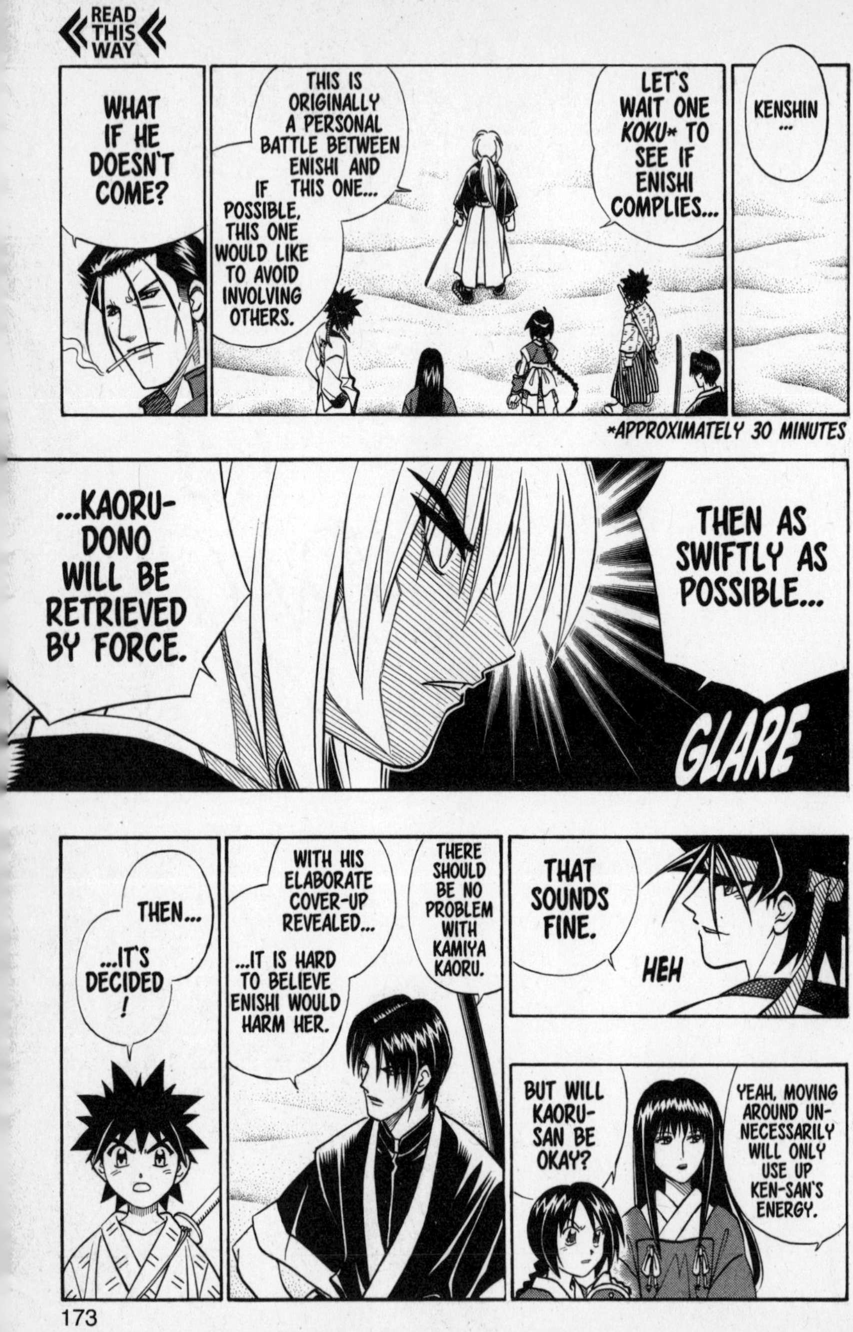
KENSHIN...
LET'S WAIT ONE KOKU* TO SEE IF ENISHI COMPLIES...
THIS IS ORIGINALLY A PERSONAL BATTLE BETWEEN ENISHI AND THIS ONE...
IF POSSIBLE, THIS ONE WOULD LIKE TO AVOID INVOLVING OTHERS.
WHAT IF HE DOESN'T COME?
*APPROXIMATELY 30 MINUTES
THEN AS SWIFTLY AS POSSIBLE...
GLARE
...KAORU-DONO WILL BE RETRIEVED BY FORCE.
THAT SOUNDS FINE.
HEH
YEAH, MOVING AROUND UN-NECESSARILY WILL ONLY USE UP KEN-SAN'S ENERGY.
BUT WILL KAORU-SAN BE OKAY?
THERE SHOULD BE NO PROBLEM WITH KAMIYA KAORU.
WITH HIS ELABORATE COVER-UP REVEALED...
...IT IS HARD TO BELIEVE ENISHI WOULD HARM HER.
THEN...
...IT'S DECIDED!

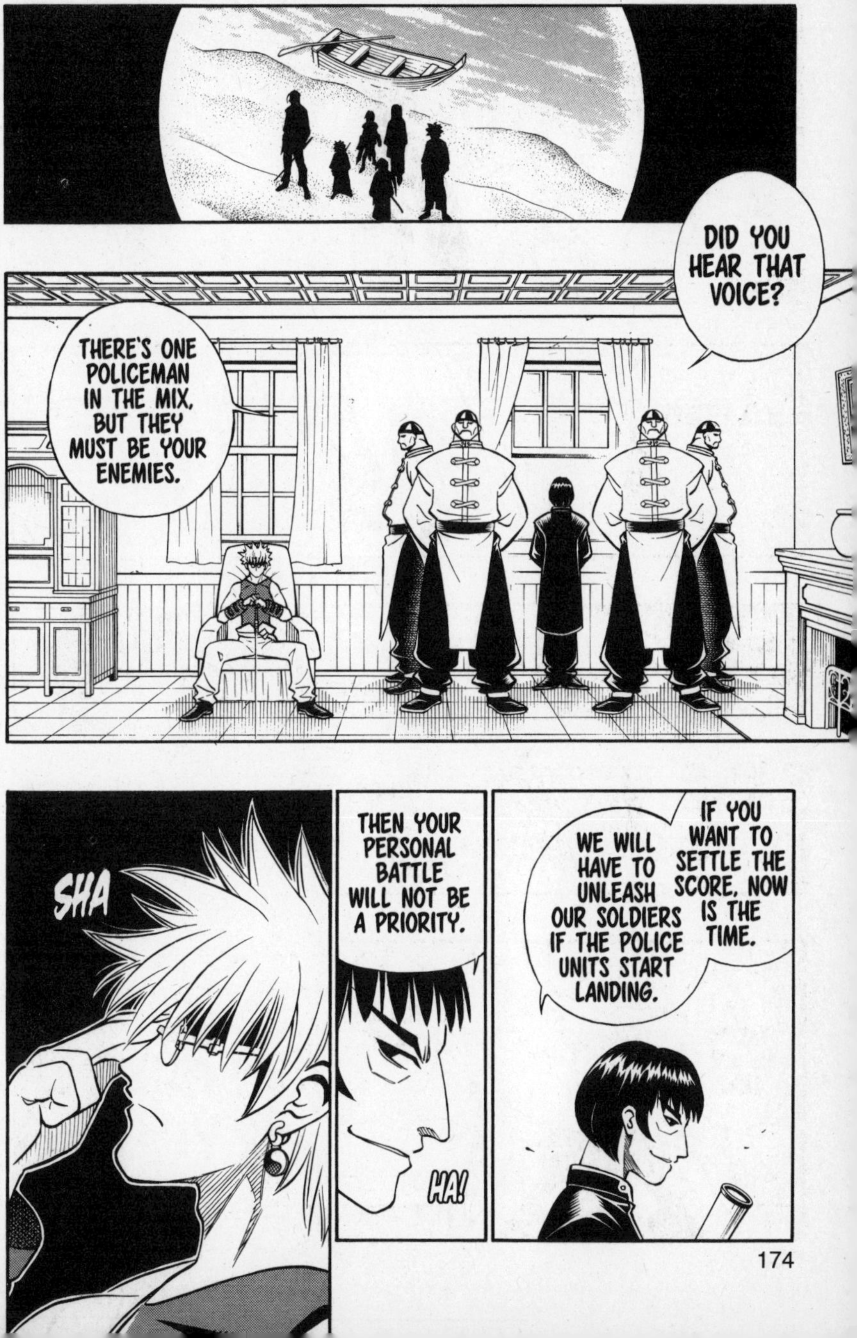
DID YOU HEAR THAT VOICE?
THERE'S ONE POLICEMAN IN THE MIX, BUT THEY MUST BE YOUR ENEMIES.
IF YOU WANT TO SETTLE THE SCORE, NOW IS THE TIME.
WE WILL HAVE TO UNLEASH OUR SOLDIERS IF THE POLICE UNITS START LANDING.
THEN YOUR PERSONAL BATTLE WILL NOT BE A PRIORITY.
HA!
SHA

READ THIS WAY

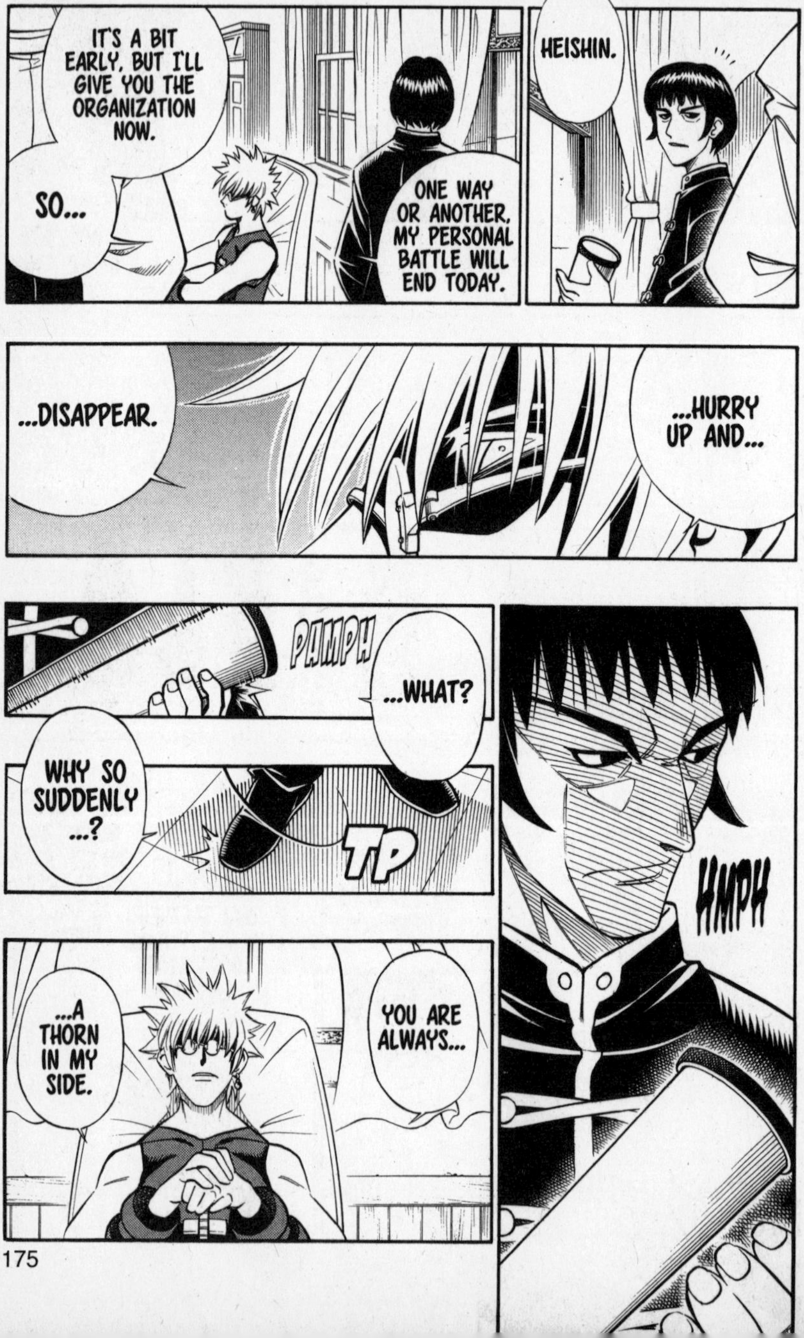

HEISHIN.
ONE WAY OR ANOTHER, MY PERSONAL BATTLE WILL END TODAY.
IT'S A BIT EARLY, BUT I'LL GIVE YOU THE ORGANIZATION NOW.
SO...
...HURRY UP AND...
...DISAPPEAR.
HMPH
PAMPH
...WHAT?
WHY SO SUDDENLY ...?
TP
YOU ARE ALWAYS...
...A THORN IN MY SIDE.

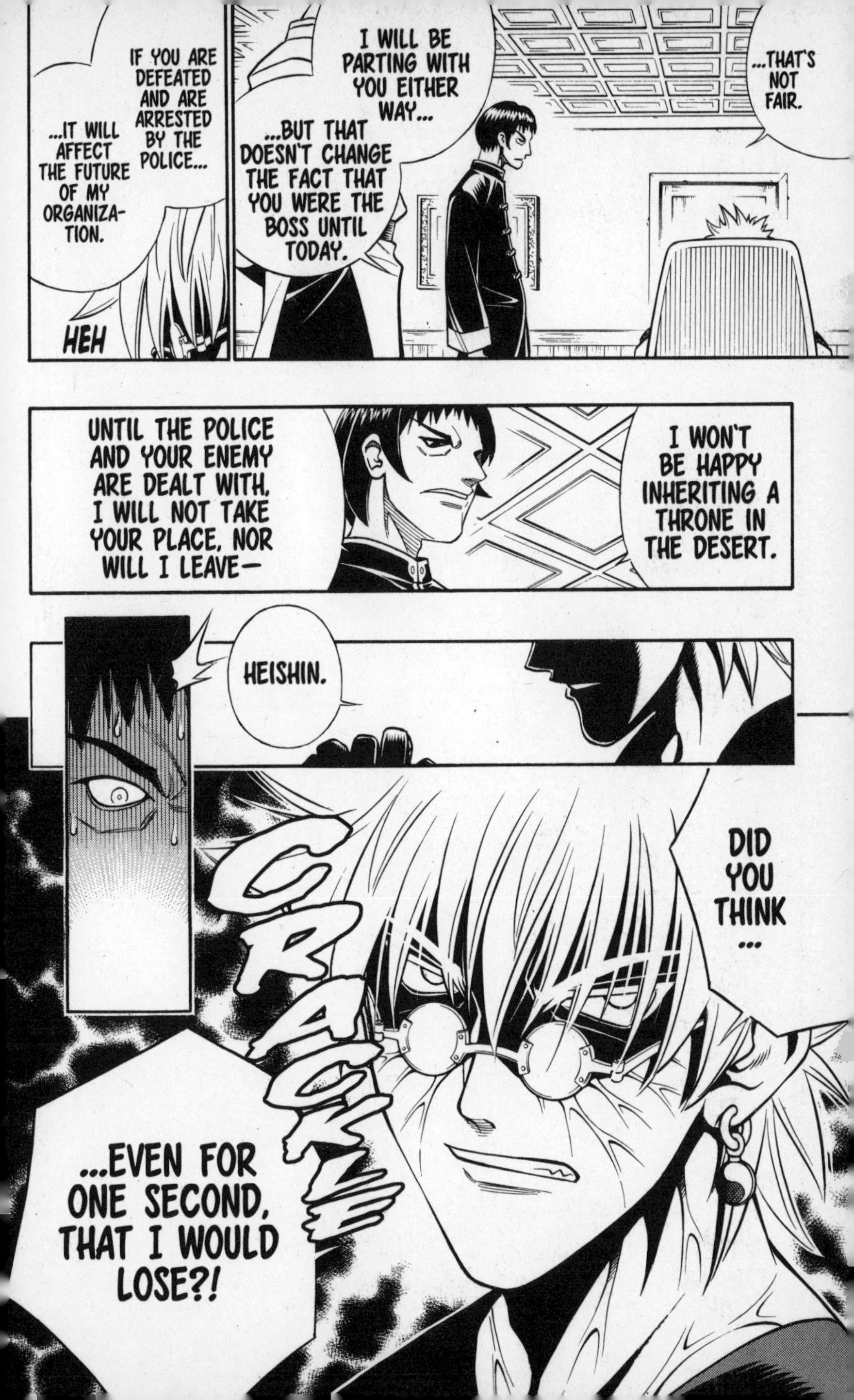
...THAT'S NOT FAIR.
I WILL BE PARTING WITH YOU EITHER WAY...
...BUT THAT DOESN'T CHANGE THE FACT THAT YOU WERE THE BOSS UNTIL TODAY.
IF YOU ARE DEFEATED AND ARE ARRESTED BY THE POLICE...
...IT WILL AFFECT THE FUTURE OF MY ORGANIZA-TION.
HEH
I WON'T BE HAPPY INHERITING A THRONE IN THE DESERT.
UNTIL THE POLICE AND YOUR ENEMY ARE DEALT WITH, I WILL NOT TAKE YOUR PLACE, NOR WILL I LEAVE—
HEISHIN.
DID YOU THINK...
...EVEN FOR ONE SECOND, THAT I WOULD LOSE?!
CRACKLE

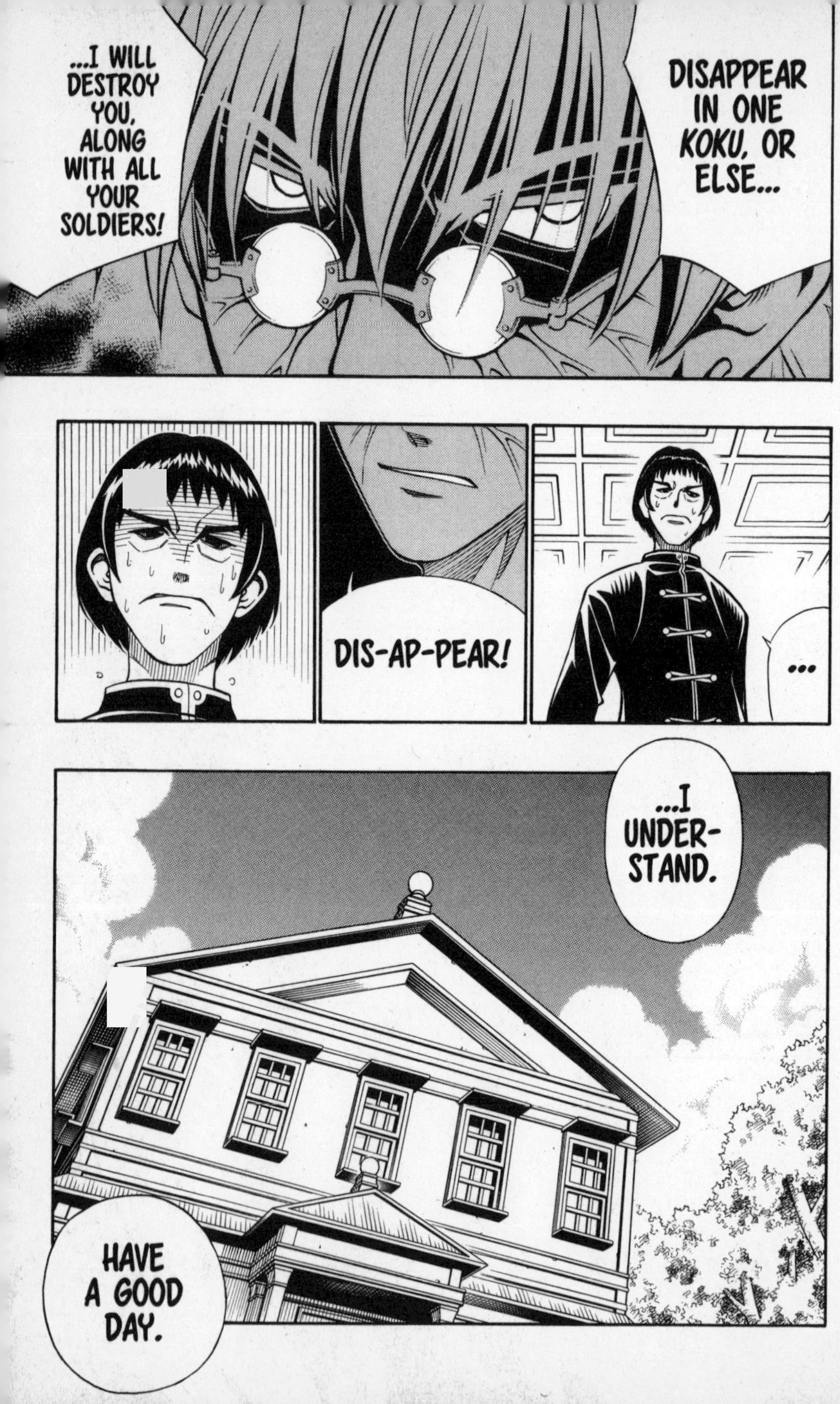
DISAPPEAR IN ONE KOKU, OR ELSE...
...I WILL DESTROY YOU, ALONG WITH ALL YOUR SOLDIERS!
...
DIS-AP-PEAR!
...I UNDER-STAND.
HAVE A GOOD DAY.

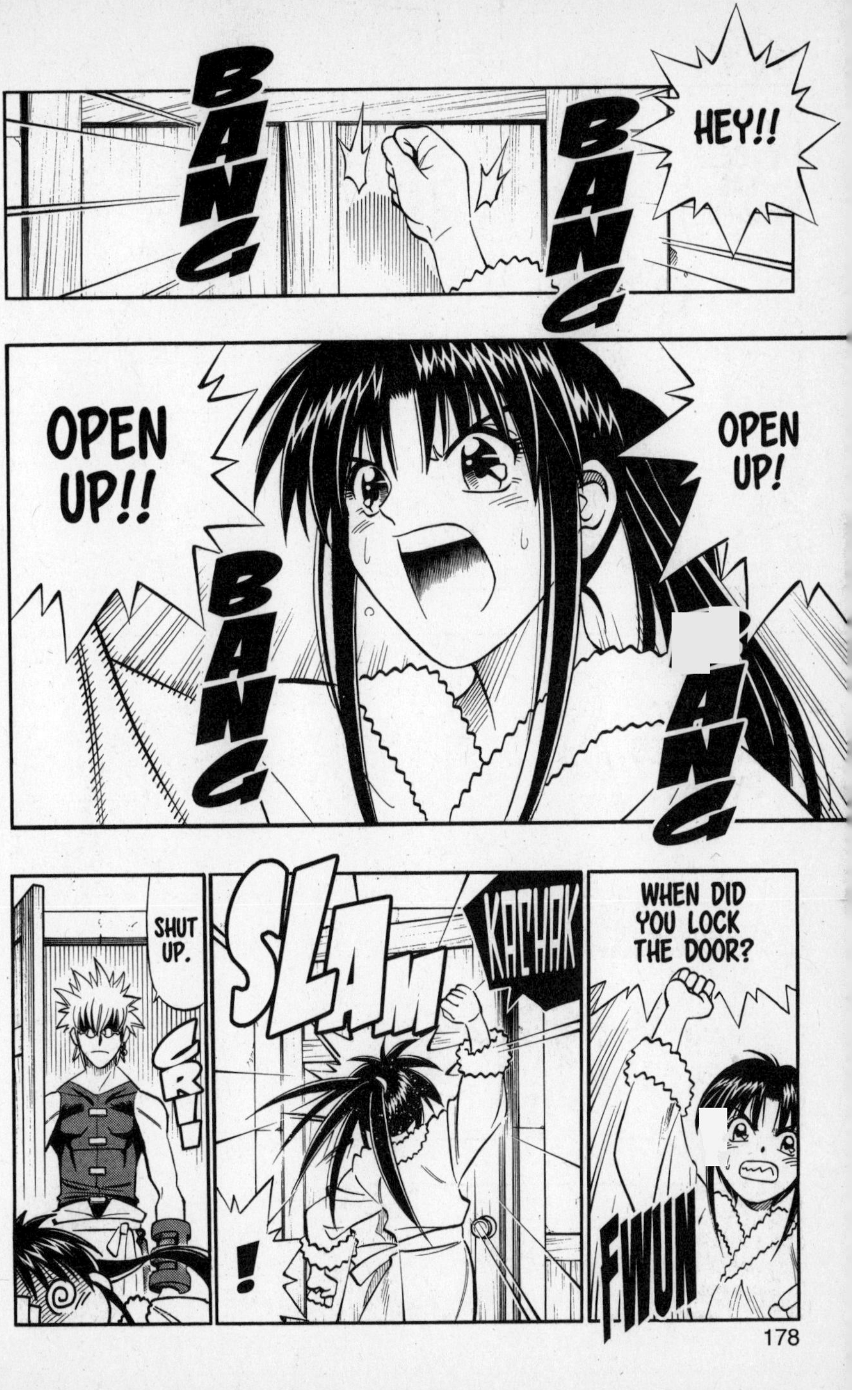
HEY!!
BANG
BANG
OPEN UP!
ANG
OPEN UP!!
BANG
WHEN DID YOU LOCK THE DOOR?
FWUN
KACHAK
SLAM
!
SHUT UP.
CR

READ THIS WAY

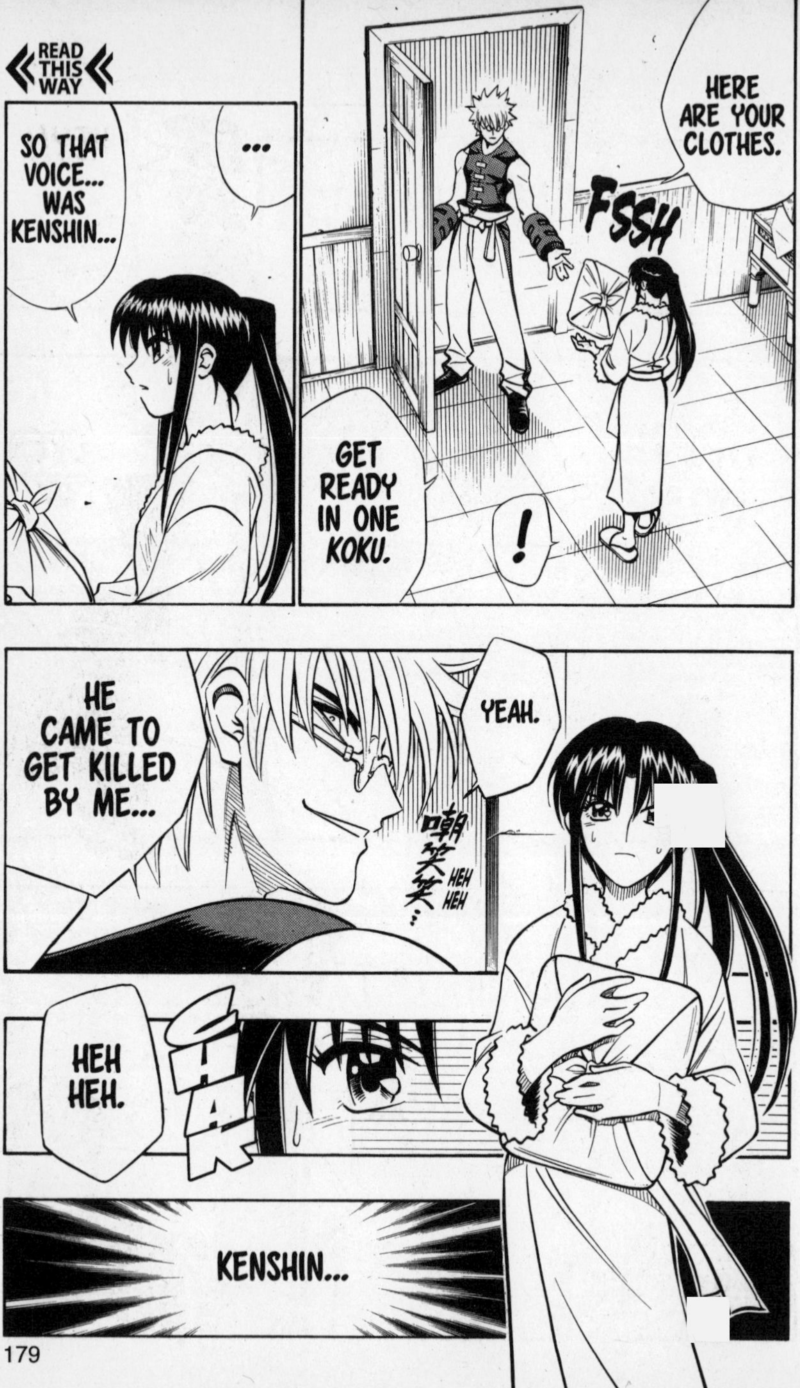
HERE ARE YOUR CLOTHES.
FSSH
GET READY IN ONE KOKU.
!
...
SO THAT VOICE... WAS KENSHIN...
YEAH.
HE CAME TO GET KILLED BY ME...
嘲笑笑…
HEH HEH
CHAK
HEH HEH.
KENSHIN...

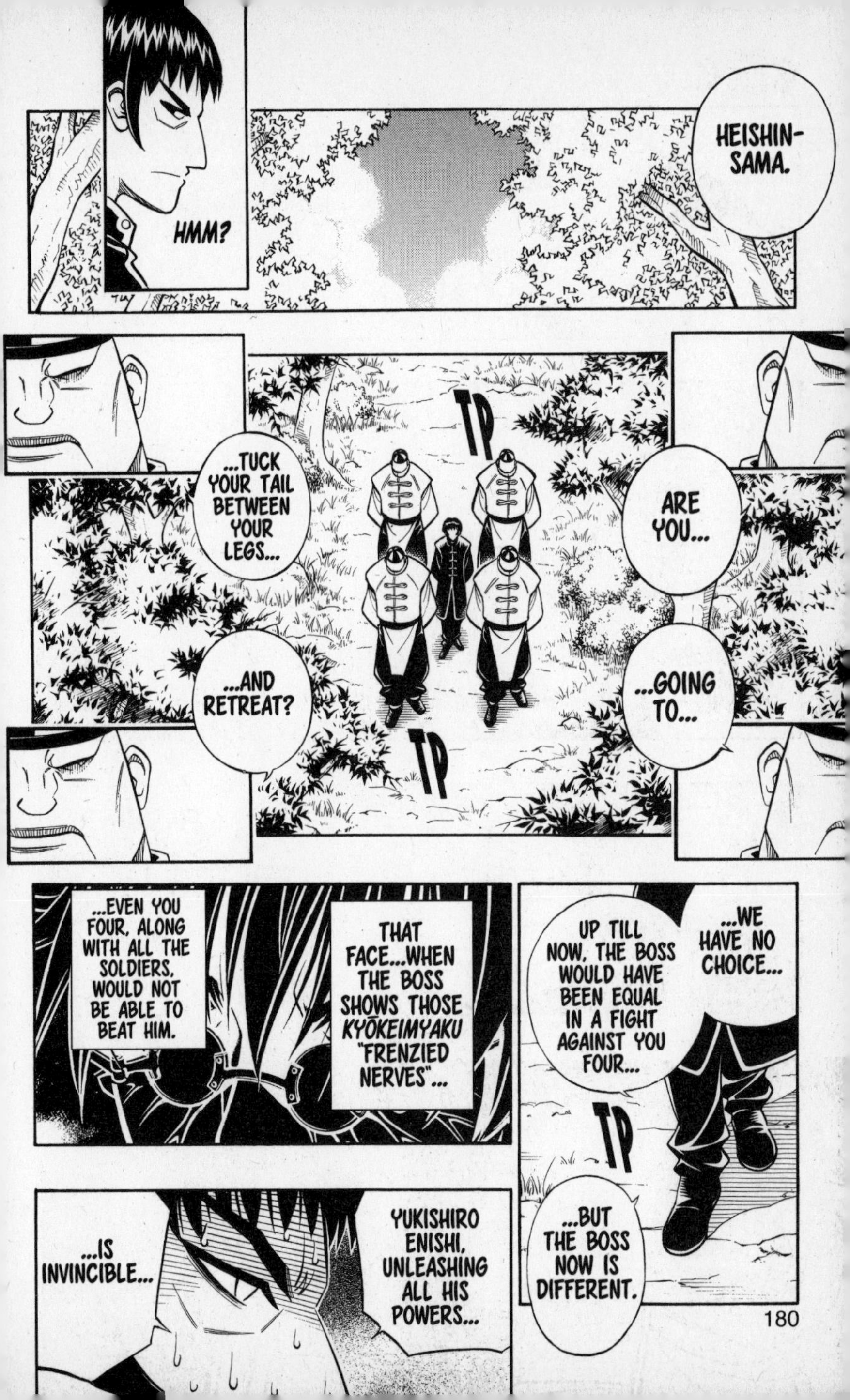
HEISHIN-SAMA.
HMM?
ARE YOU...
...GOING TO...
TP
...TUCK YOUR TAIL BETWEEN YOUR LEGS...
...AND RETREAT?
TP
...WE HAVE NO CHOICE...
UP TILL NOW, THE BOSS WOULD HAVE BEEN EQUAL IN A FIGHT AGAINST YOU FOUR...
TP
...BUT THE BOSS NOW IS DIFFERENT.
THAT FACE...WHEN THE BOSS SHOWS THOSE *KYŌKEIMYAKU* "FRENZIED NERVES"...
...EVEN YOU FOUR, ALONG WITH ALL THE SOLDIERS, WOULD NOT BE ABLE TO BEAT HIM.
YUKISHIRO ENISHI, UNLEASHING ALL HIS POWERS...
...IS INVINCIBLE...

READ THIS WAY

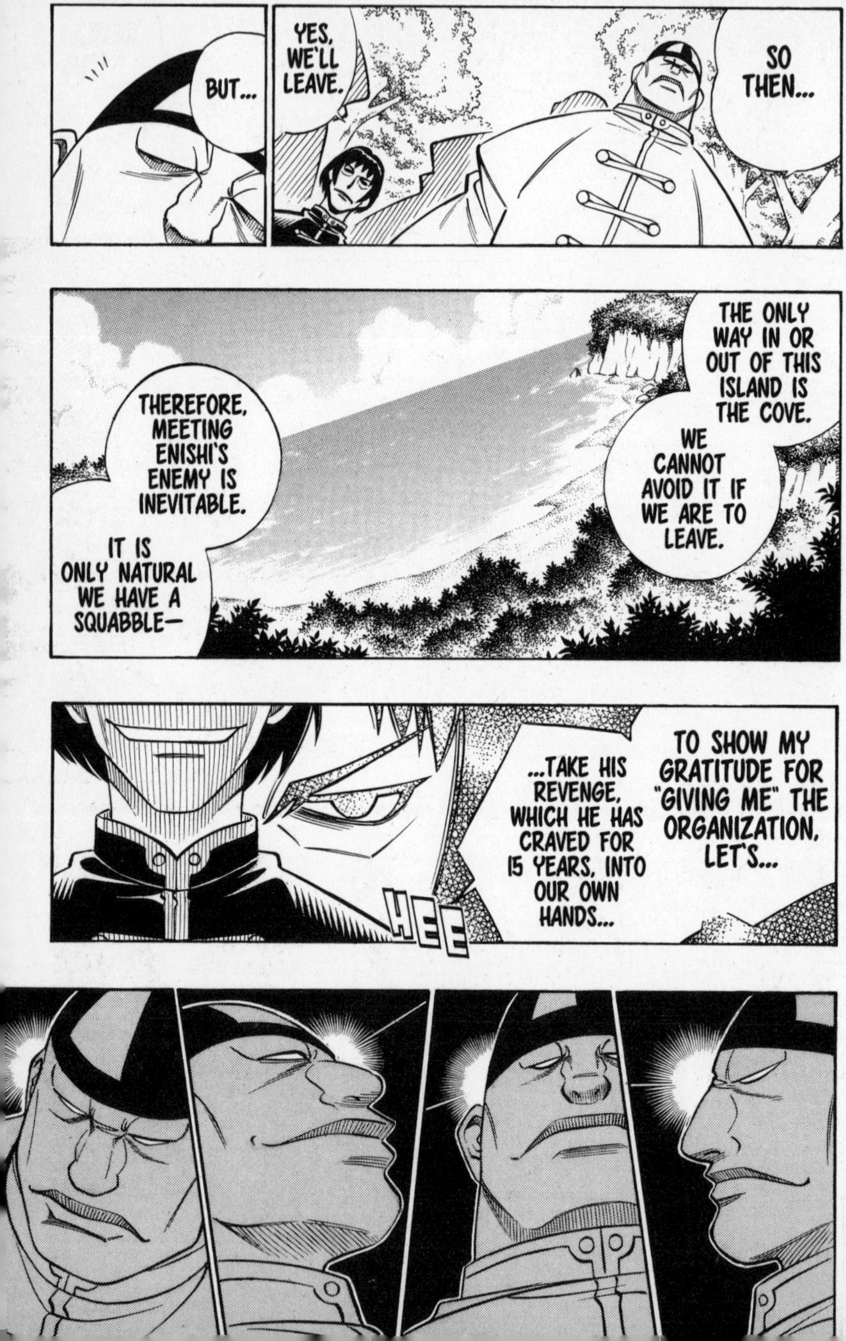

SO THEN...
YES, WE'LL LEAVE.
BUT...
THE ONLY WAY IN OR OUT OF THIS ISLAND IS THE COVE.
WE CANNOT AVOID IT IF WE ARE TO LEAVE.
THEREFORE, MEETING ENISHI'S ENEMY IS INEVITABLE.
IT IS ONLY NATURAL WE HAVE A SQUABBLE—
TO SHOW MY GRATITUDE FOR "GIVING ME" THE ORGANIZATION, LET'S...
...TAKE HIS REVENGE, WHICH HE HAS CRAVED FOR 15 YEARS, INTO OUR OWN HANDS...
HEE

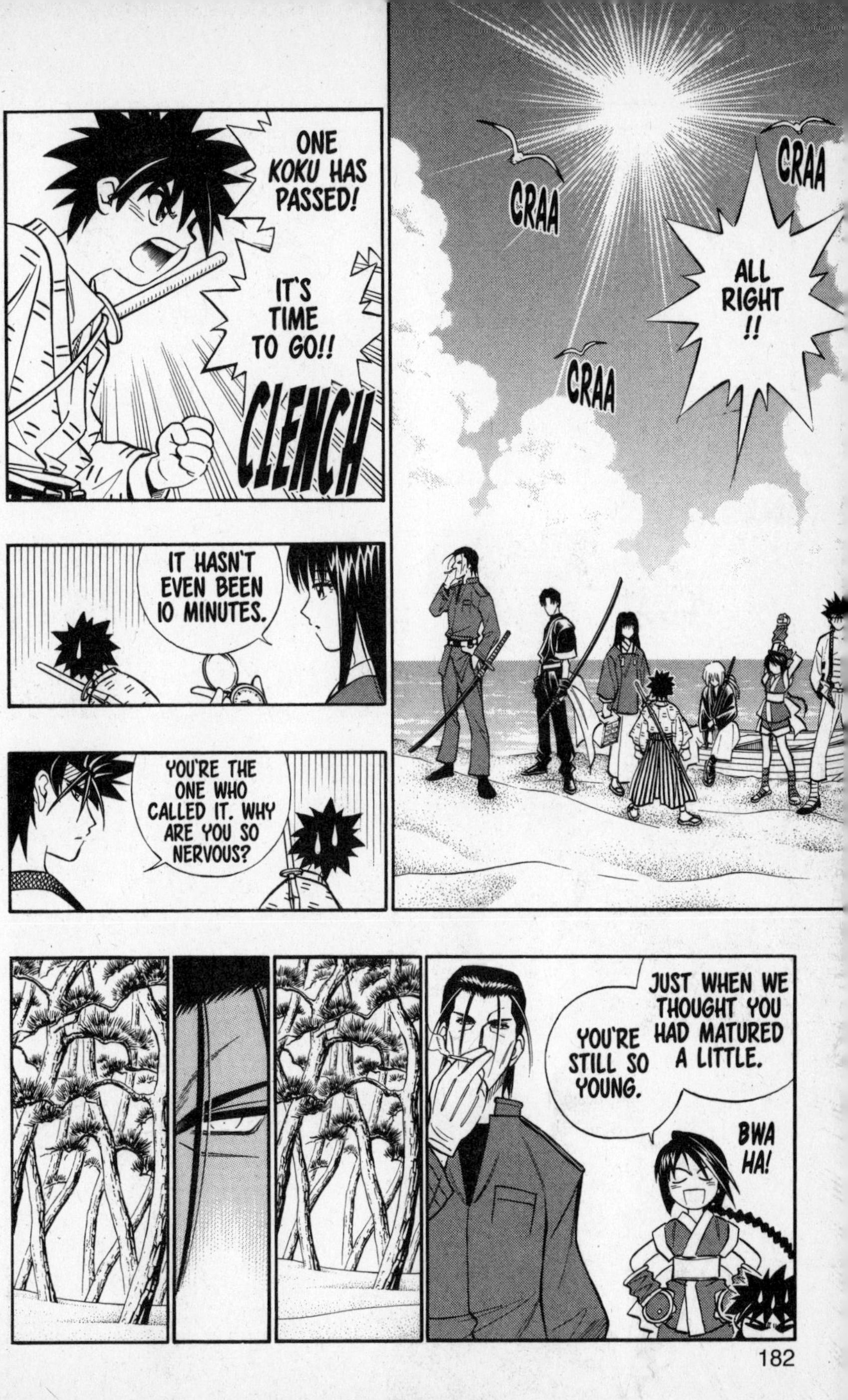
CRAA
CRAA
ALL RIGHT!!
CRAA
ONE KOKU HAS PASSED!
IT'S TIME TO GO!!
CLENCH
IT HASN'T EVEN BEEN 10 MINUTES.
YOU'RE THE ONE WHO CALLED IT. WHY ARE YOU SO NERVOUS?
JUST WHEN WE THOUGHT YOU HAD MATURED A LITTLE.
YOU'RE STILL SO YOUNG.
BWA HA!

READ THIS WAY

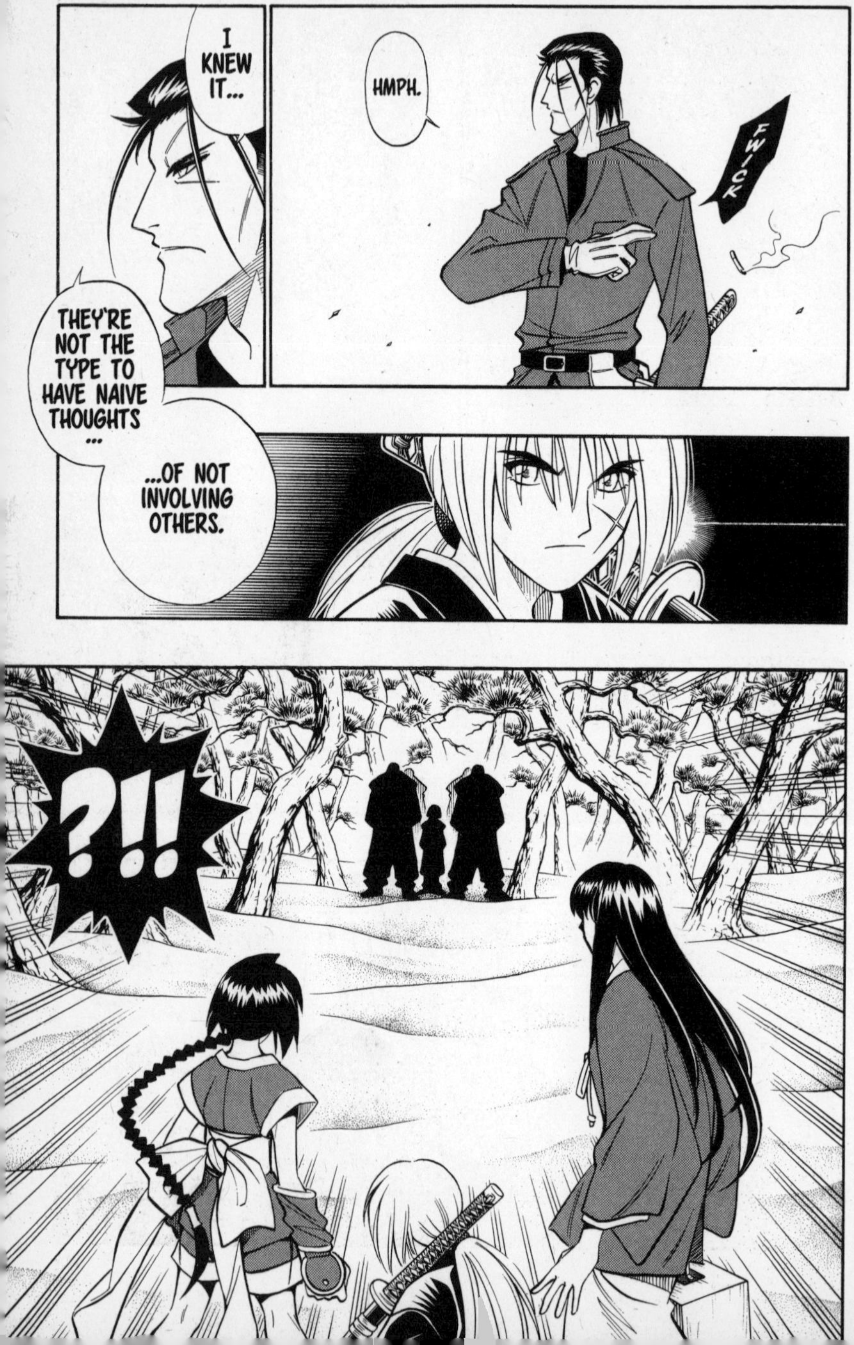
HMPH.
FWICK
I KNEW IT...
THEY'RE NOT THE TYPE TO HAVE NAIVE THOUGHTS...
...OF NOT INVOLVING OTHERS.
?!!

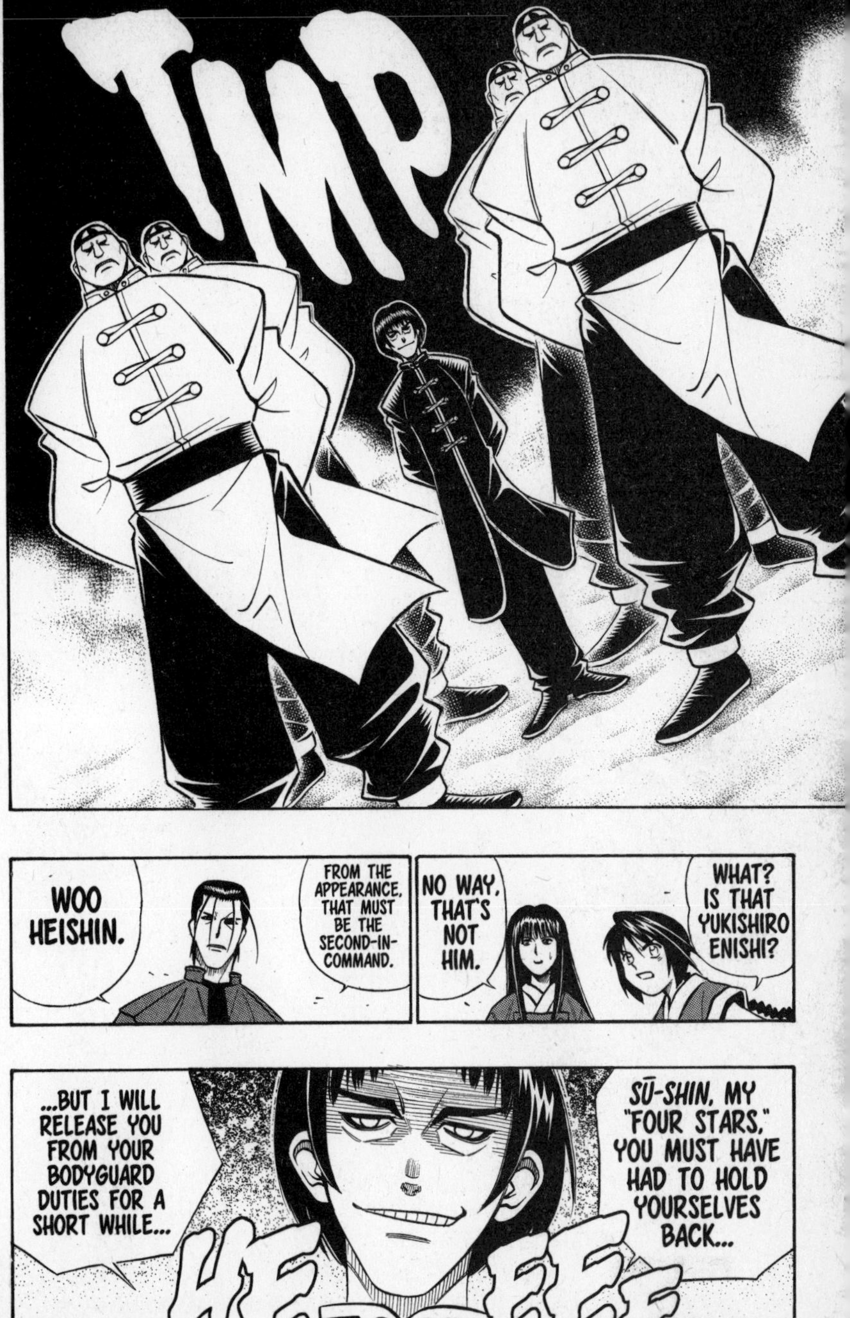
TMP
WHAT? IS THAT YUKISHIRO ENISHI?
NO WAY, THAT'S NOT HIM.
FROM THE APPEARANCE, THAT MUST BE THE SECOND-IN-COMMAND.
WOO HEISHIN.
SŪ-SHIN, MY "FOUR STARS," YOU MUST HAVE HAD TO HOLD YOURSELVES BACK...
...BUT I WILL RELEASE YOU FROM YOUR BODYGUARD DUTIES FOR A SHORT WHILE...
HE-
EEE

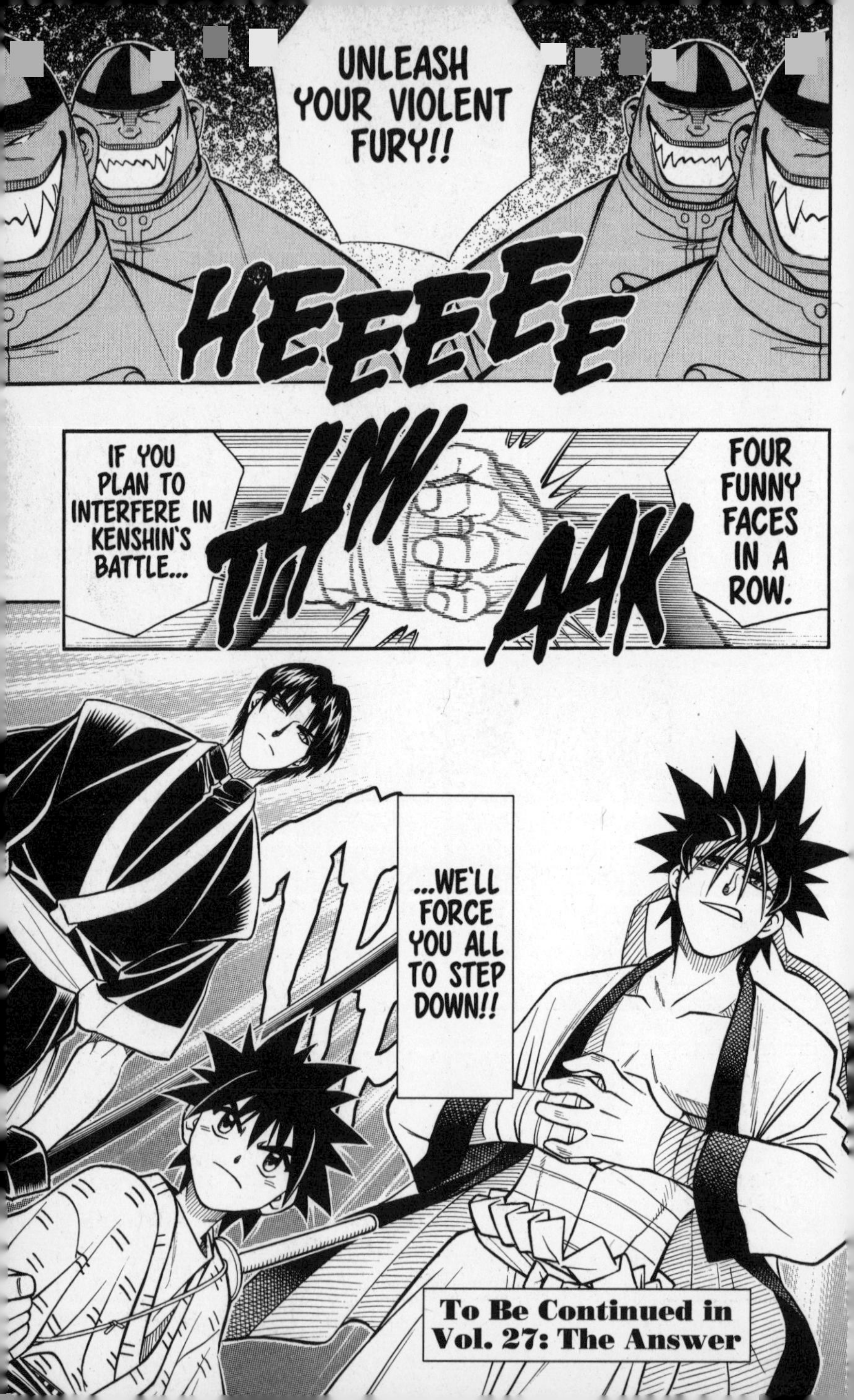
UNLEASH YOUR VIOLENT FURY!!
HEEEEE
FOUR FUNNY FACES IN A ROW.
THWAAK
IF YOU PLAN TO INTERFERE IN KENSHIN'S BATTLE...
...WE'LL FORCE YOU ALL TO STEP DOWN!!
To Be Continued in Vol. 27: The Answer

GLOSSARY of the RESTORATION

*A brief guide to select Japanese terms used in **Rurouni Kenshin**. Note that, both here and within the story itself, all names are Japanese style—i.e., last or "family" name first, with personal or "given" name following. This is both because **Kenshin** is a "period" story, as well as to decrease confusion—if we were to take the example of Kenshin's* sakabatô *and "reverse" the format of the historically established assassin-name "Hitokiri Battôsai," for example, it would make little sense to then call him "Battôsai Himura."*

Fudô Myô-ô
In Vajrayana Buddhism, the destroyer of delusion and protector of Buddhism. Also known in Sanskrit as "the Immovable One," his immovability refers to his ability to remain "unmoved" by carnal temptations. His fearsome blue visage is typically surrounded by flames, representing the purification of the mind.

Himura Kenshin
Kenshin's "real" name, revealed to Kaoru only at her urging

Hiten Mitsurugi-ryû
Kenshin's sword technique, used more for defense than offense. An "ancient style that pits one against many," it requires exceptional speed and agility to master.

hitokiri
An assassin. Famous swordsmen of the period were sometimes thus known to adopt "professional" names—**Kawakami Gensai**, for example, was also known as "Hitokiri Gensai."

Ishin Shishi
Loyalist or pro-Imperialist **patriots** who fought to restore the Emperor to his ancient seat of power

Kansatsu Tobikunai
"Piercing/Killing Flying Daggers." Misao's special technique.

aku
Kanji character for "evil," worn by Sanosuke as a remembrance of his beloved, betrayed Captain Sagara and the **Sekihô Army**

Bakumatsu
Final, chaotic days of the Tokugawa regime

-chan
Honorific. Can be used either as a diminutive (e.g., with a small child—"Little Hanako or Kentarô"), or with those who are grown, to indicate affection ("My dear...").

-dono
Honorific. Even more respectful than -**san**; the effect in modern-day Japanese conversation would be along the lines of "Milord So-and-So." As used by Kenshin, it indicates both respect and humility.

Edo
Capital city of the **Tokugawa Bakufu**; renamed **Tokyo** ("Eastern Capital") after the Meiji Restoration

-sama

Honorific. The respectful equivalent of **-san**, **-sama** is used primarily in addressing persons of much higher rank than one's self...or, in a romantic sense, in addressing those upon whom one is crushing, wicked hard.

-san

Honorific. Carries the meaning of "Mr.," "Ms.," "Miss," etc., but used more extensively in Japanese than its English equivalent (note that even an enemy may be addressed as "**-san**").

Sekihô Army

Military unit (formed mainly of civilians) who, believing in the cause of the Emperor's restoration to power, were eventually turned upon by those same pro-Imperialist forces and declared traitors

shôgun

Feudal military ruler of Japan

shôgunate

See **Tokugawa Bakufu**

Tokugawa Bakufu

Military feudal government which dominated Japan from 1603 to 1867

Tokyo

The renaming of "**Edo**" to "**Tokyo**" is a marker of the start of the **Meiji Restoration**

zanbatô

Sanosuke's huge, oversized sword which gave him the nickname of "Zanza" during his fight merchant days. It was allegedly developed for the purpose of cutting an opponent in half along with his horse.

Kawakami Gensai

Real-life, historical inspiration for the character of **Himura Kenshin**

-kun

Honorific. Used in the modern day among male students, or those who grew up together, but another usage—the one you're more likely to find in *Rurouni Kenshin*—is the "superior-to-inferior" form, intended as a way to emphasize a difference in status or rank, as well as to indicate familiarity or affection.

Kyoto

Home of the Emperor and imperial court from A.D. 794 until shortly after the **Meiji Restoration** in 1868

loyalists

Those who supported the return of the Emperor to power; **Ishin Shishi**

Meiji Restoration

1853-1868; culminated in the collapse of the **Tokugawa Bakufu** and the restoration of imperial rule. So called after Emperor Meiji, whose chosen name was written with the characters for "culture and enlightenment."

patriots

Another term for **Ishin Shishi**... and, when used by Sano, not a flattering one

rurouni

Wanderer, vagabond

sakabatô

Reversed-edge sword (the dull edge on the side the sharp should be, and vice versa); carried by Kenshin as a symbol of his resolution never to kill again

IN THE NEXT VOLUME...

Now that Sano's back with Team Kenshin, and the location of Enishi's island compound is known, Kaoru's rescue seems imminent. Waiting for Kenshin and company on the beach, however, is the nefarious and calculating Woo Heishin, Enishi's No. 2 man, and he's brought some company—his *Sû-shin* "Four Stars" bodyguards. Sano, Yahiko, Saitô and Aoshi all pair off with Heishin's mysterious and deadly fighters, and the biggest rumble the Meiji Restoration has ever seen is about to begin. If they fail, will Kaoru's life also slip through their fingers?

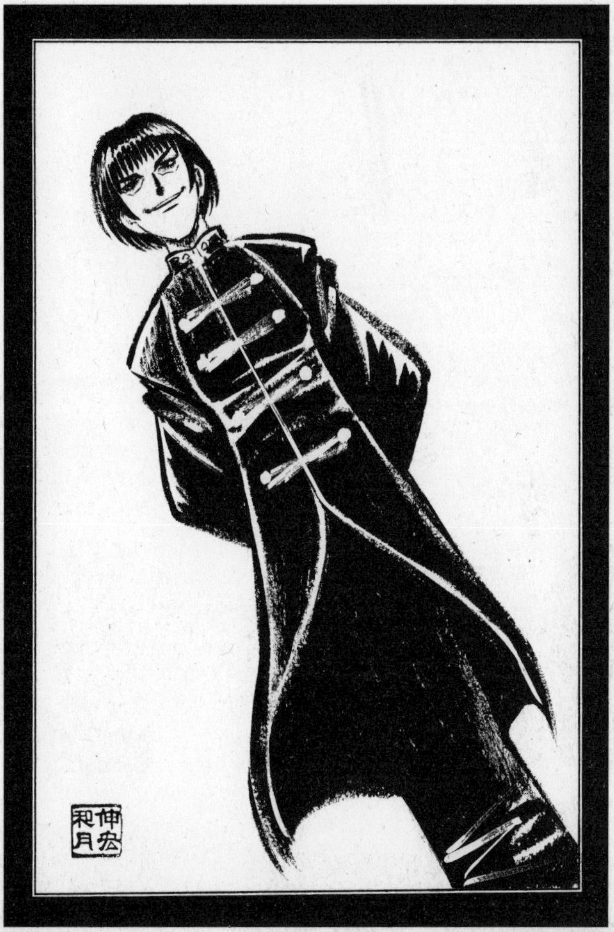

Available in June 2006

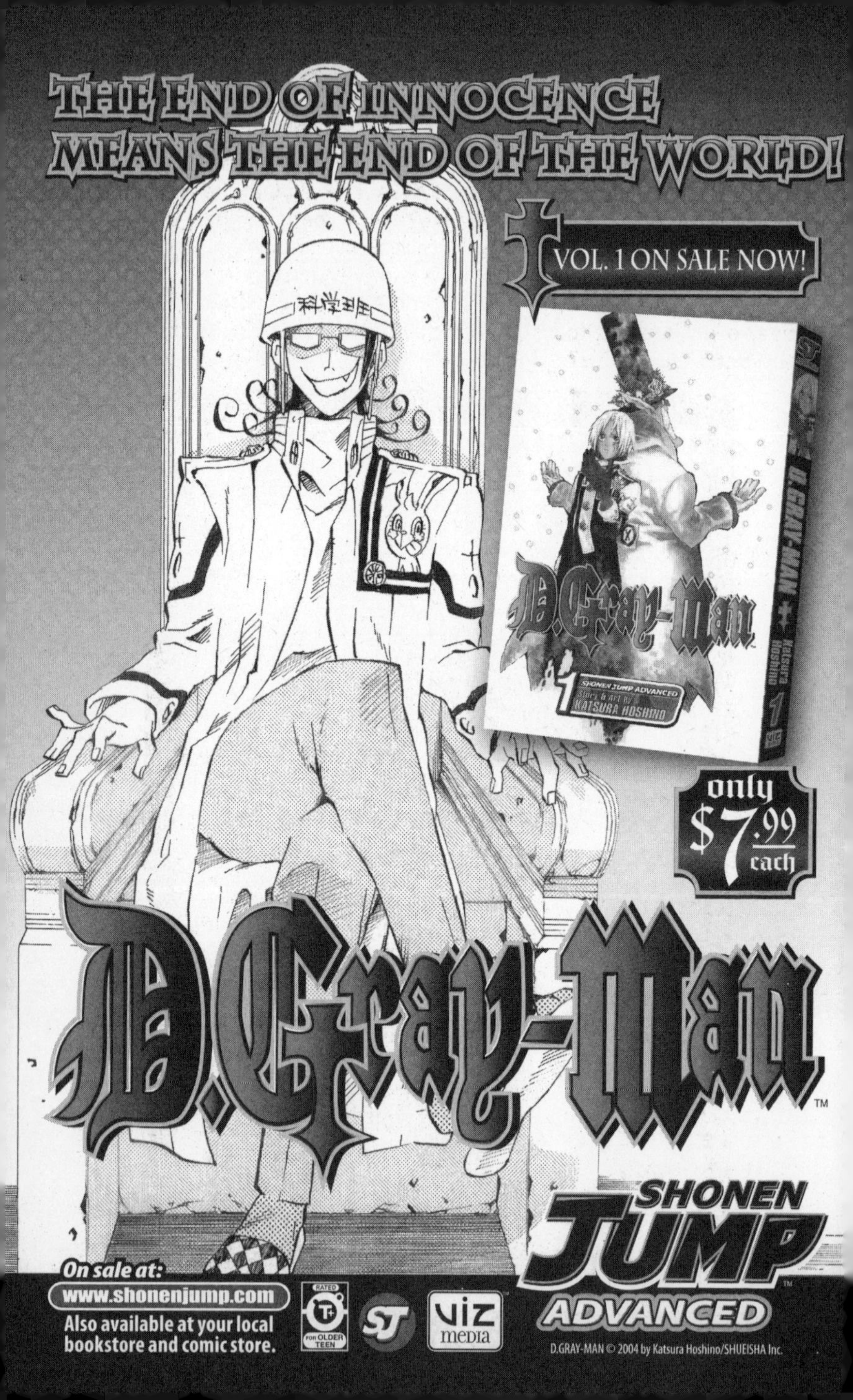
THE END OF INNOCENCE
MEANS THE END OF THE WORLD!
VOL. 1 ON SALE NOW!
D.Gray-man
SHONEN JUMP ADVANCED
Story & Art by
KATSURA HOSHINO
only
$7.99
each
D.Gray-man™
SHONEN JUMP ADVANCED
On sale at:
www.shonenjump.com
Also available at your local bookstore and comic store.
RATED T+ FOR OLDER TEEN
SJ
viz media
D.GRAY-MAN © 2004 by Katsura Hoshino/SHUEISHA Inc.

Tell us what you think about SHONEN JUMP manga!

Our survey is now available online.
Go to: www.SHONENJUMP.com/mangasurvey

Help us make our product offering better!

THE REAL ACTION STARTS IN...

THE WORLD'S MOST POPULAR MANGA
www.shonenjump.com

ADVANCED

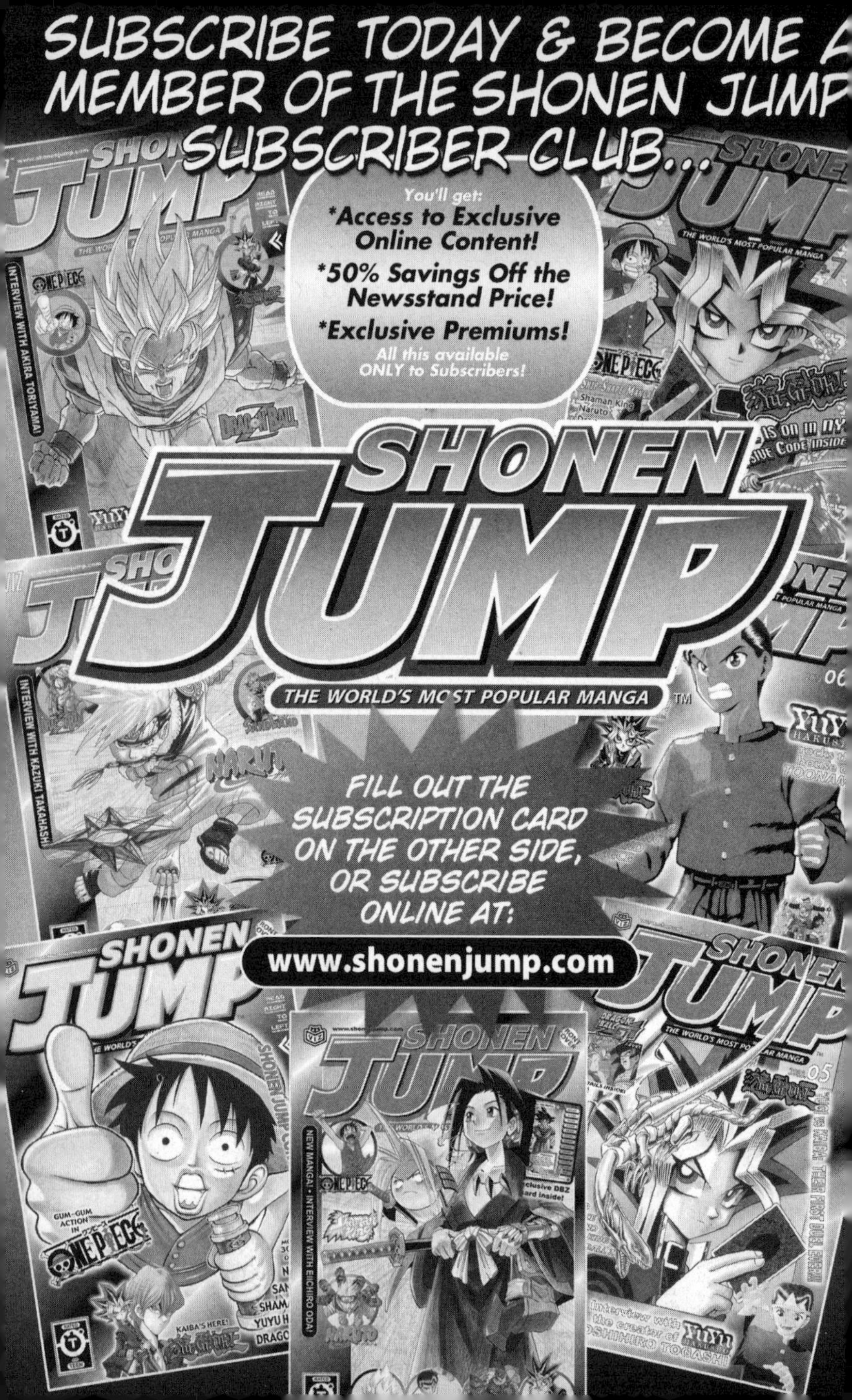
SUBSCRIBE TODAY & BECOME A MEMBER OF THE SHONEN JUMP SUBSCRIBER CLUB...
You'll get:
*Access to Exclusive Online Content!
*50% Savings Off the Newsstand Price!
*Exclusive Premiums!
All this available ONLY to Subscribers!
SHONEN JUMP
THE WORLD'S MOST POPULAR MANGA ™
FILL OUT THE SUBSCRIPTION CARD ON THE OTHER SIDE, OR SUBSCRIBE ONLINE AT:
www.shonenjump.com